Trotsky and His Critics

Revolutionary History, Volume 11, No 1
Socialist Platform Ltd
MERLIN PRESS

Revolutionary History

Founding Editor: Al Richardson (1941-2003)

Editorial Coordinating Team: Ted Crawford, Paul Flewers, Esther Leslie, John Plant

Reviews and Obituaries Editor: John Plant

Website Coordinator: Alun Morgan

Editorial Board: Toby Abse, Ian Birchall, Tony Borton, David Broder, Barry Buitekant, Mildred Gordon, Chris Gray, Simon Hardy, Dave Renton, Mike Jones, Stuart King, Richard Kirkwood, Sheila Leslie, Ben Lewis, Mike Pearn, Jim Ring, Alejandra Rios

Continental Contributing Editor: Fritz Keller

Foreign Advisory Board: Andy Durgan, Rick Kuhn, Staffan Lindhe, Jean Jacques Marie, Einde O'Callaghan, Tom O'Lincoln, Reiner Tosstorff

ISBN 978-0-85036-612-9

Copyright © 2013

Web site: www.revolutionaryhistory.co.uk

E-mail: tcrawford@revhist.datanet.co.uk (editorial)

barry.buitekant@hotmail.com (business)

trusscott.foundation@blueyonder.co.uk (text processing)

Socialist Platform Ltd, BCM 7646, London WC1N 3XX

Merlin Press Ltd, 99B Wallis Road, London E9 5LN
www.merlinpress.co.uk

Printed in the UK by Lightning Source

CONTENTS

Editorial   5

Trotsky and His Critics

Boris Souvarine, Letter to Leon Trotsky   7
Trotsky and the German Communist Opposition   84
Jay Lovestone, Soviet Foreign Policy and World Revolution   110
Christian Stalinism and Trotskyism   117
Senex (Mark Schmidt), Revolutionary Tactics In Spain   129
Trotsky and Spain: The POUM's Assessment   144

Other Material

Work in Progress   165

Obituaries   167

Hector Abaywardena — Ahmed Ben Bella — Bob Gould — Ian David Kitson — George Leslie — Terry Liddle — Theodore Melville — Akiva (Aki) Orr — Dave Packer — Dave Spencer — Alan Woodward — James D Young

Ron Heisler, High Theory for the Marxian Chattering Classes   215
Paul Le Blanc, Making Sense of Trotskyism in the United States:
    Two Memoirs   239

Reviews

Éric Aunoble, *Le communisme, tout de suite! Le mouvement des*
    communes en Ukraine soviétique (1919-1920) (Sarah Gruszka)   260
David Austin (ed), *You Don't Play With Revolution:*
    The Montreal Lectures of CLR James (Christian Høgsbjerg)   276
Nikolai Bukharin et al, *Les communistes de gauche contre*
    le capitalisme d'état: La Revue 'Kommunist' (Jean-Jacques Marie)   280
Michel Cordillot, *Aux origines du socialisme moderne:*
    la Première Internationale, la Commune de Paris, l'Exil.
    Recherches et travaux (Jean Jacques Marie)   283
Mathieu Léonard, *L'émancipation des travailleurs.*
    Une histoire de la Première Internationale (Jean Jacques Marie)   283
Alain Cuénot, *Pierre Naville (1904-1993):*
    Biographie d'un révolutionnaire marxiste (Ian Birchall)   288

Neil Davidson, *How Revolutionary Were
    the Bourgeois Revolutions?* (David Renton) — 291
Bob Dent, *Hungary 1930 and the Forgotten History
    of a Mass Movement* (Julien Papp) — 296
David Fernbach (ed), *In The Steps of Rosa Luxemburg:
    Selected Writings of Paul Levi* (Mike Jones) — 299
François Ferrette, *La Véritable Histoire
    du Parti Communiste Français* (Ian Birchall) — 307
VN Gelis (ed), *Pandelis Pouliopoulos, First Secretary of the KKE:
    In His Own Words* (Chris Gray) — 309
Ted Grant, *Writings: Volume One: 1938-1942:
    Trotskyism and the Second World War* (Alun Morgan) — 315
Ted Grant, *Writings: Volume Two: 1943-1945:
    Trotskyism and the Second World War* (Alun Morgan) — 315
Selma James, *Sex, Race and Class: The Perspective of Winning:
    A Selection of Writings 1952-2011* (Sheila Lahr) — 318
Ben Lewis and Lars T Lih (eds), *Zinoviev and Martov:
    Head to Head in Halle* (Bob Archer) — 320
John Newsinger, *Fighting Back:
    The American Working Class in the 1930s* (Paul Le Blanc) — 328
Ngo Van, *In the Crossfire:
    Adventures of a Vietnamese Revolutionary* (Gregor Benton) — 332
Tom O'Lincoln, *Australia's Pacific War:
    Challenging a National Myth* (Edward Crawford) — 335
John Riddell (ed), *Toward the United Front:
    Proceedings of the Fourth Congress of the
    Communist International, 1922* (Simon Hardy) — 340
Jean Marc Schiappa, *Buonarroti (1761-1837):
    L'Inoxydable* (Ian Birchall) — 345
Richard Seymour, *Unhitched:
    The Trial of Christopher Hitchens* (Ian Birchall) — 347
Reiner Tosstorff, *El POUM en la revolució espanyola*
    (Salvador Lou Cuartero) — 349

Letters — 357

EDITORIAL

From the very start Marxism has been noted — indeed, for many observers has been notorious — for its polemical demeanour. Nearly one-third of its founding document, Marx and Engels' *Manifesto of the Communist Party*, was devoted to a robust critique of rival socialist trends. Leaving to one side Marx's spirited attacks upon the 'hired prize-fighters', the vulgar apologists of capitalism, in *Capital*, and his book-length assault upon the now-forgotten provocateur Karl Vogt, he and Engels spent considerable time combatting the ideas and activities of Proudhon, Bakunin, Lassalle and many other contemporary radicals. Engels' presentation of Marx's ideas took the form of a lengthy polemic against the socialist Eugen Dühring, and his last political act was to defend Marx's revolutionary reputation against the efforts of the German Social-Democrats to present him as a mere reformer, a supporter of 'peace at any price and of opposition to force and violence'.

Trotsky was no stranger to the cut and thrust of vigorous debate, and throughout his revolutionary career he never hesitated sharply to criticise the views of his rivals and to offer fraternal criticisms of those of his comrades and to reply to his critics with considerable energy. However, whilst many of Trotsky's polemics have long been available to the interested reader — from his youthful arguments against Lenin in *Our Political Tasks* and *Report of the Siberian Delegation* to his final interventions in the US Socialist Workers Party collected in *In Defence of Marxism* — little of the material to which he was replying or which presented a critique of his views has been published. This edition of *Revolutionary History* is devoted to assessments of Trotsky that either have never previously been published in an English-language translation or have not reappeared since their first publication in long-forgotten journals.

Much of the material presented below — the articles by the German Communist Opposition, the open letter from the (at this juncture) dissident communist Boris Souvarine, the piece by the anarchist 'Senex' and the two retrospective articles by former POUM members — argues *inter alia* that Trotsky tended to view events rather too much through the prism of the experience of the October Revolution and the factional debates within the Soviet Communist Party, and that this seriously impaired his strategic and tactical acumen, especially in respect of the Spanish Civil War.

In reproducing this material, we are not endorsing the views expressed therein. As always, we publish previously unobtainable or long-forgotten material with the clear intention of developing understanding of historical events, presenting differing viewpoints in order to encourage discussion of the past, with the view of helping socialists today and in the future to approach analogous political situations in a fruitful manner.

It is with great sadness that we announce the death of our Editorial Board comrade George Leslie, who died last year at the age of 93. George had been a member of our Editorial Board since the very beginning and chaired our meetings with that combination of apparent ease and definite authority that only long experience in the labour movement can give. We offer our deep sympathy to George's friends and family, and especially to fellow Board members Sheila and Esther Leslie, and we dedicate to George this issue of *Revolutionary History*.

It is also with great sadness that we announce the death in July of our Editorial Board comrade Clarence Chrysostom. Clarence had been a revolutionary Marxist ever since he joined the Lanka Sama Samaja Party as a teenager in the late 1930s. An obituary will appear in the next issue of *Revolutionary History*.

Editorial Board
Revolutionary History

* * *

Corrections to *Revolutionary History*, Volume 10, no 2, page 212, paragraph starting 'The Baku workers…': the text should read 'this trait was already well known in Moscow'; page 213, paragraph starting 'Point 11': 'Orgburo' should read 'Orgotdel' [Organisation and Instruction Department]'

Correction to *Revolutionary History*, Volume 10, no 4, page 322, paragraph starting 'There are further problems': 'Theorien der Mehrwert' should read 'Theorien über den Mehrwert'.

Boris Souvarine

LETTER TO LEON TROTSKY

Boris Souvarine (real name Lifshitz, 1894-1984) was active in the anti-war socialist left during the First World War, and subsequently played an important role in establishing the French Communist Party (PCF). He attended the Third Congress of the Communist International in 1921, and became a member of the Comintern's Executive Committee. He defended Trotsky when the Soviet leadership under Stalin and Zinoviev started their campaign against him, and helped to publish a French translation of Trotsky's *The New Course* in 1924. He was expelled from the PCF and from the ECCI later that year, and in 1926 played a key part in getting Lenin's 'Testament' published in the *New York Times*. Also in 1926 he formed the Marx-Lenin Communist Circle, but refused to bring this organisation into a united Left Opposition in France. Although he offered his support to Trotsky upon his expulsion from the Soviet Union, he had many differences with him, and some of his policies were closer to those of the German Communist Opposition led by Heinrich Brandler and August Thalheimer than to those of the Left Opposition.

Relations between Souvarine and Trotsky became increasingly acrimonious, and were effectively terminated with Souvarine's lengthy letter which we present here in its first English-language rendering. Trotsky's reply ('A Man Overboard', *Writings of Leon Trotsky (1929)* (New York, 1975), pp 188-89) was brief, and, apart from a few words countering Souvarine's contention that the Soviet Union was a state capitalist society — which was hardly the central aspect of the letter — failed to engage with any of the arguments presented in it. His conclusion, however, was harsh: 'You will pass to the other side of the barricades. Theoretically, you are already there. We record a man overboard and pass on to the next point on the agenda.'

Souvarine did shift to the right, albeit only gradually at first. His drift away from revolutionary politics was noticeable in his *Stalin* (English-language edition, London, 1939). When it first appeared in 1935, Souvarine was still willing in part to follow Trotsky's analysis of the rise of Stalinism and to declare that as late as 1923 the process of bureaucratisation could have been halted and soviet democracy revived. However, by early 1939, when he added a postscript to the book, he was bluntly asserting that Stalinism was the logical and unavoidable consequence of Bolshevism. Trotsky's description of him that year as 'ex-pacifist, ex-Communist, ex-Trotskyist, ex-Democrato-Communist, ex-Marxist… almost ex-Souvarine' ('Moralists and Sycophants Against Marxism', *Their Morals and Ours* (London, 1974), p 48) was cruel but by no means inaccurate. Souvarine's postwar material, repeating the most vulgar Cold War assumptions about Bolshevism, the October Revolution and the ensuing Soviet regime, indicated a marked decline on the part of his critical faculties.

Souvarine's letter was translated by Al Richardson and Harry Ratner from the version reproduced in Boris Souvarine, *À Contre-Courant* (Denoël, Paris, 1985), pp 208-75. Al Richardson also provided the notes.

* * *

Paris, 8 June 1929
Dear Friend
Your more or less open letters of 31 March and 25 April[1] invite me to a somewhat belated exchange of views: your conclusions have preceded the debate. However, replying to them cannot be without use, if only because it offers you a theme to refute.

The way you have begun this discussion does not seem to me to be the best. By setting down as 'decisive criteria' for tendencies in international communism secondary questions of strategy, tactics, methodology and application, it implies, along with accepting things that have happened in the Russian Communist Party and the International since Lenin's removal, agreeing with ideas imposed as the official doctrine in 1924 by shadowy congresses: the Fourteenth Congress of the Bolshevik Party and the Fifth Congress of the International.[2] Now the things done and these ideas represent a break with the principles that inspired and directed our movement up to 1923. It would be more advisable to accept as a touchstone communist axioms of theory and politics after having properly subjected them to the judgement of real events.

Communism as Marx defined it has to express the general interests of the proletariat: the neo-communism of 1924, currently called 'Leninism', reflects the narrow interests of the new leading formation in Russia which contradicts the inheritance of ideas that they took over along with power, which have lost their original sense to the extent to which the leading group has given in to pressure from the most demanding classes. Obviously, we must not abstract

1. LD Trotsky, 'Groupings in the Communist Opposition' (31 March 1929), and 'Six Years of the Brandlerites' (25 April 1929), *Writings of Leon Trotsky (1929)* (New York, 1975), pp 80-05 and 111-16.
2. The Fifth Congress of the Comintern was held in June-July 1924, and the Fourteenth Congress of the CPSU was held in December 1925.

ourselves from accomplished facts, but to a certain extent political realism consists of recognising them *de facto* without accepting them *de jure*.[3] And if it is true that questions of tactics or method cannot be separated from considerations of principle, this is not a reason for starting to examine causes obliquely by studying their effects. At the end of your second letter you call for 'a correct evaluation of the epoch and its driving forces and a correct forecast of the future':[4] that is truly what is important above all, but it is also precisely what you leave obscure. You have not said the first word about it. It would have been better to have begun there.

By calling continuity in question in the sixth year of the Russian Revolution, I am not in any way trying to pretend that communism today has now gone from absolute excellence to total degeneration. There were weaknesses and mistakes in our movement before the death of Lenin. And Lenin's own responsibilities for the change in our destiny are proportionate to his position amongst us. But in the period when our International was being formed the slips and errors above all were part of the movement itself, of the historical conditions of its birth in the European chaos in the aftermath of the war, of a generalised feeling of reaction against the decadent tendencies within socialism, and of the immaturity of the cadres of our improvised parties: Bolshevik hegemony was inevitable, as well as corresponding with natural selection: by encouraging the proper development of the other parties it would normally have tended to disappear and given way to an international cooperation of conscious forces. In the second period, once the movement had been set consciously in motion, with a relative cleaning out, seasoned by the first struggles and the hard experience acquired in them, it ran up against this tutelage which, while historically necessary to begin with, tended to outlive this historic necessity and found the Soviet state an artificial means of domination, at the very time that the course of the revolution rendered it less and less qualified to exercise it. Under an authority that gradually sterilised it, from then on the International did not cease to decline. In agreement with this phase, which is still continuing, there is a composite ideology, in which traces of the old remain, but in which theories of convenience come out on top.

Nor should my observations about the evolution of Soviet power due to the pressure of certain classes be understood as condemning all concessions or compromises within that range of ideas. Let us leave to scribblers all platonic affectations to intransigence. Lenin said, when speaking of the NEP, 'this isn't a change, it is a tactic'.[5] But the duration became changed in quality, and, in

3. *De facto* means in fact, and *de jure* as law (Latin).
4. LD Trotsky, 'Six Years of the Brandlerites' (25 April 1929), *Writings of Leon Trotsky (1929)*, p 116.
5. VI Lenin, 'Report on the New Economic Policy to the Seventh Gubernia Conference of the Russian Communist Party' (29 October 1921), *Collected Works*, Volume 33 (Moscow,

the long run, the tactic became second nature. For an agrarian country isolated in its revolution, this phenomenon could hardly be avoided: at the very best it could have been minimised, and the Soviet economy ought to have been rationally pointed in the direction of industrial progress, by stimulating the activity of the proletariat, by encouraging it to make use of its freedoms, by really democratising the party and all the workers' organisations and institutions, and by helping the autonomous development of the sections of the International. The future very much depended on the European working class. The merit of the Opposition was to have understood this in time. The fault of Lenin's successors is not to have done this and to have made it incapable of being realised by the normal methods. Accepting this, it still remains that proletarian power must not be prevented from compromising with non-proletarian classes or social categories, both at home and abroad. The policy of a socialist revolution that has been isolated for a long time can only be the art of compromise while safeguarding its basic positions. It is a matter of knowing how; through giving up ground in order to survive, it can avoid losing all reason for its existence: the solution cannot be summed up in a simple formula. I only wish to say that a retreat as such does not have to be criticised in all cases; we should rather concern ourselves with the errors that made these retreats necessary when political foresight would have allowed us to avoid them. And if the Soviet administration has really got itself forced into class bargaining, that is one more reason for the majority of the communist movement to be on guard against the Leninism that inspires it.

It has become impossible in our circles to begin a speech without backing it up with a heap of explanations, corrections and restrictions. There is no longer a common language among communists. This is a very striking sign of trouble and decline. From the very first words of this letter two obvious digressions were necessary, and the risks of being misunderstood have still not been exhausted. We constantly feel that we have said too much, or not enough, whatever precautions we take. Every term seems to require explaining. And it seems to me to be difficult to make any further progress without reappraising certain interpretations of Leninism.

Let us leave aside the almost banal sense in which the word has been used since the death of Lenin, a simple form of words, and the most vulgar acceptance of it in vogue in the International. A Leninism nonetheless remains to which the whole of the Russian Communist Party lays claim, including the Opposition, which even lays claim to it with particular fervency. Let us admit, for the sake of argument, that the Leninism of the Opposition is more worthy of the name it invokes, and is even the only real thing. We can talk about this one day at our

1966), pp 83-101.

leisure. But what is represented by this recent ideology, not in advantageous definitions adopted for the sake of convenience, but in reality? And, to be more precise, can we consider this Leninism as the modern extension of Marxism? I cannot here attempt a study, or even the draft of such a study of the subject, but I do feel the need to point out the outlines of a general idea.

Marxism has suffered the eternal fate of all great philosophical, historical or social systems that have become epoch-making; and because it involves the non-experimental sciences, those who follow and explain it have a margin of interpretation with indistinct limits which they often abuse. The materialist conception of history, in particular, moreover, is more easily subject to deformation because, by taking in all the phenomena of social life, it concerns human actions that are difficult to link to historical results by the chain of causality. From time to time, it therefore needs to rediscover its true meaning by making renovations in the spirit of its method's creators. They do not feel the need to draw up treatises of their science, relying on actual usage to demonstrate their arguments; this spreads the universality of their concepts throughout their work, written or lived. They have obviously not felt the need to affirm or confirm notions that go without saying for them, without for all that allowing anybody else to consider these gaps as negations. For more than a quarter of a century now controversies have occurred over various elements in Marxism, and, even if the first were not without their use, we are obliged to admit the feckless nature of the more recent: for they repeat themselves, the arguments and the known counter-arguments are chewed over and over again. This is yet another sign of the collapse of communist thinking: always repetitions of old texts in an evolving world, whilst the physical and natural sciences do change. And we must always take the trouble to recall, from time to time, that in addition to economic causes and political effects we must also take account of how the effect in turn reacts back upon the cause, and of all that results from that. How can we explain the futility of exhausting oneself in research investigating the impact of technical innovation in reinforced concrete on the venality of a Chinese general, not to mention the impact of synthetic petrol on the psychology of a district secretary? Marxist methods of working properly used should have allowed us to have progressed beyond this stage of cultural elaboration long ago.

On the level of practical struggle, differences are happily more simple than this. In the old Russian Social Democracy, a ramification of the political Marxism then in operation, Menshevism expressed a propensity to economic fatalism then derisively called 'Mahometan', and Bolshevism a tendency towards activism sometimes called Jacobin or Blanquist.[6] Menshevism appeared more

6. The Jacobins were left revolutionary democrats at the time of the French Revolution;

orthodox because it was closer to the letter, whereas Bolshevism allowed itself more latitude by appealing to the spirit. Nevertheless, in the light of historical experience, it was Bolshevism that turned out to be the driving force of the Revolution. What accounted for its superiority? Here I note a remarkable involuntary prior explanation of it in one of Lenin's writings (*Our Programme*, 1899), which was only published after his death. This is the striking passage:

> We do not regard Marx's theory as something complete and inviolable; on the contrary, we are convinced that it has only laid the foundation stone of the science which socialists *must* develop in all directions if they wish to keep pace with life. We think that an *independent* elaboration of Marx's theory is especially essential for Russian socialists; for this theory provides only general *guiding* principles, which, *in particular*, are applied in England differently than in France, in France differently than in Germany, and in Germany differently than in Russia.[7]

This way of not conforming to the letter of Marx's formulae was really more closely in agreement with Marxist teaching. Bolshevism was the intelligent and effective application of the Marxist method for gaining power in Russia, but in Russia, and not elsewhere. When it was put into operation in other countries it was botched up. In addition, this pre-revolutionary Russian version of Marxism played no part in the International before the war. We need go no further than to note Lenin's support for Rosa Luxemburg's amendment at Stuttgart[8] to highlight the truth of this remark. Lenin delivered violent attacks upon the 'venerable' founders of his party, Axelrod[9] and others, his teacher Plekhanov[10] and his friend Martov;[11] he struggled bitterly against Rosa Luxemburg and the Polish leaders who were involved with the Russian movement, but he was careful not to treat Bebel and Kautsky, Guesde and Adler, Jaurès and Turati and

---

    Blanquism takes its name from Louis Auguste Blanqui (1805-1881), who advocated the seizure of power on behalf of the working class by a conspiratorial élite by means of a *coup d'état*.

7. VI Lenin, 'Our Programme' (October 1899), *Collected Works*, Volume 4 (Moscow, 1960), pp 211-12.
8. Rosa Luxemburg (1870-1919) was the brilliant theorist of the left of the German Social Democracy and later of the Spartakusbund and the German Communist Party. Her amendment at the Stuttgart Congress of the Second International in 1907, seconded by Lenin and Martov, advocated 'hastening the downfall of capitalism' in the event of war.
9. Pavel Borisovich Axelrod (1850-1928) was one of the founders of the League for the Emancipation of Labour in 1883, the pioneers of Russian Marxism.
10. George Valentinovich Plekhanov (1856-1918) was the founder of Marxism in Russia.
11. Julius Ossipovich Tsederbaum, known as Martov (1873-1923) was the main theorist of the Menshevik faction of the RSDLP.

Hyndman and Vandervelde in the same manner.[12] And if he spoke out against Bernstein, that was part of a general argument about socialism in Europe, on which he did not stand out separately, and is the exception that tests the rule.[13] This is a good lesson for us today: our work in our own country can alone qualify us to intervene effectively in other countries. Later, during the revolution, Lenin was often to emphasise his favourite idea of respecting the particular nature and particular features of every revolutionary movement.

Bolshevism was Marxism simplified for use in a country in which classes were well defined and in which the revolution was permanently on the agenda against a regime that had long outlived its usefulness. On the level of social science it represented an impoverished Marxism, whereas as regards practical activity it was in line with the needs of its time and place. That was its undeniable merit, and October confirmed it. But seizing power is one thing, and organising a socialist economy is another. Post-revolutionary Bolshevism is no further forward in resolving the problems of power. For as long as the Civil War[14] continued, its prime qualities could be well employed, Lenin's strategic genius performed miracles, and those who came to it from the various schools of Russian socialism based themselves upon the great party of the Revolution and emerged as the best thinkers within it. But Bolshevism showed itself not up to the task during the period of peaceful reconstruction. The recovery of Russian production was undertaken by means of a state capitalism in which a new social layer appropriated and consumed a great part of the surplus valueproduced by the wage-earners. Lenin died without being able to show that he was capable

12. August Bebel (1840-1913) was a friend of Marx and Engels, and a founder of German Social Democracy. Karl Kautsky (1854-1938) was the foremost theorist of German Social Democracy and executor of Marx's literary legacy. Jules Bazile, called Guesde (1845-1922) was the leader of the French Workers Party who opposed participation in bourgeois governments, but later supported the First World War. Victor Adler (1852-1918) was a prominent Austrian Social Democrat and friend of Bebel, who gave lukewarm support to the war. Jean Jaurès (1859-1914) was a leader of the French Socialist Party in parliament, a noted orator and an opponent of the war. He was assassinated by a fanatic just before it broke out. Filippo Turati (1857-1932) was a leader of the Italian Socialist Party who opposed participation in the war. Henry Mayers Hyndman (1842-1921) was the founder of the Social Democratic Federation, the first British Marxist organisation, who had already before the war criticised the Liberal government for not building battleships fast enough. Émile Vandervelde (1866-1938) was Chairman of the International Socialist Bureau from 1900, but joined the Belgian cabinet during the war.
13. Eduard Bernstein (1850-1932) was the German Social Democratic thinker who began the 'Revisionist' controversy in the Second International with his article 'Probleme des Sozialismus' in *Die Neue Zeit* in October 1896. It questioned the need for the armed overthrow of the capitalist state, and posited the possibility of a peaceful and gradual development towards socialism.
14. The Russian Civil War (1918-22) between the Bolsheviks and the White armies, backed by numerous interventions from abroad, can only be said to have come to an end with the Japanese withdrawal from Vladivostok in October 1922.

of turning warlike Bolshevism into creative Bolshevism. He died leaving too difficult an inheritance for his followers, who had only been trained to think as their master thought.

Whilst playing an impressive role on the Russian stage to which it was adapted, Bolshevism intervened on the international arena. After the first steps of Zimmerwald and Kienthal,[15] where the left was in a weak minority, came an activity on a great scale with delegations of emissaries, support accorded to revolutionary groups in other countries, and then the founding of the Third International.[16] Lenin's political intelligence, his understanding of the particularity of conditions in each country and of the appropriate solutions for each party were drowned by the upsurge of the movement in which he was immersed. And here are the consequences: there is an obvious contrast with the victories in Russia. There were only defeats and failures in Europe. And from an entire epoch of civil wars and bitter class struggles there do not even remain, for the future of the proletariat, communist parties worthy of the name, nor the memory of any episodes worth enriching the revolutionary tradition. Without Lenin and without you, and your 'rightist' turn at the Third Congress of the Comintern, our parties would have been drowned in blood.[17] Deprived of Lenin and cut off from you, they are reduced to impotence.

Bolshevism has failed outside Russia, and not only by ignoring the relationship of forces. It has not grasped the nature of the epoch, it does not know how to analyse the condition of capitalism, has badly underestimated the ruling classes' means of resistance, has overestimated the consciousness and combativity of the exploited classes, and has made the fatal mistake of wanting to create communist parties in its own image. It has foreseen nothing, without ceasing to prophesy. None of the apocalyptic predictions of crises, revolutions or wars that it has proclaimed with such assurance have come to pass. We, on the other hand, were far too late in understanding capitalism's re-establishing its equilibrium, American domination, fascism, the consequences of the occupation of the Ruhr, the Dawes Plan and the new stage in the Chinese Revolution, and when an insurrection took place in Vienna and a general strike in Britain, they passed us by.[18] And where communists were involved, the party was not only uselessly

---

15. The Conferences of Zimmerwald (September 1915) and Kienthal (April 1916) brought together groups of socialists from all over Europe who opposed the First World War.
16. The Third or Communist International (Comintern) was founded in Moscow in March 1919.
17. At the Third Congress of the Communist International in June-July 1921, Trotsky attempted to warn those who believed in 'the theory of the offensive' that capitalism had temporarily stabilised itself, and that the tactic of the United Front should replace the previous leftist verbiage (LD Trotsky, *The First Five Years of the Comintern*, Volume 1 (London, 1973), pp 307-13, 321-33).
18. Benito Mussolini, Europe's first fascist dictator, came to power in Italy in October 1922.

defeated, but discredited as well: after Finland, Hungary and Bavaria came Bulgaria, Estonia and China.[19] And as the events of this decade unfolded, if at times you were the most farsighted among us whilst being completely involved in the collective errors, that is no doubt because you are the man you are, but probably also because of your autonomous development outside Bolshevism.

Post-revolutionary Bolshevism needs to return to Marx. It has, on the contrary, more and more taken its distance from Marxism. Its schematic simplicity has pushed the parody of its original teaching to the point of caricature. The economic determinism of its apologists has become more and more comic. And the results of its organisational principles have produced a belated illustration of Shchedrin's prophetic views.[20] Already as militant theoreticians Marx and Engels had been obliged to emphasise some of their arguments and some features of their concepts for polemical purposes and had laid themselves open to exaggeration and economic-materialist deformations by their over-narrow followers. Engels admitted this in explicit terms. It was a Marxism as elementary as this that held sway in the Second International. Bolshevism was firmly based upon a particular simplification, necessary for the catastrophic conditions of

> When Germany defaulted on its reparation payments under the Treaty of Versailles, French and Belgian troops occupied the Ruhr in January 1923, causing widespread economic and political crises. Economic order was only created in Europe by the Dawes Plan in 1924, under which America loaned money to Germany, which paid it in reparations to France and Belgium, which paid it in war debts to Britain, which then returned it in war debts to the USA. The Chinese Revolution went on the upturn in 1925, but the Comintern, first by subordinating the Chinese Communist Party to the Guomindang, and then by staging a coup annihilated the working-class movement. In July 1927, the police fired on a workers' demonstration in Vienna held to protest against the acquittal of Heimwehr supporters who had murdered Austrian workers, leading to 85 deaths. The British General Strike of May 1926 was called off by the TUC leaders after just over a week, leaving the miners, threatened by a pay cut, to fight on alone.

19. A general strike in Finland was followed by a premature uprising on 27 January 1918, which was suppressed by General Mannerheim with the help of German troops, and thousands were massacred. The Hungarian Soviet Republic was founded in March 1919, but was crushed by a Romanian invasion in the following August. A Bavarian Soviet Republic was proclaimed on 7 April 1919, but was suppressed by the Reichswehr a month later, followed by extensive executions. In June 1923, the Peasant Union government of Alexander Stambulisky was overthrown in Bulgaria by an army and right-wing coup. The Bulgarian Communist Party refused to take any part in the fighting on Stambulisky's side. Censured by the Comintern, the Bulgarian party then attempted an uprising of its own in September, which was easily smashed. In December 1924, encouraged by Zinoviev, the weak Estonian Communist Party attempted a coup, and held Reval for a few hours. It was suppressed with some brutality, ending with the formation of a military dictatorship.

20. Mikhail Yegrafovich Saltykov-Shchedrin (1826-1889) was a famous Russian novelist, editor and publicist. He had utopian dreams of a just, rational and ordered world, but criticised ruthlessly the shallow liberalism of his time, and doubted whether it would make any contribution to it. See LD Trotsky, 'The Methods of the Leadership' (2 June 1928), *The Challenge of the Left Opposition, 1928-29* (New York, 1981), p 113.

the imminent fall of an enormous outdated empire. But after its overthrow, as Lenin said, it showed itself to be 'behind the times', and, absorbed by creating its new state, it allowed itself to fall behind even further. A state-Bolshevism had been formed without being noticed which, after Lenin's death, assumed the name of Leninism.

This Leninism was in turn an extreme oversimplification of Bolshevism after power had been seized, and was a stage even further removed from Marxism. Not only is it 'behind the times' even more than the previous doctrine, it forever prevents itself from catching up. It is a theory that has eliminated from Marxism its dialectical method, its scientific richness and its universal validity, in order to latch on to a few schemas deprived of their original content, and practices of a religious character subjecting the masses to obedience, formulae and ceremonies which go to make up both the activity of the party and the life of the state. Leninism is a mystique armed with a deterministic phraseology which lives in Lenin's ashes after having choked off his flame, just as Menshevism attached itself devotedly to the letter of Marx without grasping his spirit. It is only able to survive in Russia by way of social immobility, by living off its past successes and by stealing from the heresies it condemns, but its ventures into Europe, America and Asia are derisorily inane. All the communist factions rightly lay claim to it, for they are no more than varieties of the same phenomenon, in spite of the external influences that are beginning to be felt among them.

In 1923, the Opposition attempted to distinguish itself from Leninism, whether it was conscious of it or not;[21] in 1926, after several somersaults, it fell back into the common rut. By assuming the name of 'Bolshevik-Leninist', as if that would help achieve it, by its very existence it announced its intention of competing with the Majority in pseudo-Leninist conformity and in fidelity to the letter of Lenin's writings, moreover taken out of context, as if there were to be found in them definitive answers to all the questions posed by history. In the fairly abundant literature of the Opposition, there is not a single example of a critical allusion to any action or speech by Lenin. A single iconoclast cannot be found in the ranks of the Opposition to make public protest against the divinisation of Lenin and the canonisation of his work, or even to propose burning the entombed corpse along with its mausoleum. We find in the practices of the Opposition the spontaneous reactions, methods and habits of the Majority. Leninism further debases the men and the factions.

A detached sociological explanation for this ideology would reasonably link it with the primitive rural character of the country in which it was elaborated. Leninism is an expression of peasant ignorance endowed with a Marxist varnish. Lenin, following Kautsky, saw in Marx's theory a higher synthesis of German

21. See Alfred Rosmer, *Trotsky and the Origins of Trotskyism* (London, 2002), pp 91-92.

philosophy, English political economy and French socialism.[22] Leninism makes an abstraction of all this intellectual heritage in order to elaborate a system of beliefs. But the only Russian Marxists are those who have lived in the West or are strongly imbued with European culture. Now doesn't the present conflict between the two major tendencies in the party represent some aspect of the traditional argument between the Slavophiles and the Westerners[23] which often gives off an odour of 'true Russian' nationalism? Marxism, strongly influenced by the rationalism of the Encyclopaedists,[24] has nothing in common with the phenomenon of peasant mysticism which, after Lenin's death, has in its own way taken the advice Carlyle gave Britain, finally to accept 'its Luther and its Cromwell, its priest and its king'.[25] But what the mystical preacher never dreamed of was a spiritual and temporal fusion within a corpse, to whose illegitimate heir we then have to submit.

The superiority upon which the Opposition prides itself of having a 'left Leninist line' is illusory. To begin with, this 'line' cannot be found; then, supposing that it is Leninist, that is not sufficient for it to be accepted; finally, if it is 'left', that proves nothing. At least accepting, according to Bacon's expression, 'a bucket of definitions for the substance of things',[26] we would do well to admit the present functioning identity between the theses of the Opposition and those of the leadership as regards the connection between the things they pose and what they deduce from them, either as regards the mechanism of thought, or in its general sense. The difference in their secondary conclusions is of little importance. That is why the majority of the oppositionists were so easily capable of returning to the official 'line': it is not good enough to divide your supporters into 'capitulators' and 'anti-capitulators' in order to avoid the question in the face of this problem, above all when, on the other hand, you are pretending to explain everything in terms of class currents. Examining your basic assumptions will show if I am wrong. I am impatient to come to this. The Leninist chapter

22. VI Lenin, 'The Three Sources and Three Component Parts of Marxism' (March 1913), *Collected Works*, Volume 19 (Moscow, 1963), pp 23-28.
23. See David Riazanov, *Marx and Anglo-Russian Relations and Other Writings* (London, 2003), pp 69, 74, etc.
24. The Encyclopaedists were French savants whose rational critique of religion was one of the stimuli for the French Revolution.
25. Thomas Carlyle (1795-1881) was a famous Tory historian of the English Revolution. Martin Luther (1483-1546) was the German monk who began the Protestant Reformation, and whose writings provided the rationale for the assault of the princes upon the power of the church. Oliver Cromwell (1599-1658) ruled England after overthrowing the king in the English Civil War (1642-49), but assumed the title of Lord Protector instead of king. The two names symbolise the problem of regulating the new relations between church and state created by the Protestant Reformation.
26. Sir Francis Bacon (1561-1626), Baron Verulam and Viscount St Albans, laid down the philosophical basis for the experimental method in the natural sciences.

merits a separate work, on its own, and in depth; I will when you wish provide examples, correspondences and proofs to support the assertions above.

* * *

We are heading for such difficult times that every co-thinker, every *potential* co-thinker, is precious to us. It would be an unpardonable mistake to reject a co-thinker, all the more so a group of co-thinkers, by a careless appraisal, by biased criticism, or by exaggerating differences.[27]

This is your first affirmation, and I completely agree with it. But at the same time you give yourself the right to place 'on the other side of the barricades'[28] those who do not answer as you do the questions that you have decided to set up as 'criteria', unless it is a circular barrier, where one finds oneself in the camp of the bourgeoisie for as little as allowing oneself to interpret and resolve in one's own way certain difficulties of tactics and methods. With your idea of classes and political currents, everything is simplified and everything is clear at little cost: on the one side there is the proletariat and the left; on the other, the bourgeoisie and the right; and since this does not come about without leaving a few more complex situations, there is 'centrism' which, if it did not exist, it would be necessary to invent it in order to pour into it all awkward circumstances. As for the barricade, since it does not have three sides, it is a metaphor occasionally used in a case in which we do not have to resort to a convenient centrism.

You very rightly say that the Opposition was formed 'on the basis of principled *ideological demarcation*' and not on '*mass actions*', and that 'in a period of stagnation or ebb tide' drawing 'a clear, precise ideological differentiation is unconditionally necessary'.[29] That is my opinion completely. 'The unity of the Opposition cannot be obtained by abstract sermons on unity or by mere organisational combinations',[30] adds your *alter ego*, in the same spirit. I agree absolutely with that. These opinions very much justify the resistance mounted to the thoughtless attempts at uniting the oppositional groups in France demanded by the Russian Opposition, which you are now disavowing in various ways.[31]

27. LD Trotsky, 'Groupings in the Communist Opposition' (31 March 1929), *Writings of Leon Trotsky (1929)*, p 80.
28. LD Trotsky, 'Once More on Brandler and Thalheimer' (12 June 1929), *Writings of Leon Trotsky (1929)*, p 156.
29. LD Trotsky, 'Groupings in the Communist Opposition' (31 March 1929), *Writings of Leon Trotsky (1929)*, p 80.
30. LD Trotsky, 'Tasks of the Opposition' (March 1929), *Writings of Leon Trotsky (1929)*, p 87. *Alter ego* means 'other self' (Latin).
31. The different groups of the Opposition in France had different origins and came into existence at different times. Souvarine's Marx–Lenin Circle and Monatte and Rosmer's *Révolution prolétarienne* group had been expelled from the French Communist Party

But since you also agree that this is a time for 'ideological demarcation', what has become of your theory of necessary class influences with which all your latest writings have been filled? Do ideas have to be the rigorously automatic emanations of states, class relations and shifts? If that really is your idea you will have confirmed my argument concerning the Leninism of the Opposition which would absolve me of the necessity of any further proof. Finally, as for the clarity and precision that you have on three occasions demanded, they might very well be necessary, but not, in my opinion, in the sense in which you take them. I vaguely remember Heinrich Heine[32] talking about an author whose talent consisted of making his public shed tears, a quality he shared with the common onion. Similarly, the clarity and precision that you are hoping for are easy to attain with today's technology by means of a gramophone record. Up to now this is all you have been able to gain in the International by way of agreement. Before you had any, 'Moscow' had a multitude of such supporters of whom already not a trace remains. Allow me therefore to state that ideas must not only be clear and precise, but also well considered, assimilated and attained in an almost organic manner. That ought to be self-evident. But in these times we must dot the i's.

You contend that 'communist opportunism expresses itself in the urge to re-establish under present-day conditions the prewar social democracy', vaguely attributing this deviation to me, more clearly shown, according to you, in Brandler and Thalheimer.[33] I do not know what they think about it, or on what you base your criticism. But so far as it applies to me, you are indubitably wrong. Since you refer neither to facts nor to texts, my refutation has nothing to aim at. Is a profession of faith so urgent on this unexpected theme? My fidelity to the spirit of the four real congresses of the International must put your doubts to rest. It is you who are seriously mistaken in your definition

       earlier by the Treint–Girault group, which had supported Zinoviev, and the *Contre le Courant* group of Maurice and Magdeleine Paz and the *La Lutte de Classes* group of Naville and Rosenthal developed some time afterwards. The formation of the Joint Opposition in the USSR led Trotsky to attempt to unite the French Trotskyist and Zinovievist oppositional groups, but the attempt to call a unity conference was rejected (Damien Durand, 'Opposants à Staline', Part 1, *Cahiers Léon Trotsky*, no 32, December 1987, pp 28-31, 56-59).

32. Heinrich Heine (1797-1856) was a German revolutionary poet.
33. LD Trotsky, 'Groupings in the Communist Opposition' (31 March 1929), *Writings of Leon Trotsky (1929)*, p 81. Heinrich Brandler (1881-1967), a building workers' leader, had been a delegate to the Zimmerwald Conference, a supporter of the Spartakusbund and a founder member of the KPD. He led the KPD in 1923 and was later scapegoated for its failure at that time and expelled from the party in 1929, when he founded the Communist Party (Opposition) group. August Thalheimer (1884-1948) was one of the founders and main theoreticians of the German Communist Party and later a leader of the Communist Party Opposition (KPO) along with Brandler.

of opportunism: for several years it is you and above all your followers who have been accusing those who disagree with you and are opposed to you of opportunism; nine out of ten times wrongly. I will set against you one of Lenin's excellent formulations, since it is practically forbidden to risk contradicting you without basing oneself upon recognised authorities: opportunism means 'sacrificing the fundamental interests of the working-class movement for the sake of momentary advantages', or 'the alliance of a small section of privileged workers with "their" national bourgeoisie *against* the working-class masses'.[34] Engels briefly defined opportunism as 'forgetting of the great, the principal considerations for the momentary interests of the day, this struggling and striving for the success of the moment regardless of later consequences'.[35] This hardly corresponds with the tendency you are denouncing. Are there any among our comrades, so devoid of dialectical thinking, who after 15 years are aspiring to rebuild the old social democracy in conditions so profoundly different from those of previous times? Why not, while you are at it, have them recreating 'the Conspiracy of Equals'?[36] And in fact, some of our friends are not far from having thought that. We shall later talk about this if the occasion arises.

Speaking of the party of Bebel, you say that 'history testifies that Bebel's party became converted into the present-day social democracy. This means that Bebel's party had already become absolutely inadequate in the prewar epoch.'[37] But allow me to add: history testifies that this is what became of Lenin's party; this proves that, while Lenin was alive, this party was already sick. Now it is not I who am dreaming of reviving Bebel's party, but rather you who wish to recreate Lenin's party, as if nothing had happened for the last five years. I could attempt to prove this, but you were the first to support this argument with regard to me. I will only add one thing: all my work is an attempt to *go beyond* the stages represented by our previous parties: it is therefore the opposite of returning to them. No one is claiming to have succeeded in doing it, but the *sense* of what I am trying to do is undeniable.

Now I come to your point of view about the relationship between social classes and political tendencies. It is necessary to cast a little light on this, for all your writings of these last few years are incapable of analysis without

34. VI Lenin, 'The Attitude of the Workers' Party to Religion' (13 May 1909), *Collected Works*, Volume 15 (Moscow, 1963), pp 409-10; 'Opportunism and the Collapse of the Second International' (January 1916), *Collected Works*, Volume 22 (Moscow, 1964), p 112.
35. Frederick Engels, 'A Critique of the Draft Social-Democratic Programme of 1891' (1891), Marx and Engels, *Selected Works*, Volume 3 (Moscow, 1969), p 435.
36. The Conspiracy of Equals was the organisation led by Gracchus Babeuf during the French Revolution.
37. LD Trotsky, 'Groupings in the Communist Opposition' (31 March 1929), *Writings of Leon Trotsky (1929)*, p 81.

clarification on this. I am even tempted to argue that you have become a prisoner of terminology and that your thought is being carried away by the speed of expressing it. According to you, everything comes down to the positions of 'left' or 'right', themselves corresponding to proletarian or bourgeois currents; he who thinks otherwise in the matter is, at best, a utopian who is inclined to place himself 'above the classes', or 'between classes', and is really a 'centrist' who does not understand and wants to reconcile social antagonisms; his unstable equilibrium must sooner or later put him to one side of 'the barricade'. There have been 'three classic tendencies in socialism — 1) the Marxist tendency; 2) the centrist tendency; and 3) the opportunist tendency'; you also call them 'historical tendencies'; they are, so you say, 'filled with social content; and in 'Soviet conditions' this social content is 'precisely incontestable'.[38] (I note the nuance here because you are evidently trying to say that outside Russia this content is not quite so clear.) And you call these tendencies respectively left, centre and right. Let us look at this more closely, from a historical point of view, which is the only one which is in agreement with the methods of Marxist investigation.

In the English proletarian movement for the Charter, the Working Men's Association represented by Owen and Hodgskin made up the 'Moral Force Chartists' (what we today would call the right), and the Democratic Association, influenced by French bourgeois Jacobinism, made up the 'Physical Force Chartists' (which we would now call the left).[39] O'Connor wrote in *The Northern Star*: 'The cry of the working classes was invariably "Let us not separate ourselves from the Whigs", and since this was my main aim, I had to struggle against a mountain of difficulties.'[40] During the French revolutions of the nineteenth century, the left expressed itself in the secret societies and insurrectionary groupings inspired by Blanqui, in which predominated the influence of the petit-bourgeois, intellectuals and artisans, whereas the workers were moving more to the right, towards the religious democratism of Buchez, Cabet's pacifist

38. Ibid, p 82.
39. Robert Owen (1771-1858) was a philanthropic cotton manufacturer and utopian thinker, who originated the theory that 'conditions determine consciousness'. Thomas Hodgskin (1783-1869) was a naval lieutenant and an English social theorist, the author of *Labour Defended Against the Claims of Capital* (1825). The Moral Force Chartists led by William Lovett aimed at organising within the law to make slow progress by means of the elaboration of trades unions and working-class educational and political societies. Allied with them were the Fraternal Democrats, an organisation founded in September 1845 by revolutionary emigrants and left-wing Chartists. The Physical Force Chartists, on the other hand, led by the Irish landowner Feargus Edward O'Connor (1794-1855), were revolutionary in their phraseology, even if O'Connor himself condemned abortive attempts at insurrection in *The Northern Star*, which he edited ('The Time For Fighting Has Not Yet Come', *Northern Star*, 29 December 1838, p 8).
40. *Northern Star*, 4 May and 22 June 1839.

communism, and Proudhon's mutualism.⁴¹ After the revolution of 1848, Marx and Engels were right-wingers, because they were dispelling the illusions of the petit-bourgeois phrase-mongers, the Ledru-Rollins, the Louis Blancs, the Mazzinis and the Kossuths;⁴² one of Engels' celebrated pages remains amazingly modern in this respect:

> The vulgar democrats expected sparks to fly again any day; we declared as early as autumn 1850 that at least the *first* chapter of the revolutionary period was closed and that nothing was to be expected until the outbreak of a new world economic crisis. For which reason we were excommunicated, as traitors to the revolution, by the very people who later, almost without exception, made their peace with Bismarck...⁴³

In Germany, the Lassalleans often passed as leftists, both in their stance and on paper; as opposed to the Eisenach socialists⁴⁴ and the Marxists, their theory was apparently very radical: 'as far as the working class is concerned, all other classes only form one reactionary mass', which has been given new life in the present Leninist 'insight' of 'class against class', and their practice of support for Bismarck is carried on in the Leninist tactic of shamefaced but effective support

41. Philippe Joseph Buchez (1796-1865) was a politician, historian and Christian socialist. Étienne Cabet (1788-1856) was a utopian communist writer. Pierre Joseph Proudhon (1809-1865) was a French social theorist, the author of *The Philosophy of Poverty* (1846), against which Marx wrote *The Poverty of Philosophy* (1847). His ideas had considerable influence upon future anarchist thinking.
42. Frederick Engels, 'On the History of the Communist League' (8 October 1885), *Revolution and Counter-Revolution in Germany* (Beijing, 1977), p 187. Alexandre Auguste Ledru-Rollin (1807-1874) was Minister of the Interior in the Provisional Government of 1848 in France. Jean Joseph Louis Blanc (1811-1882) was a French socialist and historian. Giuseppe Mazzini (1805-1872) was an Italian revolutionary and democrat who founded a 'Central Committee for European Democracy' which tried to infiltrate the First International. Lajos Kossuth (1802-1894) was the nationalist leader of the Hungarian insurrection of 1848. He joined Mazzini's Committee as an émigré in London. Marx accused him of cowardice because he later disavowed his proclamations calling for revolution after the uprising had collapsed.
43. Frederick Engels, 'Introduction to Karl Marx's *The Class Struggles in France 1848-1850*' (March 1895), Marx and Engels, *Collected Works*, Volume 27 (Moscow, 1975), p 510. Otto, Prince Von Bismarck-Schönhausen (1815-1898), the 'Iron Chancellor', was the main architect of German unification under the crown of Prussia. The reference here is to Ferdinand Lassalle (see the next note), who entered into negotiations with him.
44. The Lassalleans are so named after Ferdinand Lassalle (1825-1864), the founder of the General Association of German Workers, the first successful German workers' political movement. The Eisenachers, the smaller organisation adhering to the ideas of Marx, took their name from the Congress held at Eisenach in 1869 which set up the Social Democratic Working Men's Party. The two groups united in the Gotha congress of 1875 to create the German Social Democratic Party.

for Hindenburg, Poincaré and Chamberlain;[45] moreover, the proletarian Marxist whitewash of the Erfurt programme did not prevent the Lassallean statist democratic routinism of social democracy. Marx was to the right of Bakunin in the First International,[46] because revolutionary science was too much for the tumultuous peasant temperament. After the Commune, the Blanquists who had taken refuge in London broke with the Marxists whom they accused of being lukewarm and inactive. For half a century anarchism, which had peasant origins but which had some working-class aims, attacked proletarian socialism from a point of view that has been accepted as 'from the left'. In Russia, the pioneers of social democracy, the future Bolsheviks and Mensheviks, appeared to be boring right-wingers compared with the *Narodnovoltsy*, the terrorists, the Socialist Revolutionaries and the Maximalists, the supporters of the insurrection of the 'people' and of the peasants.[47] After the revolution of 1905, Lenin was on the right of his own party and allied with the Mensheviks against its left, from whom he separated himself. In France, the tendency to the left expressed itself in Hervéism,[48] of shameful memory. In Holland, the brilliant school of left Marxists with Pannekoek and Gorter is merely an intellectual current.[49] In the present German revolution, Liebknecht and Rosa Luxemburg figured as right-wingers, and their left sunk into *Nationalbolschewismus*, or rooted themselves into a small working-class sect cut off from all activity.[50] At the time of the

45. Field Marshal Paul Von Hindenburg und Beneckendorff (1847-1934) was titular head of the German army towards the end of the First World War; his election as President of the Weimar Republic in 1925 was assisted by the refusal of the Communist Party to call for a vote for the Social Democratic candidate in the first round of the election, which split the working-class vote. The French Communist Party's tactic of 'class against class' adopted during the 'Third Period' similarly assisted the French right, led by Raymond Poincaré (1860-1934), as did the mistaken policy of the British Communist Party after the General Strike, which strengthened the hand of Austen Chamberlain (1863-1937), British Foreign Secretary between 1924 and 1929, who was the main inspiration behind the anti-Soviet policy of the Conservative government.
46. Mikhail Alexandrovich Bakunin (1814-1876) was one of the theorists of anarchism, who intrigued against Marx by forming a secret faction inside the First International.
47. The Narodnovoltsy, or Narodniks, were the Party of the Peoples' Will (Narodnya Volya), a populist organisation; the Socialist Revolutionaries and Maximalists were their linear successors, and went in for terrorism.
48. Gustave Hervé (1871-1944) was famous for his anti-militarism and verbal extravagances. But he became an extreme patriot in 1914, and later moved in the direction of fascism.
49. Anton Pannekoek (1873-1960) was a Dutch astronomer and revolutionary socialist on the extreme left of the Second International before the First World War; Hermann Gorter (1864-1927) was a poet and theorist of the German left. Their ideas can be consulted in DA Smart (ed), *Pannekoek and Gorter's Marxism* (London, 1978), and the International Communist Current, *The Dutch and German Communist Left* (London, 2001).
50. Karl Liebknecht (1871-1919) and Rosa Luxemburg (1871-1919) were the leaders of the Spartacists during the First World War, and then founders of the German Communist Party; they had considerable trouble restraining the party's left wing. The KAPD (Communist Workers Party of Germany) was formed from the expulsion

communist crisis over Brest-Litovsk, Lenin was again on the right, and Bukharin treated him like a capitulator, agreeing with the Left Socialist Revolutionaries.[51] After our defeats in Central Europe, Lenin was yet again a right-winger at the Third Congress of the International, with your enthusiastic agreement.[52] In his letter to the Jena Congress of 1921, Lenin wrote: 'In order to explain and correct these mistakes (which some people enshrined as gems of Marxist tactics) *it was necessary* to have been on the *Right* wing during the Third Congress of the Communist International.'[53] After Lenin's death, his true successors were denounced as a rightist faction for having spoken about democracy in the party, industrialisation, orientation by means of an economic plan, and for saying that the European revolution was marking time for a while.

Historical experience illuminated by a serious analysis of class tendencies therefore testifies against your schema. It shows the so-called 'left' currents as quite often expressing the impatience, combativity or ideology of the urban or rural petit-bourgeois, even when they draw elements of the proletariat along with them, within the limits of the given circumstances (which I will not discuss here, for I am in no way trying to take up the opposite stance to what you are saying). If a faction of the proletariat is going to the left, it is proof that you should be on your guard against lapidary generalisations in view of the complexity of the subject; as a general rule, the working class in its organised mass inclines towards the sense called 'the right', and this finds lasting confirmation in the imposing numerical growth of the reformist trade unions and socialist organisations, not to mention the social democratic residue within the communist parties. The crisis of capitalism engenders a dynamic

    of this left at the Heidelberg Conference of October 1919, when they opposed participation in parliamentary politics and activity within reformist trade unions. Their programme can be consulted in *International Review*, no 47, Summer 1999, pp 13-17. *Nazionalbolschewismus* (National Bolshevism) was the tendency led by Heinrich Laufenburg and Fritz Wolffheim, expelled from the KAPD in August 1920, which called for unity with the German capitalist class for a 'revolutionary people's war' against the Versailles powers (*Revolutionärer Volkskrieg oder konterrevolutionärer Bürgerkrieg?*, Hamburg, 1920).

51. The Left Communist group, led by Nikolai Bukharin (1888-1938) arose in the Bolshevik Party in protest at the signing of the Treaty of Brest Litovsk in March 1918. Its platform, the *Theses of the Left Communists*, first appeared in *Kommunist* on 20 April 1918 (English translation, *Critique*, 1977). Bukharin later moved over to the side of Stalin, and was the main spokesman for the Right Opposition within the Soviet Communist Party.

52. Both Lenin ('Speech in Defence of the Tactics of the Communist International', 1 July 1921, *Collected Works*, Volume 32 (Moscow, 1965), pp 468-77) and Trotsky ('Speech on Comrade Radek's Report on "Tactics of the Comintern" at the Third Congress', 2 July 1921, *The First Five Years of the Communist International*, Volume 1, pp 321-33) opposed the disastrous 'theory of the offensive' and the 'March Action' in Germany at the Third Congress of the Comintern.

53. VI Lenin, 'A Letter to the German Communists' (14 August 1921), *Collected Works*, Volume 32, p 517.

of class forces that escapes rigid classification or all-purpose formulae, and requires a supple, living and rich interpretation, and if you will allow me to make use of a remark by Lassalle, *armed with all the knowledge of the time*. The most authentic interpreters of Marxism are not necessarily to be classified on the left or the right, and it would be arbitrary to charge them with centrism, this label being applicable to equivocal compromises between doctrines that are incompatible; we defined our position at our Third Congress as 'neither right opportunism nor left inopportunism'; revolutionary consciousness and communist understanding cannot be forced into rigid moulds, without for all that being either 'above classes' or 'between classes'.

The two great continental revolutions, which happened in agrarian countries, and from this fact show distinctive resemblances in spite of the obvious differences of period, of internal and external circumstances, of developments, of the received ideas and influences they have undergone, could not avoid striking at their left wing after they had done so against their right. In France, the Enragés and the Hébertists were destroyed for having pushed, the former for pillaging, and the latter for war. The current opinion among communists that these amputations led directly towards Thermidor[54] would not hold up for five minutes in the presence of a serious argument. In Russia the Left Socialist Revolutionaries and anarchists were also broken for having pushed, some for pillaging, and others for war.[55] Robespierre[56] and Lenin, both of whom incarnated *their* revolution, could not have acted otherwise. Neither the one nor the other could be accused of being centrist, unless you alter the meaning of the word. They did not suppress their left in order to counterbalance their destruction of the right, but through an understanding of the risks they would run if active minorities succeeded in dragging along the masses by seducing them with unrealisable programmes. Before them in the English 'Great Rebellion' of the seventeenth century, Cromwell had to strike at the Presbyterians on the right

54. The Enragés were the followers of Jean Varlet and Jacques Roux, who led the sansculottes of Paris in attacks upon hoarding and speculation in 1793. The Hébertists were the followers of Jacques-René Hébert (1757-1794), the most extreme supporters of the terror dominating the Cordeliers Club who tried to engineer a popular uprising, only to be guillotined. Thermidor 1794 was when the Jacobins were overthrown, and the reaction against the French revolution began.
55. Some of the anarchists during the Russian Revolution went in for individual expropriations and banditry: the anarchist Black Guard was finally disarmed and dislodged from the houses it occupied in Moscow by the Cheka in April 1918. The Left SRs, who formed the first Soviet government in a coalition with the Bolsheviks, refused to accept the terms of the Treaty of Brest Litovsk in March 1918. They broke with the government and tried to reverse the treaty by shooting the German ambassador, killing members of the government such as Uritsky and Volodarsky, and wounding Lenin.
56. Maximilien Robespierre (1750-1794) was the Jacobin leader of the French Revolution at the height of the terror.

and the Levellers on the left,⁵⁷ for the industrial revolution was not able to give birth to the classes in modern society until the following century. A conscious revolutionary policy has to hold back any pressures, even of the class whose rise it expresses, or of classes allied to it, that risk diverting it from its historic paths.

With reference to the social content of the 'three tendencies', it is, whatever you might say, very debatable, even within 'Soviet conditions', even if you confine your focus to the communist movement. In 1925, one of the main theoreticians of the Opposition, an expert in the use of your method, thus defined the party's political and social currents in accordance with the ideas of their leaders: Zinoviev, Kamenev and Sokolnikov represented above all the right, the peasants; Trotsky, Piatakov and Preobrazhensky represented the left, the proletarians; and Stalin the centre, the bureaucrats.⁵⁸ Six months later, the three 'most authentic' right-wingers were on the left. After that, an entire series of your left lieutenants or left allies went off towards the right, the majority of them halting in the centre. Other people who represented a class, according to your orthodox interpretation, have experienced enigmatic vicissitudes: Rykov, reflecting the mentality of the technicians, and Tomsky, that of the skilled workers, should have supported a policy of industrialisation; it was the opposite that took place.⁵⁹ Rakovsky and Radek, supposed to be right-wingers, were to be found on the left, each with his own reasons, whilst waiting to return to where they had come from or changing places.⁶⁰ All these

57. Cromwell effectively ruled England after the execution of Charles I. When the Presbyterians, who represented the rich merchant oligarchy, attempted to halt the further progress of the revolution, Cromwell dissolved the 'Rump' parliament dominated by them. The Levellers, on the other hand, wished to press the revolution further in the direction of representative government. Their final army mutiny was suppressed at Burford in 1649.
58. Grigory Yevseyevich Radomysslsky, known as Zinoviev (1883-1936), and Lev Borisovich Rosenfeld, called Kamenev (1883-1936), were to begin with more prominent than Stalin in the government of Russia after Lenin's death. Allied with them was Grigory Yakovlevich Brilliant, alias Sokolnikov (1886-1938). Yuri Leonidovich Piatakov (1890-1937) and Yevgenii Alexandrovich Preobrazhensky (1886-1937), on the other hand, led the Left Opposition along with Trotsky. All later fell victim to Stalin's Terror.
59. Alexei Ivanovich Rykov (1881-1938) was President of the Council of Peoples Commissars on the death of Lenin. Mikhail Pavlovich Efrimov, known as Tomsky (1880-1936) was the head of the Soviet trades unions. Both were allies with Bukharin as leaders of the Right Opposition. Tomsky committed suicide, but the others perished in the Terror.
60. Christian Georgevich Rakovsky (1873-1941) spent much of his diplomatic career in the 1920s negotiating trade agreements for the Soviet government, and so could have been expected to support the right in the Communist Party, but was in fact a close associate of Trotsky's in the Left Opposition. Karl Bernhardovich Sobelsohn, whose pseudonym was Radek (1885-1939), had initially supported 'National Bolshevism' in Germany, as well as making the notorious Schlageter speech in 1923, and so could be expected to support the right, but was also a member of the Left Opposition. Both of them later perished in the Terror.

crossovers are badly explained by means of a theory which makes political programmes and social interests strictly inseparable. On the contrary, we can find approximate explanations by allowing subjective factors to intervene, while remaining in the spirit of Marxist sociological ideas. Ideas, even those springing from class necessity, acquire their own life, interacting back on their origins and reciprocally influencing each other. Personalities, in their turn, and to various extents, also play their part. It requires serious crises for economic and social forces to override secondary causes and allow great collective social interests to prevail. Between two crises, as in the present period, it is not at all rare for less important motives to predominate over deep determinants. The true Marxist is precisely he who discerns the successively essential 'moments' in the cycle of causes and effects.

The conventional terms of left and right imply very diverse meanings (positive and negative, as they say in Russia), and this is so true that they can sometimes take a positive and sometimes a pejorative meaning, according to the circumstances in which they are used or the nuance given to them in a particular setting. (In the revolutionary movement, 'right' almost always implies an unfortunate idea, and you have to be a Lenin to choose calmly a place on the right, which his friends of the most established tendency attempt to pass themselves off as... the real left). In 'left' we can read revolutionary spirit, brave militancy and class intransigence, but also romantic boasting, thoughtlessness, demagogy and adventurism. In 'right' we can find a spirit of biding our time or compromising, a fear of blows, opportunism, but also an exact knowledge of realities, a proper estimation of an obstacle, and tactical foresight. The same faculty can be a quality for some and a defect for others; a party on the attack must know how to temporise, but temporisation elevated to the level of a principle, as the English do with the cult of Fabius Cunctator,[61] becomes bourgeois liberalism. Moreover, a Trotsky can allow himself in his studies expressions needing explanation, but he must not put them into circulation as political formulae capable of being transformed into poison by the interpretations of vulgar Philistines.

As for 'centrism' — it is difficult to understand exactly what you mean by that. 'We have more than once', you say, 'appraised the general line of the Comintern leadership as *centrism*.'[62] You have not appraised anything at all.

61. The Fabian Society in Britain, which was the most right-wing component of the Labour Party in the 1920s, took its name from Quintus Fabius Maximus Verrucosus, called Cunctator ('the delayer'), the Roman consul who wore down Hannibal's armies in South Italy during the Second Punic War by refusing to accept battle. By taking this name, the *Fabian Tracts* signalled their desire to move slowly to socialism by gradual reform.
62. LD Trotsky, 'Groupings in the Communist Opposition' (31 March 1929), *Writings of Leon Trotsky (1929)*, p 80.

On the contrary, centrism serves as an expedient for you to avoid appraisals. How, for example, did the Reval outbreak and the Sofia explosion[63] express centrism? Or even more so, the tactics in electoral political contests that tend to favour the reactionaries and clericals in France, and the Conservatives and jingoes in Britain? Or denouncing the Kellogg Pact[64] as a threat of war against the Soviet republic at the same time as the Soviet government was signing it? In this theoretical, tactical and often bloody chaos are mixed up all sorts of personal and collective aberrations, physical and moral degeneration, intellectual disarray, ignorance and presumption, emanations of a real social mess where the proletariat's lack of understanding fights it out with petit-bourgeois incoherence. I know that you have a very ready response, always the same, for each embarrassing example: a zigzag, sometimes to the right, sometimes to the left. This is an answer that is not an answer at all. For the zigzag remains to be explained, to be given a social content, whose existence and origin you are sure. During the war, Lenin was fighting against a 'centre' that he had defined: it was a question of a position intermediate between out-and-out reformism and consistent Marxism. The 'centre' in bourgeois parliaments also represents a tendency sufficiently intelligible to all. But your centrism remains, if not inexplicable, at least unexplained in spite of occasional explanations that have not supported the comparison.

To bank upon the decline of capitalism, when production and technique are in full swing; to predict the next revolution when, under our eyes, the communist parties are isolating themselves and degenerating; to foresee a war during a period of peace — this may well be very 'left', but it is not the act of conscious revolutionaries fit to lead the masses. Lenin publicly called this sonorous verbiage 'communist conceit' (*comchvanstvo*)[65] and, in private, expressed himself in a yet more severe manner. Obviously, repeating for two or three decades predictions of violent social turmoil will always end up finding an apparent justification in a capitalist world which has a history of recurrent crises; nonetheless, the event surprises those who profess to forecast it. In order seriously to account for the future of capitalism by the development of its productive forces, the real threats of war and the possibilities for successful

63. In April 1925, the Bulgarian Communist Party's military section exploded a bomb in Sofia cathedral during a state funeral. The king and the government escaped, but over a hundred others were killed, and hundreds of others wounded. Hundreds of communists were then rounded up and tortured, and many were executed. For the insurrection in Reval, see note 19 above.
64. By signing the Briand-Kellogg Pact of 1928, so called after the French and American foreign secretaries, the signatories agreed to outlaw war as an instrument of foreign policy.
65. VI Lenin, 'The New Economic Policy and the Tasks of the Political Education Departments' (17 October 1921), *Collected Works*, Volume 33, pp 77-78.

revolution, there is a need, not only for a class point of view and a Marxist method of analysis, but self-discipline, study and a modicum of modesty. This is not incompatible with a combative spirit, or with sound audacity. In default of this, even in catastrophic situations, communism would be synonymous with bankruptcy. And if this means inclining to the right, then go to the right. Happily, the reverse has not been proved, and an enlightened communism will find its class orientation without falling into either inveterate infantilism or premature senility.

The three 'criteria' you advance in your first letter for understanding the present tendencies in communism appear to me to be chosen arbitrarily and devoid of value in themselves. You are expecting a French, Czech or Italian communist to be able to give an impeccable answer to basic political problems in Britain, to economic ones in Russia, and to tactical ones in China. Failing this, you class him on that side of 'the barricade' where according to you are to be found the bourgeoisie, the social democracy and the 'Centre-Right Bloc'. And correcting his position is based upon his agreement with your own point of view, which is no doubt considered as the standard laid down in advance. All this relates to nothing solid. Independently of his view of the overall epoch, a communist must be judged more in accordance with the foresight he shows in the affairs of his own country. For all that his international views will not be negligible, but they will be worth all the more if the individual in question shows himself to be up to his task in the country where he happens to be. In the modern world there is no encyclopaedic brain capable of taking in all the vital questions. Specialisation, connected with general knowledge, becomes as necessary in politics as it is in production. The advantage of having an international collectivity is rightly to associate competences whose equivalent does not exist inside one head alone. In certain historical circumstances the decisive criterion can be found elsewhere: the Paris Commune, the war of 1914 and the Russian Revolution could test the quality of a communist from Sweden, Spain or Holland. But the history of the 'Anglo-Russian Committee',[66] the comings and goings of the Guomindang and the complications of the NEP remain very obscure to all the communists in two hemispheres, apart from some in each country who happen to be directly involved. As for the very rare comrades who have a panoramic view of the world and sufficient training, of which you are the most eminent representative of the type, they have more chances to deceive themselves, as your example precisely demonstrates, which I will try to prove, since you insist.

66. The Anglo-Russian Trade-Union Committee was set up in April 1925, initially to campaign for the readmission of the Soviet-led trade unions into the social-democratic-dominated Amsterdam trade-union centre. It was hailed by the Russians as a move to the left on the part of the British trade-union leaders.

Marx and Engels, whose work has stood the test of time and the gnawing of bourgeois erudition, and whose stature grows to the extent to which history distances them, lived in England and made a special study of this classic land of capitalism. They followed the development of the classes there in relation to the evolution of technology, and the consequences of their antagonisms. However, their faculties of foresight were perhaps found to be defective there. Lenin, whose political sense and 'realism' is even recognised by bourgeois statesmen, and whose mastery of Marxist analysis and tactical subtlety we know, also lived in England and allowed himself predictions that were contradicted by the events. He believed in a British revolution after the war, and saw in the network of shop stewards' committees the embryo of a soviet system.[67] He wanted the various communist parties and groups of England and Scotland to unite into one section of the International, and we know what became of that, helped by other mistakes. But you expect men who have none of the qualities of these masters to approve your views on the course of events in the British Empire and your tactics in one of its crises. But even if you were right, which the present and future will show, what would be the sense of having illiterates confirm you in the matter? The most qualified people in the revolution have argued for five years about economic policy in the USSR, hurling statistics and percentages at each other without being able to resolve anything: yet you are calling for the agreement of who knows what illiterates with theses whose signatories cannot even agree among themselves as to how to interpret them. Finally, on China, from whom in Europe are you hoping for a validly considered agreement? And do not attempt, for the purposes of reply, to attribute to me the idea of a mandarinate dividing out cerebral functions between highly qualified specialists. You know very well what I am trying to say. This is not a matter of theorising, but of stating a matter of fact. Our movement is disorganised, dislocated and practically everywhere in pieces. It is without heads, without cadres, and without the masses. It is also without information, and without training. The publications of our parties are stained by illiterate scribblers. A few dispersed people remain who are striving to 'keep up to date', and only very relatively succeed in doing so. The little oppositional groups determined to eke out a living in the shipwreck cannot but support the opinions of their most venerable or advanced member without really convincing anybody. And the way to encourage the rank and file to rise higher is not by imposing your dilemmas upon them. I only know of two or three comrades in France who can usefully be consulted about Britain or Russia. I do not know of any for China. And none would allow himself to set up his own opinion as a criterion. In other

---

67. VI Lenin, 'Speech at the Opening Session of the First Congress of the Communist International' (2 March 1919), *Collected Works*, Volume 28 (Moscow, 1965), pp 455-56.

countries, apart from Russia, the situation may not be any better. That is why I cannot conceive of a worse manner than yours of posing the problem of criteria in general. And you do not deal with it any better in each particular example.

There is no recognisable difference between your theses on the economic, social and political tendencies in the British Empire and those of the Russian Politbureau. It was, moreover, you who fed ideas about Britain to the two opposing factions in your book of 1925.[68] The excessive schematism of this book, the far too strict transposition of continental revolutionary processes into the British setting, lie at the basis of the errors committed on both sides. (I am obviously talking about publicised opinions and public resolutions, and not about afterthoughts, such as must have been in Tomsky, details of which I do not know).[69] The general identity of analyses, of understanding and of tactical conceptions is obvious. The difference only rests upon the timing of the split with the Anglo-Russian Committee and of the denouncing of the attitude of the trade-union leaders. Now the question of timing can have a decisive importance in a generally well-led operation, in which a rapid turn could make its mark at the appropriate time. But in a continuous collection of misunderstandings and mistakes, in which the Bolsheviks only yet again demonstrated the noxiousness of their interventions in situations which they were powerless to foresee and were incapable of supporting the interests of the proletariat, the question of the time to break can only be of scant significance. You have got very heated up about it, nobody understands you, and, moreover, they have difficulty in understanding what it is all about, so poor is your criterion. You have, both leaders and Opposition, gone astray in a direction in which it was impossible to go a step further without making a false step, and, finding yourselves at a dead end, you are arguing with each other over an imperceptible nuance.

You both believed that the British industrial crisis was opening up a revolutionary period. You deceived yourselves. You believed that the Labour Party felt favourable to Bolshevism in its majority. You deceived yourselves. You stuffed the skulls of the trade-union delegates in Russia and you fed them with illusions whilst catching them yourselves in turn. You deceived yourselves. You extolled the leaders of the left of the trades unions as revolutionaries and semi-communists after having first of all denounced them as 'left social democrats' and as being worse than those of the right, and then you thought you had sovietised them. Here you deceived yourselves twice over. You formed an Anglo-Russian Trade-Union Committee on the basis of mutual deception, in which the Bolsheviks tried to pass themselves off as British-style trade unionists,

68. LD Trotsky, *Where is Britain Going?*, in *Trotsky's Writings on Britain*, Volume 2 (London, 1974), pp 3-123.
69. Tomsky gave a belated description of several British trade-union leaders as 'traitors' in an interview in *Pravda* on 8 May 1927.

and the trade unionists tried to pass themselves off as Russian-style semi-communists. You deceived yourselves. You took the General Strike for the first stage of a revolution. You deceived yourselves. You conspicuously sent subsidies believing that you were rendering service to the movement and increasing the value of your interventions. You deceived yourselves. You then denounced as traitors the British trade-union representatives whom you had hoisted without reason on the Soviet masthead. You deceived yourselves yet again. You did not stop deceiving yourselves. After that the Opposition called upon the universe to bear witness that they had demanded the public repudiation of the 'traitors' and an appeal to the masses at the appropriate time, whereas the Politbureau obviously did it too late. The whole world remained indifferent, and for good reason.

The situation might have been revolutionary in your mind, but not in Britain. In any case, but not in the sense you understand it, we might accept it in Kautsky's, when he wrote 25 years earlier that the social revolution could no longer be premature. There can be no question of a revolution if there are no revolutionaries, for history is made by men. You know as well as I do that communists do not exist in Great Britain. But there is something worse than the absence of communists; and that is the presence of a party of a few hundred pseudo-communists who discredit their flag and repel workers tempted to join them. It would be better to have a clean slate than this obstacle. The revolutionary workers of the Clyde and of Wales will never join a servile group discredited in the sight and knowledge of all. You expected the struggle to create a layer of new militants capable of supplanting the old trade-union leadership; cadres cannot be improvised in this way; it needs years to educate and temper them. We know the balance sheet of the Bolsheviks with regard to this: in 10 years the International lost all its outstanding individuals and all its valuable militants in every country, and has not been capable of training a single one. You talk about British communism as if it were an abstraction in line with your definitions; but in reality it is derisory, not only quantitatively, but qualitatively. The old Social Democratic Federation[70] at least had the abolition of the monarchy in its programme: the Communist Party isn't even as brave as this; that is the amount of progress that has been made. It is true that this skeleton genuflects in the direction of Moscow, and claims to be very Leninist. But it is obvious to all that that is why the proletariat holds it in contempt.

You counted upon a drive to the left determined by unemployment: Marxist thinking should have spared you this type of illusion; poverty does not inevitably give rise to the understanding of poverty; sometimes the thinking

---

70. The Social Democratic Federation was the original Marxist organisation in Britain, founded by HM Hyndman in 1881.

and activity of a class are in inverse proportion to its reasons for rebelling. You think it is sufficient to denounce the leaders in order to win over their troops; the former are contemptuous of your insults, and the latter do not want to hear them anymore. I remember the astonishment of Taine in the presence of miserable British proletarians who were paying one and a half shillings to listen to a meeting about Macaulay;[71] the Comintern's extravagances have no hold on so educated a public. You do not know how to talk to the British workers. Nor do I. But if hypothetically I did have to talk to the British, I would perhaps have a chance of being heard, for I would begin by studying my audience. Whereas you, by persisting in not reckoning on any difference between the workers of London and those of Moscow, are wasting your time and effort. Yet again, do not attempt to ascribe to me an idea that is absent from me of being the educator of the workers who had been open-mouthed before Macaulay. I am only recommending the use of an intelligible language, and yours is not that. And you can 'denounce', expose, etc, as much as you like, but the proletariat has taken no notice of it. And rightly so.

For whilst being in the wrong to exist politically on the prejudices inculcated by its bourgeoisie, it is in the right in aspiring to lead itself. It believes it is doing so by giving itself leaders like JH Thomas; that proves the extent to which the Tom Manns can be separated from their class. Thomas is deceiving nobody; he has even published a book, *When Labour Rules*, in order to affirm his loyalty to the monarchy.[72] The British railwaymen vote for him in full knowledge of this. This might not be in conformity with Leninism, but it is Leninism that is defective in the face of the facts. Thomas represents his trade-union federation, which elected him. Tomsky was elected by no one, and represents nothing. A telephone call from Stalin was enough to overthrow Tomsky;[73] but no matter how much Stalin might have telephoned, Thomas would have remained in place. Let us remember that Thomas was nearly overturned at his last conference, but by the railwaymen who had elected him, and not by Stalin. It was an intervention of the communists against him that saved him. All this is full of lessons.

The Labour Party had a very special liking for the Bolsheviks: that of industrialists and traders towards important clients. You know this — you

71. Hippolyte-Adolphe Taine (1828-1893) was a prominent French historian and positivist thinker; Thomas Babington Macaulay (1800-1859) was an English historian and a Whig MP.
72. James Henry Thomas (1874-1949) was the leader of the railwaymen's trade union who played an important part in engineering the defeat of the General Strike; his book, *When Labour Rules*, was published by Collins in 1920. Tom Mann (1856-1941) had a long and honourable record in the socialist movement, having led the great dock strike of 1889, and been a founder of the British Communist Party.
73. Tomsky was dismissed as head of the Soviet trades unions in May 1929, and replaced by Chvernik.

must know this. You only have to think. If you took this community of interests between the unemployed and the employers for solidarity between proletarians, the lot of you are unforgiveable. And if you were not deceived, why have you based a policy upon a misunderstanding or a deception? From whatever angle you look at it, you are in the wrong. The trade-union representatives in Russia, at your suggestion, published a vast report full of exaggerations; they were promised orders in Moscow for 'their' industry. But they nevertheless concluded that Bolshevism is excellent for the Russians, but repugnant to the British: this proves in what contempt they hold you and what an elevated notion they have of their own island. The Politbureau got nothing for its money; that should teach it to want to buy everything.

The leaders of the trade-union left did not become communists by virtue of their honorary nomination to various soviets, any more than they had been social democrats previously: they remained what they had always been, liberals, evolutionists and disciples of Mill and Spencer.[74] They remain labourites. That is the sum total of what you blame them for. This is a ridiculous accusation: you must not take them for what they are not. Repudiating them as traitors because they came into your Anglo-Russian Committee not as Bolsheviks, but as trade unionists, and behaved as trade unionists and not as Bolsheviks, is senseless: they cannot betray a cause that they have never embraced, or break agreements that they never made. It is you who are wrong for reproaching these legalists, parliamentarians and evangelical pacifists for not having led an economic strike like insurrectionists and revolutionaries. And do not tell me that all economic activity has a political character: I know this as well as you do, but the British proletarians do not know this, and it is a question of making them understand it. With your way of going about things you are confirming them in their traditions. In your motion on the Anglo-Russian Committee for the Party Central Committee, which alone takes up two pages of the *Bulletin Communiste*,[75] I counted the words 'traitors' and 'betrayal' 25 times, without taking account of 'felony', 'perfidy' and other expressions. You are wrong 25 times over to emphasise your lack of arguments in this way. If this motion had contained more ideas, it would have needed fewer adjectives.

In all this political–tactical mess-up, in spite of your efforts, you have completely lost sight of the split in the Anglo-Russian Committee. It is no longer just a question of your way of looking at the British workers' movement in relation to communism, but of your position as regards the non-communist

74. John Stuart Mill (1806-1873) was an English economist and philosopher, a utilitarian and a free trader; Herbert Spencer (1820-1903) was a positivist and a psychologist.
75. LD Trotsky, 'Resolution to the Joint Plenum of the Central Committee and Central Control Commission on the General Strike in Britain' (July 1926), *Trotsky's Writings on Britain*, Volume 2, pp 189-95.

working class of every land, and consequently the problem of the relations between proletarian parties, the idea of the United Front, and the attitude to be taken up towards the trade unions. The way of going about things called 'of the left', adopted by the Politbureau as well as by the Opposition, with insignificant variations, appears to me to be completely contrary to the spirit of Marxism; it isolates the communists more and more, makes them alien to the mass of the proletariat, and sets them as opponents of the masses. It is not enough to judge it as sectarian: a sect, at least, lives for itself and gets in nobody's way. But the Leninist sect tries to impose itself everywhere upon the workers' movement and impose upon it its wishes dictated by a Russian 'bureau' which passes itself off as the supreme expression of revolutionary understanding. Totally lacking in the higher qualities that could confer upon it the necessary prestige and ascendancy, it can pursue its enterprises only by making use of underhand politics and base manoeuvres. The proletariat ends up seeing it as an enemy, and treats it accordingly. Such is the result of the left's higher thinking.

To this aberration, which actually does not even have the virtue of representing an elemental momentary upsurge of the proletariat, since it is the work of professional revolutionaries and hardened functionaries, I oppose our real class policy in the accepted tradition: the alliance of the proletariat with the social layers more or less hostile to the ruling bourgeoisie, common action between the parties and the workers' trade unions, and an 'honest United Front', as Radek put it (even if he then retracted) on the basis of a minimum programme, by virtue of precise agreements reserving the right of criticism and our freedom of action in the future. This may well include breaking alliances and clashes between previous allies but in healthy competition. Outside this path, I do not see anything that can save our movement from disaster.

From the pronouncements in various forms of the Opposition on the international workers' movement, it emerges that anyone who contradicts it is more or less a traitor or a counter-revolutionary. Sometimes it takes the trouble to distinguish between 'objective' betrayal and 'conscious' counter-revolution, but this merely further obscures a theme that is already well tangled up. While the expression changes, the sense never alters. 'The offensive of the bourgeoisie, the social democracy, and the right-centre bloc in the Comintern' are, so you say, 'phenomena of one and the same order.'[76] And the metaphor of 'the barricade' serves to place on the bad side men about whom, by a singular contradiction, we read an eulogy in your latest 'Letter to the Workers of the USSR' as companions of Lenin in the course of the first and hard years of our

---

76. LD Trotsky, 'Six Years of the Brandlerites' (25 April 1929), *Writings of Leon Trotsky (1929)*, p 115.

International.[77] The most curious thing is that on the other hand you do not let an occasion pass to discover under every expression of opinion a class basis which, in strict logic, would exclude the explanation of betrayal. It is time to put an end to this confusion, which is made worse by an unjustifiable method of classification. If the war induced those of us, who rejected the Sacred Union[78] in the way we did, to repudiate our old leaders as traitors, that is easily explained. We had the speeches they made at Stuttgart and Basel,[79] and at their national conferences: we were right to denounce them for such a flagrant going back on the promises they had given. However, our anger at the time could not take the place of politics or doctrine. When a 'betrayal' is made by several million people all at once, it is not a betrayal in the usual sense: it is an historical development or change, the social reasons for which it is necessary to study and draw all the conclusions from them without resorting to formulae that empty and simplify, but explain nothing. British Labourism, Austro-Marxism[80] and postwar social democracy need a bit more than a label. Moreover, the communists, in the state of indescribable decay into which they are sinking, really do not have the right to criticise the whole world and his father. Isn't it distressing to see a party, and an International, whose most famous representatives have been expelled as different sorts of traitors in the course of 12 years, arrogating to itself the right to denounce traitors in neighbouring parties? To start off with, the oppositions must set an example in decency and objectivity.

Distinguishing between leaders and followers does not provide the key to the difficulty: it is far too easy to identify generals and troops in seeking to pit the former against the latter. This comparison is rarely valid in the social movement of the West. The masses and their elected leaders react on each other and are often inseparable. There are leaders who follow their troops and others who go ahead of them; it very much depends upon the circumstances. But in general, the consciousness and activity of the class are for better or worse expressed through political and trade-union cadres, and even when the workers are discontented with their usual representatives, they prefer them to people who attack them and whose hostility from outside has the effect of drawing them closer to those from whom people want to separate them. In the capitalist world, armies do not elect their generals, but proletarian organisations choose their representatives

77. LD Trotsky, 'Open Letter to the Workers of the USSR' (29 March 1929), *Writings of Leon Trotsky (1929)*, p 79.
78. Sacred Union (union sacrée) was the term used by the French socialist leaders to justify the support of the working-class institutions for the First World War.
79. The Stuttgart (1907) and Basel (1912) Congresses of the Second International both passed resolutions threatening widespread working-class opposition to any attempt to cause a European war.
80. Austro-Marxism occupied a position between the mainstream of social democracy and that of the Comintern.

within the framework of democratically-inspired rules whose limited and oblique character we know, but which are nonetheless more or less, according to country and period, compatible with the real freedom of choice that the rank and filers exercise. In any case, they at least are of the opinion that they have chosen their representatives. It is in Russia that nobody has been elected for 10 years. The balance of power between the leaders and the masses is not conceived in our minds in the way it is conceived in the collective opinion of those whom we wish to influence. Judging by the results over 10 years, communists could not have gone about trying to get them to share our views in a worse way.

Working-class reformism is deeply rooted in the economy of capitalism, and its ideology is fed from abundant and diverse streams which you will in no way uncover by crying betrayal, or choke them off by indiscriminately condemning all who contradict you by using one and the same sentence. I do not deny anyone the right or duty to insult people in order to undermine the credibility of their ideas; but you are not doing it with proper insight, and the disorder as well as the sameness of your judgements renders useless whatever useful things they may contain. To cut short the argument, let us project your argument into the past and apply it to a subject already dealt with by other people: Marx and Engels devote a remarkable chapter in their *Manifesto* to analysing the types of socialism of their time, their complex origins, their contributions, and their concealed or open tendencies. They mention Sismondi and Grün, Proudhon and Babeuf, Saint-Simon and Fourier, and Owen and Cabet,[81] and make reference to others, in order to criticise their writings and activity in the light of their 'scientific' criticism. In the language of today's Opposition, this chapter would be reduced to a short paragraph which would inform us that Sismondi was a traitor, Proudhon a traitor, Saint-Simon a traitor, and so on. Let us now suppose that a new Marx is dealing with the present-day tendencies within socialism: would he explain them by writing that Otto Bauer and Sidney Webb, de Man and André Philip, Eastman and Roland-Holst, Bukharin and Thalheimer[82] were traitors or semi-traitors of various types? To ask the question

81. Jean Charles Léonard Simonde de Sismondi (1773-1842) was an early Swiss economist. Karl Theodor Ferdinand Grün was the pen name of Ernst von der Haide (1817-1887), a German writer who became a 'true socialist' in the 1840s. François Noel 'Gracchus' Babeuf (1760-1797) led the Conspiracy of Equals during the French Revolution. Claude Henri de Rouvry, Comte de Saint-Simon (1760-1825) was an early French utopian thinker. François Marie Charles Fourier (1772-1837) was the founder of the French school of utopian socialists.

82. Otto Bauer (1881-1938) was the leader of Austrian Social Democracy and the main theoretician of Austro-Marxism. Sidney Webb (1859-1947), later Lord Passfield, was one of the foremost thinkers of British Fabianism. Hendrik de Man (1885-1953) was a leader of the Belgian Labour Party. André Jean Louis Philip (1902-1970) was a French economist, Socialist parliamentarian and government minister. Henrietta Roland-Holst (1869-1952) had been a leader of the left of the Dutch Social Democracy before the First

is to answer it.

'It is not the same sort of thing' is all a 'Bolshevik-Leninist Oppositionist' (unfortunately!) will find himself replying. But the extent to which 'it is not the same sort of thing' is what goes against you even more. Can it be showed that the mistakes and illusions from before the *Manifesto* no longer have any reasons for existing now? On the contrary, they have more than ever before, and even more so. And if 'Feudal Socialism' and 'True German Socialism' have disappeared with the growth of the capitalist system, varieties of petit-bourgeois, conservative or utopian socialism continue in new developments, and the rapid degeneration of communism has strengthened them. Parliamentary successes have made the proletariat hope for peaceful progress, and the fate of the most recent revolutions that bear the stamp of communism has confirmed it in this hope. It does not see itself faced with a choice between death and revolt, but between an uprising defeated before it starts and a life of bearable mediocrity. Its ideology of things getting gradually better rests upon an economic basis and a social structure that obviously correspond to a period of industrial civilisation that Lenin did not know how to analyse. Marx perhaps had a glimmer of genius by perceiving that convulsions could be produced at the far extremities of the bourgeois system before reaching its heart, where there are greater possibilities of equilibrium.[83] Confronted with the events today, we can by rediscovering this idea find an important explanation for the historical phenomena that we are witnessing: the fact that revolutions with communist leanings are in our days taking place in agrarian countries encourages us to look in that direction.

The idea of betrayal corrupts supposedly orthodox communism in all its rival variations and renders impotent in advance its repeated attempts to win over the minds of conscious proletarians. It can only latch on to the power of ignorance and prepare disappointing tomorrows. We must finish with this primitive sociology. And since Lenin is leading us back to this side of Marxism, I will not exhaust myself referring to Marx and Engels when our ideas have proved incapable of going beyond them. In their first article in the *New York Tribune* on the revolution of 1848, they begin by precisely refuting the accusation of treachery directed at Louis Blanc and Ledru-Rollin in the same way that you have directed against Purcell and Citrine:[84] the causes of the uprising and its

World War, and then a communist; she broke with the Comintern in 1927. Max Eastman (1883-1969) first revealed to the world the conflict between Stalin and Trotsky after the death of Lenin, and was later the translator of Trotsky's *History of the Russian Revolution*, but he never joined the revolutionary movement.

83. Karl Marx, *The Class Struggles in France, 1848-1850* (Moscow, 1972), p 126.
84. Arthur A Purcell (1872-1935) was a leader of the General Council of the TUC during the General Strike and of the Anglo-Russian Trade-Union Committee; Walter McLennan Citrine, later Lord Citrine (1887-1983) was General Secretary of the TUC from 1926 to 1946.

defeat, they write:

> ... are not to be sought for in the accidental efforts, talents, faults, errors or *treacheries* of some of the leaders, but in the general social state and conditions of existence of each of the convulsed nations. ... but when you enquire into the causes of the counter-revolutionary successes, there you are met on every hand with the ready reply that it was Mr This or Citizen That who 'betrayed' the people. Which reply may be very true, or not, according to circumstances, but under no circumstances does it explain anything — not even show how it came to pass that the 'people' allowed themselves to be thus betrayed. And what a poor chance stands a political party whose entire stock-in-trade consists in a knowledge of the solitary fact that Citizen So-and-So is not to be trusted.[85]

We might almost believe that we are reading an exact criticism of your arguments about the Anglo-Russian Committee:

> No man in his senses will ever believe that 11 men, mostly of very indifferent capacity either for good or evil, were able in three months to ruin a nation of 36 millions, unless those 36 millions saw as little of their way before them as the 11 did.[86]

This accurately applies to the poor gentlemen of the General Council in their lamentable conduct of the strike.

I do not intend to go into detail here about those of your views on Britain I believe to be erroneous. It is sufficient to point to two aspects of the problem. You have accepted the current view about the disappearance of Liberalism, and this common ground is one of the main elements of your argument. Now the facts ought to make you think about it. The Liberals had 5.25 million votes in the last elections out of 22.5 million, and a proportional electoral system would undoubtedly have given them two million votes more that are at present gathered up into the two branches because of the well-known peculiarities of voting in Britain, and therefore they would have gained about a third of the votes. But this is still nothing compared with the rebirth of liberalism inside 'Labour'. The differences between the Labourites and the Liberals have diminished to the extent of allowing people to pass over from one party to the other as naturally as the Russian Oppositionists return to a Leninesque conformity. Cobden[87] did

85. Frederick Engels, *New York Daily Tribune*, 25 October 1851, *Revolution and Counter-Revolution in Germany*, pp 4-5.
86. Ibid, p 5.
87. Richard Cobden (1804-1865) was an English manufacturer and MP, a leader of the free

not embarrass Owen's illegitimate disciples, and *vice versa*. Similarly in France, where Radicalism has survived several intermittent attempts to bury it, it is still reviving in a new form within the Socialist Party. You will have to reckon with this in the next edition of your work. Finally, you take it as proven that British imperialism has begun to come to an end; but this moribund structure is taking its time to disappear, and is still giving us repeated lessons that we will precede it in its fall if we do not decide to profit from them. A few torpedo boats on the Yangtse and a few bundles of dollars judiciously distributed to Stalin's faithful supporters in the Guomindang have made short work of all the Leninist theories with regard to China. More recently the 'progressive king' in Afghanistan so dear to the ineffable Politbureau has felt the little finger of this dying man.[88] The boasting of the left can neither foresee, nor counter, nor repair such blows. Perfidious Albion is not important enough to produce theses. But the Kremlin's scribblers can still learn from its empiricism.

Where is Britain Going? We are still lacking in certainty about this. In default of this there only remains the expediency of digging into hypotheses. And here is one by Marx that is worth noticing (*Speech on the Hague Congress*, 1872):

We know that heed must be paid [in the struggle for political power] to the institutions, customs and traditions of the various countries, and we do not deny that there are countries, such as America and England, and if I was familiar with its institutions, I might include Holland as well, where the workers may attain their goal by peaceful means.[89]

Twenty years later, on the occasion of the Erfurt Programme, Engels confirmed the same idea:

One can conceive that the old society may develop peacefully into the new one in countries where the representatives of the people concentrate all power in their hands, where, if one has the support of the majority of the people, one can do as one sees fit in a constitutional way: in democratic republics such as France and the USA, in monarchies such as Britain, where the imminent abdication of the dynasty in return for financial compensation is discussed in the press daily and where this dynasty is powerless against the people.[90]

traders within the Liberal Party.

88. In 1919, Amanullah Khan (1892-1960) succeeded in regaining the right of the Afghans to conduct their own foreign policy from Britain. He subsequently visited Moscow, was greatly fêted there, and signed a treaty of friendship with the USSR. But a tribal revolt instigated by Britain forced his abdication and exile in 1929.
89. Karl Marx, 'Speech on the Hague Congress' (8 September 1872), *The First International and After* (Harmondsworth, 1874), p 324.
90. Frederick Engels, 'A Critique of the Draft Social-Democratic Programme of 1891' (1891), Marx and Engels, *Selected Works*, Volume 3, p 434.

As opposed to Stalin, Marx and Engels were not infallible. But even when they were mistaken, their 'mistakes' contain more fruitful fare than the present truths of the ineffable 'agitprop'. In this example, is it so certain that the perspective they sketch out must be illusory? I have other ideas in addition to this that I will share with you if you will accept me on your side of the 'barricade'. It is, moreover, more risky when I come to the second 'criterion': the Chinese.

Nevertheless, on the points that are at first sight the essential ones, our concepts of the progress of the revolution in China have coincided. I do not take it upon myself to decide now if this is due to the insufficiency of my competence in Chinese affairs or to the superiority of the Bolsheviks in the peasant Oriental sphere, as opposed to the industrial West. We have both of us attempted to reassert a general truth about the necessity for having a class party of the proletariat, with its distinct identity, its socialist programme, its independence in action, its own aims, its independent organisations, its right of criticism of its temporary allies, and its freedom of manoeuvre, without prejudicing the limits that occasional agreements or occasional political necessities might impose upon it. We denounced as an unforgivable abdication the subordination of our movement to the military leaders of the national bourgeoisie, the substitution of the republican programme of Sun Yat-Sen[91] for the communist programme, the complicity of our Chinese party in the massacres of workers and revolting peasants, and in the ferocious repression of spontaneous strikes.[92] The incorporation of the communists into the Guomindang, conveniently identified with the Labour Party, the 'Bloc of Four Classes',[93] giving up communist propaganda, suppressing agrarian uprisings, collusion with generals and dujuns[94] connected with foreign imperialism or domestic reaction, all this shows how alien 'theoretical and practical Leninism' is to Lenin's work. We rightfully recalled his thinking on the relations between communists and national revolutionary movements, clearly explained at the Second Congress

91. Sun Yat-Sen (1866-1925) is generally regarded as the founder of modern Chinese nationalism.
92. Communists held the posts of Minister of Agriculture and Minister of Labour in the Wuhan government of 1926 at a time it was suppressing strikes and peasant insurrections.
93. The Guomindang was the Chinese Nationalist Party founded by Sun Yat-Sen in August 1912. The Chinese Communist Party was accepted into the Guomindang in January 1924. Bukharin justified their continuing membership in an article in *Pravda* on 10 July 1927 by saying that 'communists must defend their positions inside the Guomindang as they do inside the British Labour Party'. The Comintern authorities defined the Guomindang, not as a bourgeois party, but as 'a bloc of four classes' — bourgeoisie, petit-bourgeoisie, workers and peasants.
94. The Dujuns (Tukiuns) were the warlords who gained local power during the decline of central authority that attended the fall of the Manchu dynasty. Many of them were clients of one or another of the imperial powers.

of our International: Lenin forcefully insisted that communist support must exclusively be given in the case in which we have the complete possibility of bringing a complete revolutionary education, organisation and preparation to the exploited workers and peasants.[95] I have myself already referred to his theses on the Rif war, which took place well before the tragic episodes of Shanghai and Hankou, in order to attack the French pseudo-communist policy during the events in Morocco and its apology to 'Abd el-Krim, a fitting prelude to the glorification of Chiang Kai-shek.[96]

As regards being preoccupied with the day-to-day tactics about which you appear to be so keen, I will not allow myself to enter into a discussion until I am in a position to make a worthwhile or informed judgement with enough understanding of the matter. The background to the events, the economic geography, the social complexity, the history and the politics of China are things I have only recently learned about. I would not venture an opinion about the correct timing for 'a slogan for soviets' in China without finding out by mutual consultation with some reliable Chinese people, in default of an on-the-spot enquiry, how the idea that produced the word 'soviet' came into the minds of the proletarians over there, whether it was translated into Chinese or not, and without knowing what idea this system represented in the understanding of the masses. I will only point out that in Russia soviets did not come about as a result of a 'slogan', but were a spontaneously generated product which the Bolsheviks later learned how to take over, and if soviets did not arise in China from the irresistible needs of the people's movement no 'slogan' would make them viable, even if the communists did succeed in setting them up here and there. We are by no means short of examples of ephemeral committees and councils set up solely on the initiative of communists in various countries that vanished into thin air without leaving any further trace. The Bolsheviks are over-inclined

95. VI Lenin, 'Report of the Commission on the National and Colonial Questions to the Second Congress of the Communist International' (26 July 1920), *Collected Works*, Volume 31 (Moscow, 1966), p 242.
96. 'Abd el Krim was the leader of the Rif rebellion in Morocco that defeated the Spanish army at Anual in 1921; because it threatened to spill over into French Morocco, the French army combined with the Spaniards in suppressing it. After first being lukewarm in its support, the French Communist Party on 11 September 1924 published a telegram in *L'Humanité* congratulating 'the courageous leader 'Abd el Krim'. On 5 April 1927, Chiang Kai-shek declared martial law in Shanghai, and on 12 April began the suppression of the working class and the Communist Party in the city with a series of frightful and barbaric massacres. On 30 March 1927, large-scale executions of workers accused of invading the British concession had taken place in Hankou (see Victor Serge, 'The Class Struggle in the Chinese Revolution', *Revolutionary History*, Volume 5, no 3, Autumn 1994, p 71). The Guomindang had been accepted as a sympathising section of the Communist International in March 1926, and Chiang had been made an honorary member of the Praesidium of its Executive Committee.

to want to decide everything by 'slogans', and out of the thousand slogans launched into the void by our parties, 999 of them were completely useless, and the thousandth rarely produced any effect. A slogan must be the conscious expression of the thinking that lies latent amongst the masses, or must define a demand intended to collect their forces together; the continuous elaboration of slogans by the bureaux of the International and its sections betrays the caste mentality of parasitic functionaries who believe themselves destined to think instead of and in place of the proletariat and only give themselves the illusion of playing a part when the course of events passes by their proclamations. Finally, it is debatable whether the stage of soviets is inevitable by virtue of the precedent of the Russian Revolution and the temporary infatuation among revolutionary circles for an institution about which nobody outside Russia can form an exact idea; to the extent to which the truth about the internal state of politics within the USSR has been made clear, the attraction of soviets has become dissipated; we have had to realise that soviet administrative and governmental machinery has no virtue in and of itself; it is only a structure whose content depends upon the extent of consciousness and level of development of the labouring masses and can be used even better than the old parliamentary apparatus to stifle the sovereign people. In Russia soviets took the place of the impotent Duma, the zemstvos, and the municipalities.[97] It is not inevitable that in the West they will be the successors of classical parliaments. In the East, it is very possible that the Russian model might become an example, in the way that the British parliament became for Europe. The proof of this has still to be made, and ought to come from the local people. Having said this, it remains that Stalin proved you right by calling for soviets far too late, when the revolution was in full retreat, but confirming this is of scant value.

By abstaining from following to the letter your arguments as the eminent theoretician and strategist of the class struggle on the process of revolution in China, I am not attempting to avoid a difficulty. At a first reading, your articles and arguments appear to me to be correct and on the whole well directed, but I feel that I am neither well enough informed nor sufficiently in command of the subject to venture a detailed discussion of it. On the other hand, where I am very sure of being in the right, it is when I am resolutely opposed to the basic tendency common to both the right and the left of our Russian party — for as long as Leninism is common to you — that impels both of you to want to impose a Russian leadership upon a Chinese movement. This seems

97. The Duma was a constitutional assembly to be elected on the lines of differential class voting granted by the Tsar in October 1905 to defuse the demand for a democratic parliament; the Confederation of Cities, called the Zemstvos, was a system of provincial and county self-government set up in 1864 and administered by the local gentry. Neither wielded any power, which was monopolised by the Tsarist autocracy.

to triumph over all other considerations. The revolution in China has to be Chinese, and the emancipation of the Chinese workers will be the work of the Chinese workers themselves. The socialist and communist parties of the world, the Internationals and the Soviet state, must provide them with help and solidarity, advice and discussion, but should not seek to take over their movement. The best directives of Stalin or Trotsky would never be so valuable as those of the leaders chosen by the Chinese proletariat themselves. A mistake dreamed up in Canton is preferable to a truth from Moscow in the relative sense that those who gave birth to it will learn from their experience and will be able in return to guide the revolution, but while they take their inspiration from abroad they will not make it fruitful. It is inadmissible for real communists to take part in tactical arguments as regards revolutionary activity in China in which the Chinese communists have never had a say. (Obviously I am not talking about delegations fabricated in the corridors of the Comintern, but of real representatives from youthful Chinese communism.) The struggle between Russian factions cannot bear any weight in the face of the opinion of militants who spring from the proletarian and peasant effervescence in China. If there is a Chinese Communist Party there, it is for it to take charge of the operations. Much can be saved in the way of mess-ups and mistakes for any new party by profiting from the lessons of other revolutions and the maturity of other parties, and nothing could be more necessary, but the Bolsheviks of the decadence should not believe that they are on the earth to dictate the conduct of revolutionaries anywhere on the globe. And if there is no Chinese Communist Party, or if it is so small that we cannot take it seriously, we should not be talking about setting up soviets in China, nor of leaping over the stage of capitalism.

I am not advising waiting in the face of events that are so important for the future of the world and, more immediately, for the Soviet Union and its imperialist rivals, nor allowing a new communist party to be left to its own devices. But any obsessive meddling from 'Moscow' there and elsewhere must inevitably result in the heaviest disasters, in spite of any inherent value its theses may have in themselves, and would disqualify any even necessary intervention of that sort. And I am not even talking about the manner in which Moscow offices cobble together revolutionary recipes for the use of minor parties: you know them as much as I do, they can prepare only defeats. This needs no further proof. I am completely convinced that even if the Communist International had been able to experiment with its right or left tactics in Mexico the Mexican revolution would have lived; what is existing now is not soviet-style, but at least it has the merit of existing.[98]

98. The Mexican Revolution was a long drawn-out process (1910-20) begun before the Russian Revolution, which cannot be said to have been completed even today.

A lot more could be said about the connection between the foreign policy of the USSR and the International's policy as regards China, the innumerable 'betrayals' notched up during the civil war, the trade-union activity, how the communists played with the Nationalist fire, and the outlook for the future. You are now insisting upon the slogan of a Constituent Assembly for the period following the smashing of the proletarian vanguard,[99] with perhaps well-founded reasoning in the abstract, but I do not know how it will come to be applied in the present conditions in China, about which I would like to know what our Chinese comrades are thinking, if there remain any of them. But you have just published a whole volume of your arguments on the Chinese revolution, and I cannot attempt a parallel examination of it in a few pages.[100] The situation at present rather forces me to start on your third 'criterion': the political economy of the Soviet Union.

* * *

You are also preparing a book on this theme that we will all read with great profit.[101] No doubt Stalin has already secured his own copy, for we would not wish to deny him a particular ability for stealing ideas from those who have them, and, to this day, he has laid you under obligation to such an extent that we do not know who is the more compromised by it. It is risky in a few lines to deal with a subject worthy of an octavo volume. Nonetheless, counting upon your good will, I will try to sketch out my outline correctly without needing arguments that go all the way back to the republic of Novgorod[102] or extending to the furthest corners of the matter.

The economic policy in force since the end of so-called 'War Communism' (that is, in essence consuming products previously accumulated under capitalism) is accepted in Russia by the various party factions. The differences arise in determining the proportions, the methods, and the means of applying it. Questions of *how far*, in this sphere, are of prime importance, for the nature of the regime has come to depend upon the amount of emphasis in one direction or another. The NEP was a tactic, not a change, as its promoters intended to begin with; but in addition to the fact that a tactic cannot be prolonged indefinitely without involving a molecular organic transformation, lack of regulation is

99. LD Trotsky, 'Democratic Slogans in China' (October 1928), *Leon Trotsky on China* (New York, 1976), pp 342-44.
100. LD Trotsky, *Problems of the Chinese Revolution* (London, 1969). The English edition first came out in New York in 1932.
101. Trotsky's *La Révolution défigurée* came out in France in 1929. The English version, *The Third International After Lenin*, was published in New York in 1936.
102. The independent trading republic of Novgorod was only subjected to the rule of the Tsars by Ivan III (1462-1505). See D Riazanov, *Karl Marx and Anglo-Russian Relations and Other Essays*, p 65.

giving rise to two dangers depending on the direction in which the NEP is leaning: to the right, an evolution towards capitalism, or to the left, an étatism putting a brake on production. Hence the bitterness of the tendency conflicts about disagreements about which the public knows nothing. (It should be said in passing that it is constantly clumsy of the Opposition to become involved in conflicts that seem far removed from the concerns of the masses, which even make them appear to be hostile to the interests of the great majority.)

At the start of the NEP, nobody knew what the facts amounted to. Theoretical definitions did not give a concrete idea of them. It was laws and decrees, spaced out in the first years, responding to the most urgent requirements which sketched out more or less precise contours. Successive economic difficulties, partial crises and general miscalculations then imposed corrections. One groped in the dark, in the empirical manner of which Stalin is very much the representative. The removal of Lenin made you the only leader capable of looking at the thing as a whole and of thinking up long-term policy. You shook up the inertia of the party that followed the Civil War, and directed its attention to the pressing necessity for industrial progress. The revolution owes to you the fact that it has avoided a complete break between town and countryside, the pronounced drive towards industrial production, and the general economic plan, for your programme was put into operation by those who defeated you, just like the higher civilisations overcame their less cultivated conquerors.

The Opposition projected an annual investment of a thousand million roubles in industry. Stalin, after having proved by means of the GPU the utopianism of this project, found the means to invest two thousand million. The Opposition denounced the insufficiency of the Five-Year Plan of 1926-31; Stalin, after having sent those who would change his figures to Siberia and into prison, arranged a new plan for 1928-33 in comparison with which the old demands of the 'Industrialisers' seemed to be timorous. The Opposition sounded the alarm about the effects of a badly-thought-out agrarian policy favouring a class differentiation in the village in the sense previously intended consciously by Stolypin: the development of rural capitalism;[103] Stalin, after having choked off its voice, declared war on the kulaks. The Opposition combated a 'right' danger in the party, represented by a tendency to reduce investments in heavy industry in favour of light industry and individual rural exploitation, to concede too much to foreign capital, to tax too heavily the poor and middle peasants, and to pay too much for the corn of the rich peasants;

103. Count Pyotr Arkadyevich Stolypin (1862-1911) was the Tsar's Chief Minister and Minister of Finance. Between 1906 and 1910 he carried out a policy of breaking up the rural commune to the advantage of a minority of the peasants, in the hope of encouraging the development of a rich peasantry that would become a layer of support for the regime.

Stalin charged his official spokesman Bukharin with drawing up a resolution against the rightist danger, and used the theory to shoot down the theoretician. Nonetheless, the Opposition was not disarmed, even if a number of its supporters were. You have emphasised the minor infractions of principle, experimental oscillations, internal contradictions, gaps and weaknesses in the official policy, but you cannot deny that your concept has been put into practice in its broad lines. Moreover, in the presence of this change in direction, the current opinion among our Moscow comrades before they received your instructions was to wait for the imminent coalition of the Left with the leading Centre; the defections in your forces are only the result of this way of thinking.[104] Why has the basic antagonism remained?

It is because its criterion resides not in 'political economy', as you claim, but in politics pure and simple, obviously inseparable from the other. The question posed in the party since the death of Lenin is that of power. By advancing political economy as a criterion, you hope to avoid vulgarising the conflict, to remove from it its personal character, and to respect formal Marxism. But in reality you are falling into the puerile materialism of Leninism. Politics here does not proceed from economics: it is preceding it. As a Marxist you have to state one fact to start off with, and then to clarify it, which is easy because the politics under observation flow from the *previous* economics, not the immediate ones; the subjective superstructure does not arise immediately from the objective infrastructure like a lift leaves the ground; before the subterranean processes of the countryside make themselves felt in governmental decisions across several obstacles, there has to be time for repercussions, cross currents, and even influences in the opposite direction. As a Leninist you have inverted these phenomena. The result of this has been the extreme confusion felt in your latest writings.

The Opposition occupied the main positions in the leadership of the Soviet economy, and it was up to it to achieve *de facto* almost a monopoly by the value and competence of its personnel, notably by avoiding wasting its time in diplomatic functions in which it made itself the instrument of the general policy which it condemned in its theories. It could thus have exercised a preponderant influence effectively equivalent to managing the state, even with a Politbureau it did not want. Stalin, who was never troubled by principles or doctrinal views, did not dispute your authority in this matter; on the contrary, he hoped to see you manage all the higher economic organisations, and he allowed oppositionists to work at the top of the Council of Commissars, the Economic Council, the State

104. The leadership of the Joint Opposition in Russia began to break up in the late 1920s. Zinoviev and Kamenev made their peace with Stalin at the end of 1927, Pyatakov, Krestinsky and Antonov-Ovseyenko in 1928, and Preobrazhensky, Radek, Smilga and 400 others in 1929.

Planning Commission, the Concessions Committee, and the great production combines. He firmly opposed your exclusion not only from the party but from high positions, as long as you were not a danger to his political hegemony, and he sought to get you to assume the highest responsibilities in economic affairs. What he did not at any price want to allow you was the possibility of threatening him in the Secretariat, the Politbureau and the Party Central Committee. His later implacable struggle against the so-called Leningrad Opposition, your furious enemies who had become your allies out of tactical considerations, and then against the so-called Right Opposition, who both had every latitude as you did to work at the 'tops', cannot be understood otherwise.[105] Talking about a proletarian current as regards an apparatus of Petersburg functionaries in the face of their more than cold relations with the workers whom they have harshly persecuted is a real offence against the truth; explaining the main concentration of the so-called Left Opposition in the two capitals by referring to the working-class base is specious; the various tendencies of the Opposition are recruited from the political autocracy and the administrations of state, in other words from among the privileged who enjoy a modicum of civic rights. As for accusing the proletariat of lassitude, if it had the slightest freedom to express itself, it would indubitably support those who appeared, rightly or wrongly, to represent internal and external peace, and more well-being and freedoms.

It is obvious that all these questions are connected, and that all the levers of command are interdependent, but since you confine the criterion to 'political economy', I say that you ought to have had every possibility in fact of making your own policy prevail, for no Politbureau would ever be able to draw up an indictment against a programme agreed by its own leading economic organisations. But with your Leninist concept of the party, you did not see any other way than gaining control over the central political positions, an undertaking out of all proportion to the means of an isolated faction, in a period of apathy in which the most sincere and freest speaking must sound hollow. The demarcation between political and economic power cannot be traced, but an undeniable functional specialisation has arisen, and, yet again, you yourself are deriving political economy from politics in general. (I, in any case, am subscribing to this very conventional and relative distinction in order to make study easier.) Under the pretext that any class struggle is a political struggle intending to make use of power, you have converted this indubitable generalisation into an immediately realisable possibility, overestimating the possibilities, the real facts and the conditions for carrying them out. This led

105. The Leningrad, or Left-Centre Opposition, was led by Zinoviev and Kamenev, who had been far more hostile to Trotsky in 1923 than Stalin had been. The Right Opposition led by Bukharin, Rykov and Tomsky had been in charge of the economy and the Comintern after 1927.

you to give way to short-term considerations of manoeuvre, and to submit to the pernicious influences of the most impatient people. You came to forging theories to justify a tactic instead of putting tactics at the service of theory.

The main problem of the Russian Revolution is that of political power. This is an authentic criterion for the whole International. Can the Soviet regime only survive by suppressing all the labouring classes, beginning with the proletariat, and imposing silence upon an entire people? The proletarians and revolutionaries of all countries, incapable as they may be of saying how many roubles are available for industry, or what taxes can be sustained by a middle peasantry, understand this question very well. It is even the only clear one for everyone, even in Russia. Now the Opposition has always feared posing it. And it never raised it because it did not feel capable of resolving it in the eventuality that it would have taken, or at least shared, the power. You already asked for 'inner-party democracy' in 1923; three years later you stammered out quite timid democratic demands in favour of the trade unions; then three years after that you advocated a secret ballot in the party and, to a lesser extent, in the trade unions. But all these partial demands throw light on your hesitations in confronting the difficulty in its full extent.

Unless you were thinking about substituting purely and simply the dictatorship of one clan for that of another, it would have been better to define, however approximately, the limits, forms and extent of the dictatorship and what guarantees there were to protect the citizens. The Soviet Constitution, this museum piece, will never come about without legislation that would assure the execution of its principles, and without a brigade of men determined to fight to impose it. A slogan of giving force and life to a constitution appears to me to be the only one capable of attracting the adherence of the masses and preparing them to act. If a state of emergency, an all-powerful police and the full powers of the Politbureau are permanently admissible, the communist oppositions do not have to be exempted. And if this emergency regime could only be justified by the extraordinary circumstances of the Civil War, nothing can be more urgent than to subject all citizens and all parties to revolutionary legality. Without this, governmental arbitrariness will only find a rebuttal in a new October or in counter-revolution. But it is not my criterion that is at issue: let us return to yours.

The economic programme of the Opposition has imposed itself upon the party in its broad outlines, even if the present leadership was incapable of taking in its concept in its entirety and deserves no confidence at all for applying it intelligently. You rightly emphasise that the Soviet economy must not be cut off from the world market, and it is its rhythm and development that will decide its future. Stalin was lost in the exchange of theoretical views, but he yielded *afterwards* to the evidence and accepted the measures that flowed from it: that would not be for the first time. His state capitalism presupposes a certain anarchy empirically corrected, like the other capitalism, and this will go on for as long as a deep crisis does not rudely provoke a return to principles. But as for confirming the essential ideas of the Opposition, the about-turn of the leaders, reflected above all in the Five-Year Plan, is not necessarily a justification. A communist must be allowed to have objections to present to both of them, precisely over the question of its proportions, its rhythms, and how it is to be applied, which cannot be resolved by speeches, but by practical work. If they do not go off the point in general and respond to concrete necessities, it is of scant interest as to whether they coincide with the observations of factional opponents, or even of political enemies: the Mensheviks were not wrong in every detail, and Milyukov's articles can still be read with profit;[106] Lenin collected a certain number of bourgeois appreciations without being excited by them; are we forced to contradict systematically whoever is not on our side?

From the sole fact that the Oppositions of Left or Right have a critical attitude, they can see better certain aspects of things than the self-satisfied people in power. On the other hand, the inner logic of the struggle often tempts them to demagogy and denigration. It would be tedious and fastidious to discuss all the motives dictating the contrary affirmations or the lightly improvised theories of those who profess Leninism. The Left Opposition has accused the government of being inclined to recognise the old debts: but was it not Rakovsky, Preobrazhensky and Pyatakov who designed and approved the project of an agreement with France based upon settling these debts? It has denounced the seven-hour day as impractical: so why did it demand it in its agitational leaflets distributed in the factories? It denies being a threat to the peasants, declaring itself to be an enemy of the kulaks alone; but what does it then say about the left zigzags with regard to the administrative acts of violence, police raids and primitive operations that are now pitting the peasant masses against the regime? The Right Opposition condemns the ambitiousness of the Five-Year Plan: but Rykov made the official reports to justify it. It finds the development of industry to be too steep, and makes use of fallacious statistics to pretend that no capitalist country has ever experienced such a growth: but Bukharin is lying on the points of comparison and forgetting that that the countries that came late to industrialisation leaped over the earlier stages; thus Japan's production has gone up 83 per cent since 1913. It shares the responsibility for all the mistakes made over six years, and off the record utters views which would make the Whites blush. By what right do either of them presume to make us pass examinations

---

106. Pavel Nikolayevich Milyukov (1859-1943), the leader of the Cadets during the Russian Revolution, was a noted historian.

and apply criteria to us?

I say that questions of proportions and extent have a crucial weight in the plan we are discussing. An excessive exaggeration can compromise everything. Requisitions can be increased, and this was Kronstadt; the offensive can be extended, and this was Warsaw; taxation can be increased, and this was Georgia.[107] If concessions were to be excessive, it would mean the invasion of finance capital. Exaggerations, where they are not fatal, are always paid for by an excessive reaction. The latest repressive administrative excesses in the countryside have welded together the rural classes and produced a 'right-wing mentality' in the whole country. It then became necessary to reduce the extent of agricultural taxation, increase the price of wheat, reduce the proportion of the tax-paying peasants, and give subsidies for the sowing; in Stalin's place you would have had to do the same in the given circumstances, whoever may have been the previous people in charge. In his letter to the Jena Congress already quoted, Lenin warned the German communists thus: 'Exaggeration, if not corrected, was sure to kill the Communist International.' (And that is in fact what happened.) 'Exaggerating', he added, 'however slight, means preventing victory.' And he added, as if he had foreseen your mistakes today: 'Exaggeration of the struggle against Centrism means *saving* Centrism, means *strengthening* its position over the workers.'[108] (Again a prophecy that came to pass.) This warning seems to me to retain its value as regards economic activity. And here very briefly are the reasons.

Your emphasis on accelerating industrialisation always depended upon finance. Now, however important as this problem may be, it is not the only one, and it cannot be separated from the others: the level of technique, the state of the equipment, how rational the organisation is, how well-qualified the workforce is, how competent the management is, how much manufacturing experience there is, and how well coordinated the various branches of production are. It needs not only money, but time to sort these out. To make faster progress we need to learn from our predecessors and contemporaries. Soviet industrialisation is impossible without the contribution of resources of every sort that Western capital enjoys. Your mistake is to insist obstinately upon investments without giving sufficient attention to the rest and yet, in drafting out your texts, you know how to refute the insanity of the 'autarky' of the Russian economy. Under your

107. Forced requisitions during the Russian Civil War provoked an uprising in the fleet base at Kronstadt in March 1921. Spreading the army further to the south caused a gap between the Russian armies and resulted in defeat at the Battle of the Vistula and the failure to capture Warsaw during the war with Poland in August 1920. High taxation enabled Georgia to declare its independence of the USSR under Menshevik rule in May 1919.
108. VI Lenin, 'A Letter to the German Communists' (14 August 1921), *Collected Works*, Volume 32, pp 520-21.

impulsion, the budgetary contributions for Russian industry have been and are being increased for each financial year; but you know how this industrialisation is being carried out, in what chasms capital is being swallowed up, and what incredible wastes are the result of bureaucratic methods and a lack of trained personnel. Obviously something will come out of this disordered effort and this chaotic creation, but for whom? The astronomical figures that decorate the Five-Year Plan do not fail to impress, and the Left Opposition in Russia does not fail to be so impressed: I have, moreover, looked for evidence for the origin of the funding, and I have found none: my imagination supplies a good part of it, and I admit that, for what I cannot prove, I am unable to do so; but I feel that I am on firm ground when I ask by what means the hundred thousand new engineers and technicians that are envisaged by the super-industrialisers are to be trained.[109] And I have stopped short of posing the many questions that are of themselves posed around this miraculous project: you know them better than I do.

Soviet industry will not reach the output and perfection of the advanced countries by depriving itself of profiting from the world division of labour. The NEP and the relations between the USSR and the external market imply at the same time an antagonism and a collaboration with capitalism. These necessities require cultural means of communication and commercial exchanges appropriate to the novelty of these relations; the present methods of achieving a monopoly of foreign trade and the type of discipline imposed from within, far from satisfying them, constitute an obstacle for them. The Soviet state has not yet been able to realise the principle of its monopoly effectively, and no opposition has proposed the root and branch reform that it requires. Just as the state in general must be educated before it can aspire to be an educator, the Soviet state in particular is nowhere near rationally accomplishing the role of an all-purpose buyer and seller. Only a combination of customs barriers and import and export licenses could give the monopoly the indispensable play and elasticity, choke off the axis of corruption that the present étatised commercial department amounts to, and restore and develop in the appropriate institutions a feeling of individual responsibility (given that, at the same time, the internal regime becomes more tolerant). Protected by such a system, industry could and should grow in quality and quantity on condition that it begins at the beginning, that is to say, with the raw materials and partly manufactured products whose sale would allow it to buy merchandise in the average conditions of the world market in goods, above all machines, from countries with specialised products

---

109. Later published by Boris Souvarine in 'The Five Year Plan', *Bulletin Communiste* no 31, February 1930 (English translation in *What Became of the Revolution?* (London, 2001), pp 90-129).

that Russia cannot compete with. In a quarter of a century, the Soviet Republic would reach the required level of industrial growth, if it were a democracy and not an autocracy, and bearing in mind the possibility of war. The problems of credit and the circulation of money and of exchange and concessions still need to be tackled, but I am not a reporter to the All-Russian Congress, and it is you who are writing a book.

You have in a letter denounced the tendency to slide over to a line of least resistance, sacrificing future advantage for immediate gains.[110] No communist can contradict this. But is this a reason for the proletariat, in the twelfth year of the revolution, to submit to interminable deprivation in the present in the hope of hypothetical improvements? How many generations must resign themselves to existing on these unpleasant arguments? In another document you very rightly argue that the fact that lifting the standard of living cannot be put off indefinitely, and that the productivity of labour depends on the health and morale of the working class.[111] We should therefore be on our guard against abstract generalisations. No ideal perspective is on offer, and we will only make progress by overcoming, by skill and tenacity, all sorts of contradictions. The long-running lack of goods calls for an urgent contribution from abroad, which is possible without the role of the Soviet state being reduced to that of an intermediary between two capitalisms; if this state, which possesses a sixth of the world's land surface, with incalculable wealth beneath the earth, and almost all the industry and buildings, transport and forests, became a simple intermediary, this would not only mean the failure of Stalin's government, but that of the Bolshevik party itself.

The possibilities for industrialisation cannot be measured solely by the purchasing power of the countryside, as you have done; on a hundred occasions you have warned of the danger of a widening gap between supply and demand in the peasant market in the event of a good harvest: by forgetting to take into account all the elements for successful production, as outlined above, and to resort to the foreign market, you are vastly increasing the risks that have to be avoided. At the same time you are allowing yourself, as Lenin said, to be too preoccupied with the administrative side of things,[112] with the functioning of state planning, which you rightly described five years earlier as a plan of general orientation with regulatory tasks. In a country like Russia, the bureaucratisation of the work of the plan will lead to irreparable damage. Finally, as regards the

110. LD Trotsky, 'What Now?' (12 July 1928), *The Third International After Lenin* (New York, 1972), p 244.
111. LD Trotsky, 'Crisis in the Right-Center Bloc' (November 1928), *The Challenge of the Left Opposition (1928-29)* (New York, 1981), pp 328-29.
112. A reference to Lenin's *Testament*: see VI Lenin, 'Letter to the Congress' (23 December 1922), *Collected Works*, Volume 36 (Moscow, 1966), p 595.

classes of peasants, you are falling into an exaggeration of the same sort, the consequences of which are all too clear. Even if the rich peasant stores were concealing the thousand million poods that you were not able to estimate, the resort to constraint in the given situation has counter-effects. This forcible seizure, then, is the equivalent in the thinking of the peasants to measures being taken to bring to an end the arrangements of the NEP. You say that class peace is impossible; there's no doubt about that, but the class struggle is not a game, and in a state that has to maintain a certain social equilibrium, for the NEP was a compromise, such a struggle should not take a violent form unless there is good reason.

You defend yourself from the charge of misunderstanding the need for the NEP, and of 'underestimating the peasantry': it is no longer a matter of your theses, but of the view the population takes of your practical proposals. You are not confined to a laboratory, your interventions take place in public; make yourself understood, or accept the unpopularity of your proposals. It is very likely, and personally I am convinced of it, that putting the Opposition's suggestions into practice at the proper time would have avoided the crisis in question (not by virtue of your economic programmes, but from progress towards Soviet democracy, because 'all the world knows more than M Voltaire',[113] and the workers would have been able to correct the learned projects of all the Piatakovs); but whoever was to blame, in the given state of affairs, we must take account of reality, and not indulge in an overbidding to the left that would end up in a reduction in cereals, the disappearance of corn, scarcity, and lead Soviet power to retreat in the face of peasant capitalism.

Denunciatory literature is useless for counteracting kulak growth. We must not lose sight of their origins and their position in order to understand their present and future significance. The Opposition had the merit of tearing away the veil of mystery that concealed a countryside so resistant to penetration, whose needs and tendencies of which the government was ignorant to the extent of being forced by the investigations of veritable explorers (like the Yakovlev Expedition in the province of Kursk)[114] to take its temperature and discover its secret aspirations. It in time awakened the party, which, by allowing things to go on by the law of least resistance, had misunderstood the obscure phenomena of the social differentiation among the peasantry. But it has, from the evidence, obviously overestimated the numerical extent and economic power of the kulaks (according to it, amounting to 10 per cent of the rural population, a thousand million poods of wheat laid by, without including

113. François Marie Arouet de Voltaire (1694-1778) was France's leading enlightenment thinker.
114. Yakov Yakovlev (1896-1939) was the Commissar of Agriculture under Stalin who was placed in charge of the forced collectivisation. He perished in the purges.

buildings, stocks and money), and has misunderstood their links with the other categories of peasants. It shares responsibility for the repressive policy striking at the middle peasantry from which the class enemy has profited. It is above all inexcusable to have forgotten that the kulak was an effect before he became a cause, corresponding to a definite stage in the development of the productive forces which no administrative and fiscal measures could eliminate.

The kulak is inevitable for as long as a better mode of production does not conquer him. He was able to become an exploiter again thanks to a human selection that makes him more conscious, and because of his ownership of the instruments of work and above all draft animals, the lack of which makes the peasant poor. Collective farms, factories of wheat, alone could overcome him, but fantastic plans do not create the conditions necessary for intense cultivation of the socialist economic type. The mass of the peasants is pressurised, not so much by taxes (better spread out recently) as by usury and high industrial prices; neither the state nor cooperation could noticeably lighten this, given the general present economic and political orientation; the kulak thus had a reserve of proletarians at his disposal from which to recruit his producers of surplus value, which he alone could use to intensify the productivity of agriculture on redistributed lands thanks to their locations. Such exploitation brings in far more than the extensive agriculture of the tiny holdings of the *obshchina*:[115] it will have the last word if the state only opposes it with the operations of the militia. The party, after having taken over the programme of the Socialist Revolutionaries on the nationalisation of the land, thus seems to have returned to the social democratic principle of the collectivisation of labour;[116] this is a long and exacting task in which I wish it every success, but it will be no more accomplished by decrees, circulars and sloganeering than industrialisation will be.

Is the economic system in the USSR leading towards capitalism or towards socialism? To this question you have given replies which, if not contradictory, are at least noticeably different in the space of a year, and very qualified. You doubtless had passable reasons and weighty arguments for them. But you should not expect from ordinary westerners, cut off from Russia for many years, deprived of the best materials and lacking the leisure to study them, a firm and definitive answer in formulaic form when no two expert leaders of the Russian Opposition agree on what is the case.

115. The *Obshchina* was the Russian system of communal village agriculture.
116. By adopting the programme of nationalising the land and granting it to the peasants during the Russian Revolution, the Bolsheviks had, in fact, taken over and implemented what had been originally the policy of the Socialist Revolutionaries, traditionally rejected by the Marxists in favour of cooperative farming (see Karl Kautsky, *The Agrarian Question*, Volume 2 (London, 1988), pp 329-35, 445).

* * *

You have devoted almost an entire letter to an indictment against a faction of German communism expelled from the party, the old Spartacist nucleus commonly called the 'Right', as if you regard it necessary to rejoice over its expulsion and to give us a foretaste of the democracy we might expect in an International that corresponds with your views.[117] I am not in direct contact with Brandler and Thalheimer, for there is no hurry, and we have too much work to do in our respective countries before we can usefully make contact. We are not connected by any particular agreement, and it is inexplicable why you are addressing yourself to me about them. However, as you are expelling them on a second occasion, this time on your own authority (following their bad example in this, for they also expelled you), I will reply to you point by point, to the extent to which I am acquainted with the questions that have been brought up.

1: In 1923 this group was unable either to understand or to utilise an exceptional revolutionary situation.[118]

This is an inconsistent accusation. This group in 1923 did not have any particular policy of its own; it was subordinated to the Executive, whose policies it followed faithfully, perhaps wrongly. The responsibilities for it therefore come down entirely to the Executive, in the last analysis the Russian Politbureau, that is. You yourself, as you later recall, opposed the attempt to make Brandler the only one to blame;[119] I have a similar point of view, and it has not changed. But it is inexact, because it is too simplistic to blame the defeat on a 'Zinoviev–Stalin' leadership of the International. It was Radek who had the responsibility for German affairs on the Executive, and his opinion prevailed practically all the time. You were a member of the Politbureau just as much as Zinoviev and Stalin were, and share their responsibilities. I know very well that the troublesome division of work due to Lenin and the state of personal relations between the leaders had practically removed you from the affairs of the International, apart from those of France, but on the Political Bureau your opinion had great weight. As for Stalin, a stranger to foreign affairs, he used to leave them to Zinoviev, who most often handed them over to Radek as far as German matters were concerned; and on this occasion he was making his first hesitant moves on the European plane by relying on the reports of his Russian and Polish comrades,

117. LD Trotsky, 'Six Years of the Brandlerites' (25 April 1929), *Writings of Leon Trotsky (1929)*, pp 111-16.
118. Ibid, p 112.
119. LD Trotsky, 'The Draft Programme of the Communist International: A Criticism of Fundamentals' (June 1928), *The Third International After Lenin*, p 95.

exceptional agents whom the Politbureau considered to be the best men to send to the spot. (Dzerzhinsky[120] was playing a more important role than Stalin in this instance.)

Radek was not only the Politbureau's expert: his advice prevailed most of the time. In August-September 1923, the Politbureau made a decision to take control of German affairs, practically dispossessing the Executive. In the council of war we held in Moscow in September, Brandler, Eberlein and Thälmann[121] were in agreement; the most 'left' of them was Brandler, whom you and Radek on several occasions had to bring back in line with reality. A hidden conflict arose when Brandler asked the Politbureau to send you to Germany; Zinoviev took the move as a personal offence and never forgave either Brandler or you. The decision to pull back at Chemnitz was taken unanimously, all tendencies included, in agreement with Lozovsky and Guralsky;[122] Radek and Piatakov, the representatives of the International in your place, approved of this tactic. The Executive confirmed it. It was only in January that Zinoviev attempted to discredit Brandler because he had refused to support the campaign being carried on against you in the Russian party. Such were the facts.

Before the German October miscarried, as afterwards, I always thought that Brandler had made two mistakes: the one allowing a dualism and an antagonism to be created and developed between the leftist organisation in Berlin and the leadership of the party; and the other, arising from the first, for having transferred the Central[123] to Saxony, where the perspective was not valid for the rest of the country. This was explained by the suspicion that concerned Maslow, whom documents extracted from the *Polizeipräsidium* in Berlin showed to be

120. Felix Edmondovich Dzerzhinsky (1877-1926) was a Polish aristocrat placed by Lenin in charge of the Cheka. He died of a heart attack after denouncing the Left Opposition at a meeting of the Central Committee. For the activities of his agents in the crisis year of 1923 in Germany, see Walter Krivitsky, *I Was Stalin's Agent* (London, 1939), pp 53ff.
121. Hugo Eberlein (1887-1944) was a supporter of the Spartakusbund and a founder member of the KPD, which sent him to the First Congress of the Comintern in 1919 with instructions to oppose its foundation. He was shot in a concentration camp in the USSR. Ernst Thälmann (1886-1944) came from Hamburg and supported the Berlin left and was appointed chairman of the KPD in November 1925. He resigned during the Wittorff scandal, but was reinstated on the intervention of Stalin, and became his unquestioning tool, as a result of which he led the party to its annihilation by Hitler and his execution in Buchenwald.
122. Solomon Abramovich Dridzo, called Lozovsky (1878-1952) was on the Praesidium of the Comintern; August Guralsky was one of the pseudonyms of Abraham Heifertz (1890-1960), one of the Comintern delegates sent to Germany during the crisis year of 1923. Brandler argued against a general strike at the conference of the factory councils at Chemnitz on 21 October when the central government was preparing to send in troops to overturn the Communist-Socialist coalition government in Saxony.
123. The Central (Zentrale) was a smaller body than the Central Committee, consisting of 24 members.

in the position of a provocateur or, on the best interpretation, a dangerous adventurer.[124] But this explanation is not enough of a justification. In any event, nobody, in Germany or in Russia, can claim to have been more farsighted than Brandler. The faults were shared, and the responsibilities for them were equal.

You yourself, in a chapter in *The New Course* ('Tradition and Revolutionary Policy') written at the end of 1923 expressed the idea that the main mistake of the German Communist Party was not to have known how to accomplish a tactical change in the period opened up by the 'passive resistance' to the occupation of the Ruhr, and not having taken its opportunity in May or July as the Bolsheviks had done in April 1917.[125] Whatever the value of this explanation, it cannot be denied that it was thought up after the event, thanks to an overview of the period that had unfolded. I do not think that you would have set the date in May or in July. Your argument is from December, and supposing that it was made before then, and accepting that it might be irrefutable, in what way can your former enemies, who today are your followers in the German communist movement, take the credit?

2. In 1924 Brandler tried to see a revolutionary situation lying directly ahead and not behind.[126]

If Brandler had this illusion, he shared it with the leaders of the Russian Communist Party and the International. You yourself cherished hopes of the same order. In the chapter in *The New Course* already cited you wrote:

> We have every ground to believe that the German proletariat will not pay too dearly for its omission, for the stability of the present German regime, resulting above all from the international situation, is more than doubtful.'[127]

Perhaps you were then making a concession to the general mood, but why do you refuse Brandler the same excuse? It is true that you were one of the first to abandon this illusion: Rosmer and myself were the only people to agree with you, which earned us the accusation of not 'believing' (sic) in the German revolution by your enemies of yesterday, who in France are your followers

124. When Arkady Maslow had been arrested in 1922, he had told the German police that he had come into Germany by sailing boat from Norway, thereby giving them the impression that he had been sent by the Comintern. He was brought before an investigation committee in Moscow in September 1923 which included Clara Zetkin and Souvarine, accused of being an agent of Severing to discredit the KPD.
125. LD Trotsky, *The New Course* (Ann Arbor, 1965), pp 47-58.
126. LD Trotsky, 'Six Years of the Brandlerites' (25 April 1929), *Writings of Leon Trotsky (1929)*, p 112.
127. LD Trotsky, *The New Course*, p 50.

of today; the one who was the most heavily deceived, as usual, was Zinoviev, whose imprudent writings remain. As for Brandler, he no longer believed in an imminent revolution when I saw him in Moscow in May 1924.

For as long as there have been revolutionaries, it has occurred to them to have inopportune expectations of this type: in spite of their extraordinary foresight, Marx and Engels were not free of them, and Lenin was more than once deceived in this direction. The optimism inherent in every revolutionary's temperament predisposes him to mirages. You yourself at the present time appear to entertain hopes that I believe to be vain. But that is another story.

3. In 1925 he decided that there had been no revolutionary situation at all, and that there was an 'overestimation' on the part of Trotsky.[128]

(The phrase is equivocal: I am interpreting it as dealing with the situation in 1923.) As far as I understand it, you are here one-sidedly interpreting Brandler's opinion in two ways. He did not deny that a revolutionary situation had existed, but attempted to explain that the forces behind the party had been exaggerated and that the means of the bourgeois state, the Reichswehr, the social democracy, the secret military organisations, etc, had been underestimated. To sum up, they had been mistaken as to the real relationship of forces. And by 'they' is meant not only Trotsky, but the Executive, the Russian Politbureau and the German Central. At least that is how I understood Brandler's intervention at the Fifth Congress of the International. I do not know whether he has explained himself more fully since. Even your outline of the German situation in 1923 in *The New Course* appeared to be very correct to me at the time, it is all the same too summary to be considered to be the last word, and it would be inadmissible to refuse Brandler a say in the matter. Now no discussion worthy of the name took place in the communist movement on the German question; it is a veritable crime on the part of Zinoviev to have choked off all honest debate about it and to have exploited the defeat in Germany for the ends of the internal struggle in Russia, so sacrificing the present and immediate future of the communist movement in Germany and trampling upon the interests of international communism. As long as a healthy and loyal explanation has cast no more light on this aborted October, I will not allow myself to pass a definite opinion, or, for an even stronger reason, to condemn anybody whomsoever. The speech Brandler made at the Fifth Congress in the face of a band of real madmen who had sworn to prevent him from speaking and among whom there were those

---

128. LD Trotsky, 'Six Years of the Brandlerites' (15 April 1929), *Writings of Leon Trotsky (1929)*, p 112.

who tried to have him killed cannot exhaust the subject.[129] Nearly everything remains to be said.

Finally, if you had had the possibility of personally coming to a definitive opinion, thanks to your position in Russia, your sources of information, your contacts and even your personal ability, that does not give you the right to suppose that this opinion must be automatically considered as valid for anybody else. Your situation is unique, or nearly so. Those who repeat your lessons do not know the first thing about the matter. It needs an exchange of views between experienced comrades to clarify this episode in our history.

This is all that you blame Brandler for in the context of the German movement. In strict concern for the truth, and solely in the interests of our cause, I believe that I have shown that your assertions are not convincing. But before passing on to your other criticisms, there remain a few observations to be made on the relations between the Russian Opposition and the German oppositions.

In 1923, when we were talking about the leaders of the German Left, you explicitly treated them as 'adventurers'. I can still hear you pronouncing the word. That was also Lenin's opinion, who was aiming at Maslow & Co in his letter to the Jena Conference in diplomatic terms, scarcely concealing his brutally pejorative condemnation. And this was before the revelations that brought Maslow before the Commission of Enquiry in Moscow. In the course of the Russian discussion of 1923, Molotov, attacking the Workers Opposition and some expelled clandestine groups before a meeting of the Zamoskvorechie regional assembly (I think) accused Miasnikov of being in league with Maslow, Ruth Fischer and others in attempting to create a Fourth International (Andreychin was present, and I am repeating what he said).[130] I understood that Maslow had had discussions to this effect with Lutovinov,[131] who committed suicide the following year. At the Commission of Enquiry into the Maslow

129. The theme of the Fifth World Congress of the Comintern (June-July 1924) was the struggle against 'the right danger' as exemplified by Brandler, and the proceedings were dominated by the political theses expounded by Ruth Fischer.
130. Vyacheslav Scriabin, called Molotov (1890-1986), a relative of the famous composer, was one of Stalin's oldest and closest allies. He later became notorious for signing the Nazi–Soviet Pact in 1939. Ruth Fischer (1895-1961) and Arkady Maslow (1891-1944) led the left of the KPD in the early 1920s based upon the Berlin District. Georgi Andreychin was a Bulgarian who had been an IWW militant in the USA before the war, and went to Russia in 1917, becoming a supporter of the Left Opposition. Gavril Miasnikov (1889-1946) joined the Bolsheviks in 1906. He was expelled from the CPSU in 1922 for forming an 'anti-party group', the Workers Group, a split from the Workers Opposition. He later went abroad, and made overtures to Trotsky in Prinkipo.
131. Yuri Khrisanovich Lutovinov (1887-1924) was a metal-worker who had joined the Bolsheviks in 1904, and was one of the leaders of the Workers Opposition in the USSR. He made the acquaintance of Maslow on a trade mission to Berlin in 1923. He committed suicide in despair at the degeneration of the Russian Communist Party.

affair in September, it was one of the most prominent representatives of the Russian Opposition, Piatakov, who proposed Maslow's immediate arrest, a demand Radek, Terracini[132] and I rejected. I am only mentioning this as a reminder of Radek's over-exaggerated hostility, political as well as moral, towards the Fischer–Maslow grouping, as well as its own irreconcilable hatred towards Radek and virulent denunciations of 'Radekism'. And after all that do we have to regard Maslow & Co, who had been accepted in 1924 as orthodox Leninists by the Stalin–Zinoviev–Molotov leadership of the Russian party, as orthodox oppositional 'Bolshevik-Leninists' by the Trotsky–Zinoviev–Piatakov leadership of the Opposition? In the meantime, Brandler and Thalheimer, who had comported themselves with dignity during the Russian crisis of 1923-24 by refusing to become involved in an intrigue hatched against you, allowed themselves to repudiate you, after the publication of *The Lessons of October*, in circumstances in which personal tact and dignity required silence. All they gained for themselves was a certain amount of discredit and blame from close friends such as Radek and Clara Zetkin. Following upon this, she was again to do her worst, on account of her hostility to Maslow and his outfit, whom you made your allies, by keeping a complicit silence at the time of the deportation of the Oppositionists.[133] Finally, Brandler and Thalheimer themselves, by voting for your expulsion from the party, lessened themselves to no avail by the thoughtless calculation of believing that it was necessary to pay this price for their readmission onto the political scene.

In this succession of to-ing and fro-ing without credit for anybody I look vainly for the famous 'left Leninist line' of which you so often speak, nor do I find much of 'the barricade'. In fact, instead of the barricade, I see a whole series of petty intersections in an inextricable mess in which he who finds himself on the left of one side is at the same time on the right of the other. But of the symbolic class barrier, there is no trace. And I defy any conscious proletarian, any élite proletarian, to find the way to his emancipation through

132. Umberto Terracini (1895-1983) was a member of the anti-war Socialist left in Italy, and afterwards of the Italian Communist Party, which he represented on the Praesidium of the Comintern. After a long imprisonment under Mussolini he was expelled from the party, but accepted back after the fall of the regime. He later became one of the party's senators.

133. Clara Eisner Zetkin (1857-1933) was the prewar leader of the German Social Democratic women, a supporter of Rosa Luxemburg and Paul Levi within the KPD, and later of Brandler and Thalheimer. For her hostility to Fischer and Maslow, see Ruth Fischer, *Stalin and German Communism* (Harvard UP, 1948), p 553 n 13. By then very ill and blind, she remained silent during the attacks made on Trotsky in 1924 (ibid, p 374) and 1927, and his contempt for her was thinly disguised (LD Trotsky, 'Who is Leading the Comintern Today?' (September 1928), *The Challenge of the Left Opposition, 1928-29*, pp 188-89, 200; 'Foreword to the 1929 French Edition' (15 April 1929), *The Third International After Lenin*, p xxxii).

this complicated labyrinth, or to find himself in this tangle of manoeuvre and tactics anywhere where there is any longer the slightest place for principles.

Adventurers in 1922, splitters in 1923, Leninists in 1924, Oppositionists in 1925-26, capitulators in 1927-28, and always vulgar demagogues and harmful blunderers, Maslow and his associates have been invested with as much of the confidence of the Russian Opposition as they would have wanted. On what account? Is it because they made the German Communist Party lose two-thirds of its members, destroyed its place in the unions, and succeeded in hoisting Hindenburg to the presidency of the republic, not to mention the decisive part they played in the 'Bolshevisation' that bled white the International?[134] It was enough for them to repeat obediently your formulae and slogans, or to seem to do so, for them to be on the 'left Leninist line'. Their example, like so many others, testifies to the fact that this line obviously does not represent either Marxist thinking, or a class tendency; it can lead to the most peculiar results. We can see why Brandler is not particularly anxious to follow it.

You write that you gave Brandler a negative appraisal only when you 'became convinced that he lacked the desire or the ability to learn even from the greatest events'.[135] But on what criterion do you base yourself to decide in this way? Solely upon the basis of the differences in your views. So far your concept has been purely personal. No debate, and no study, has yet been allowed to make it a collective one. Only in Germany do people know what it is based upon, but across what distortions? Not a text has appeared on this subject in France, apart from yours, not even Brandler's speech at the Fifth Congress. It is the same in other countries. Have you forgotten your letter from Alma-Ata of 21 October 1928, where you wrote:

> A broadly extended and systematic exchange of theoretical and political experiences, a collaboration in the sphere of Marxist analysis of ongoing processes, and a working out of slogans for action — that is the place to start.[136]

I am not proposing anything else. Let us not start off with the conclusions.

134. Placed in charge of the KPD by Zinoviev in 1924 and 1925, Fischer and Maslow embarked upon a 'leftist' course which involved renouncing the United Front and the slogan of a workers' government, and founding split trade unions. They were to blame for refusing to support the SPD candidate in the second round of the presidential elections, leading to the election of Hindenburg. When Stalin broke with Zinoviev they were expelled from the party, and formed the Leninbund along with Urbahns.
135. LD Trotsky, 'Six Years of the Brandlerites' (25 April 1929), *Writings of Leon Trotsky (1929)*, p 112.
136. LD Trotsky, 'The Danger of Bonapartism and the Opposition's Role' (21 October 1928), *The Challenge of the Left Opposition, 1928-29*, p 284.

Finally, you said that Brandler's 'retrospective appraisal of the 1923 German situation is completely analogous to the criticism which the Mensheviks made of the 1905 revolution in the years of reaction'.[137] I only want to believe you, but please supply proof to begin with, that is to say, quotations and references and arguments. Even a coincidence, apparent or fundamental, or a similarity of opinions with the Mensheviks does not impress me *a priori*. I am not among those who make it a point of honour to reckon that the Mensheviks were wrong at all times, in all places and in all circumstances. After the revolution of 1905, and precisely during the years of reaction, Lenin went along with the Mensheviks against the rest of his party, which was more 'to the left'. I am not saying that Lenin was right, or that Brandler was not wrong. I am only quoting a classic example to warn against a certain way of discussing of which you yourself have all too often been the victim. But let us go on to the rest of your criticisms:

4: In 1925-26 he [Brandler] considered that the course toward the kulak, the Stalin-Bukharin course of that time, was correct.[138]

In the years in question, Brandler was a sort of prisoner on parole in Russia. He was not free to express any other opinion than the official point of view. Did he really approve a 'course toward the kulak', or was he pretending to approve it as a tactic? In both cases, he was to be very heavily mistaken, but I would like to know more. It is likely that his opinion on the Russian economy had been formed by Radek, of whom you say that 'up till 1923 Radek held that it would be impossible to carry through any economic policy other than that of Stalin and Bukharin'.[139] Why should you expect Brandler to be better able to judge Russian affairs than Radek, who was in permanent contact with you? Yet again you reveal that your criterion lacks validity when you expect a German communist to be a better Russian communist than a Russian communist, and how inane your classification of right and left is as regards problems that are not suited to them. It is also possible that Brandler went in the direction of the official thinking under the negative influence of the Opposition, whose correct criticism did not justify a certain amount of demagogy to which Zinoviev gave a particularly repulsive expression. If it were a choice between the monstrous errors of the one side and the irresistible truth of the other, everything would be simple. But the choice was different. Those in power took a certain amount of notice of the Opposition's warnings, borrowed clauses more or less badly

137. LD Trotsky, 'Six Years of the Brandlerites' (25 April 1929), *Writings of Leon Trotsky (1929)*, p 112.
138. Ibid.
139. LD Trotsky, 'Radek and the Opposition' (26 May 1929), *Writings of Leon Trotsky (1929)*, p 139.

from its programme, but did not really follow a 'course toward the kulak'; the Opposition had the merit of sounding the alarm only for it then to pursue the chimera of uncovering millions of poods of wheat and of manipulating the social composition of the countryside by means that would inevitably have given rise to cereal strikes, the reduction in harvests, and all the rest; between the Opposition on the one side and the power on the other, in the face of problems as difficult as these, it is pardonable for an old German building worker, lost in Russia, to make a mistake in the same way as such unchallenged leaders of the Opposition as Piatakov, Krestinsky and Antonov, and to which such veteran oppositionists such as Preobrazhensky, Smilga, Radek and many others inclined.

5: In 1923-25 Thalheimer as a member of the programmatic commission supported Bukharin against me on the question of the character of the programme (a bare schema of *national* capitalism instead of a *world* economy and *world* policy).[140]

I do not know the first thing about this difference. Obviously, a communist programme must be based upon an analysis of the world economy. This is a truism. Is there really anything to fight about in that? I can scarcely believe you, above all when I see you in the specific cases in which you are putting me to the test, attributing to those who contradict you ideas they never had. Thalheimer's concept was surely more complicated than what you say. In the unlikely event that the man whom Lenin regarded, rightly or wrongly, as Germany's 'best Marxist' had forgotten the rudiments of Marxism, do you have outside of Russia among oppositionists attracted by the 'left Leninist line' a comrade, one alone, with whom you can usefully discuss the programme without charging him with deviation?

Bukharin's programme, complicated by the 600 amendments from the Mamelukes of the pseudo-Sixth Congress of the International, remarkably documents the degeneration of the Leninist 'old guard'. You have had no difficulty after this in uttering a few remarks full of sense. But by pointing to the gaps, by suggesting corrections, proposing changes, and projecting proportional adjustments, you are implicitly revealing a general agreement with the direction of thinking which brings you so much closer to agreement with Bukharin and Thalheimer than you seem to suspect. Neither the suffocating atmosphere of the International nor the Opposition's tainted orthodoxy at present allow the useful expression of a concept that frankly diverges from that of the official factions: ready-made ideas, yet again, are for a time holding back ideas in gestation; that

---

140. LD Trotsky, 'Six Years of the Brandlerites' (25 April 1929), *Writings of Leon Trotsky (1929)*, p 112.

seems to me to be very prejudicial for our future, for I am probably not the only one to think considerations out of line on my own and, among all those that are being elaborated, there are certainly some that are worth being known and will make our activity fruitful. If working out a programme only meant translating class feeling, the work would have been completed long ago, but it is nowhere near producing a result that is really worthy of our insights, because that requires a noticeable development of communist thinking. We are not helping this development by denouncing as heresy in advance any transgression of some supposed 'left Leninist line'.

6: Brandler and Thalheimer have nowhere, to my knowledge, raised their voices against the theory of socialism in one country.[141]

This is no doubt because they did not feel it their duty to push against an open door. Is it enough for Stalin to make fun of the world for us to feel obliged to repeat an elementary course in Marxism? Radek seems to me to have brilliantly refuted the official thesis with his quip about 'socialism in a single canton'. This reminds me of the cry of Victor Considérant to the Assembly of 1848: 'Give us just the Forest of St Germain!'[142] But I doubt if Stalin shares the naivety of the pacifistic Fourierist: he does not believe a word of his story about socialism any more than his leitmotiv about an imminent war: he is exploiting reasons of state to maintain the dictatorship of the Secretariat... Instead of wasting our time repeating or paraphrasing truths acquired over half a century, we should have fresh answers to provide for new questions. At the Fourth Congress of the International, the last of them that mattered, we all declared in a unanimous resolution:

> The Fourth World Congress reminds proletarians everywhere that the proletarian revolution can never triumph within the limits of a single country; it can triumph only internationally, by developing into world revolution.[143]

---

141. Ibid, p 122.
142. Prosper Victor Considérant (1808-1893), an officer and journalist, was a disciple of Fourier and a member of the International. He edited *Le Phalanstère* from 1832 onwards, advocating self-contained workers' cooperatives. Considérant gave critical support to the laws restricting the right of assembly that were passed by the National Assembly in the aftermath of the June Days uprisings in 1848, on the grounds that the constitutional reforms that had earlier been granted would be endangered should oppositional meetings lead to further disturbances.
143. 'Resolution of the Fourth World Congress of the Comintern on the Russian Revolution' (5 December 1922), in B Hessel (ed), *Theses, Resolutions and Manifestos of the First Four Congresses of the Third International* (London, 1980), p 428.

Nothing that has happened since that warrants repudiating the entire communist teaching, unless one of Stalin's lucubrations can be considered as an event.

7: Brandler and Thalheimer tried to worm their way into the party leadership by assuming a protective Stalinist colouration (like Foster in America).[144]

You are right there, and I did not have to wait for you to express my thinking. But the whole thing should be said: their mistake was to lower themselves to a compromise with a particular component of 'Leninism', the justification for which I have often experienced on the part of the leaders of the Opposition under the label of *tselesoobraznost*,[145] something like the English *expediency*, for which French has no equivalent, but which quite closely corresponds in fact to the formula ascribed to the Jesuits: 'The end justifies the means.' Every time it was necessary to denounce some enormity of Bolshevik neo-Machiavellianism, I owed it to the truth to recognise the joint responsibility of the official Opposition for the moral weakening of communism. Have you forgotten the mutual denials and insincere disavowals of the Opposition in 1925 and 1926? It is true that part of the oppositionists came to their senses in the following year and gave proof of a healthy ability to react against the degeneration that was contaminating it: this proves that men are worth more than their elastic ethics. Marxism requires an agreement between theory and practice. Not everything in Lenin has to be sacred to us, and particularly what he implied in his formula 'we are not competing for a Montyon prize',[146] for if Lenin is Lenin, you see what the epigones amount to who believe that they are allowed to do anything by invoking higher ends to justify inadmissible means. About deceitful Leninist ploys, you wrote excellent things in *The New Course*,[147] and as far as morality is concerned, I read with pleasure in your letter of 3 January 1928: 'We do not accept any abstract morality that dominates reality, the classes and their interests. But this does not mean that we do not recognise any morality.'[148] If this last statement is not a stylistic turn of phrase, it demands that we should not require from the lone Brandler a principled rectitude in which politics, tactics and ethics merge into each other. We should set an example and investigate a little those who are in the 'left Leninist line'.

144. LD Trotsky, 'Six Years of the Brandlerites' (25 April 1929), *Writings of Leon Trotsky (1929)*, p 112.
145. *Tselesoobrazhnost* means 'expediency' or 'advisability' in Russian.
146. Jean-Baptiste-Antoine, Baron de Montyon (1733-1820) was a philanthropist who founded prizes for moral value and acts of virtue (1782) to be awarded by the Académie Française. See Marx and Engels, *The Holy Family* (1844) (Moscow, 1975), p 223.
147. See LD Trotsky, *The New Course*, pp 55-56.
148. LD Trotsky, 'Des Témoignages sur l'origine de la légende du "Trotskysme"' (3 January 1928), *Oeuvres*, second series, Volume 1 (Institut Léon Trotsky, 1988), p 52.

8: On the question of the Chinese revolution Brandler and Thalheimer dragged at the tail of the official leadership.

9: The same on the question of the Anglo-Russian Committee.[149]

I have replied above to these two points. We might note here that you also apply your strictures to Radek, Preobrazhensky and Smilga over the policy in China, and to Radek over the Anglo-Russian Committee.[150] And you are not mentioning everybody. Thus Rakovsky was equally in disagreement with you over Britain. Why attack Brandler in particular? Even if you were right on this basis, you were wrong to be talking about criteria, unless it was to purge your ranks.

Let us move on to your discussion.

* * *

You have taken from a report by Thalheimer with which I am not acquainted a phrase describing a 'shameful position' for a Marxist: 'Trotsky's programme calls for a tighter financial squeeze on the peasantry.'[151] This formulation makes you angry because the peasantry is not one whole thing, and because a class struggle is taking place there that gives birth to two tendencies, a capitalist one for the kulak, and a socialist one for the exploited. Now on this I very much doubt whether Thalheimer needs these revelations. We commonly use general terms assuming that everyone involved understands them in the same way. This isn't the first time that the poverty and semi-fixed quality of our vocabulary have formed an obstacle preventing thinking from being expressed. There are certain cases, and very much so in this one, where there are more inconveniences than advantages in making use of restricted or too precise words that correspond to schematic views. You know just as much as I do that in today's Russia, with a shortage of manufactured goods, high industrial costs, growing unemployment, a parasitic bureaucracy, credit weakness, fiscal arbitrariness, police brutality, party corruption and government interference, social differentiation among the peasantry does not reflect itself in distinct political currents, and that on the contrary the mass is temporarily tending to become united against the state, against 'the town', as a result of actual circumstances. In this sense we can speak of the peasantry, with a mind filled with *ifs* and *buts*. A little bit of Marxism shows class differentiation in the countryside, but too much Marxism makes clear the risk of class coalition. With a mechanical concept of social phenomena you

---

149. LD Trotsky, 'Six Years of the Brandlerites' (25 April 1929), *Writings of Leon Trotsky (1929)*, p 112.
150. Ibid, p 115.
151. Ibid, p 113.

cannot explain the part played by the poor peasants in the Vendée insurrection.

This is now the state of affairs in Russia: the discontent of the great majority of the peasants. The Opposition cannot but take account of this, even if it is not responsible for it. Tax the rich, treat the middle with consideration, and help the poor, that is quickly said. I am likewise completely of your opinion about it. But beyond this, everything remains to be done. And it all has to be done in Russia such as it is, with the party such as it is, with industry such as it is, and with the soviets such as they are. Nothing is fixed, that is obvious. The party must be purged, awakened and democratised, industry must be made to advance, and the soviets must be revived. I agree. But it will not take place by decree, it is necessary to work, struggle and manoeuvre for it, and it is right that it is important for us to explain the ways and means of this long process. A precondition for this is not mutually to condemn each other in advance without a sufficiently valid reason.

We have all used such general phraseology as 'peasantry' and 'the peasants' without for all that repudiating the teachings of Marxism. If we were to apply to you the way of describing that you have used, how blameless would you emerge? Allow me to examine a text by way of example: your theses on the economic situation in Russia for the Fourth Congress of the International, the last to be properly held, and in which one was allowed to speak without fear of tendentious interpretations. On several pages we find a dozen times expressions like 'the peasant economy', 'the peasants', 'the peasant masses', 'peasant exploitation', 'the peasant class' and 'the peasant'. Here are your phrases:

> The counter-revolutionary events of February 1921 showed that it was absolutely impossible to postpone any longer a major adjustment of the economic methods of socialist construction to the needs of *the peasantry.*
>
> All land belongs to the state. Approximately 95 per cent of the arable land is at the disposal of *the peasantry.*
>
> And just as the contest in the Civil War involved in the main which side would succeed in attracting *the peasantry* politically, so today the struggle revolves chiefly around the *peasant* market.
>
> The most important political and economic result of the NEP is that we have obtained a serious and stable understanding with the *peasantry*, etc.
>
> The inclusion of *the peasantry* within the planned state economy, that is, socialist economy, is a task far more complicated and tedious.[152]

152. LD Trotsky, 'Theses on the Economic Situation of Soviet Russia from the Standpoint of the Socialist Revolution Presented to the Fourth Congress of the Comintern' (1 December 1922), in B Hessel (ed), *Theses, Resolutions and Manifestos of the First Four Congresses of the Third International*, pp 339-41, 343; LD Trotsky, *The First Five Years of the Comintern*, Volume 2 (London, 1974), pp 267, 269, 271.

A less scrupulous opponent could have appealed to the Marxist system and reminded you on every occasion that 'the peasants' are of different sorts, that 'the peasant class' is differentiated, and truths of like character that all of us, you, Thalheimer and myself know very well. I am not questioning your good faith. But I am saying that you are obsessed with fixed ideas. Instead of changing them in the light of the facts and a friendly discussion you are repeating them with a sort of desperate eagerness which makes them less and less convincing. That is why I had hoped that you would in some way have freed yourself from the quite particular mentality formed by the atmosphere of the internal struggle, underground work and being deported, and that you would profit, if I may venture to say so, from your exile to check, renew and rejuvenate our views.

You write that 'the middle peasantry is a social protoplasm. It develops invariably and interruptedly in two directions: toward capitalism through the kulaks, and toward socialism through the semi-proletarians and the agricultural labourers.'[153] This is an old Marxist hypothesis which history has not confirmed. You are repeating it here in far too simplistic and absolute a manner. In the bourgeois countries the concentration of capital and the proletarianisation of labour has not taken the expected course in the countryside. Statistics, economic science and experience all confirm this. A small and medium rural property has arisen which develops neither in a capitalist direction through the kulaks, nor in a socialist direction through the semi-proletarians and day labourers. Obviously, this is not a question of asserting that this form of agrarian production is eternal, but it is obviously going to last for a certain stage of human development when it corresponds with technique and market conditions. Will we have in Russia a special development of the 'middle peasantry'? That will depend upon the general development of the Russian economy as a whole, in its relations with the world economy. A policy that attempts to encourage the poor peasants by ameliorating taxation, offering them credit, helping them with seed and equipment and lowering the prices of industrial products — supposing that the Soviet state is capable of succeeding in it — would only end up lifting the poor peasants up to the level of the middle peasants and in consolidating the type of rural exploitation called 'middle'. And if, in addition, the growth of kulak enterprises of the capitalist type could be reined in or repressed by administrative and fiscal coercion, the 'middle peasantry' would be reinforced even more. Then your protoplasm would take shape in a third direction which you did not foresee. It is only by creating a new, collective mode of production, which would consequently be neither kulak nor proletarian, that would allow us to direct the agrarian economy in a fourth direction, a truly socialist or

153. LD Trotsky, 'Six Years of the Brandlerites' (25 April 1929), *Writings of Leon Trotsky (1929)*, p 113.

communist direction. But to arrive at that we need a combination of conditions and means which are nowhere near being brought together in the way Stalin has embarked upon, and which will not be found in the 'left Leninist' bloc either.

After your insights on the 'middle peasantry' you turn quickly to the situation inside the party. I am following you.

Thalheimer had described as 'Menshevism' your demand for a secret ballot in the party. He was very wrong to have used an expression that involves too many troublesome interpretations and risks inflaming the controversy, but that does not make you right on account of this. (Let us note in passing that on your side you do not hesitate to dismiss anyone who disagrees with you as a social democrat or an opportunist without replying to his arguments.) Obviously, your overriding intention in this matter has only a superficial aspect in common with the Menshevik point of view, but your argument does not prove this; on the contrary, it emphasises its weakness. You are demanding a secret ballot in the party in the hope that the precedent would then allow it to be introduced into the trades unions of the proletariat, in other words, if I have understood you correctly, only in the trades unions of the industrial workers, and perhaps later in the soviets depending on the preceding results. But why are you giving this preference to the party to start off with? Obviously because you consider the party to be the élite of the working class, its vanguard and its most conscious section, in accordance with the accepted definition. This is very much an abstract and non-dialectical view of the question.

In order to refute Thalheimer you yourself are obliged to place the party workers on a level with non-party workers by saying that they are afraid to vote as they feel, fearing the apparatus and its reprisals. In short, the élite is afraid and the vanguard is on its knees. And I am not trying to be ironic; this is a matter of historical fact. An example of a revolution has never been known before in which the tenacity of the combatants has had to be maintained for so long. In a tragic symbolism, Lenin's death coincided with the exhaustion of the party's revolutionary strength. Your political elimination put the seal on the 'turn'. Physical exhaustion, moral fatigue, privation, unemployment, want of culture, the backward state of the economy and the pressure of class enemies have all contributed to make the party what it is today. And we must not take it for what it no longer is.

If you had gone a little further into this theme, you would not have been able to avoid noting the following: the 'Lenin levy' weighed down the party with hundreds of thousands of backward, non-communist members, and with further levies, nearly a million automata have submerged the conscious membership; an infinitely small number of these remain: the extinction and senility of the 'old guard', the surgical elimination of the oppositions, the corruption and bureaucratisation of the cadres, the bourgeoisification of the functionaries, the systematic exclusion of healthy, enlightened and critical elements, as a result of successive purges and the lethargy of the remainder; the majority of those who vote take the party as an insurance against unemployment, an improvement in their living conditions and something of a strengthening of their civic rights; legitimate *self-defence*, an instinct for self-preservation that is vulgarly translated by the epithet *shkurniki*.[154] (This mass is not very different from that which fills the socialist organisations in the West that control the public services, the local authorities, the co-ops, etc.) It goes without saying that this state of affairs and these people will not remain fixed; in new historical conditions even automata will free themselves, and I bet that they will regard you as a rightist. But for the time being it is a question of the party such as it is and what it will become in a given period. And is it to such a party that you want to assign a vote, which even a truly communist one, true to its principles, would find it hard to fulfil? And you believe you can revive it via a secret ballot. Are you sure that a secret ballot would not rather have the most likely and irreversible effect of opening the way for the influence of those class enemies whom you are incessantly denouncing?

In a country where one party monopolises political power, which was never laid down by any communist programme, all class influences work upon it, and consequently that of the peasants is enormous. Revolutionary potential still remains today in the depths of the working class, of which the ruling apparatus must take account, as the leftist phraseology of the officials proves, and which, even in spite of the bureaucratic screen, is still to a certain extent held in respect by the scouts of the counter-revolution: a secret ballot would open the floodgates to the flood of peasant ideology, and what remains of the Opposition would not be strong enough to contain it. The party of today, with its privileged caste mentality, placed above the classes, is not selected from the proletariat; the revolutionary élite is outside the party, some of them expelled, others left of their own accord, and the rest reluctant to enter it; it is from among the masses that we must find fresh forces and rediscover well-seasoned cadre elements for renewing communist activity. By calling for a secret ballot in the party because its members dare not open their mouths, you are accepting the fact that the party is no longer the party, while arguing as if it still were. But if this party were the genuine party, your proposal would have no reason for existence. And if the workers were capable of imposing a secret ballot upon the oppressive apparatus, they would likewise have become masters of their own fate again and would have carried out a reform that would have been the equivalent of a revolution.

154. *Shkurniki* means those who are only concerned with their own personal advantages (Russian).

It is a vicious circle. Moreover, you are launching a slogan that is devoid of interest for over 99 per cent of the population. Nobody is forced to enter the party, joining it is regarded as voluntary, and whether they are free to speak or not is of no interest to the 150 million Soviet 'citizens' who are not party members; and this also applies to the immense majority of party members who understand nothing about the 'Anglo-Russian Committee' or the 'Guomindang', but faced with imperious necessity would prefer a little more butter upon a little more bread to the secret ballot. And that is not all: for the secret ballot to have any value whatsoever, it must be preceded by a certain amount of freedom of information and discussion, without which it would only serve to confirm, in a secret vote whose validity you would already have accepted in advance, the outlawing of the Opposition decided by a public count. It therefore poses the question of the press, correspondence, individual security, limiting the dictatorship, revolutionary legality, and soviet democracy in general.

This is a question that interests the majority, and which would catch their enthusiasm. But you are approaching it from the side, by way of a secondary aspect instead of expanding it to its full extent. This is because in this particular case you have made yourself the interpreter, without being conscious of it, not of the general interests of the exploited classes, but of the particular interests of the Opposition. Your slogan is the expression of a restricted idea of the interests of your faction. It would have been better, on the contrary, for the Opposition to make itself the spokesman of the working masses in the widest sense. It would have been better to talk less about the proletariat and poor peasants and think more about them, rather than continuing to talk about them on every occasion, day in, day out, whilst almost always misunderstanding their aspirations.

Not so long ago I took part in Paris in a discussion between Lazarévich, an anarcho-syndicalist, and Rosmer, a communist syndicalist.[155] The former was for the secret ballot and the latter against, and to make your predecessor think, Rosmer made an allusion to the Mensheviks, obviously tactfully. Lazarévich held fast to a position better than yours; he took the trades unions as his point of departure, an excusable concept for a syndicalist, but he defended the secret

155. Nicolas Lazarévich (1895-1975) was born to a Russian revolutionary family in Belgian exile. He became a syndicalist before the First World War. He went to Russia in 1919, and was active in the Civil War and later worked in factories, but fell foul of the Soviet authorities in 1924. Expelled from the Soviet Union in 1926, he spent the remainder of his life as a syndicalist in Western Europe. His wife Ida (1901-1973) is better known as Ida Mett, the author of *The Kronstadt Commune* (1938: English translation Solidarity pamphlet no 27, London, 1967). Alfred Griot, whose pseudonym was Rosmer (1877-1964) had worked with Trotsky in Paris, and supported him from the very beginning in the struggle against Stalin. See Alfred Rosmer, *Trotsky and the Origins of Trotskyism*. For Guesde and Jaurès, see note 12 above. The Guesdists, or 'Impossibilists' were the left, and the Jaurèsists, or 'Possibilists', the right of the two groups that came together to form the French Socialist Party.

ballot for all the exploited, and therefore for a considerable proportion of the active population. Nobody saw this debate as between left and right, or even about 'centrism', but only between two revolutionaries of different leanings who were looking for a solution in the interests of the proletariat, the revolution and communism. And if you had had the opportunity to discuss your proposal in a meeting of the Russian Opposition, it is perhaps you who would have been seen as an opportunist.

You say that social democracy supported Stalin and Bukharin on the essential questions of the world revolution to which you refer. Without wanting to defend these particular gentlemen, it is necessary to establish the truth: your assertion has no more value than that of Stalin and Bukharin when they accuse you of being defended by the social democrats. With the exception of the Russian Mensheviks and some rare individuals, most of the socialists do not understand a word about the majority of the disputes in Russian communism, and they do not generally take sides in them; when it comes about that some of them offer an opinion, of a strictly personal and mostly of a journalistic character, it is to approve of those that appear to be the most 'moderate'; thus both Trotsky and Stalin have in turn received their share of conditional and hardly compromising praise. With the obvious intensified increase in its orientation to the left and the revolutionary phraseology of the Opposition, a sort of 'public' education has slowly gone on and has inclined the socialists towards a certain preference for Stalin, as they chose the lesser of two evils. But it would be quite arbitrary to see in this a matter of an identity of social content being reflected in a common political tendency.

Even a coincidence or a similarity, whether passing or lasting, of more or less well understood interests would not necessarily have the sense that you put on it. We witnessed in the past the unification of the Marxists and the Lassalleans, the Guesdists and the Jaurèsists, and the Bolsheviks and the Mensheviks; it is not at all ruled out that the future would hold out for us dislocations within existing workers' parties and unifications between fragments, viable or not, but temporarily inevitable. The Socialist Party and the Communist Party of our days notoriously represent, under divergent and often antagonistic forms, the disarray of a proletariat bled dry by war, devastated by the failure of the Second International, the aborted revolutions in Central Europe, the deceptive course of the Russian Revolution and the rapid decomposition of the Communist International; a disarray that is further complicated by bourgeois influences, transmitted by means of the privileged groups of workers, the full-timers of the trades unions, the cooperatives and the already won parliamentary and local government positions. A future economic crisis and the rise of a new generation will throw up different conjunctures. But the first fruits can already appear and produce their effects. Why are you here forgetting to apply your preferred reasoning and are unable to accept that the immense working-class majority of the socialist movement, weighing down heavily upon its leadership in specific cases, could produce a convergence with the aims envisaged by the communist movement? And how do you reconcile your idea of a Stalin unconsciously and indirectly reflecting the tendencies of the peasantry with your second contention of a basic identity between Stalin and… MacDonald,[156] whose character as a representative of the peasantry you would find it difficult to show? We know what restrictive qualifications, casuistic changes, nuances and subtleties the resources of a creative mind can oppose me with; I could perhaps in your place, by way of a mock-up, write a justification of your point of view. But let us not try to give here definite answers to badly-posed questions, I am only reacting against a propensity to settle everything far too hastily and simplistically.

Your point of view on this topic would be understandable if, to the extent to which social science allows, we had established that bourgeois society had entered the final phase of its existence; we could then consider as episodic the complexity of class relations and political antagonisms and expect in the near future decisive conflicts in their pure state, or nearly so. In this eventuality, the historic meaning of the socialist and communist parties would be easy to establish. But it obviously remains for us to give a deep and tested characterisation of the epoch we are in, unless we are content to live off Lenin's phrase that defined it as an epoch of wars and revolutions.[157] But in the meantime it can well be said that whereas it took the socialist parties half a century to degenerate, five years were enough for the communist parties to decline. That is worth thinking about.

With reference to the successive defections that have cleaned out the ranks of the Opposition and are still going on, you make summary references to previous disagreements with the comrades who broke, seeing in them the source of their present deviation from your 'line'. We are far from accepting this. What is your touchstone for taxing the people who disagree with you with 'errors'? You have no pretensions to infallibility, and if you erect your point of view into a doctrine, or a 'line', it should be on the grounds that you have shared it with your companions-in-arms, to the extent to which the Soviet autocracy allowed a common thinking to be elaborated. Now the extent of this has in fact been meagre. Moreover, there is such a disproportion between you and your supporters, and such a difference of means and abilities that your

156. James Ramsay MacDonald (1866-1937) was prime minister in the Labour governments of 1924 and 1929-31, after which he deserted the Labour Party to set up a 'National Labour' component in the Conservative-dominated 'National Unity' government of 1931-35.
157. VI Lenin, 'Opportunism and the Collapse of the Second International' (January 1916), *Collected Works*, Volume 22, p 111.

success in this sphere is not the equivalent of a real agreement. To prevail does not mean to convince. You are not cautious enough about your magnetism, whose effects cannot prevail for a long time under the impact of great social and political currents. In reality, the Opposition, for intrinsic and extrinsic reasons, has never had the continuous 'line' to which you refer as if to a talisman, although it would be going a bit too far to say that it was heterogeneous, and that it really lacked principles. Obviously incapable of avoiding the general deformations of Bolshevism, in spite of its initial inclinations, it has endowed it still further with its own mistakes and contradictions. It was more Marxist than Leninist until the 'bloc' of 1926 was formed: with the bloc, Leninism took over. The joint *Platform*, a compromise document,[158] obviously represented a more advanced stage of your thinking as regards the problems of the Russian Revolution, but on the other hand it amounted to a deficiency in the presence of international questions. The dislocation of the bloc, foreseeable because it was foreseen, showed how valid were your famous 'criteria' and tactical creativity. The continued decline in your forces does not stop being instructive. In vain do you console yourself by alluding to Lenin's phrase about the inevitability of splits and desertions when faithful followers and unreliable people are as alike as brothers.[159] The people who speak in your name in various countries have given a very sad picture of the last battalion of irreconcilable people in the USSR if we judge it according to them. In France we refused your invitations to imitate the Russian model (for the Opposition behaves exactly like a miniature Comintern), and we soon discovered that we had made a 'bloc' impossible. This spared us psychological and literary exercises about so-called capitulators.

To make a provisional conclusion about Brandler and Thalheimer, I will thus oppose my criterion to yours: given the state of the International, we must in every country save what can be saved for the future of socialism and communism, and to start off with this presupposes that we free the healthy and young people from the leaderships, whether right or left of 'Moscow', and allow them to lead themselves, to go beyond imperative outside instructions, to think out their policies and to gather together a real working-class élite for class activity. If Brandler and Thalheimer contribute effectively to this task, if they only set up a living party which knows how to defend the German workers in the thankless day-to-day struggle and to prepare them to march towards the great final aim, they could well be mistaken as much as you and me about the

158. The Joint Opposition was an alliance between the Left Opposition led by Trotsky and the Left/Centre or Leningrad Opposition led by Zinoviev and Kamenev concluded in 1926. *The Platform of the Left Opposition* was released in September 1927. See LD Trotsky, *The Challenge of the Left Opposition, 1926-27* (New York, 1980), pp 301-94.
159. LD Trotsky, 'Six Years of the Brandlerites' (25 April 1929), *Writings of Leon Trotsky (1929)*, p 115.

Anglo-Russian Committee or the Guomindang, but would nonetheless have proved themselves worthy of the proletariat and the revolution. We will judge them, and they will also judge us, from the work done.

* * *

'In the last analysis what decides is the correct political line', you conclude.[160] That depends. The best 'line' is of no value for action if it is conceived abstractly, if it does not express a collective experienced will, and if it does not have at its disposal enlightened individuals to follow it and to modify it if necessary. In another letter you say, speaking about Russia, 'the classes will decide'.[161] Excuse me. If it is classes that must decide, a long time ago the peasant classes decided against us, in a country in which nearly the entirety of its citizens are semi-peasants of various varieties, and moreover where peasants properly so-called make up more than five-sixths of the population. Fortunately, the outcome is the result of interests, actions and influences reciprocally interacting with each other in which a more conscious and more resolute faction of a class rather than classes in general can influence the whole thing. At the end of the day, it is the need to develop the productive forces to satisfy the most urgent needs of society which will have the last word.

> The conflicts of innumerable individual wills and individual actions produce a state of affairs in the domain of history entirely analogous to that prevailing in the realm of unconscious nature. The ends of the action are willed, but the results which in fact follow from these actions are not; or when they do at first seem to correspond to the end willed, they ultimately have consequences quite other than those willed.[162]

You must excuse this frequent resort to the classics, but it is your too rigid formulae that force me to do this, and it has not finished. There is a time for everything, for simplified schemas as much as for subtle nuances; it is a question of using them at the right time. You are often giving excellent lessons in dialectics, as when you addressed yourself to Sapronov's friends,[163] but you soon fall back upon a scholastic formula; hence our disagreements.

160. Ibid.
161. LD Trotsky, 'Crisis in the Right-Center Bloc' (November 1928), *The Challenge of the Left Opposition, 1928-29*, p 335.
162. Frederick Engels, *Ludwig Feuerbach and the End of Classical German Philosophy* (1888) (Beijing, 1976), p 46.
163. Timofei V Sapronov (1887-1939) was the leader of the Democratic Centralists. The reference here is probably to Trotsky's 'Letter to Borodai' (11 November 1928), or perhaps to 'Philosophical Tendencies of Bureaucratism' (December 1928), *The Challenge of the Left Opposition, 1928-29*, pp 292-300, 389-409.

Among your criticisms with regard to me is one of falling over into a subjective deviation by putting too much importance upon the merits of men and the criticism of ideas, as if economic structure and class factors must of necessity predominate over all other subjects. This was already an old dispute before my modest part in it. The main thing is to know within what limits and at what point we are to think about a question. We already have enough to do constantly explaining this to others without having to remind each other of this every day. Men make their own history, but within given circumstances. We must recognise the place that men and groups occupy during periods of stagnation or in the aftermath of conflicts when the great social tides are not submerging individual wills and we wait for classes and multiple social forces to be set in motion. We can talk about people without losing sight of classes or of political positions; and it is not necessarily a correct class concept which refers to classes *ad nauseam*. Among Marxists there are accepted things that do not need to be made explicit. I would submit that you very often come to exaggerating the importance of personalities, such as with the pitiful British trade-union leaders to whom you attribute so many calamities; but you believe yourself to be sheltered behind some 'well understood', 'it goes without saying', 'naturally', calling for the record upon historical materialism, a useful precaution as regards the abundant disloyal people who disagree with you, but useless for a friendly, unbiased and experienced reader. The present inertia of the masses — for as far as I am concerned you are deceiving yourself in talking about their 'left leanings' or 'radicalisation' — encumbers us with mediocrities from which the first tremors will doubtless free us; but this is not a reason for making them wait or even more for settling them down and showing them no interest. And under the pretext of reducing individuals to the appropriate position of their historical importance, it can only complicate our work by mixing them in with people 'who are more intent on escaping their duty than in softening the blow'.

'The materialist doctrine concerning the changing of circumstances and upbringing forgets that circumstances are changed by men and that it is essential to educate the educator himself.'[164] Lenin, who was not a Leninist, gave yet more proof of his far-sightedness by describing in his *Testament* the men of the Central Committee between whom he foresaw that the political game must be played. Marx, in a period that has more than one thing in common with ours, wrote to Engels these lines that could have been written to Rakovsky:

Old comrades… are no more, others have fallen by the wayside or gone to the bad and, if there is new stock, it is, at least, not yet in evidence. Moreover, we now know what role stupidity plays in revolutions, and how they are

---

164. Karl Marx, 'Theses on Feuerbach' (1848), *Early Writings* (Harmondsworth, 1975), p 422.

exploited by blackguards.¹⁶⁵

The same man wrote to Sorge, at a time when the First International was in a relatively similar state to that of the Third today:

> As I view European conditions, it is quite useful to let the formal organisation of the International to recede into the background for the time being, but, if possible, not to relinquish control of the central point in New York so that no idiots... or adventurers... may seize the leadership and discredit the whole business.¹⁶⁶

And again, the same person 23 years earlier, had said to the Communist League: 'You have 15, 20, 50 years of civil wars and people's struggles to go through, not only to change the conditions but in order to change yourselves and make yourselves fit for political rule.'¹⁶⁷ This is how I understand the question of people, without abstracting it from any other, and that is why I disapprove of your behaviour towards the Western communists; it seems to me to illustrate an Eastern proverb according to which 'it is better to have an army of asses led by a lion than an army of lions led by an ass'. Now the party is only an army at certain points in history, and even an army, in a situation of peace, becomes transformed into a school; and in modern war, even a civil war, armies do not resemble the hordes of the proverb. On the other hand, under the heading of a supplementary contradiction, you are denouncing the expulsion of the most experienced militants from our movement.

> There remains hardly one country in the world where at the head of the communist party today stand those revolutionists who led the party in the days of Lenin. They are almost all expelled from the Communist International... After the death of Lenin, almost all the participants, at any rate all without exception of the influential participants of the first four congresses, were expelled from the Comintern.¹⁶⁸

You return to this statement on several occasions (whilst excluding yet again those who were excluded for not conforming as regards the Guomindang).

165. Karl Marx, 'Letter to Frederick Engels' (13 February 1863), Marx and Engels, *Collected Works*, Volume 41 (Moscow, 1985), p 453.
166. Karl Marx, 'Letter to Friedrich Adolphe Sorge' (27 September 1873), Marx and Engels, *Collected Works*, Volume 44 (Moscow, 1989), p 535.
167. Karl Marx, 'Revelations Concerning the Communist Trial in Cologne' (1852), Marx and Engels, *Collected Works*, Volume 8 (Moscow, 1977), p 412.
168. LD Trotsky, 'Open Letter to the Workers of the USSR' (29 March 1929), *Writings of Leon Trotsky (1929)*, p 78.

The final call by Lenin to the International at the Fourth Congress, in which he uttered his final advice with his last strength, was to 'understand'.[169] Yes, individuals who believe that they are called upon to lead the proletariat must above all understand, as Lenin advised them, how to transform themselves and make themselves worthy of their task, as Marx advised them. This is what the *Bulletin Communiste* tried vainly in France to make an opposition understand that would rather be influenced by the Russian Opposition and the poison of Leninism, sinking to the level of the party that had expelled it, and whose miserable fate it will share.

All your reasoning about the present of the communist parties and oppositions in Central and Western Europe suffers from an enormous gap: forgetting the essential fact of the epoch for the revolutionary movement, which is to understand that the extermination of 10 million men, the great majority of them proletarians, and the demoralisation of the 40 million survivors is a dead weight that will paralyse our activity for a long time to come. In France, where the male able-bodied population was almost totally mobilised, and the percentage of losses considerable, the phenomenon appears more noticeable to me, and it was hardly affected by keeping war industry workers in the rear — physical and moral corpses, for those who escaped the front and had the privilege of being behind it are generally lost for the revolution, and in the best instance go towards socialist pacifism, swamping our little circles. It is only now that the physiological consequences of the war, about which we could not have had an accurate idea in the aftermath of the Armistice, are beginning to be heavily felt.[170] We must work to gather together and win new generations whose buoyancy remains intact, and not exhaust ourselves in trying to reanimate disenchanted, disorganised or corrupted elements. The rare Marxist revolutionaries who are not discouraged and who are matured by the defeat can only aspire to a role as transmitters; it would already be a great achievement to ensure the continuation of our thinking, our traditions and our culture, and hand on to the young people the torch passed on to us by our predecessors. Such are the ideas I have supported against the majority of the comrades of the Opposition since the beginning of our crisis in 1924, against the Russian Opposition above all, adding that our stagnation has now gone on for about 10 years, ideas which I am nowhere near giving up.

Every day that has passed for five years now, and half the time foreseen, has confirmed my conviction. The internal crises, the splits, the losses and the pulverisation of our movement have unceasingly convinced me that I am right

169. VI Lenin, 'Five Years of the Russian Revolution and the Prospects of the World Revolution' (13 November 1922), *Collected Works*, Volume 33, p 431.
170. The Armistice putting an end to the First World War was agreed in November 1918.

as against those who are telling irrelevant tales about left and right and class influences when it is precisely class influences that are lacking. Now I want to remind you of a passage from the letter of Marx to Sorge quoted above:

> Events and the inevitable development and intertwining of things will of themselves see to it that the International rises again in an improved form. For the present it suffices not to let the connection with the most capable in the various countries slip altogether out of our hands.[171]

This was written after the fall of the Commune. The defeat of 1848 suggested to Engels 20 years before the reflections that you know:

> If, then, we have been beaten, we have nothing else to do but to begin again from the beginning. And, fortunately, the probably very short interval of rest which is allowed us between the close of the first and the beginning of the second act of the movement, gives us time for a very necessary piece of work: the study of the causes that necessitated both the late outbreak and its defeat…[172]

You well understand that these quotations cannot serve as very complete responses to the questions of the day, but on the contrary I am quoting them to support my own arguments. Anyone can vary the interpretation of them.

Keeping the links with the best men in every country, even those with different orientations, without wanting to create an international organisation prematurely, until comes the inevitable rebirth we are working to hasten on; beginning again at the beginning, taking advantage of an interval that will be long, studying the causes of our defeats, foreseeing a return of our strength, getting down to researches of sustained effort and preparing a new generation; this is the general sense of a valid undertaking for incorruptible revolutionaries between two great convulsions in the capitalist system. Remember that we don't even have a serious work on the German Revolution, nor on the Bavarian Soviet Revolution, nor on the Hungarian Revolution. And on the Russian Revolution? It is necessary to make an effort with the dozens of volumes of denigration and apologetics, equally incomprehensible and servile, in order to extract useful information from them, and that almost requires specialists. Speaking of the European revolution at the Third Congress of the International, you expressed yourself thus: 'In 1919 we told ourselves: it is a matter of months.

---

171. Karl Marx, 'Letter to Friedrich Adolphe Sorge' (27 September 1873), Marx and Engels, *Collected Works*, Volume 44, p 535.
172. Frederick Engels, *Revolution and Counter-Revolution in Germany*, p 4.

Now we are telling ourselves it is a matter of years.'[173] It is clear today that it was a matter of decades, and that cannot but have an influence upon our work. It is a matter of decades, and even if the crisis of overproduction that you don't need to be a great economist to see coming owes us a general conflagration, it is not imminent, and it is out of the question that there would be so soon in existence communist parties homogenous and conscious enough to face up to the events. We know from our own experience what the present sections of the International are good for, formed by a reverse selection; they only serve to discredit communism, and to delay the birth of parties corresponding to the 'historic mission of the proletariat'.

It is difficult to take account of realities without adapting to them. But the one who best resists bourgeoisification is not obviously he who most strongly denounces the cool-headed observer. And the one who daily announces the storm, apart from the fact that he is discredited by days of flat calm, like a meteorologist whose opinion ends up being interpreted in the opposite manner, risks being completely exhausted by the time the event that he had for so long prophesied in vain happens. Camille Desmoulins[174] expressed his discouragement at the apathy of the Parisians on the eve of 14 July. In 1847, Proudhon proved that the era of revolutions had already passed, whereas Marx predicted 1848. In October 1870, Bakunin left France and wrote: 'I have no faith in the revolution in France, this people is no longer revolutionary at all.' The Commune took place without him. I like the image of Rosa Luxemburg, who compared the popular masses with the calm sea and the farsighted revolutionary with a pilot capable of foreseeing the swell. Obviously the world proletariat has in you an indomitable and wise leader, who will always be ready for the struggle. But you must control a temperament which impels you to sound the charge at a time it is necessary to beat a retreat. The dialectic of our movement is not a philosophy of the offensive, and it seems to me to be clearly expressed in Goethe's saying: 'It is not enough to take steps which one day will lead to an end, because each step must be an end in itself at the same time as it carries us forward.'

173. No statement with these exact words was made by Trotsky at the Third Congress of the Comintern, but one like it was made at the Fourth: 'The year 1919 was the most critical year in the history of the European bourgeoisie… it was possible to cherish hopes for a swift liquidation of bourgeois rule, within a few weeks or months.' (LD Trotsky, 'The Fifth Anniversary of the October Revolution and the Fourth World Congress of the Communist International' (20 October 1922), *The First Five Years of the Comintern*, Volume 2, pp 193-94)
174. Lucie-Simplice Camille-Benoist Desmoulins (1760-1794), one of the French revolution's most prominent pamphleteers, led the moderate wing of the Jacobins along with Danton, and was guillotined with the others.

* * *

Since Marx and Engels have we learned anything, elaborated our doctrine and perfected our methods? What lessons are we capable of drawing from the great events of our century: the dividing up of the world between the imperialist powers, the awakening of the oriental peoples, the world war, international socialism's adaptation to bourgeois legality, the revolution in Russia, in Germany and in Austria-Hungary, the revolutionary dictatorship in Russia and the reactionary dictatorship in the other agrarian countries, the balkanisation of Europe, the economic supremacy of the United States, the birth and disappearance of the Communist International, the Chinese revolution, the crisis of the British Empire, and the gigantic progress in science and technology? Where are our solutions to the problems posed under new aspects by the consequences of all these things, those of cycles of crises, of outlets, of unemployment, of rationalisation, of the classes, and of the absolute increase of the share of the proletariat in the total product in spite of its relative decline? Our literature on the line, in botched analyses, in pedantic affirmations, and in lightweight prophecies, is a response to nothing. Will it be given to Wall Street to impose a peace, if only for a time, on the Pacific and the Atlantic, like that of Rome upon the Mediterranean world? And have the old capitalist states of Europe any other resource for assuring their rate of profit than to open up to the fullest extent the markets of the European and Asiatic East? Moscow's soothsayers, of both right and left, have for years happily announced every day an immediate war, an artificial warning that will not for much longer substitute for an international policy. (Four years ago I briefly refuted the vague and far too obscure thesis that an imminent war was being prepared by Locarno, and two years later refuted in more detail the more precise thesis of the Russian Opposition, shared by the leadership, of a war against the Soviet Union being the only way that Britain could resolve its industrial crisis. It is possible that these views may be those of a 'Rightist', but events have confirmed them rather than the so-called 'left' warnings which proved to be well off the mark.) I would have preferred to discuss with you the problems of the future rather than return to the questions of the past, whatever interest they may still hold, and which your writings show to be at the centre of your preoccupations. At least I hope that these retrospective explanations will not nullify future possibilities for work and common activity.

As for the present, it appears to me to be dominated by an essential 'moment' about which I have two things to say to you, in spite of the inconvenience of too precise a formulation. Out of the whole revolutionary effort of our time, all that remains for us is the Soviet Union (and, if you like, the negative balance sheet of the Communist International, teaching us how we should not organise and lead the proletariat). The existence of this state forces us to think of a policy and a tactic generally conforming to its interests, which must not contradict those of the international workers' movement; and in any case the alternative cannot be to be forced to sacrifice the one for the other, and if the contradictions of the situation often apparently present the appearance of this, it is those of the Soviet state which must take precedence, on the supposition that they have been well understood, and on condition of there being complete understanding of what is done. The present divergence between the policy of the International and that of the Soviet state, even if it persists under the disguise of identity, will lead both of them to a fall. The Opposition is mistaken, believing itself to be proving its revolutionary intransigence, in subordinating the tangible necessities of the Soviet state to the doubtful needs of some occurrence that is apparently revolutionary elsewhere. There is nothing more important for the whole international workers' movement than the economic success of the Soviet Union, whose state capitalism represents the first attempt to organise economic production in the absence of private ownership; this state capitalism is not socialism, but it represents an undeniable advance over imperialist capitalism, in what it is trying to do rather than in what it is succeeding in doing. The Opposition must show that it is willing to work in its service before aspiring to get back into the party, for its present position comes down to a useless heroism without being of use to either the party or the state. Our overall mistake under your influence was to want to be reintegrated into a party in which there was no longer any place for Marxists, and the most particular mistake of the Russian Opposition was to persevere in this, which some have individually succeeded in doing by giving in, while others hoped to succeed as a group by martyrdom while they awaited the awakening of the proletariat. I am sure that a Lenin would not have given himself up to this romanticism and would have preferred, to the artificiality of the uncertain homage of a vague posterity, the slightest possibility for practical work in the service of the proletariat, without withdrawing any of his ideas, and without renouncing any of his plans. Knowing how to wait is as necessary as knowing how to fight, and it is even possible to keep silent without losing the ability to act, as though we can give ourselves the illusion of acting when we exhaust ourselves with words. As irrational as this may appear to a Russian communist, you can be of service to the revolution without being a member of the Politbureau, the Central Committee or the party. There is no shortage of tasks. The quickest way to the rebirth of the party may not, among other eventualities, pass via the party. The labour of men and the work of the time must also be coordinated, and the work of the silent forces. Think of it, that while there still remains in Russia a courageous team resolved to hang on, it will be dispersed in all directions if you cannot take the initiative of saving it for our future by an intelligent retreat.

TROTSKY AND THE GERMAN COMMUNIST OPPOSITION

We present below five articles from *Gegen den Strom,* the theoretical journal of the Communist Party (Opposition) of Germany (KPO) and one from *Der Internationale Klassenkampf,* the German-language journal of the Internationale Vereinigung der Kommunistischen Opposition (IVKO — International Union of the Communist Opposition), of which the KPO was a key affiliate. They have been translated into English by Mike Jones.

These articles are important as they outline the central points of the KPO's attitude towards Trotsky and the Left Opposition in particular respect of the relationships of the oppositional groups towards the Communist Party leaderships in Germany and the Soviet Union.

By the late 1920s, the leadership of the German Communist Party (KPD) was divided into three factions: the 'Right', whose most prominent figures were August Thalheimer and Heinrich Brandler, who had both recently returned from the Soviet Union, the 'Conciliators', and the 'Left', who were favoured by Stalin and who supported the ultra-left orientation that was rapidly developing within the Communist International. In September 1928, the KPD's leadership voted to suspend the party's General Secretary Ernst Thälmann, a leading 'Left', for his covering up of a case of corruption in the party branch in his home city of Hamburg. Stalin furiously defended his protégé, and although the KPD leaders retreated, Moscow used their original insubordination to attack both the 'Right' and the 'Conciliators'. The former started to organise themselves as a faction, the Comintern's Executive Committee responded on 19 December 1928 by issuing an Open Letter calling for their expulsion from the KPD, and 10 days later they held a conference that declared themselves as an opposition within the party. A subsequent purge in the KPD resulted in around 6000 'Rightists' being expelled. Although the KPO considered itself as an opposition within the KPD, it effectively operated as an independent group. One of its key orientations was maintaining a consistent opposition to the ultra-leftism of the Third Period, and it called for a united front of workers' organisations against the Nazi threat. After the Nazis' victory in 1933, the KPO worked in clandestinity, but Nazi oppression eventually led to the demise of its activities.

Thalheimer and Brandler lived in exile in France until the German invasion, and then in Cuba. Thalheimer died there in 1948, but Brandler returned to Germany to help rebuild the movement, and he was active in left-wing politics until his death in 1967.

There is very little information in English-language publications about the KPO. Robert Alexander's *The Right Opposition: The Lovestoneites and the International Communist Opposition of the 1930s* (Greenwood Press, Westport, 1981) is, as the title suggests, biased towards coverage of the Communist Opposition in the USA, and it devotes 122 pages to that group compared to a mere 20 pages to the KPO. It does not draw upon any of the KPO's publications, relying largely upon secondary material and reports in the US *Workers Age*, and makes no reference to the fact that, unlike the US group, which folded in 1941, the German current revived after 1945, and indeed still exists today.[1] Readers with a knowledge of German, however, can find much material on the KPO, particularly Karl Hermann Tjaden's pioneering *Struktur und Funktion der KPD-Opposition (KPO): eine organisationssoziologische untersuchung zur Rechts-Opposition im deutschen Kommunismus zur Zeit der Weimarer Republik* (Meisenheim am Glan, 1964), and Theodor Bergmann's *Gegen den Strom. Der Geschichte der KPD (Opposition)* (Hamburg, 2001), which includes a substantial biographical section on KPD(O) members.

I: Trotsky on the German Opposition

From *Gegen den Strom*, Volume 2, no 16, 20 April 1929, pp 10-11. We present here a letter written by Trotsky to the Leninbund. It is preceded by an introduction bearing the title 'Is That Really Accurate? (About the "Collaboration" of the Right and the Left in Germany)', which was presumably added by the *Gegen den Strom* editors.

Trotsky's letter had apparently been sent to the Leninbund but not published

---

1. There are misconceptions that have become part of the mythology of rival tendencies. The notes to Trotsky's *The First Five Years of the Communist International*, Volume 1 (Pioneer Press, New York, 1945) state baldly: 'In the early 1920s Thalheimer with Brandler became one of the leaders of the Right Wing of the Communist Party — whose counterpart in America was the Lovestone group. The Brandlerites were expelled from the CI in 1929 and survived for a while as a centrist movement headed for the camp of the bourgeoisie (where they finally landed).' This travesty was repeated in the New Park (London) edition of the book which was published in 1973. It is true that Jay Lovestone and various other leaders of the US section of the IVKO rapidly deserted any recognisable form of left-wing politics after their group dissolved itself in January 1941, with Lovestone and several of his colleagues subsequently becoming key figures in the establishment of pro-US, anti-communist labour organisations around the world, and others, most notably Bertrand Wolfe, becoming Cold War ideologues. This, however, was not the case with either Thalheimer or Brandler, who remained Marxists until their deaths.

by them until its appearance in *Gegen den Strom*. It is undated but refers to an extract from the Soviet trade union paper *Trud* of 10 November, which, in turn, allegedly quotes from a leaflet by Thalheimer of 6 October. Obviously, that can only be 1928. In referring to the crisis over the attempt by Ernst Thälmann, the pro-Stalin leader of the German Communist Party (KPD), to cover up the corruption in the Hamburg branch of the party (the Wittorf Affair), Trotsky expresses no faith in the 'Right' genuinely challenging Thälmann. It did, however, and in late 1928 and early 1929, the expulsions from the KPD of 6000 or so 'Rightists' began. Trotsky was clearly unaware of this fact. That also would seem to place the writing of the letter in late 1928 during his exile in Alma Ata, prior to his deportation to Constantinople. It appears that no English-language version of this letter exists in print.

The letter from Engels to Marx quoted by Trotsky as appearing in *Gegen den Strom* is perhaps taken from an earlier German version or translated back into German from Russian, as it is different in phrasing, though not in sense, to the German version in the *Marx-Engels-Werke*. The English version in the *Marx-Engels Collected Works* (Volume 38, p 290) is not entirely successful so here a translation from the *Werke* (Volume 27, p 190) is used instead. The italicised part of the last sentence is in English in the original.

Hugo Urbahns (1890-1946) had been an adherent of the Zinovievite left wing of the KPD led by Ruth Fischer and Arkady Maslow. Expelled from the KPD in 1927, he was subsequently the main leader of the Leninbund, which was launched in April 1928. It published *Volkswille*, a daily paper, and *Fahne des Kommunismus*. More details on the Leninbund can be found in Pierre Broué, 'The German Left and the Russian Opposition', *Revolutionary History*, Volume 2, no 3, Autumn 1989, pp 20-28.

* * *

a: Is That Really Accurate?
(About the 'Collaboration' of the Right and the Left in Germany)

We publish here a letter by Trotsky, in which he takes a position towards our opposition.

Trotsky writes this letter in order to warn his German adherents in the Urbahns group against getting together with us.

Upon the outbreak of the Thälmann crisis, Urbahns had, as is known, called for his adherents to support the 'right' in the struggle over party democracy.

From that the official party press discovered the 'unprincipled bloc between Urbahns and Thalheimer'.

This bloc never existed. It was impossible for the simple reason that we directed our struggle against the ultra-left policy, and the Urbahns group was, and is, merely the most consistent representative of this policy.

Certainly we have done everything in order to win, through ideological conviction, workers who, out of loathing for the misdeeds of the party bureaucracy, have wandered into the Urbahns camp, for a correct, fruitful opposition. We will also continue to do that.

But a political getting together with Urbahns was, and remains, out of the question for us.

Trotsky's warning very likely contributed to the *Volkswille* changing its tone in relation to us. The ultra-left recognised more and more that the 'new line' of the party was nothing other than the policy that it had always advocated. Thus, for example, in *West Saxony*, we see how the ultra-left seize the leadership in the struggle against 'rightists'. No wonder! The rejection of the united front tactic, the 'struggle leaderships',[2] etc — all those are venerable white elephants from the junk-shop of Maslow's[3] policies called the Leninbund.

The *Volkswille*, which usually prints every line by Trotsky, has omitted to publish this letter, which deals not with Russian but German questions. It surely is influenced by the knowledge that Trotsky's position is the most stupid imaginable confirmation of the ultra-left policy. It is so for the reason that Trotsky is the most consistent representative of ultra-left politics in the international Communist movement.

Trotsky's argumentation against us is very simple, even primitive.

The first main sin of Brandler and Thalheimer is their attitude to 1923: 'If these people want to wait until history brings them a more ripe, more favourable situation for victory, than in the autumn of 1923, then they will never engage in the decisive struggle.' Thus, a more ripe revolutionary situation than in October 1923 cannot exist! This is the ultra-left October Legend[4] as set out in its crudest fashion and in the ECCI Open Letter.[5]

2. Struggle leaderships (*Kampfleitungen*) were rank-and-file bodies that were set up by the KPD during this period to lead struggles in opposition to the official trade union organisations.
3. Arkady Maslow (Isaac Yefimovich Chereminsky, 1891-1941) was a Russian of Jewish extraction. Together with Ruth Fischer (1895-1961), he headed the ultra-left in the KPD from 1921. He was leader of the KPD in 1924, was imprisoned during 1925-26, and was expelled from the party in 1926. He was co-founder with Fischer of the Leninbund, and went into exile in 1933. His death in Cuba may have been in suspicious circumstances.
4. For Thalheimer's account of the events of 1923 and his analysis of the October Legend, see his '1923: A Missed Opportunity? The Legend of the German October and the Real History of 1923', *Revolutionary History*, Volume 8, no 3, pp 90-124.
5. The Executive Committee of the Communist International sent an Open Letter to the KPD on 19 December 1928 calling for its leadership to open an all-out attack upon the 'rightists'. The letter included a leftist critique of Brandler and Thalheimer for their role in 1923. A purge of the 'rightists' soon followed, and about 6000 people were expelled from the KPD.

Secondly, Trotsky reproaches Brandler and Thalheimer because they are — not *Trotskyists*.

We have certainly thought that the policies of the Trotskyists for Russia were erroneous and dangerous, without therefore, as Trotsky claims, seeing in Stalin's policies the perfect solution. Moreover, we have already written amply about these matters. Here we only want to state that Trotsky, just like Stalin, judges the whole movement in the other countries only from the viewpoint of his *narrowest* Russian factional interests. The only difference is that Trotsky, with an unshakeable naivety, expresses it openly.

Trotsky's warning to Urbahns was superfluous. At least two are needed for the 'bloc'.

We have, however, a somewhat longer aversion to unprincipled blocs than Trotsky, whose latest attempt in this field, the bloc with Zinoviev, belongs to only the very recent past.[6]

b: Leon Trotsky, Letter to the Leninbund

I received an extract from *Trud* of 10 November, from Comrade Valentinov,[7] devoted to the groupings in the German party. From this extract I first learnt of Thalheimer's leaflet of 6 October, in which he speaks of the necessity of supporting oneself 'on the left and even ultra-left workers', as also about the words allegedly spoken by Urbahns in a Leninbund conference that this organisation 'cannot rule out a factional collaboration with the right and must strive for such a collaboration'.

I do not know to what extent this information is correct. The official press is filled with falsified quotes in general, and in questions that concern the Opposition quite particularly. However, some private letters force me to insinuate that there is a certain element of truth in this information. This is also quite enough in order for the voice of warning to be raised with all determination. Each oppositionist, each group and each organisation, that takes this route must unavoidably perish.

Thalheimer says in his leaflet that the right must show the left and ultra-left workers 'the complete hollowness' of the terms 'left and right'. These words show only the complete hollowness of Thalheimer himself. In the year of 1923, together with Brandler, he demonstrated that he was not equal to the revolutionary situation. One could explain that then by insufficient preparation, lack of revolutionary experience and steeling. However, at that time also, of

---

6. A reference to the Joint or United Opposition in the Soviet Communist Party, which brought Trotsky's and Zinoviev's factions together. It lasted from April 1926 to December 1927.
7. G Valentinov was a Soviet trade union journalist and member of the Left Opposition, exiled in 1928.

course, one should not have made the slightest principled concession to the passive, fatalist views of Brandler, Thalheimer, Klara Zetkin, among others. One may and must demonstrate that they bear no more blame for the catastrophe of 1923 than the whole official leadership of the CI, and we have rendered this 'defence' to the right. But no more than that. However, as B and T, at the Fifth Congress and later, began to demonstrate that the situation in Germany at the end of 1923 was not sufficiently 'ripe' for a revolutionary offensive with the aim of seizing power, as they together with their antagonists declared that 'we have overestimated the revolutionary character of the situation, etc', it was clear that these people are not capable, or not willing, to learn from their mistakes, which are linked to gigantic defeats of the proletariat. In such a state of affairs it is out of the question for the Bolshevik-Leninists to orient towards B and T. If these people want to wait until history brings them a more ripe, more favourable situation for victory than in the autumn of 1923, then they will never engage in the decisive struggle.

The behaviour of B and T was no better in Russian affairs. Both lived for a number of years in the USSR. The whole period of the right-centrist backsliding passed before their eyes. That did not hinder them from solidarising themselves throughout the whole time with the ruling course. In the golden age of the course of the 'strengthening' of the middle peasants and against industrialisation, they were of the view that no other policies could be conducted than those pursued by the right-centrist bloc. Together with Dan,[8] they were of the view that the line of the Opposition is dangerous. Possibly they wanted, in this way — disregarding everything else — to assume a protective colouring, as the Polish centrists did (Warski, Koszucka,[9] among others), in order to get into power in the party. Even if this had only been a manoeuvre, then it would also have been a sign of alarming national narrow-mindedness and lack of principle. In reality, however, their attitude to the Russian questions corresponded to their intrinsic attitude, which expressed itself clearly enough in the German questions during the year of 1923 and later. That there are good workers who could be driven out by the unprincipled and irresponsible, utterly poisonous politics of the leadership of the right — there can be no doubt. But these workers can only be brought back to the correct route through a pitiless struggle against Brandler and T.

So what kind of factional collaboration with the Bolshevik-Leninists is in

8. Fyodor Ilyich Dan (Gurvich, 1871-1947) was a leading Menshevik. Exiled in 1922, he co-edited the Menshevik journal *Socialist Courier* until 1940, when his increasingly pro-Soviet orientation led to a split with the rightward-moving Menshevik majority.
9. Adolf Warski (Warszawski, 1868-1937) and Maria Koszucka (known as Wera Kostrzewa, 1879-1939) were both pioneer Polish Social Democrats and founders of the Polish Communist Party. Both moved to the Soviet Union, and perished in the Great Terror.

question? What is the aim of this collaboration? On what sort of principled basis can it be realised? Cde Urbahns has allegedly said that the Leninbund does not reject the factional collaboration, 'if this collaboration brings us closer to our aim of conquering the party'. It is difficult, without knowledge of the whole speech of cde Urbahns, to understand the sense of these, at first glance, wholly incomprehensible words. That our aim is to conquer the party and not to create a second parallel party, in that Urbahns is naturally absolutely right. But how can one conquer the party? Obviously through a clear and distinct principled line, which more and more circles of the party, by means of their own experience, become convinced is correct and make their own. If that is correct in general, then it is ten times more correct in conditions where the opponent disposes over truly limitless technical possibilities for the distortion and falsification of the views of the Opposition. Complete ideological clarity and absolute ideological intransigence are here a law of self-preservation. So how can factional collaboration with the right, which occupies an opposing principled position, bring the left nearer to conquering the party? It is clear that what it concerns here can only be an organisational combination that damages the principled position. Only a group that aspires and hastens itself to occupy a place in the party that does not absolutely correspond to its ideological-political strength could engage in such a combination. But that is a route to suicide and no further. More than once I have had to observe how political impatience became the source of opportunist politics. The aspiration to harvest unripened fruit leads to all kinds of blocs and coalitions with this or that part of the enemy class. The German Social Democracy is bound to break its neck in doing so. Groupings within the CP are no more than social tendencies which have yet to develop and ripen, but which are, however, class lines tending towards division. One should not fool around with these lines. The least ambiguity is dangerous. Also one should never put the factional mechanics of the struggle, even if it is only for an hour, above its principled content.

The organisational aim of collaboration between the left and right would not lead to the conquering of the party by the left, but simply to the fall of the bureaucratic-centrist Thälmann[10] group. But even if this aim was achieved at the price of forming the bloc (which is out of the question in the near future), then the weight of the left wing in the party after this victory would be less than at present. Any coalition that obliterates the principled line always brings advantages to the right at the expense of the left, just as the coalition of the SP with the bourgeois parties is, without question, grist to the mill of capital. That

10. Ernst Thälmann (1886-1944), a Hamburg dockworker, led the KPD after the deposing of Fischer and Maslow in 1925. A dedicated Stalinist, he led the party until the Nazi takeover. Arrested in March 1933, he was murdered in Buchenwald concentration camp.

is particularly important and correct now, when the left wing must swim against the current. The whole mechanism of bourgeois society, the automatic workings of all its powers and institutions, as well as finally the traditional ideology, which penetrates into every pore, ensures that every obscurity, ambiguity and half-measure of the revolutionary wing without fail brings advantage to the class enemy, or the agency of this class enemy, or the sub-agency of this agency in the guise of the left socialists or the centrists within the CP. Therefore a factional collaboration with the right is out of the question. Of course, that does not exclude parallel voting from time to time in respect of questions of the party regime and the party procedure. The proletarian revolutionary will vote against a vote of confidence in the Teddy [Thälmann] clique of course, without thereby being deceived into thinking that the Brandlerists will also vote against Thälmann. In parliaments all over the world it happened more than once that in such negative (critical) votes against the centre the revolutionaries had to step through the same door as the ultra-reactionaries.

Just like the present-day Social Democrats, the liberals have always raised a wild clamour on the occasion of such apparent 'blocs'. However, it takes no great effort to expose such charlatanism. In such votes the emphasis is on the motivation of the vote, that is to say, in clear and accurate references as to the purpose of the vote.

In all cases where the centrist bureaucracy goes behind the back of the party and uses the poisonous weapon of calumny, maliciousness and intrigue against the right, the left will raise the voice of implacable protest, not on account of abstract moral, nor out of sympathy for the right of course, but for the reason that such methods and tricks dangerously poison the party and cause abscesses, as in Smolensk and Hamburg.[11] If the Bolshevik-Leninists demand an open and all-round party discussion about the three lines: the right, the centrist and the left — they will unconditionally point out that the Thälmann regime has international roots, that its source is the regime in the CPSU, that the regime in the CPSU is a functional organ of the policy of the right-centrist bloc, that B, T and company have always and consistently supported this policy, and still do in its essentials.

Once more: one should never let oneself be led by impatience and thereby strive to overtake oneself in politics. In April 1917, Lenin, as he arrived in

11. In 1928 an investigation into agricultural problems in Smolensk discovered serious misdemeanours, with factory managers, some of whom were CPSU members, being accused of corruption, bribery and abuse of their official positions. John Wittorf was Thälmann's brother-in-law and an inveterate gambler. Thälmann tried to cover up the fact that Wittorf paid his debts with party funds. The affair was revealed in the Leninbund's *Volkswille*. At first, Thälmann's rivals in the KPD leadership voted to remove him, but reversed their decision after Stalin intervened.

Leningrad, saw himself faced with the fact that the leaders of the party, frightened by the fact that they found themselves in the minority [in the Soviets], not only thereupon strove to unite with the majority in every possible combination, but were uniting with defenders of the fatherland. Moreover, at the March Conference in 1917, Stalin declared that it was possible to fuse with Tsereteli[12] and Dan in one party. He [Lenin] immediately posed the question in its full extent. He said:

> We are no charlatans. We must base ourselves only on the consciousness of the masses. Even if it is necessary to remain in a minority — so be it. It is a good thing to give up for a time the position of leadership; we must not be afraid to remain in the minority. (March Conference, Session of 4 April)

That was under the conditions of the growing revolutionary surge. This rule is now for us all the more an obligation, when the surge is not rising, when we are all swimming against the stream. Whether Thälmann sits in the CC for a few months more or less is unimportant. It is a matter of welding together the proletarian revolutionaries on the correct position, the rest will follow. No nervousness. One should not be taken in by bureaucratic provocations. One should not chase after official positions, as long as their conquering is not prepared for among the masses. In this context, I want to quote some powerful and truly refreshing words from the letter Engels sent to Marx on 13 February 1851:

> Not only no official *government* position, but, also, as long as possible, no official *party* position, no seat on committees, *per procura*, no responsibility for asses, pitiless criticism of everyone, and thereby that cheerfulness which all the conspiracies of blockheads can surely not deprive us. And we can do that. We can always, in the nature of things, be more revolutionary than the phrasemongers, because we have learnt something and they have not, because we know what we want and they do not, and *because, after what we have seen for the last three years* [six years — LD], *we shall take it a real deal more coolly than anyone who has an interest in the business.*

L Trotsky

* * *

---

12. Irakli Georgievich Tsereteli (1882-1959) was a leading Menshevik and a minister in the Provisional Government. He was prominent in the Menshevik government in Georgia, and went into exile in 1923.

II: August Thalheimer, The Leninbund and Trotsky

From *Gegen den Strom*, Volume 2, no 19, 11 May 1929, p 15.

* * *

On the initiative of Trotsky's letter about the relationship of the Leninbund to our opposition, which was first published in *Gegen den Strom* and then in *Volkswille*, no 10, the latter has started a discussion about the line set out by Trotsky. In the following we will touch on it, above all, since it illustrates how the Leninbund (and not just it, but the 'left' opposition in general), by carrying out an uncritical adherence to Trotsky, will be led further and further into a blind alley and be damned to barrenness. On the other hand, it shows that where these lefts follow their own judgement, as a rule they arrive at much more sensible conclusions, such as now in the question of Communist trade union policy, and in the evaluation of the May Day action of the KPD[13] (in which then, of course, it is not a left or ultra-left, but a somewhat 'right', that is, the correct communist line, even if with occasional inconsistencies, that becomes evident).

The uncritical falling in line behind the Trotskyist Opposition is, in the final analysis, only the *latest stage of the uncritical relationship of the Communists outside the Soviet Union towards the leadership of the Communist International, that is, to the leadership of the Communist Party of the Soviet Union.* If the [KPD's] officials follow, at any given time, the dominant tendency in the leadership of the CPSU, uncritically and slavishly, then the international left just as uncritically falls in line behind the respective directives of the Opposition in respect of the Russian and the international questions. If the latter undoubtedly evidences more character and steadfastness, it is nevertheless, politically, *only the same uncritical relationship, even if with reversed signs.* But if one thing is clear today, then it is that the Communist parties outside the Soviet Union must learn to see with their own eyes and to stand on their own feet. That in no way means underestimating the significance of the Soviet Union for the international Communist movement or an indifference to the Russian questions. Precisely the opposite. *One can only talk of a serious and valuable influence on the Russian questions as on the leadership of the Communist International by the Communist parties outside the Soviet Union when it rests on independent judgement.* The mere echo of the present majority or the Opposition of the CPSU is worthless and meaningless. What should differentiate the attitude to the Russian questions of the Communist parties outside the Soviet Union from the Russian party is, obviously, not their inferior evaluation but their *different viewpoint,* which is

---

13. The KPD decided to stage a march in Berlin on May Day 1929 in defiance of an official ban on all demonstrations. The police, for which SPD Police Chief Karl Zörgiebel was responsible, opened fire, killing 25 and injuring 160 unarmed marchers.

all the more important and indispensable, as the Russian comrades themselves, in the nature of things, are unable to have it. This viewpoint is the *attitude to the Russian questions from the angle of the revolutionary movement and on the basis of the revolutionary experiences in their countries*. Only on this basis can the Russian viewpoint be *supplemented, can a real, broad, international attitude to the Russian questions come about*. This indispensable task will be neglected through the uncritical trailing of the left behind the Trotskyist Opposition, as much as by the attitude of the officials. The result is the same in both cases: the subordination of the international and the national Communist movement to the, at any given time, factional interests and factional manoeuvres of this or that grouping within the CPSU.

Therefore, it is a characteristic of all left oppositions that the questions of the Communist movement of their own countries, which must constitute the *basis* for the *maturing of their parties*, are repressed by the actual Russian questions. In actual fact, so far, every opposition that set out on Trotsky's course has been led into the wilderness and ruined. That is not primarily to do with Trotsky as a person, but rather by the application of the standards of the Russian ultra-left factions to the Communist movement of the other countries. If the Leninbund persists in its present dependent relationship to the Russian Opposition, then strange and dangerous escapades will be in store for it. The Trotskyist group in the Soviet Union has, as is known, split. *Radek* and some others have split away and are evidently getting closer to Stalin.[14] The attitude of this group to the currents within the international Communist movement will also change accordingly, and the Leninbund will have to ask itself: 'Where should I turn to, I the dim little brother?' It is obvious that such an attitude is full of contradictions, untenable and senseless.

Stimulated by Trotsky's letter, the Leninbund now takes up again the left October Legend in its most absurd form, namely in the form that objectively all the conditions were ripe for the seizure of power and that only the party leadership failed in October 1923. *Evidence* for this assertion, which can only rest on a fundamental analysis of the class relations of the year of 1923, has *never even been attempted* to be advanced, either by Trotsky or by his blind adherents. They are content with the repetition of the *assertion*; while the economic and political facts, from which the opposite can be decisively demonstrated, are piled up mountain high today. The argument that up to the Chemnitz

---

14. Karl Radek (1885-1939) had been prominent in the Left Opposition. In the summer of 1928, he wrote documents that distanced himself from the policies of Trotsky and the Left Opposition, particularly in respect of the concept of Permanent Revolution. On 30 May 1929, *Izvestia* announced his capitulation to Stalin's leadership.

Conference[15] even the then leadership of the CC deceived itself about the real situation is, of course, no argument, it cannot substitute for a real investigation of the then objective situation. We, the 'right', are not in the least afraid of such an investigation. We have already produced a not inconsiderable amount of factual material for it, and more will follow. Of course, that cannot be done in one or two newspaper articles, it will be produced at the necessary length.

This new reheating of the October Legend is *today all the more dangerous, as precisely the party's May Action delivers new and conclusive material for it*, like the idea that the party, independently of the real relationship of class forces, only needs to wish, in order to drag along the class as a whole or in its majority — *as this idea either makes the party incapable of struggling at all, or pitches it into putschist adventures*. The May Action delivers the proof for the second part of this sentence. If a real and profound discussion of October 1923, based on the facts, had occurred, both within the party and in the Communist International, then the fiasco of the May Action would not have been possible. It is more and more manifest that without the final theoretical clarity over the party's own actions in the past, a more correct and more certain course for the party, a real mastering of the tasks of the revolution in any country is impossible.

The *Volkswille* is simultaneously reheating again the legend which *Geschke*,[16] in his time, promoted, whereby the 'right' had been responsible for the course of splitting the trade unions, while the left had fought and liquidated this course. It is certainly an advance when the left today, like scalded children, oppose the course of establishing independent 'revolutionary trade unions', but where the past is concerned, then the facts speak an only too clear language here. We must soon devote a specific essay to this matter.

The October Legend needs to be dealt with once and for all, not because we are obstinate, but because adhering to it hinders the discarding of false opinions, and blocks the road to the future.

Before the May Action, the Leninbund had expressed criticism and made proposals which, in essence, coincided with our own. We welcome that. But after the action, when simultaneously with the ultra-left brainwave of armed demonstrations, in the spirit of Heinz Neumann and Remmele,[17] it comes with

---

15. A congress of workers' organisations took place in Chemnitz on 21 October 1923 in order to plan the defence of Saxony against the threat of military intervention by the Reich government. Brandler called for a general strike in the eventuality of military action, but his proposal was rejected.
16. Ottomar Geschke (1882-1957) was a founding member of the KPD, and was in the ultra-left wing of the party in the early 1920s. He joined its Central Committee and Politbureau in 1925. He was imprisoned for the entire Nazi period, and held high posts in the DDR.
17. Heinz Neumann (1902-1937) and Hermann Remmele (1880-1938) rose to the leadership of the KPD alongside Thälmann after the removal of Fischer and Maslow. They fell foul

the purely opportunist proposal of a militia, then that shows only too clearly the confused contradictions in which the Leninbund flounders.

In order to escape from these contradictions one must liberate oneself just as much from one's own factional legends as from the dependence and uncritical adherence to the Russian Opposition or one of its factions. If the Leninbund is unable to free itself of these self-imposed fetters, then it will remain a sect and never find its way into the open channel of the Communist mass movement.

* * *

III: Reply to Urbahns

Unsigned article from *Gegen den Strom*, Volume 2, no 21, 25 May 1929, p 12.

* * *

In the *Volkswille*, Urbahns relates all sorts of things about the 'fiasco' of the Brandler meeting. The Leninbundists had averted Brandler's thrust into Berlin. We recommend Urbahns and his friends not to follow the example of the CC and boast about successes they have not gained. Urbahns was allowed to speak in our meeting, just as an adherent of the CC would have been, if prepared calmly to discuss. Urbahns has certainly abused this freedom of speech. He spoke about all sorts of things, but not on the theme of the evening, the elections in Saxony and the events on May Day. The reason why he did not do so is very simple. He had nothing to say about it. He admits himself in his paper: that Frölich's[18] criticism of the CC's May Day tactics is wholly correct. What Urbahns contributes in the way of positive proposals is a foolish mixture of slogans from the Opposition and from the CC. Urbahns' situation is very precarious. An increasing number of his adherents recognise that in Germany no other practical Communist policy is possible than that of the so-called 'Rights'. But if Urbahns were to admit that, then he would have to renounce his ultra-left past. Since he avoids the German questions in order to mask the complete ideological bankruptcy of the Leninbund, he continually responds with the counter-retort: we avoid the Russian questions.

Here we want to answer him once and for all, so that the next time when we encounter each other in a meeting, he no longer has an excuse to avoid the German questions.

We were, and remain, opponents of Trotsky's policies. Are you for Stalin then?, asks Urbahns. Not at all. It has never occurred to us to approve of everything

---

of Moscow in 1932 for advocating a harder anti-Nazi approach.

18. Paul Frölich (1894-1953) was a founding member of the KPD. He became a leading member of the KPO, and then moved to the Socialist Workers Party (SAP). He wrote a biography of Rosa Luxemburg in the late 1930s, an English edition of which was published in 1940. He moved to the USA, but returned to West Germany in 1949.

Stalin does, particularly not the activities of his bureaucratic apparatus or his Comintern policies. However, Trotsky's policies would bring the Soviet Union to the edge of the abyss and further increase the bureaucratism.

In order to evade the practical questions of Communist politics, Urbahns has hidden himself behind the theory of the building of socialism in one country. For him this theory is tantamount to the role of original sin in theology. And see, we Brandlerists have also sinned. It seems to us that this whole dispute over the theory of the building of socialism in one country was not worth the paper required in setting it out for his sake. It was conducted purely scholastically by both sides. Both sides, Stalin and Trotsky, posed the question falsely. However, if the question has any meaning, then Trotsky is incorrect.

The question of the building of socialism in one country is not a purely economic question. It is a political question. The most important precondition for the building of socialism is the dictatorship of the proletariat. And vice-versa, the dictatorship of the proletariat can only exist if it creates an economic basis for itself, that is, if it builds socialism. The question is not: 'Can one build socialism in one country?', the question is: 'Can the dictatorship of the proletariat maintain itself in one country?'

It is clear that one cannot answer in general in the affirmative for all countries and for all time. If capitalism in the rest of the world is not in the epoch of its decline but finds itself in a rising development, then a dictatorship of the proletariat in a single country will not be able to endure. Also in a country like Austria or Bulgaria or Holland the dictatorship of the proletariat cannot maintain itself in isolation. The Mensheviks take the same view in respect of Russia, on account of the numerical weakness of the Russian proletariat. Lenin continually opposed this view and said that the dictatorship of the proletariat in Russia is quite able to maintain itself in spite of the numerical weakness of the working class, namely with the precondition that the proletariat conducts a correct policy towards the working peasants. And in this question Trotsky has completely failed.

That will have to satisfy Urbahns for now. Now we expect from him that he gives us a quite clear answer to where he stands on the practical questions of revolutionary politics in Germany in general and on our proposals in particular. Constantinople is a very beautiful place, but perhaps Urbahns will turn his gaze towards areas nearer home.

Urbahns knows very well that the Leninbund will not live long with its present politics; what the Leninbund does today is to stagger to and fro between the politics of the Opposition and of the CC; Urbahns expressed this frequent ideological and political gratitude to the Opposition, since he offers it an 'unprincipled bloc'. Comrade *Hausen*[19] has clearly answered him, that we are not thinking about that. Clarity, critical accounting with the past — that is the only way in which the ultra-left worker can advance. Besides the *Volkswille*, the *Vorwärts*[20] also occupies itself with our meeting. It also carries out some shameless falsifications in order to hush up the bloody guilt of its party comrade Zörgiebel. The following correction by comrade Paul Frölich will shut its lying mouth.

* * *

IV: Trotsky, the Counter-Pope

From *Gegen den Strom*, Volume 2, no 28, 13 July 1929 pp 7-8. The two letters which appeared in *Fahne des Kommunismus*, the organ of the Leninbund, were replies by Trotsky to letters from Boris Souvarine. English renditions of each, 'Six Years of the Brandlerites' (25 April 1929) and 'Once More on Brandler and Thalheimer' (12 June 1929), can be found in *Writings of Leon Trotsky (1929)* (Pathfinder Press, New York, 1975), pp 111-16 and pp 155-60. The quotes from the letters are translated from *Gegen den Strom*, presumably the texts as published in *Fahne des Kommunismus*, as where a comparison was made with the Pathfinder version there were minor inaccuracies and errors. For example: 'one must know how to approach events in their development' (p 157) for 'one must understand how to observe phenomena in their development' ('die Erscheinungen in ihrer Entwicklung zu sehen').

* * *

The *Fahne des Kommunismus* carries two letters from Trotsky, in which he takes a position on our group.

Trotsky sums up his general evaluation of us in the following sentences:

> Truly I needed no time... in order to ascertain that the Brandler-Thalheimer group stands on the other side of the barricades... Our task consists in explaining that the Brandlerite faction is only a new gateway to the Social Democracy...
>
> Of course one can say that this is an exaggeration: Brandler and Thalheimer are not yet Social Democrats. Of course, they are not *yet* Social Democrats and, of course, they are not the *present* Social Democracy, but one must understand how to observe phenomena in their development... Permit me

---

19. Erich Hausen (1900-1973) was a fitter who joined the KPD from the USPD. He held various senior posts in the KPD, and was expelled in December 1928 when he refused to back down when summed by the ECCI over the Wittorf affair. He later emigrated to the USA.
20. *Vorwärts* was the daily paper of the German Social Democratic Party.

to remind you once more that young, particularly oppositional, opportunist factions are no 'nicer' in relation to the old social chauvinist parties, than a little piglet is 'nicer' than an old swine.

In order to make such a 'ascertainment', Trotsky, of course, did not need much time. He has simply repeated what the official Comintern press says. The only original thing in his 'ascertainment' is the choice of abusive terminology, which demonstrates in Trotsky an otherwise wholly unusual preoccupation with rustic psychology and the problems of livestock farming.

This manner in which Trotsky treats the questions of the international labour movement shows how right we were in describing him as the most *consistent representative of ultra-left politics.*

While those faithful to the party line still attempt to cobble together an 'analysis' of the objective situation out of scraps of theses and newspaper clippings in order to conceal their nakedness, Trotsky scorns all such apparel, even those reminding him from afar of the pedantic customs of earlier times.

He does not even make an attempt to examine the objective situation in the different countries, the relationship of class forces, or the perspectives of the class struggle. He has his own infallible yardstick with which he separates the righteous from the unrighteous and places them on the different sides of the barricades.

The decisive questions for him are the attitude towards 1923, to the Anglo-Russian Committee, to the Chinese revolution, and to the theory of the building of socialism in one country.

Here anyone not swearing on the Trotskyist formula stands on the other side of the barrier — pardon, the barricade — which separates the small Trotskyist groups from the earthly world and its problems. The present questions of the international labour movement, the present tasks of the revolutionary workers, are absent from the Trotskyist creed. Here the slogan holds good — to paraphrase Heine: 'The earth we relinquish to the piglets and the swine.'

Trotsky literally says: 'Today it is an honour for any genuine revolutionary to remain a "sectarian".'

We, the Opposition in Germany, are also a minority, and we are not afraid of being a minority. But we are not a sect and have no wish to be one. We agree with Marx who, at the beginnings of the labour movement when it did not yet contain masses, always fought sectarianism with all his strength. A minority does not need to be a sect. It can become one at the moment it, instead of participating in the movement of the great masses, instead of seeing its aim as looking after their interests, boxes itself off from it, if it concerns itself with problems not connected with this movement, but which have been *especially chosen for a specific purpose.*

Trotsky's confession of sectarianism is therefore much nearer the truth than he himself suspects. Sectarianism is the content of the activity of Trotsky and his adherents. For example, it is characteristic that Trotsky states, *by the way*, the necessity of a platform of transitional demands and a correct tactic in the trades unions. But he does not believe that to be decisive. What is decisive is *how one stands regarding his creed*. What one should do today, the practical tasks, are secondary for him. How that manifests itself can be seen with Trotsky's adherent *Urbahns*. The Leninbund is one day in favour of work in the trade unions, another day for the struggle leaderships. They get their day-to-day slogans now from the KPD CC, and then from us. They do not know what they want. If one is a bit sharp with them, then at each opportunity, however appropriate or inappropriate, they fire off the Trotskyist article of faith, whereupon the theory of the building of socialism in one country is the source of all evil. That is the purest type of sectarianism.

Today the conflict over the united front tactic and the trade union question is occupying all sections of the Comintern. But these are not decisive questions for Trotsky. Decisive are 1923, the Anglo-Russian Committee, etc, etc. As long as the world has not recognised that Trotsky was correct in all these questions, he generously leaves it to itself in its own filth, until then he does not concern himself with *the situation today and what is happening today*.

But now to the content of the Trotskyist article of faith. On 1923 he says: 'It [Brandler's policy] led to the great catastrophe in late 1923... This catastrophe is the political precondition for the subsequent stabilisation of European capitalism...'

In a word: Brandler has stabilised capitalism. No one else has yet formulated the October Legend so crudely. One arrives at such conclusions when one is, like Trotsky, of the opinion that in 1923 all the preconditions for a victorious armed uprising were present, and that it all failed only because Brandler and Thalheimer had overslept. The question of whether the conditions existed in October 1923 that Lenin named in 1917 as the preconditions for the uprising, is not posed by Trotsky. An examination of the objective situation in 1923 does not interest him.

In respect of the question of the Anglo-Russian Committee[21] we took a position at the time (in the circle of some comrades, as a public appearance was not possible) against Stalin, as well as against Trotsky and Zinoviev. We are of the opinion that negotiations at the top level with the reformists cannot

---

21. The Anglo-Russian Trade Union Committee was formed in May 1925 by the leaderships of the Soviet and British trade unions. It collapsed after the latter departed from it in September 1927.

be fundamentally opposed, but under certain circumstances are necessary and useful. Only one should not, of course, want to sit at a table with the reformists merely for conversing together, but only when it concerns a distinct practical aim. During its first stage of existence the Anglo-Russian Committee served just such a distinct aim, namely the struggle for a united trade union international. Later, however, as this slogan was dropped, the Anglo-Russian Committee ceased to have any immediate practical significance and actually transformed itself into an opportunist top-level combination. It adopted decisions on all sorts of questions, and everyone knew that they were only generalities which committed nobody to anything. Trotsky's attitude to the Anglo-Russian Committee is, however, different to ours. He represented the viewpoint that it was inadmissible to sit at a table with Purcell,[22] that is, *the old ultra-left attitude towards the united front tactic.*

Neither were we in agreement with Stalin or Trotsky in the *Chinese Question*. We were against the policy of unconditional support to the Kuomintang. We criticised that in order to get unity with the Kuomintang, one paralysed the proletarian class struggle in China, held the mass movement back, throttled strikes, etc. We were, however, simultaneously against the attitude of Trotsky and his friends, who were against any, even transitory, collaboration with the national-revolutionary bourgeoisie. By the way, today Karl *Radek*, who in his time was in agreement with Trotsky on the Chinese Question and was the China specialist of the Opposition, also states that Trotsky's attitude to the Chinese Question stood in direct contradiction with that of Lenin. Recently Trotsky has namely advanced the view that in China only the slogan of the socialist dictatorship of the proletariat is valid, but not that of the democratic dictatorship of workers and peasants.[23] According to Trotsky then, the bourgeois, the national, the agrarian revolution in China has already been concluded.

In a previous issue we have already taken a position on Trotsky's hobby-horse, the *theory of the building of socialism in one country.* As far as we are concerned, as regards the Soviet Union, another question seems to be decisive. Namely, that of whether the Soviet Union is a dictatorship of the proletariat or not. Among the Russian Trotskyists the discussion over this question resulted in sharp differences and has led to a split in the group. In one letter, Trotsky advanced the view that the Stalin–Rykov bloc was an expression of the middle peasants and the kulaks. His closest Russian adherents are of the view that

22. Albert Purcell (1872-1935) was a leading official in the furniture workers' union. A left-winger, he was active in the Anglo-Russian Trade Union Committee and was a member of the TUC General Council during the General Strike.
23. Possibly a reference to LD Trotsky, 'The Political Situation in China and the Tasks of the Bolshevik-Leninist Opposition', *Leon Trotsky on China* (New York, 1976), pp 402-08. This article appeared in the *Bulletin of the Opposition*, July 1929.

Soviet Russia is governed by a 'bloc of the reactionary elements of the town and the village'. That is not our view but that of the Social Democracy. We are by no means inclined to identify with Stalin's policies from A to Z, nor to ignore the deficiencies of the CPSU's policies, but the starting point for our criticism is the fact that the Soviet Union is a Workers' State. We criticise that which is inappropriate from the standpoint of the maintenance and the strengthening of the proletarian dictatorship and the socialist construction. However, we stand with the Soviet Union against the capitalist world on one side of the barricade! But here Trotsky has lost his way.

Trotsky turns against our criticism our position on the peasant question in Russia and writes:

> The middle layer of the peasantry represents a social protoplasm. It uninterruptedly and unalterably assumes certain forms in two directions: towards capitalist ones through the kulaks and towards socialist ones through the semi-proletarians and agricultural labourers. Anyone who ignores this fundamental process, anyone who speaks of the peasantry in general, anyone who does not see that the 'peasantry' has two hostile faces, is irretrievably lost.

The confirmation that a differentiation occurs among the middle peasantry, that it unceasingly separates out proletarianised and capitalist elements, should on no account induce us to overlook the fact that today the majority of the population of the Soviet Union consists of neither agricultural labourers nor of kulaks, but of middle peasants. Trotsky disregards this fact, and that is what we criticise him for.

Therefore Trotsky's article of faith does not accord with our conception. We are unable to adhere to any of the points mentioned by him. The falseness of this article of faith is also shown by its *blocking the way of Trotsky and his adherents from dealing with the present political problems*.

Trotsky has, for his part, gained sympathy with many, particularly outside Russia, who were dissatisfied with the regime of the ruling party. This sympathy holds good for those persecuted by Stalin. Numerous groups in different countries which otherwise uphold the most contradictory conceptions adhere to Trotsky. However, personal sympathies for a leader who has gained great merit in the past are not a suitable basis for a political association. That requires principled agreement. All the groups adhering to Trotsky have necessarily ended up in the *channel of sectarianism*. All the groups not wanting to pursue ultra-left politics have gradually distanced themselves from Trotsky.

At the moment in which Trotsky makes the attempt to set up his Trotskyist

International from Constantinople, a large part of his adherents in almost all countries have already left him or are about to do so.

That which is gathering around Trotsky is a sect, which swears allegiance to the great leader and his article of faith. Anyone who has doubt will be rejected, as with Souvarine in France, who did have great personal sympathies for Trotsky, but in some questions dared to have his own opinion.

Trotsky is infallible after all. In one of his recent articles 'The Permanent Revolution and the Line of Lenin', he states that Lenin polemicised against him without having read his (Trotsky's) fundamental work on the Russian Revolution of 1905.[24]

Those who refuse to go along with such a game — ourselves, for example — get excommunicated by Trotsky.

This method seems familiar to us. It is not patented by Trotsky. It is a poor imitation of the methods of the Comintern apparatus.

It is a sad image presented by Trotsky, when he sets himself up in Constantinople as a Counter-Pope and dispatches his excommunications. He will not gain anything for the future by that, but only blot out the memory of his past.

* * *

V: The Crisis in the Leninbund

Unsigned article from *Gegen den Strom*, Volume 2, no 40, 5 October 1929, p 10. Trotsky's pamphlet *The Defence of the Soviet Republic and the Opposition* is reproduced in *Writings of Leon Trotsky (1929)* (Pathfinder Press, New York, 1975), pp 262-313.

* * *

A grave crisis has broken out in the *Leninbund*. The majority of the national leadership, with *Urbahns* at the head, has *fallen out* with *Trotsky* in respect of the question of their attitude towards the *Russian-Chinese conflict*. Trotsky is now having a *pamphlet*, *The Defence of the Soviet Republic and the Opposition*, produced in Grylewicz's[25] publishing house (not by the *Volkswille* publishing house), which represents one single attack on Urbahns. Trotsky states that the *Fahne des Kommunismus*, as it is today, is not a suitable organ of the Communist left, it is necessary to create a new organ.

---

24. This resembles a passage in Chapter 1 of *The Permanent Revolution* (Pathfinder edition, New York, 1969, pp 166-67). However, this book did not appear until after this article was published. There is no reference to the title of the article in Louis Sinclair, *Trotsky: A Bibliography* (Aldershot, 1989).

25. Anton Grylewicz (1885-1971) was a KPD militant who was expelled from the party in 1927. He became a leader of the Left Opposition group in Germany after the Leninbund expelled the Trotskyist minority.

The argument essentially concerns whether one should take up the defence of the Soviet Union or not in the Russian-Chinese conflict. Trotsky is right when he, in relation to Urbahns, demands the unconditional defence of the Soviet Union as of the proletarian state. But his criticism touches not only Urbahns. It touches on himself. That which for Trotsky today reproaches Urbahns, Radek recently reproached Trotsky himself. If Trotsky today demonstrates that Thermidor is still not accomplished in the Soviet Union, that the proletarian dictatorship rules there, then Radek recently reproached him, that one could hardly take up the defence of the Soviet Union, when one saw in the present Soviet government a representation of the interests of the middle peasants, as Trotsky does, thereby denying its proletarian character. If Trotsky rebukes Urbahns, that his demand for the freedom of assembly in Russia is Menshevik-like, because it was a demand of bourgeois-capitalist democracy, then that also applies to his own demand for the secret ballot. The other reproaches Trotsky makes against Urbahns are also similar. He is correct when he rebukes Urbahns and his supporters for still being engrossed in the ideology of Maslow from 1924-25, but this ideology of Maslow is after all based on the October Legend, and in his latest pamphlet also Trotsky makes a fervent avowal of the legend.

If he dictates to Urbahns the Trotskyist version of the October Legend instead of the Zinovievist one, then he will certainly not cure him of ultra-left errors. If Trotsky today takes up the struggle against ultra-leftism, well that seems less convincing and everyone will easily be able to ascertain that the preacher of repentance himself is afflicted with the sins which he rails against. Trotsky wants to delimit himself, firstly from the 'right', secondly from the 'centrists', and now also from the 'ultra-left'. We believe that then, out of the patented Marxist 'left' which he demands, a creation will remain that one will be able to describe in some words that Trotsky once used, unjustifiably in fact, against Lenin: the organisation according to the principle, 'the individual and his property'.

Trotsky has also not allowed this opportunity to pass by without directing a few attacks against us. He credits himself with the merit of having warned Urbahns against getting together with us. We want gladly to allow him the merit. In addition he writes:

> By its very nature, opportunism is nationalistic, since it rests on the local and temporary needs of the proletariat, and not on its historical tasks. Opportunists find international control intolerable, and they reduce their international ties as much as possible to harmless formalities, imitating therein the Second International. The Brandlerites will salute the conferences of the Right Opposition in Czechoslovakia; they will exchange friendly notes with the Lovestone group in the United States, and so on, on the proviso

that each group does not hinder the others from conducting an opportunist policy to its own national taste.

All that is pure fantasy. We have never at any time gone in for the national independence of the parties. We want a stronger centralisation of the Comintern in the sense that it leads real international actions and not, as now, mere international factional struggles. What we do not want, however, is that the Comintern's politics are decided exclusively by the factional groupings in the CPSU, and that the parties will get the possibility to elaborate their concrete struggle tasks inside their countries. That is not a return to the Second International, but a strengthening, a consolidation of the Communist International. It is almost amusing how Trotsky copies precisely the methods of the Stalinist apparatus in relation to the different national Trotskyist groupings. He also shifts right and left about. Stalin is now the kulak ruler, now the representative of the proletarian dictatorship — however in relation to all these shifts one thing does not interest Trotsky: what position his adherents take on the concrete struggle tasks in their countries. His pamphlet contains not a word on the tactic of the Leninbund in respect of the German questions, except by chance that he declares himself against separate lists in the elections. The same goes also for his criticism of various French Trotskyist groups. What Trotsky imagines as international cooperation is unconditional followers for his Russian faction. Nothing of that even changes in the meagre comfort Trotsky finds for his adherents. He writes:

> The hypertrophic internationalism of the Comintern could arise — on the basis of the former authority of the Russian Communist Party — only thanks to the existence of state power and state finances.

Certainly, Trotsky has no cash-box, but the whole Trotskyist current is merely constructed on the personal authority of Trotsky. That is the basis of its whole cohesion and therefore it will remain a barren sect.

* * *

VI: Comments on an Agent's Report

From *Der Internationale Klassenkampf*, Volume 2, no 3, September 1937, pp 11-12. Anonymous but the references point to August Thalheimer as the author.

* * *

In issue 3/4 of the *Internationale*, published by the KPD, the report of an agent is made public, under the title 'Brandler–Radek'. Content and style betray the author: 'Oskar'. After his unsuccessful attempts to dislocate the KPD(O), he was employed by the KPD bureaucracy with Comintern expenses as a spez against the IVKO.[26] As the KPD bureaucracy was so careless as to publish this agent's report, we want to use the opportunity to throw some light on this sort of activity.

The general instructions now issued by the CI to its agents sound roughly as follows:

1. The Trotskyists are not a rival political group to be fought with political arguments, but spies, Gestapo agents, etc. All agents have the task of delivering 'material' for this thesis.

2. All political groups and currents, insomuch as they do not belong to the partners of the People's Front, are to be treated as allies of these spies and Gestapo agents, if they dare to express some doubt about these assertions. The agents have to deliver 'material' on its behalf.

3. In the cases where that is impossible, the agents have the task of delivering 'material' positing that all who dare to doubt the assertion that all Trotskyists are spies, all spies are Trotskyists, and all not in agreement with the 'great' Stalin are semi-Trotskyists and two-faced, are accomplices, conscious or unconscious tools of Trotskyist spies.

As a spez for combating the IVKO, agent 'Oskar' went to work. Our declaration on the Zinoviev–Kamenev and Radek–Pyatakov trials proceeded from the possibility and probability that the confessions were based on facts and deeds, which seemed to justify the verdicts according to the severe Soviet legislation. We defended the verdicts as legally admissible, declared them politically as false and harmful to the interests of the world Communist movement and declined to see the condemned men as counter-revolutionary criminals. In this attitude, agent 'Oskar' discovered the required two-facedness. On page 99, first column, he writes: 'The two-facedness of such an attitude immediately struck one.'

Instruction 3 was thus accomplished.

This 'strikes one' has led agent 'Oskar' to the further following discoveries: 'The leaders of the Brandler group have not only indirectly, but also directly, cooperated with these traitors and their agents… already in earlier years.'

26. Internationale Vereinigung der Kommunistischen Opposition (IVKO — International Union of the Communist Opposition). This was the coordinating body of various Communist Opposition groups. It was first mooted in March 1930 at a meeting in Berlin attended by representatives of the Swedish Communist Party, the German and Czech Communist Oppositions and MN Roy from India. A conference held in December 1930 in Berlin was attended by delegates from Alsace, Czechoslovakia, Germany, Norway, Sweden, Switzerland and the USA. A second conference took place in July 1932 in Berlin. The IVKO produced a Platform, extracts from which can be found in RJ Alexander, *The Right Opposition* (Westport, 1981), pp 279-83, as can a brief account of its activities.

We are shocked, we cannot deny to having known Radek for 30 years and having worked together with him before and during the war. We cannot deny, too, that we have worked together with Radek, Trotsky, Zinoviev until 1924 in the Executive of the CI, where they represented the CPSU and we the KPD.

If, however, agent 'Oskar' also claims that we have had factional links with the Trotskyists and Bukharin then he is cheating. When 'Oskar' wormed his way into our company in 1927-28, he was a Trotskyist and had links with the Trotskyists. As a condition of his joining the KPD(O), we demanded both an ideological and organisational break with the Trotskyists.

Out of his dirty fingers he also sucks the claim, on page 101: 'During the latter period of his Moscow residence Brandler had stood in particularly close contact with Rykov.'

Neither of us has had any factional or personal links with Rykov and Bukharin at all. Brandler and Thalheimer have negotiated twice with Rykov and three times with Bukharin, as both had direct instructions from the CPSU Politbureau regarding these negotiations with them. Agent 'Oskar' is incapable of providing even one item of proof for his claims. The means by which he tries to give a semblance of proof is to point out that the KPD(O) provided its members for information texts of both the Trotskyist platform and the political conceptions of Bukharin and Rykov. In contrast to the present Comintern methods, we were and still are of the perhaps old-fashioned opinion that one must know the conceptions of the opponent, if possible in his own description, the more so if one wants seriously to combat him politically. We have even reproduced the agent's report by 'Oskar' and made it available to all groups of the IVKO. That we had links of a factional sort neither with the Trotskyists nor with Bukharin–Rykov is proved publically not only by our publications against them, but also by those of the Trotskyists and of the Bukharin group.

The agent methods are best illuminated by the following passage in the article 'The Brandlerists and their Communication to the ECCI', contained in the *Kommunistische Internationale* for 5 September 1934, which represents an official reply of the CI authorities to the proposal from the KPD(O) and other IVKO sections, in which the admission of our delegation to the Seventh World Congress was demanded. It says there:

> As concerns the Brandler Group [the KPD(O)], then we can consider as certain conditions:
>
> a) The intervention of the Brandler group against the Social Democratic and Trotskyist evaluation of the international situation, as well as against the Trotskyist defamation of the Soviet Union and the CPSU.
>
> b) The fact that the Brandler group has undertaken a revision of its

evaluation of the Social Democracy and recognises that the defeat of the working class in Germany and Austria is a result of the Social Democratic policy.

c) That the Brandler group has admitted that the 'left' Sozialistische Arbeiterpartei (SAP)[27] and the Trotskyists supply ideology to the reformists, in order to hinder the transition of the workers to Communism.

The whole agent-stupidity shows itself when 'Oskar' chalks up against us as a crime and evidence of two-facedness that in 1926 we protested against the way Ruth Fischer and Maslow were expelled — 'only some ultra-left leaders have been exposed as bankrupt, not the ultra-left course' — although, or exactly because, we were their severest political opponents. We have not only opposed the method of creating political scapegoats for covering up false political measures by the CI, as these methods were used in 1923 against us, but because we consider the self-critical exposure of mistakes made as the only means of curing the world Communist movement, and fought against the policy of scapegoating already then at the beginning of the decline of the CI.

If this struggle for inner-party democracy must be a 'criminal struggle' against the CPSU, then we are guilty in the past, present and future.

In the past we have 'fought against the CPSU', for example, as in 1922, when we caught a colleague of 'Oskar' drafting informer reports on behalf of Zinoviev. We protested against these methods to the ECCI and demanded their cessation. Lenin supported us at the time. The agent was recalled. Unfortunately the method was not suppressed. According to agent conceptions, we have also 'fought against the CPSU' when, for example, in 1922, we opposed Lozovsky's recall from the leadership of the Profintern and his replacement by Rudzutak, in spite of the unanimous decision of the CPSU Politbureau. In the Profintern conference we brought about a majority against this CPSU Politbureau decision through pertinent arguments. Lenin did not see it as a 'criminal struggle' against the CPSU, but proposed the annulment of the CPSU Politbureau decision, though Zinoviev went wild. We never felt and still do not consider ourselves as revolutionary civil servants who collapse before the frown of a CPSU representative, but as representatives of our organisation with equal rights who were ready to learn from the revolutionary experience of the Russian comrades. We did not conduct ourselves as obedient fools, but were of the opinion that the experiences of the workers' movement of our own country had to be represented

---

27. The Socialist Workers Party (SAP) was formed in October 1931 after the SPD expelled some of its left-wing Reichstag deputies. It was joined in 1932 by some former KPD(O) members, who took over its leadership. It cooperated for a while with the Left Opposition.

by us, if we wanted to bring our party up to the level of its revolutionary tasks. Such an attitude is high treason and criminal under the Stalin regime. Lenin repeatedly encouraged us to criticise the measures of, among others, Zinoviev or Trotsky. We also still today believe Lenin's method as correct, that of Stalin as dangerous. For that reason, we also opposed a proposal from Stalin in 1926, conveyed to us by Béla Kun, which demanded from us unconditional adherence to Stalin in Russian questions in exchange for a free hand for us in Germany. At the time, we were in agreement with Stalin's general line in Russian questions and had rejected an offer from Trotsky, Zinoviev and Radek, who, in their turn, wanted to forgive us all the sins which we had supposedly committed in 1923, if we would adhere to their unprincipled bloc and advocate it in the KPD. In relation to both Stalin and Trotsky, we have *rejected orienting our politics to the factional struggles in the CPSU*, because in such a method, regardless of whichever faction implements it, we foresaw only the greatest harm for the world Communist movement.

Because we did not want to become an appendage of those Russian factional struggles, in 1929 we were excluded as 'deserters to the Social Democracy and accomplices of the social fascists'. Today we are labelled as accomplices of 'Trotskyist and Bukharinist Gestapo agents'. The nuance in the invectives against us only shows the degree of degeneration of the CI that is caused by this method.

Jay Lovestone

SOVIET FOREIGN POLICY AND WORLD REVOLUTION

We present here Chapter 7 (pp 24-27) of Jay Lovestone's pamphlet *Soviet Foreign Policy and World Revolution*, which was published by Workers Age Publications of New York in August 1935.

In the latter half of the 1920s, Lovestone (1897-1990) had become the predominant figure in the Communist Party of the USA, taking on the post of Executive Secretary in September 1927. His group dominated the CPUSA for the next two years, but his closeness to Bukharin on the Executive Committee of the Communist International was to prove a problem for him once Stalin moved against the Right Opposition in the Soviet Communist Party, and threw his authority behind Lovestone's rival in the CPUSA, William Foster (not that this deterred Lovestone and Foster from uniting to purge party members who supported the Left Opposition). Although Lovestone's faction kept control of the CPUSA at its congress in February 1929, Stalin's forthright attack on his faction at the ECCI meeting in the following May sealed his fate. Lovestone and about 200 others were expelled. The CPUSA (Majority Group) was set up in October 1929, and, although considering itself as a party opposition (and later became known as the CPUSA (Opposition)), effectively operated as a separate organisation, aligning itself with the International Communist Opposition.

Lovestone's pamphlet is a defence of Soviet foreign policy against left-wing critics, and against Trotskyists in particular. The text reproduced below brings out the core of the author's arguments. It is true that Lovestone was not entirely uncritical of Moscow's policy, as the final paragraphs of the extract show. Elsewhere in the pamphlet, he condemned 'the false, sectarian, adventurist — and now the confused and opportunist — policies of the Comintern' (p 29). These, however, were minor details, little blemishes on an otherwise faultless orientation. Lovestone's fire was mainly aimed at the 'self-acknowledged "pure revolutionists" (Trotskyites)' who mixed 'malice with their "analysis"' in order to 'condemn Soviet foreign policy as outright betrayal of the world revolution' (p 3), and insisted that the 'Trotskyite theory' that there was 'a fundamental cleavage between the interests of "Russian state policy" and the interests of the international proletariat' was 'false from top to bottom' (p 27). (Readers will recognise the various distortions in Lovestone's text, such as the 'the Trotsky programme for civil war in the USSR'.) For Lovestone, the Soviet Union remained 'the land of the proletarian dictatorship' and 'therefore, the base, the centre, the inspiration of the international revolutionary movement' (p 29). Soviet foreign policy was thus 'primarily a weapon of the Russian section of the international proletariat in the world struggle against imperialism' (p 30).

Even though Lovestone recognised that Stalin was 'the symbol and decisive and almost sole leader' of the Comintern (p 26), he drew back from placing upon him the onus for the contradiction between, on the one hand, the Comintern's sectarian Third Period policies and its subsequent opportunism and, on the other, what he saw as the inherently progressive nature of Soviet foreign policy. He did allude vaguely to the 'lack of collective leadership' in the Comintern, and to the 'method of mechanically transferring tactics' that were correct for the Soviet regime, namely, exploiting differences and rivalries amongst capitalist powers, into the Comintern (p 21), but rather than draw the conclusion that rooted the problems of Comintern policies and activities within the framework of the relationship between that body and the Soviet leadership, he effectively drew a distinction between them.

This was by no means a transient notion. In 1937, when the opportunism of the Comintern was manifesting itself in outright class collaboration, Lovestone's pamphlet *The People's Front Illusion: From 'Social Fascism' to the 'People's Front'* (Workers Age Publications, 1937), attacked the policies of the parties of the Comintern in terms not that far from those of the Trotskyists and other left-wing critics of Stalinism. He declared that the Comintern's line was 'an open and violent contradiction to the elementary principles of Marxism and Leninism'. On the other hand, he asked rhetorically, whether one might conclude that socialism could be reached through the bourgeois democratic republic, then answered: 'At the last All-Russia Soviet Congress, Stalin said the opposite. The new Soviet Constitution is a glowing refutation of such a theory.' (pp 55-56) So why should Stalin and the Soviet leadership — heading a regime that the international working class was 'lucky' to have 'to remind it of what a proletarian dictatorship is and should be' (p 10) — instruct the parties of the Comintern to engage in the gross class collaboration that was so closely examined in this work? Apart from an oblique reference to the Czech Communist Party having 'transferred mechanically' a policy that was suitable for the Soviet Union to its own area of operation, no explanation was forthcoming, and once again he was forced effectively to divorce the Comintern from the Soviet leadership.

This dualism in Lovestone's analysis therefore served to absolve the Soviet leadership from the Comintern's disastrous policies. Hence, in the text below, Stalin's acceptance of French national defence and the French Communist

Party's ensuing endorsement of it are seen as a 'mistake', rather than a logical consequence of Stalin's theory of 'socialism in one country'. The Comintern's ultra-leftism of the Third Period — which is dishonestly attributed to Trotsky — is viewed as a mistaken revolutionary policy. However, alongside its general role of allowing Stalin to outflank the Left Opposition, it was a tactic in the key country of Germany that was intended to bring about a pro-Moscow government by undermining the pro-Western Social Democrats. Third Period ultra-leftism was thus a product of Soviet *realpolitik*, no less than the opportunism of the ensuing Popular Front. Stalin's theory of 'socialism in one country' resulted in *realpolitik* becoming the driving force behind both Soviet diplomacy and Comintern policies — something which was recognised by the Left Opposition whilst Lovestone was still sowing illusions in Stalin's beneficence.

Events were to shake the Lovestone group's faith in the good nature of the Soviet regime. The Moscow Trials, or, to be more accurate, the second and third Moscow Trials, hit them hard, but their rapid disillusionment with Stalinism led not towards their adopting a genuine Marxist approach, but to a steady slide to the right. The group changed its name first to the International Communist Labor League, and then to the International Labor League of America, and, seeing no further purpose for its existence, voted in December 1940 to dissolve itself. Lovestone and several other leading members of his group subsequently played an important role in organising pro-US anti-communist currents in trade unions in many countries around the world, whilst another leading figure, Bertram Wolfe, became a prominent Cold War ideologue.

* * *

Soviet Foreign Policy and the Comintern

To the splenetive and rash in the labour movement there appears to be the following arrangement between the USSR and the imperialist powers: In return for capitalist trade, concessions and recognition, the CPSU, leading the Soviet government, is to de-revolutionise and finally to give up the Comintern.

There isn't the slightest foundation in fact for this conclusion. Until a few months ago, the entire line of the Comintern was atrociously ultra-leftist; there was pursued a strategic course based on a totally false estimate of conditions, based on an exaggeration of the degree of development of the class struggle and the objective possibilities for revolutionary conflicts in Western Europe and the United States. We were in the 'Third Period', in the period of revolutionary upsurge and wars and revolutions on all sides! The Comintern strategy was adjusted to this fantastic conception. Nor was this merely a paper evaluation. The various sections of the CI, vigorously pushed and aided by the ECCI, dominated by the CPSU, unfortunately set to work on this basis in their respective countries. Yet, it was precisely in this period that the capitalist powers accorded more and more recognition to the USSR.

The foreign policies of the various bourgeois powers are in no way determined by the tactical course of the Communist International. It isn't at all true that the less vigorous, the less revolutionary the CI, the more concessions and the better the terms the imperialist powers accord the USSR. In fact, the first capitalist recognition of the Soviet government came in the crimson days, the first years, of the CI. Furthermore, it was precisely in these days that the Soviet government had to pay the highest price in its foreign relations.

Countries having far more fear of revolution than the US recognised the Soviet government long before Uncle Sam did. And the Soviet Republics made far greater concessions than today to bourgeois countries when their regimes were far less stable, far more in danger of being overthrown by their proletariat than at present. Witness the treaties with Estonia (1920), Poland and Latvia (1921), and the Treaty of Rapallo with Germany in April 1922. These were the days of Lenin and Trotsky and not the days and nights of Stalin.

Of course, the factionally-perverted might say that the CPSU, dominating the CI, deliberately forced an ultra-left, sectarian line on the Comintern in order to hide, with a revolutionary cover, as it were, the very aim of giving up the Communist International. The crass hypocrisy of these distorters is revealed by the fact that it was precisely they who conceived and initiated the ultra-left course. At the peak of this ultra-revolutionism in August 1929, Rakovsky and Trotsky emphasised to the CPSU that 'there had been a softening of opinion between us [Stalin and Trotsky] through circumstances'. A little later, in his letter to his so-called Leninbund of Germany, Trotsky boasted that: 'To be a sectarian today is an honour for every real revolutionary.' And Trotsky's most persistent parrot in the US not so long ago uttered the following words of truth, though not of wisdom: 'Stalin had to borrow copiously from the ideological arsenal of the Left Opposition.' (*Ten Years of the Left Opposition*, p 60)

More than that. If these critics honestly attribute to the Soviet government and its leadership such nefarious motives and dastardly plans of betrayal, then they should logically condemn the USSR as the most dangerous type of anti-proletarian state which is not only against its own working class at home but also camouflages itself in order to undermine and poison the working-class movements throughout the world. Trotskyist logic should then impel these latter day saints of 'pure revolution' to call upon the entire international proletariat to wage a holy war against this ogre known as the CPSU, this unholy monster called the Soviet government. The Trotsky programme for civil war in the USSR is in line with this logic. And a blood brother of the Trotsky family, like the United Workers Party, is consistent enough to declare:

Russia will enter the next world war, as it now prepares for it, as an imperialistic force lined up with other imperialistic forces and it is not possible for the working class to have any other position towards Russia than towards any other country. The answer of the revolutionary movement to war is revolution; so, too, must be the answer of the Russian workers to a war in which Russia participates… (*Council Correspondence*, July 1935, p 13)

Too many speak too often of the world revolution as if it were some Messianic conception. The social revolution isn't something that will happen all at once, that must come on a certain date, but is something that is happening, is developing. As Lenin saw it, 'the social revolution cannot ensue save in the form of an epoch…'. Historically speaking we are in that epoch now. That doesn't mean, however, that every moment of that epoch is equally appropriate for 'civil warfare on the part of the proletariat'. Altogether too often do many talk too loosely of the world revolution. They seem to think that all that is needed for the world revolution to happen (in one act, perhaps) is for the USSR 'not to hold back' the working classes of other countries. This is plain poppycock. The slowness of international revolutionary development is not due to the 'bad intentions' of the Soviet leaders as reflected in Soviet foreign policy. Rather, this slowed-down development is due to a whole series of factors; to wit, treacherous role of Social Democracy, consequent immediate postwar defeats of Bolsheviks, CI mistakes in tactics, economic possibilities for and political ability of bourgeoisie to recover and hit back, etc.

The fundamental problem involved here is that of the relationship between the interests, aims and tactics of a Communist Party already in power and those of the CPs still struggling to win a majority of the workers for taking power. Both types of Communist Parties have identical interests. Both types of Communist Parties seek the destruction of all capitalist forces and the state powers which protect and seek to perpetuate the bourgeoisie as ruling classes.

In this light, the revolutionary class struggle is thoroughly international. We must, however, distinguish between the various stages of the class struggle in the different countries. This means that we must differentiate between and must allow for differences in the tactics employed by the CPs in the sundry countries for the achievement of the common identical objectives.

This process of differentiation is rooted not only in the uneven development of capitalism itself, not only in the distinct class relations prevailing in different countries, but also in the degree of strength developed by the various Communist Parties. Thus the victorious CPSU faces today two problems — viz, the wiping out of the remaining capitalist elements within the Soviet borders and the aiding and abetting of the destruction of all capitalist forces outside Soviet territory.

In the first case, it is the Soviet power against the remnants of one capitalist class; in the second instance, the CPSU tackles a job in which, controlling an armed Soviet power, it is facing many or all capitalist classes and the countries which they dominate. As a section of the world party of Communism, the CPSU thus faces the problem of Red 'Intervention'. Any other Communist Party in power would face the same and other problems. For us Communists it is categoric that every CP in power, that every proletarian state not only has the right to such 'intervention' but is duty bound to exercise this right. In fact, the Red Army today in the USSR — tomorrow in another country — is so trained and organised as to be able to fulfil this duty at the proper moment. The only problem involved here is a political and technical one, the propriety of the moment, the ripeness of the occasion for such Red 'intervention'.

Would any of the opponents of Soviet foreign policy really propose that the USSR and the CPSU, which leads it, should today exercise this right, should declare that now is the proper moment for fulfilling this duty, let us say, in Germany or England? Obviously this would mean pitting the USSR not against one capitalist power but against the whole capitalist world today — when the proletariat of the different bourgeois countries is still not only far from being able to do its share in the way of rendering armed aid to the Soviet government, but is even still largely nationalistic in a bourgeois sense. Clearly, this would be suicidal and impractical. It would mean certain disaster for the USSR and its victorious working class. Just now, Hitler would welcome such an attempt by the Soviet government. That's precisely what Nazi Germany is seeking. Indeed, Hitler's powerful propaganda machine is trying desperately to sell the capitalist world the idea that the USSR is about to launch such a war against all capitalist countries. Fortunately, Soviet foreign policy has been able, so far, to thwart the Nazi bandits in their manoeuvres against the USSR, in the moves to put Germany at the head of the armies of the big powers on march against the USSR.

We must, therefore, recognise that the USSR is compelled to find some *modus vivendi* with the imperialist and capitalist powers. This *modus vivendi* is expressed in certain compromises by the Soviet government, by the Russian proletariat already in power, in certain economic relations, pacts, treaties and diplomacy resorted to by the USSR. The same would hold for the CP in the US if it were today a party in power and in the international position in which the USSR now finds itself.

But because the state politics of the USSR (laid down by the CPSU) *necessarily must be different and cannot be identical* with the politics of the various other sections of the CI, one should not conclude that there is a fundamental, necessary or unavoidable conflict between the interests of the CPSU as the leading party of the CI, as the sole victorious party, and the other sections of the CI. We cannot stress too strongly that *the methods and tactics of the various individual sections of the CI and of the Comintern as a whole towards bourgeois governments must today be totally different from the methods and tactics laid down for the Soviet government by the CPSU.*

When we grant this necessary difference of tactics in the pursuit of common aims, in defence of common interests, it doesn't, for even a fraction of a second, mean that the CPSU cannot make mistakes in the tactics it works out for the Soviet government, that the Soviet state cannot make mistakes in its diplomatic relations, in its foreign policy. Nor does it mean that when such mistakes are made by the CPSU and the Soviet government which it controls, we should close our eyes to them and not criticise them. The very opposite is the case. Only the most unequivocal but constructive criticism can hasten the overcoming and prevent the recurrence of such mistakes.

For instance, Stalin's joining Laval in the communiqué accompanying the necessary and correct signing of the Franco-Soviet pact was the gravest of errors. Being the symbol and decisive and almost sole leader of the CI today, Stalin made a fatal mistake in joining Laval in a declaration that he 'understands and approves fully the national defence of France in keeping her armed forces at a level required for security'. The French CP immediately took this not merely as a diplomatic declaration but as a line of policy for the CI.

Likewise, we must condemn Radek's recent declaration in the Japanese press assuring the world that the Soviet Union will not resort to armed force in the inner Chinese complications and that the freedom of the Chinese people is the concern of the Chinese nation itself. In the face of reality and for strategic reasons, it is not wrong in principle to say that the USSR is not contemplating armed intervention in China, but the form of Radek's declaration is impermissible.

Besides this, it is also possible for individuals who symbolise and speak solely in the capacity of Soviet diplomats to make mistakes. In this light, Litvinov's declaration in the League of Nations, hailing Germany's victory in the Saar plebiscite,[1] was not sound from the point of view of the best interests of Soviet foreign policy. To say the least, it was uncalled for and clumsy.

---

1. The Saar was detached from Germany in 1920 as part of the Versailles agreement, and placed under League of Nations stewardship, with a referendum after 15 years to decide its fate. The vote was 90 per cent in favour of reunification with what was by then Nazi Germany. At the League Council meeting on 17 January 1935, Soviet foreign minister Maxim Litvinov declared that the peaceful solution to the question of the Saar — that is, its absorption into Nazi Germany — was a contribution to world peace.

CHRISTIAN STALINISM AND TROTSKYISM

The two articles below originally appeared in *The Christian Left*, the newsletter of the Auxiliary Christian Left, a left-wing group within the Church of England. We are grateful to Ron Heisler for bringing these documents to our attention. Although the first piece distances itself a little from some of the views of the official Communist movement, it nonetheless presents a typical Stalinist representation — or, to be more accurate, misrepresentation — of Trotsky's ideas. It was simply not true that Trotsky concealed the reality of his programme, unless one considers (as the author of this piece does) that this was represented by the confessions wrung out of the defendants at the Moscow Trials about economic sabotage in the Soviet Union and the partition of the country amongst the fascist powers, rather than the writings of the Trotskyist press. There are, however, serious misrepresentations even in respect of Trotsky's public statements, which indicates either ignorance or malice on the part of the author. A passing knowledge of them would reveal that he *did not* consider that war or civil war must automatically result in a working-class victory. He *did not* deny that fascism was a grave danger to the working class; indeed, he was far more astute on this question than most other left-wing theoreticians. He *did not* consider that there was nothing worth defending in the Soviet Union. To condemn Trotsky's call for heavier taxation of the richer peasants — for that is the reality behind the phrase 'the Russian peasantry should be exploited in favour of the industrial proletariat' — whilst praising Stalin's brutal methods of collectivisation is indeed hypocritical.

Ultimately, however, the gulf between this author and Trotsky was unbridgeable: if one considered that socialism had been achieved in the Soviet Union, then Trotsky's portrayal in *The Revolution Betrayed* of the ascendancy of a privileged élite over Soviet society was untenable. This, however, did not necessarily draw a critic of Trotsky into accepting all the falsifications about him that emanated from Moscow. That the author happily accepted these distortions shows the manner in which Stalinism managed to insinuate itself amongst unlikely sections of British society during the Popular Front era.

The second article is a truly remarkable product of the Stalinist campaign against Trotsky: an attempt to justify *on the basis of Christian theology* the Moscow Trials and the monstrous allegations made against Trotsky by the trials' prosecutors and defendants. By any standards, this must rank as one of the most bizarre documents in the history of the British left-wing movement and perhaps in the history of the Church of England as well. Textual analysis strongly suggests that it is the work of Dr John Lewis, a Unitarian minister in Ipswich who subsequently became an official in the Left Book Club, joined the Communist Party of Great Britain, edited its theoretical journal, the *Modern Quarterly*, and was a leading advocate of the 'Marxist–Christian dialogue' in the 1960s.

* * *

I: The Trotskyite Problem

From *The Christian Left*, no 13, May-June 1938, pp 2-5. An editorial note states: 'This article is taken from a draft statement which has been prepared by a Christian Left group.'

* * *

The Crisis in the Working-Class Movement: The present crisis, of which Trotskyism is an expression, is due to the fact that we have a partial achievement of Socialism in the world through the successful establishment of Socialism in the USSR — not yet a Socialist society, but a Socialist economic order.

This fact brings the Socialist working-class movement up against a new situation. It is faced with the necessity of conserving the Socialist achievement in part of the world, while remaining revolutionary in the rest of the world. The ordinary Marxian outlook contains no solution to this problem.

The Trotskyite answer to the dilemma is the denial of the Socialist character of the achievement in the USSR and the consequent readiness to sacrifice that which has been achieved to the abstraction of a Socialist utopia.

The usual Communist answer is the denial of the existence of such a crisis as the result of the Socialist achievement in the USSR. Yet the Russian working class is forced by Fascist pressure — itself a result of the achievement of Socialism in Russia — to put the exigencies of the military safety of the USSR before the support of the revolutionary working-class movements in other countries.

The right approach must start from the recognition that the establishment of Socialism in the USSR, while only partial, is a real achievement which must be defended and conserved at almost any cost by the working-class movement of the West, yet without the sacrifice of their Socialist class-consciousness in the process.

Hence the Popular Front issue can be reduced to this: anti-Fascism is not a sufficient slogan. If the defence of Socialism in the USSR remains unmentioned in the propaganda for the Popular Front, the Socialist class-consciousness of the workers will be dimmed.

In Fascist countries like Germany and Austria the Popular Front is the right policy, because anti-Fascism in such conditions is necessarily a revolutionary attitude. In Spain, for instance, anti-Fascism implies active participation in the civil war. In capitalist democracies these conditions do not obtain. In these countries the propaganda for the Popular Front must put foreign policy and the defence of the USSR in the forefront.

The Situation in the Face of an Advancing Fascism: Although the defence of the Soviet Union calls for an anti-Fascist concentration in all countries, it remains open to doubt whether the Popular Front is the most effective way of achieving this end.

The argument in favour of the Popular Front is mainly based on an interpretation of the German experiences which implies that National Socialism won through by virtue of numbers.

Such an interpretation of German events is, however, superficial. The strength of Fascism in a country cannot be gauged according to numerical standards. A country can go Fascist although the Fascists are few. Experience shows that lack of determination on the part of the working class to oppose the progress of Fascism has at least as much to do with its success as the numbers of its adherents. Fascism is the only alternative to Socialism in a definite situation which is typical of the capitalist development in our period. This situation is that of a deadlock between democratic institutions and the capitalist system, a deadlock which may actually threaten to paralyse the working both of the political and the economic system of a country. Unless the working class is prepared and able to put a Socialist economic order in the place of the capitalist, the Fascist 'solution' is inevitable. The only chance of the working-class movement to oppose Fascism successfully lies therefore in its readiness to stand for a full solution of the deadlock through the establishment of Socialism.

The so-called Fascist solution is brought about under the leadership of a capitalist oligarchy. Nationally, it consists of the destruction of the political and industrial influence of the working class while retaining capitalist economics in a non-liberal form, so as to make it more resistant against the attacks of the proletariat; internationally, in the Empire that is to say, it is the solution of the problem of international economic organisation by means of conquest.

The Socialist solution of the deadlock lies, nationally, in the extension of democracy to the whole of society, involving a transformation of the property system, that is, the end of the private ownership of the means of production and the establishment of their communal ownership; internationally, in the institutional cooperation of Socialist countries.

In the clash of Fascist and Socialist forces clarity and purpose count for more than numbers. The latter are, indeed, ultimately dependent upon the former, when and where therefore the Popular Front is established at the price of this clarity and purpose, it tends to increase and not to diminish the chances of a Fascist victory.

Trotsky's Position: Neither Trotsky nor his opponents provide us with a full statement of the facts of the Trotskyite crisis. Trotsky's method implies secrecy of his actual plans and even of his programme: mainly on account of this, his opponents refuse to accept Trotskyism as a tendency in the working-class movement. The Communists disdain to conceal their ideals and aims — cf the *Communist Manifesto*.

Trotsky claims to base his policy on the world revolution which he expects as the result of world war. The activities of the POUM in Spain; the sabotage of economic construction in the USSR; the bargaining with Fascist powers — Germany and Japan — for the partition of the USSR and for the accomplishment of a 'retreat' from the advanced Socialist position in it are parts of this policy. In this Trotsky is not inconsistent; indeed his theory of the 'permanent revolution' almost constrains him to follow such a line under the given circumstances. But this theory itself has been proved false, for it implied the dogmatic assumptions: (a) that Socialism could not be established in the USSR; (b) that in capitalist countries today war or civil war must result in the victory of the Socialist Revolution. The first supposition was refuted by the success of the Five-Year Plans including collectivisation; the second by the success of Fascism in a number of leading countries.

By ignoring these two facts Trotsky can uphold his theory of the permanent revolution and deny: (1) that the working class has built in the USSR something worth defending; (2) that Fascism is a new development which the working-class movement has to face.

The theory of the permanent revolution implied 'that backward Russia would begin the Socialist revolution and be saved from the consequences of its own backwardness by the Socialist revolution in Europe'. Trotsky had rightly foreseen since 1905 that no purely middle-class revolution was possible in Russia and that a revolution in Russia would necessarily be Socialist. But he was mistaken both in the assumption (1) that Russia could not overcome her backwardness and (2) that the Russian Revolution would be followed by a successful Socialist Revolution in the West of Europe. He was refuted by the facts. But these two great mistakes led to a series of misconceptions, every one of which would have been fatal if acted upon, for example, that the Russian peasantry should be exploited in favour of the industrial proletariat; that we were on the brink of world war on account of the inevitable military clash between England and the USA, that armed risings of the German workers in

1924 had any chance of success. Trotsky's greatest mistake, however, was not that he made these assumptions (they were more or less implicit in the position of all majority Social Democrats, that is, Bolsheviks at the time): but that he adhered to them in a dogmatic fashion in a situation in which new decisions had become inevitable.

Up to the time of Lenin's death nobody in the Bolshevik Party believed that Socialism could be established in Russia alone; world revolution was an essential part of the Bolshevik perspective. But after Lenin's death the economic 'retreat' represented by the NEP[1] began to become unworkable. It was never meant to be permanent; the world revolution, it was hoped, would save Russia from her isolation before economic collapse forced her to capitulate to the Kulak's counter-revolution. But the world revolution did not come, and the pressing needs of the towns and of the Socialist sector of industry compelled the Soviet government to interfere with the peasant households to a degree that was incompatible with the working of the NEP. Fundamentally, the question was whether a new interim programme should be set up, or whether the Bolsheviks should give up waiting for the world revolution and settle down to a long-term policy. Trotsky, who had never wholeheartedly accepted Lenin's theory of the necessity of an alliance of the workers and the poorer peasantry in an agricultural country, and had never disowned the theory of permanent revolution, was logically led to stand for a new interim policy until world revolution should materialise, and to suggest the ruthless exploitation of the peasantry by the workers as the means of tiding over all difficulties. For a long-term policy only two roads were open. The one was suggested by the right-wing opposition of Bukharin, Rykov and Tomsky; it consisted in a further retreat on the lines of the NEP, even at the price of liquidating Socialism altogether (this opportunist policy could obviously be combined with a 'waiting for world revolution' line). The other was Stalin's policy of trying to build Socialism in Russia, to 'catch up and overtake' Western capitalism: in fact, the policy of the Five-Year Plan and collectivisation. Stalin's line did not imply that Russia could remain permanently the only Socialist country in the world; but it did imply that in the new situation Russia must take the risks of an attempt that had hardly been envisaged by anybody before. The striking success of this attempt and the subsequent emergence of Fascism in Italy and Germany as a powerful anti-Socialist force, both in the national and the international sphere, determines the line of the USSR.

The Revolution Betrayed: The remainder of this article is an attempt to summarise Trotsky's book *The Revolution Betrayed*. If there is any apparent

1. NEP — New Economic Policy, introduced by Lenin in 1921. [Author's note]

discrepancy between what is set out in this summary and matter referring to the same subject elsewhere in this article, the reason lies with Trotsky himself. That is to say, this is a summary of what Trotsky himself says in his own work; the previous sections are an objective review and statement of Trotskyism in relation to the world situation.

The centre of the Trotskyite criticism of the Communist International, and therefore of the USSR and Stalin, lies in the fact that it has not sponsored revolution in other countries; that it has thrown over the idea of world revolution. The reasons for Trotsky's attack could take one of two main lines, viz (a) that it was economically impossible to build Socialism in one country, in a country like Russia alone, or (b) that it was due to the reactionary bourgeois nature of those in power in Russia, that is, Stalin & Co, who did not wish to risk their own power and position by helping or fostering revolution in other countries. The former implies a judgement on theory, or at the least a difference of opinion between Trotsky and Stalin on matters of tactics and theory; the latter implies a personal judgement, a human judgement. Throughout his book Trotsky does not specifically attack Stalin as a bad Marxist, but as a reactionary; and, because of that, as an opportunist.

Trotsky attempts to show that the revolution has not been a success and that the reversal of the idea of world revolution is a carefully calculated step on the part of Stalin to consolidate his own power in the Soviet Union and to 'introduce into the social consciousness of the people the idea that the revolution has been completed'. He suggests that the policy of the leaders has been one of zigzag, completely lacking in consistency and method: from headlong collectivisation to a milder form, from legalising abortion to prohibiting it, the change in the policy of the Comintern itself, and so on. Trotsky *admits* that new conditions have arisen, but declares that this is no excuse for reversals and changes of policy. Adequate leadership should have foreseen such new conditions and taken steps to overcome them! In fact, all the examples of 'zigzagging' which he takes have been fully admitted by Soviet leaders. Trotsky seems to rely almost entirely for his material on speeches of self-criticism and admission of incomplete success in one direction or another by leaders in the Soviet Union.

Considerable controversy has existed between orthodox Communists and Trotskyists as to whether Lenin believed in the possibility of Socialism being achieved in one country. Trotsky attempts to dispose of this by quoting Stalin in 1924 (after Lenin's death) as declaring that Socialism could not be achieved in one country. Trotsky declares that NEP was not an indication that Lenin had given up the idea of world revolution, but that it was a 'necessary retreat' dictated by the conditions then existent. Trotsky admits that great headway has been made in the Soviet Union in terms of industrial production, but complains that it is still a long way behind other capitalist countries like the USA and Great Britain. He declares that Russia is actually attempting to tackle pre-Socialist conditions with Socialist methods (p 61). This and succeeding statements are tantamount to saying the revolution should never have happened.

Trotsky's most fruitful source of material for an attack on Stalin and the other leaders in the Soviet Union, lies in their statements to the effect that 'Socialism has been finally and irrevocably established in the Soviet Union', and that 'the last elements of capitalism have been liquidated'. Trotsky declares this to be sheer hypocrisy in view of the social inequalities which he says exist in the USSR at the present time. It is deliberately calculated to lead the mass of the people to the belief that now the struggle is over and matters can be safely left in the hands of the leaders; in other words, an attempt to further strengthen the power of the state.

Stalin had said that the 'dictatorship of the proletariat has been strengthened'. In view of the fact that 'Socialism has been finally and irrevocably established in the Soviet Union' and that 'the last elements of capitalism have been liquidated', this, Trotsky declares, is illogical and indicates only that the state is strengthening itself, consolidating the inequalities that exist and creating a new caste system.

The Red Army is not immune from criticism. In the Red Army we have the caste system in its most blatant form: a huge mass of trained fighters carefully insulated against any discontent and ready to defend the state against attack from without — or within. At the time of intervention the Soviet Union relied on the people, on a volunteer army. The fact that Stalin cannot now rely on a volunteer army is a further indication in Trotsky's opinion that Stalin is fearful of the discontent which he is stirring up in the masses. 'He dare not give them rifles.'

On the new constitution Trotsky has a word to say: there is no need for secrecy of the ballot if the country is really Socialist. Secrecy of voting is a method adopted in capitalist countries, in countries where class systems exist and where protection is necessary for the workers in registering their votes. The adoption by the Soviet Union of a capitalistic method of voting is a further indication, in Trotsky's opinion, of the relatively reactionary nature of the Soviet Regime.

The main part of this book was written before the 'big group' of trials took place. His only reference to them is in his speech 'I Stake My Life' reprinted at the end of the book. In that speech he attempts to show that most of the old guard have now been shot or imprisoned and that most of the present leading representatives of the Soviet Union were reactionaries at the time of intervention or at the time of the revolution.

Trotsky's book is not convincing. He sets out to prove that Stalin & Co have betrayed the Socialist cause, but he really succeeds in proving the opposite. His book serves mainly to emphasise the enormous difficulties entailed in building up a Socialist state in a country like Russia which was backward in every sense and, by implication, helps one to more fully appreciate the advances in Russia. Most of these advances Trotsky himself admits. The book is, for the most part, confused, illogical and self-contradictory. It is only when Trotsky has the speeches of self-criticism of the Soviet leaders as his material that he approaches lucidity.

* * *

II: Perfectionists and the Moscow Trials

From *The Christian Left*, no 6, 28 February 1937, pp 3-5.

* * *

Orthodox Christianity is rightly suspect to the Socialist. He cannot help regarding it as the ideological defence of a Church, the economic and financial structure of which makes it dependent upon the vested interests of property.

But still more perhaps than the orthodox creeds, it is their idealist interpretation in current Christian thought that binds organised Christianity to the existing social order. Of all the spiritual allies of Capitalism, the perfectionist interpretation of Christian ethics is the most dangerous foe of the working-class movement today. If being a Christian means the acceptance of an obligation to be perfect as our heavenly Father, not merely in the sense of a directive in the light of which we can comprehend the true nature of man and his community, but as the definition of our actual duty in society here and now, then two attitudes only are possible to the Christian in this imperfect world: either to retire from this sinful world into *pietism*, or to resign himself to the sinfulness of this world in a spirit of *quietism*. The results are the same in either case. For both he who shrinks from contact with the coarseness of his surroundings, and he who trains himself to passive indifference towards its revolting realities, equally sacrifice action in an imperfect world to the ideal of absolute perfection. No third alternative is open to the Christian perfectionist. To try to stay in an imperfect world, while struggling to overthrow it by the instrument of perfection, is mere self-delusion. State and society are imperfect by their nature. He who would resolve to restrict his attempts at revolutionising them to the use of such methods as would allow him to remain perfect himself could achieve nothing better than a delusion as to the worth of his own activities. In trying to evade the Scylla of moral complacency he would risk being shattered on the Charybdis of despairing futility. Christianity thus emasculated is no longer a force that can reshape the world; it is simply an instrument of class-rule, blocking the road to radical change, while sanctifying existing evils through a perversion of the doctrine of original sin. It is Christian ethics ridiculing itself. For even the use of force and violence is held to be justified as long as it serves to maintain an evil order; while even the rescue of the innocent victims of torture and debasement from the hands of their tormentors would not, in this view, justify the use of means other than those which most, in the nature of things, be unavailing against the oppressor.

This social perfectionism, nurtured by the Methodist revival, 'saved England from a revolution'. The British working class was the victim of a perfectionist ethic which exalted the virtues of passivity and suffering into the highway of salvation. During the first decades of that most barbarous of revolutions called the Industrial Revolution the capitalist class could safely rely on a people indoctrinated by their ministers with the idealist conception that nothing was worth troubling about but perfection. As long as such poisonous teaching was not expunged from the consciousness of the workers, the domination of an inhuman and un-Christian system of economic autocracy could neither be challenged nor overthrown. The working-class movement itself was doomed to oscillate helplessly between a sound but necessarily limited trades unionism and a vague Utopian Socialism.

Not even the tremendous experience of triumphant Russian realism was able to shake British labour out of its perfectionist day-dreams. Witness the confusing reactions to the Moscow Trials in England. Here again the pseudo-Christian ethics that have almost become part of the fabric of British labour (Socialism) have played their fateful role.

For the Christian Left these trials could never have assumed a decisive importance in judging the religious significance of Soviet Russia in the present period of history. There is a fundamental difference between the personal sphere of *community*, in which religion has its existence, and *society* which is the sphere of functional organisations. No society can be perfect. In our conviction Socialism will abolish the immediate economic obstacle to a more complete fulfilment of community today. Industry in Russia is based on the national ownership of the means of production. This is an objective truth. This fact in itself raises Russia to a higher plane of social existence, introducing the Socialist epoch in the history of the world. For the sake of this next step we must take upon ourselves freely our share in the collective sin inseparable from human existence in society. We must not refuse to take this step — towards the realisation of the eternal meaning of life in community — on account of the imperfections attached to all social embodiments of such a life. Or in terms of the working-class movement just as we must reject the reformist deviation which would have us tinker with the partial and disconnected problems of a society to which we as Christians are not, nor ever can be, committed, so we must also resist the opposite temptation which would debar us from a creative transformation of society as a whole on account of the sin inherent in all society. No realisation of the faults or mistakes committed by the Socialist government of Soviet Russia can make us deviate an inch from our recognition of the final significance of this first embodiment in our time of a higher social existence of mankind. As Christians we know ourselves safe from the danger of idolising the state or society. But as Christians we answer the call to community, though this must involve us in the risk of having to share in the responsibility for blunder, suffering and crime. If there had been blunder or crime on the part of the Russian authorities we would acknowledge it freely without any attempt at justification, while continuing to struggle to the utmost to help Russia to overcome her material weakness and moral blemishes.

Having said that we can state simply that there was neither blunder nor crime; that the ruthless judgements in the Moscow Trials were a protective reaction against the most reckless political conspiracy that was ever directed against the lives and existence of a whole people; that at no previous stage in history could the treasonous act of idealists have struck as deadly a blow to a vast population, for nowhere had political and industrial power been concentrated in one centre before; that this conviction of ours is the outcome of the second Moscow Trial, while the first left us bewildered and saddened by our utter inability to comprehend the motives both of judges and the accused; that Trotskyism has to be eradicated from the body politic at whatever cost, once it had degenerated from a divergence of opinion about the line of Soviet policy to an active secret cooperation with German and Japanese authorities to blow up the power stations, the bridges and railway centres in case of war, and to strike panic into the heart of the people by assassinating their leaders and destroying the gigantic chemical and metallurgical plants behind the front.

This latter charge sounded so incredible as almost to remove the trial into the realm of criminal fiction. The men against whom it was levelled had belonged to the élite of revolutionary Russia.

But precisely herein lies the explanation of all the apparent contradictions and inconsistencies of these trials. These revolutionaries had never accepted the possibility of Socialism in one country. They had rejected Stalin's thesis of the inevitability of attempting to establish Socialism in Russia. To attempt this was not only to embark on a, theoretically and practically, impossible task but was tantamount to a betrayal of Socialism. Socialism was international by definition; it could never be established in one country, partly on account of economic interdependence, partly on account of the inevitable clash between the capitalist powers and the isolated Socialist country. In this unequal struggle, the Socialist country must succumb, unless it can rely on the help supplied by the working-class movements of the capitalist states in deliberately undermining the military strength of their own countries. In this old-time Marxian view, the power of the working class in Russia could be saved by a successful world revolution only; but any attempt at establishing Socialism in Russia would necessarily divert the attention of the Russian Bolsheviks from this supreme task, if not abolish it as a task altogether. For in more than one manner (so they reasoned) the aim of achieving Socialism in Russia must interfere with the propaganda for world revolution. This group of revolutionaries could not for one moment admit that Stalin's contention of the possibility of Socialism in one country was anything but the ruin of the revolution.

This being so, they did not hesitate to do what in duty they were bound to do, *if they had been right*. They resolved to remove Stalin and his supporters from power in order to change the policy of Russia, stop industrialisation and collective farms, reverse the development towards democracy in Russia both internally and externally. As the masses could not be won over to this fantastic policy of self-destruction, they had to be manoeuvred into supporting the conspirators. In a country where the government was responsible for the planning and running of industrial production, the apparently fortuitous destruction of industrial plant was bound to undermine confidence in the government. These wrecking activities of the Trotskyites ran parallel to the endeavours of the German and Japanese secret agents. The temptation to make use of them was great. It became irresistible after Leon Trotsky, the creator of the Red Army, had got into touch with the German and Japanese authorities in view of an eventual war.

Thus the incredible came to pass. For the Trotskyite thesis left no other alternative than the defeat of Russia in case of war. In order to save the cadres of the revolution, it was imperative that defeated Russia should remain under the sway of the revolutionaries. Some territorial sacrifices and a measure of retreat from the Socialist position was inevitable. But Socialism being impossible in one country capitalism would have to be restored to some degree in Russia, anyway. So, step by step, the conspirators were driven on to more and more extreme conclusions. They did not shrink from drawing them. Yet only a few of them were committed to the responsibility for the series of railway and colliery disasters that had been engineered by the conspirators in high office. An even fewer number had actually been in touch with the German Embassy in Moscow, confirming personally the mandate of Leon Trotsky to negotiate in the name of the conspirators in Russia with the German and Japanese governments. The manly speech of Radek, in which he finally revealed the tragedy of the conspirators as well as their utter moral failure, has cleared up this background of the trials. The Russian people in their wonderful effort at constructing a new world had been stalked by a deadly enemy within their own ranks. While they were suffering from lack of shelter and clothing, while powerful enemies were preparing to invade their country, their food had been destroyed, their defences had been sapped by a group of determined foes hiding masked as trusted friends. No wonder that in the newspapers and books in which Trotsky defended his thesis he never so much as breathed a word of the ghastly work of death and destruction his agents were wreaking in Russia. He has denied to the last his lunatic attempts to save Socialism by delivering Soviet Russia to the mercies of Hitler.

We rejoice with the Russian people in their deliverance from deadly peril.

In the face of the epic of the Russian people the outcry of our Labour perfectionists against the alleged horrors of the Moscow Trials comes as a pitiable anti-climax. Unconsciously, they sympathise with the Trotskyite idealist who is prepared to destroy Socialist reality for the sake of his perfectionist fantasies.

For both the Reformist and the ultra-revolutionary are at heart perfectionist. They both shrink from the consequences of the inevitable alternatives of social reality, only in different ways. The Reformist tries to evade the risk and responsibility of radical social change by resigning himself to capitalism; the ultra-revolutionary flies from the actual realisation of Socialism on account of the imperfection of reality. Both hate Soviet Russia because it is not perfect. But while the Labour reformist inveighs against the 'cruelty' of the Soviet tribunals in words, the Trotskyite is more consistent. He proceeds to blow this imperfect embodiment of Socialism out of existence.

The Moscow Trials commit us to strike at the perfectionist fallacy, in whatever form it presents itself.

Senex (Mark Schmidt)
REVOLUTIONARY TACTICS IN SPAIN

The article below, a critique of Trotskyist tactics in the Spanish Civil War by means of a review of Felix Morrow's *Revolution and Counter-Revolution in Spain*, was written by Mark Schmidt under the pen-name Senex, and appeared in *Vanguard*, Volume 4, nos 5-6 (November 1938) and 7 (February 1939). We thank Ron Heisler for bringing it to our attention.

Vanguard was the journal of the anarchist Vanguard Group, which emerged in 1932 from the small Bronx-based Friends of Freedom and became the leading anarchist group in the USA during the 1930s, but fell apart after 1939.

Mark Schmidt came from a Russian background, he returned there in 1917, but moved back to the USA after becoming disillusioned with the Soviet regime, and worked as a textile salesman. He was a founder member of the Vanguard Group, and was, according to his former comrade Sam Dolgoff, 'the oldest member and guiding intellect of the group'.

Many former members of the Vanguard Group remembered Schmidt with distinct distaste, and their opinions were recorded in detail by Paul Avrich in his *Anarchist Voices: An Oral History of Anarchism in America* (Princeton, 1995). Whilst praising him as 'a highly intelligent man... well-read and well-informed' with 'great energy and drive', Abe Bluestein declared that he became 'an apologist for Stalin', an opinion shared by Louis Slater, and Louis Gerin added that 'we sometimes even felt he was a Communist planted in our midst'. Clara Solomon claimed that he was arrogant and wanted 'an intellectual anarchist élite' and 'trained cadre', Sidney Solomon considered him 'deeply authoritarian', Jack Frager felt that 'there was an element of Nechaev in Schmidt's make-up, a sign of his growing Stalinism', whilst for Franz Fleigler he was 'a nut, a psycho'. Indeed, Schmidt called on the Vanguard Group to work with the Communist Party, and actually supported the Molotov–Ribbentrop Pact of August 1939, which was one of the reasons the group disintegrated. Schmidt's own contribution to *Anarchist Voices* clearly shows his adaptation to Stalinism.

It is a moot point as to whether Schmidt's critique of the Trotskyist standpoint on the Spanish Civil War directly anticipated his future adherence to Stalinism. Whilst the Stalinists at this juncture concentrated upon portraying

Trotskyists as outright counter-revolutionaries and agents of fascism, they did at less frenetic moments criticise all those on the left who saw the civil war in Spain through the prism of its being a social revolution rather than a narrow anti-fascist conflict, which included Trotskyists and dissident Marxists such as the POUM, in terms rather similar to those used here by Schmidt. On the other hand, notwithstanding the concern eventually shown by some anarchists about the consequences of the CNT's accommodation to the reformists and bourgeois republicans and its joining the Catalan government, the fact remains that prominent leaders of the powerful Spanish anarchist movement did openly betray their revolutionary principles at a time of profound social revolution, and continued to adapt themselves to the right-wing forces within the Spanish republic even as they unceremoniously rebuffed them, and one should not be surprised that this gross opportunism might be reflected within the anarchist movement on an international scale, as with Schmidt's article here, and also with unexpected consequences, not least his drift into Stalinism. Although Schmidt's subsequent political alignment stands in contrast the CNT's sorry fate as victims of the manoeuvres of Stalin's affiliates in Spain, they can both be seen as the result of the opportunism that had arisen within the anarchist movement.

* * *

A few months prior to its final suppression, the official organ of the POUM (the Communist Opposition of Spain), *La Batalla*, began publishing a series of articles dealing with the irresponsible campaign waged against it by the agents of the Fourth International. And by way of characterising the pretentious claims of those emissaries, the paper cited a very typical instance telling how 'the infallible line' was laid down for it in the first period of the revolution.

The 'legate' carrying the instructions embodying this 'line' arrived immediately after the great historic events of 19 July. He was received in a spirit befitting a fraternal organisation. Men with revolutionary experience were needed, and it was expected that, given a certain period of time necessary to acquaint oneself with the new environment and the specific conditions created by the revolutionary events — and the fraternal delegate would be able to contribute his alleged knowledge and experience to the common effort of solving the urgent problems of the day.

Such a preliminary period of study and observation was deemed the more necessary in the case of this particular delegate who proved ignorant of the Spanish language, the history of the Spanish labour movement and especially of Catalonia. To the emissary, however, those were mere trifles, counting but little against the superior virtues of an error-proof tactical line which he handed down rather peremptorily to the astounded leaders of the POUM. As the paper pointed out, the didactic attitude was both dismaying and highly amusing. It was dismaying, for the rejection of his ultimatum meant not only a rift with a fraternal organisation but the unloosening of a vituperative campaign by the Trotskyite leaders on an international scale. And at the same time it was amusing to listen to this emissary holding forth in his pontifical manner on the tactics of the Spanish revolution, while lacking the most elementary information not only in regard to the present situation, but in regard to the immediate background of the events, the alignment of forces, the relative strength of the various movements, the nature of the terrible difficulties besetting the revolutionary sector of the proletariat from the first days of the revolt.

But… he had his theses — crude generalisations from the development of Russian events in the period of February-October 1917 — and along with those theses, which the emissary produced immediately after he had landed in Spain, went a surprising faith in their magic potency and ability to exorcise the crushing difficulties besetting the Spanish workers from the very first days of the revolution.

Trotskyite Claims

What was the nature of those theses? This question is important in view of the preposterous claims now put forth by the Trotskyites — and seemingly finding ready acceptance in the wider circles of the left Marxists — to the effect that the solution offered by those theses held out the possibility of a full triumph for the revolutionary forces of Spain, and that the tragic reverses suffered by the Spanish proletariat were due to the 'cold shouldering' of the delegates of the Fourth International, who had formulated a clear plan of proletarian victory based upon past revolutionary experiences.

Let us analyse one of the latest attempts made to present those claims in the systematised form of a coherent historic account of the epic struggles of the Spanish workers during the last two years. We have such an attempt in Felix Morrow's book *Revolution and Counter-Revolution in Spain*, written mainly with the purpose of proving the fatal nature of the errors committed by the revolutionary forces of Spain as a result of their rejection of the course urged upon them by the 'only and true Leninist vanguard'.

The Russian Pattern

Roughly, the contention of the author is that the situation in Spain after 19 July was in its main aspects similar to the one which obtained in Russia between February and October 1917. In both cases it was 'a regime of dual power', one in which the existing governments 'lack the indispensable instrument of sovereignty: armed force', while the armed proletariat which has the actual power is not conscious enough of the necessity to dispense with this state of dual power and to erect a government of its own instead of the one dominated by the bourgeoisie.

It is clear that a state of dual power can be only of short duration, the logic of the situation impelling a solution along the lines of consolidation of a single power, whether it be that of the existing government or the newly-emerged forces of the revolutionary proletariat. In Russia, according to the author, the latter solution prevailed, while in Spain the pendulum swung back to the old bourgeois rule, the reason thereof being the atomised state of workers' power:

> The workers' state remained embryonic, atomised, scattered in the various militias, factory committees and anti-fascist defence committees jointly constituted by the various organisations. It never became centralised in Nationwide Councils as it had been in Russia in 1917, in Germany in 1918-19.[1]

And this in turn 'has a simple explanation: there was no revolutionary party in Spain, ready to drive through the organisation of soviets boldly and single-mindedly'.[2]

This lack could be remedied if the voice of the 'glorious heirs' of the Russian tradition were heeded. 'The Fourth International', the author declares, with the modesty becoming his sect, 'offered the rarest and most precious aid: a consistent Marxist analysis of Spanish events and a revolutionary programme to defeat fascism'.[3] Alas, the bearers of that wonderful aid were told to learn Spanish first and then find out a little about the Spanish labour movement, its revolutionary background. And they were also told that while Trotsky's *History of the Russian Revolution* is quite a good book insofar as the dynamics of the pre-October events is concerned, it certainly cannot serve as an infallible guide to a situation which is more complex, beset with greater difficulties and essentially different from the one of February-October 1917.

Let us see whether the organisation of Soviets in Spain following 19 July would have constituted a determining factor in swinging the revolution from its course of self-limitation to the victory of a socialist form of society.

Fetishisation of Soviets

In one of his earlier pamphlets on Spain, Trotsky warned the Communists

---

1. Felix Morrow, *Revolution and Counter-Revolution in Spain* (New York, 1974), p 87. Notes provided by *Revolutionary History* unless otherwise stated.
2. Morrow, *Revolution and Counter-Revolution*, p 88.
3. Morrow, *Revolution and Counter-Revolution*, p 105.

against 'raising the Soviet into a super-historic divinity'.[4] By 1936 this warning was conveniently shelved by its author; and, in fact, the fetishisation of this form of labour organisation indulged in by his disciples, as revealed by Felix Morrow in his book on Spain, went so far as to blind them to the elementary realities of the Spanish situation.

In Russia the Soviets were practically the only form of mass organisation rooted in the revolutionary experience of the past. The trade unions developed as a mass organisation only after February 1917, and, inasmuch as they were controlled by the political parties, they were kept from expanding beyond the narrow field of trade-union struggles and organisational matters which drew heavily upon the energies of the young, immature organisations. The political parties embraced only a thin layer of workers and intellectuals: they certainly did not possess the cadres of trained and indoctrinated members which, for good or bad, exercise such a powerful influence over the mass organisations of the European proletariat. And even in Russia the political parties nearly succeeded at one time in emasculating the Soviets to such an extent as to drive Lenin into despair over the future of this type of organisation. As is known, Lenin, immediately after the July events, began to raise serious doubts in the Bolshevik press about the fitness of the Soviets as organs of free crystallisation of revolutionary energy.

In Western Europe the Soviets, although meeting greater difficulties and being less of an imperative necessity, also had an important function to fulfil in the revolutionary period of 1919-21. They had a wider mass basis than the trade unions, which were confined only to the better-paid workers and which could not give expression to the revolutionary energies of the masses because of the top-heavy bureaucratic control and the reformist mentality of its leadership.

Soviets Had Little to Offer to Spanish Labour Movement

In Spain, however, both unions — the CNT and UGT — embraced almost

4. Trotsky's text actually reads: 'Every time the masses are involved into struggle, they invariably feel — cannot but feel — an acute need for an authoritative organisation rising above the parties, factions, sects, and capable of uniting all the workers for joint action. One must know how to put forward this slogan [of building soviets] to the masses at a suitable occasion — and such occasions are now met at every step. But to counterpose the slogan of soviets as organs of the dictatorship of the proletariat to the realistic struggle of today, means to convert the slogan of Soviets into a super-historical divinity, into a super-revolutionary icon, to which only individual saints may kneel but which the masses will never follow.' (LD Trotsky, 'The Spanish Revolution and the Dangers Threatening It' (28 May 1931), *The Spanish Revolution (1931-39)* (New York, 1973), p 129) Trotsky was arguing in favour of the formation in Spain of councils as organs of struggle, but arguing against an ultra-left standpoint that was proposing their formation as a part of an immediate move for seizing power, which he considered was not on the agenda at this juncture.

the entire working class of the country. Half of the working class is enrolled in an organisation which, unlike the reformed trade union of Western Europe, is oriented upon revolutionary action and immediate building up of the workers' commonwealth. Insofar as this organisation (CNT) is concerned, there is no need of a more democratic mass organisation enabling the revolutionary will of the proletarian masses to find its own channel, free from bureaucratic trammels. Even prior to their complete emasculation by the Bolshevik Party, the Russian Soviets *were less and not more democratic* than the CNT syndicates, with their frequent Plenums, their federalist structure, the limitations placed upon power-absorbing tendencies of the Central Committees and the libertarian spirit, which is more fundamental to the functioning of democracy than any formal organisational principles.

Of course, Felix Morrow, quite in keeping with the irresponsible demagogy of the Fourth International, makes frequent allusions to the 'CNT bureaucracy' and the necessity of building up Soviets in order to 'wrest control from this bureaucracy'.[5] But the value of this assertion can be properly assessed when we come to consider that it comes from a disciple of a man who more than anyone else was instrumental in dissolving the soldiers' and workers' committees of Russia, in reducing the Soviets to organs of party dictatorship — a man who was upholding such 'democratic' measures as compulsory labour service, militarisation of labour unions and the 'substitution of the principle of selection for election'. Whatever opinion one may hold of the course pursued by the CNT, there can be no question of its mass support within its organisations. There were no splits, rifts, popular upsurges or any significant current of opposition during those most difficult years of adaptations, retreats and concessions.[6]

Pacts a Superior Form of Mass Unity

The CNT, of course, embraced only one-half of organised workers and peasants. It had to face the problem of finding a way of working together with the remaining half of organised workers so as to draw it into an ever greater participation in

5. The closest phrase to this in *Revolution and Counter-Revolution* is on page 133: 'The Friends of Durruti were organised to wrest leadership from the CNT bureaucracy.'
6. The Trotskyites make much ado about the 'friends of Durruti'. But the latter, contrary to its name, did not consist of people who were near to Durruti. Nor was it an anarchist or a CNT organisation. It was a loose formation, headed by an ex-Catalonian nationalist whose conversion to the libertarian ideas was of but recent origin. That the CNT had a right to demand that this alien organisation, strongly permeated with Marxist elements, stop camouflaging its activities by using the CNT or FAI colours can be censured only by people who reject the very elementary principles of organisational life. Had this organisation — or rather conglomeration — have any roots within the CNT unions, it would have made its voice felt at its plenary conferences and conventions. But 'the friends of Durruti', whom the Trotskyites hailed — rather suspiciously so — as 'a significant anarchist movement', vanished as suddenly as it came to life [Author's note].

the struggle to preserve and expand the revolutionary conquests. The method chosen was *that of pacts* and establishing close organisational contacts with the other great economic organisation of Spanish workers — the socialist-controlled UGT. In this connection, it is argued by the Trotskyites, a Soviet form of organisation would allow the creation of genuine mass unity, a 'united front from below' and not agreements with the bureaucratic leadership. But certainly the German experience should warrant us against such exaggerated expectations. The Soviets and for that matter the factory committees as well, were just as much dominated by the reformist leadership as the trade unions. Would the power exercised by the Socialist Party of Spain over a considerable section of the Spanish working class vanish because of the Soviet form of organisation?

Formal Soviet Democracy No Guarantee Against Party Usurpation

Felix Morrow, in his naive idealisation of the Soviet type of organisation, is prone to think that the recall and new (frequent) elections characterising the Soviets 'reduce the time-lag of political development to a minimum',[7] thus leading to the elimination of those movements and parties which fall behind this time lag.

But, as is known, this did not happen in Germany. Nor did the arch-democratic form of the Soviet organisation prevent their utter deterioration as independent mass organisations as soon as the Bolshevik Party attained power in 1917. One can almost foresee what would have happened had the 'line' urged by the Fourth International been adopted by the revolutionary forces of Spain. The socialists would have retained a considerable control in the Soviets, using their influence in the same way in which they employed it in the UGT. The Communists, whose main power lay in the terrific pressure exerted by Soviet Russia as the sole country upon which Spain depended for arms, would have obtained the same controlling positions in the ruling apparatus of the Soviets as in the governmental set-up of the country, and how much of the recall and other democratic features would remain in those Soviets with the Stalinists in the control of the commanding positions? After all, even the UGT of Catalonia possessed a comparatively democratic form of organisation. It was democratic enough to enable the POUM to function quite successfully for some time within this organisation. What happened to this union democracy as soon as the Stalinists, catapulted into a position of power by the long arm of the Soviet government, obtained control of this organisation is too well known to leave any doubts as to the similar results in Soviet form of organisation.

One can easily see that the Socialist–Stalinist control of the Spanish Soviets

---

7. Morrow, *Revolution and Counter-Revolution*, p 137.

— had this type of organisation come to prevail — which, given the political set-up of the early period of the revolution and the humiliating dependence upon the Soviet government in military matters, was inevitable in the first period, would have a paralysing effect upon the struggle of the revolutionary forces. The totalitarian claims put up by the left Marxists, and especially by the Trotskyites, on behalf of the Soviet as 'organs of proletarian power', as 'a nascent proletarian government' would have been appropriated by the Stalinists and Socialists in control of the Soviets. It is the struggle against such totalitarian claims made possible by evolving a different and more democratic form of unity *through pacts* between labour organisations, each having and retaining a clearly pronounced individual character of its own — that saved Spain from the absorption of all its social life by a monopolistic organisation *ostensibly representing the general will of the proletariat but serving in fact as the camouflaged organ of a Party dictatorship.*

Compromise Forced by Circumstances

Let us, however, grant for argument's sake, the greater effectiveness of the Soviet form of organisation as the medium through which the dual regime of the first period of the revolution would be transcended. Would it be possible to make use of this medium along the same revolutionary lines as in Russia of the year of 1917? In other words, would it be possible to adopt from the very beginning the same intransigent irreconcilable attitude toward the existing coalition government which Lenin advocated upon his arrival from abroad and which was gradually adopted by the leading Soviets of the country?

Those, who like Felix Morrow, believe that given a Soviet form of organisation — and an active Communist minority to advocate the tactics of 1917 — and the course of Spanish events would lead to a successful Spanish October, overlook a very essential difference between the Russian situation of 1917 and that of Spain after July 1936. To ignore this difference is in fact to indulge in abstract theorising about revolutionary strategy and not to make a serious attempt to understand the Spanish events.

Wherein Spanish Situation Differed from the One of 1917

In Russia the policy of combatting the Provisional Government led to a breakdown at the fronts and the deepening of economic and social chaos. But the war was an imperialist war, one in the continuation of which the revolutionary forces were not interested. When the hopes of immediately unloosing a revolutionary wave in Western Europe, and especially in Germany, failed to materialise, the new Soviet government was forced to fall back upon the horrible expedient of a shameful and humiliating peace in order to gain some sort of respite.

This is no place to enter into the discussion of the relative merits of this step undertaken at the most critical juncture of the October revolution. It is clear, however, that this course could not be followed by the Spanish revolutionary forces. The war which was thrust upon them was not an imperialist war. They were most vitally interested in the struggle against the fascists and no policy could be adopted by them which would weaken the struggle to any extent. *But obviously one cannot have both: an efficient organisation of military struggle against the fascists and a policy designed to weaken this struggle, a policy of fighting the existing government by the Soviets* — or any other equivalent organisation — carrying in its train demoralisation and chaos, for the time being at least.

There were three possible ways to be followed by the revolutionary forces of Spain. One way, that of immediate elimination of the existing government, of the liberal and reformist elements of the so-called Popular Front. Even Felix Morrow recognises, by implication at least, that in the days of 19 July the relationship of forces were not such as to make possible this course. Catalonia was the only exception, but Catalonia had to keep in step, to some extent at least, with developments in the rest of the country.

Revolutionary Spain could not avoid at that period the phase of what Felix Morrow calls 'the dual power'. But circumstances demanded *immediate* cooperation with this power since the second possible course, the one of undermining it for the purpose of its ultimate displacement would necessarily lead to the kind of demoralisation which was brought about in Russia of 1917 and which placed the revolutionary forces at the mercy of the German imperialism. Without this cooperation Valencia and Alcoy would have been lost — no one knowing the situation can fail to see that it was only the united efforts of all the anti-fascists that saved those cities, and consequently the entire province of Levante, from the tip of Southern Andalusia; the Basque province would have joined the reactionary Navarre from the first days of the revolt, and even Catalonia, torn by inner strife, would have offered a target for the rebellious forces concentrated at Zaragossa.

The United Front During Kornilov Revolt

As we pointed out in one of the recent issues of the *Vanguard*, the starting point for any comparison between the Spanish events and the Russian situation of 1917 should be the Kornilov revolt, which offers many more similarities to the situation imposed upon the Spanish revolutionists than the Russian October revolution. As is known, the revolutionary forces of the pre-October period, headed by the Bolsheviks, responded to the situation brought about by the Kornilov revolt in the same manner in which the Spanish revolutionists dealt with the similar revolt of their reactionary generals. The Trotskyite critics of the

CNT have to do a great deal of explaining in order to make palatable to their partisans the united front with the Kerensky government and other democratic elements formed at that time by the Bolsheviks for the purpose of crushing the rebellion of the counter-revolutionary generals.

What a Military-Technical Union with Kerensky Government Implied

'Lenin', Morrow writes in his pamphlet, 'was ready to collaborate with Kerensky himself in a military-technical union. But with this precondition already existing: the masses organised in class organs, democratically elected, where the Bolsheviks could contend for a majority.'[8]

There is no attempt, however, on the part of all the Trotskyite writers to think out the implications of such a 'military-technical union'. Can modern war — and Kornilov's revolt could have easily developed into as big an affair as Franco's rebellion — be conducted on a military-technical basis only? Does it not require economic, political and social bases as well? Could the Soviets enter into a military-technical union with Kerensky's government and refuse its cooperation in economic matters? Would any sort of cooperation be possible were the guidance of the struggle left exclusively in the hands of the Kerensky government? That is, wouldn't participation in this government be imposed upon the revolutionary forces as the necessary condition for an effective struggle against the Kornilov rebels?

Had the revolt drawn out longer, the implications of the 'military-technical union' with the Kerensky government would have been brought out much clearer, forcing the Soviets and the Bolshevik Party along the same line of compromises which 19 years later were adopted by revolutionary forces of Spain.

For the key to the understanding of the 'strange behaviour' of the CNT does not lie in its doctrinal premises but in the specific nature of the situation itself which placed before it the alternative of either working with the government — on conditions of its own, of course — or weakening and undermining the desperate struggle against the rebels. This in turn was aggravated by the dependence upon Stalin's government in point of armaments.

Shortage of Armaments a Determining Factor of Revolutionary Tactics

In this connection it is quite characteristic that Mr Morrow, who deals in his pamphlet at great length with so-called betrayals, deviations, tactical errors of the CNT and POUM, has hardly anything to say about the tragic shortage of armaments in face of a foreign invasion of imperialist powers.

Where were the revolutionary forces to obtain those armaments? How could

---

8.   Morrow, *Revolution and Counter-Revolution*, p 89.

they face an army equipped with the latest armaments pouring in from Italy and Germany, if all they had at the beginning was a nondescript assortment of rifles, machine guns and a few outdated aeroplanes! In vain one will look for all answer in Felix Morrow's pamphlet written for the ostensible purpose of showing how the Spanish workers could have won their struggle had they but followed the advice of the Fourth International strategists.

But here is what another writer (William Kremer, 'Revolution and Counter-Revolution in Spain'), who shares the premises of Felix Morrow and other critics of the CNT, has to say on this matter in the capacity of an eye witness:

It was the Russian arms [he writes] *that saved Madrid.* The badly equipped militias that had retreated from Toledo and Talavera, suddenly, at the very gates of Madrid, found themselves supported by artillery and aviation. For the first time in two months were they able to meet the Fascists under reasonable conditions.

But if the Russians saved Madrid (the same holds true about the aid extended at other critical junctures), *they had to be paid their price for it.* That it was a Shylock price, goes without saying. That the shipment of arms was timed with the critical phases of the struggle, enabling the Soviet government to extort a heavy price in terms of political dominance — this by now has become a commonplace with everyone conversant with the Spanish struggle of the last few years. But what other alternative did the revolutionary forces of Spain possess?

There is no comparison in this respect between the Spanish and the Russian situation. The October revolution followed a long war which bequeathed to the revolution not only trained military cadres, but considerable supplies of war *matériel*. In point of military supplies the disparity between the Red and White armies — if there was any — was not of decisive importance. Aviation played an insignificant role, tanks were brought in only towards the end of the civil war, and as to artillery, the lack of which is so painfully felt by the Spanish loyalists, the Soviet forces — that is, the regulars and not the partisan forces — had in many cases a decided advantage.

Could Revolutionary Tactics Change the Passive Attitude of European Workers?

It will be pointed out in this connection that accepting aid from the Soviet government upon the humiliating conditions imposed by the latter was not the only choice left to the Spanish workers. It is often alleged by the revolutionary romantics of the Fourth International that had the Spanish workers struck out boldly for an uncompromising revolutionary line, they could have dispensed with the Russian aid; the response of the international proletariat would have been so spontaneous, direct and overpowering in its effect that no government would dare to halt the flow of armaments to revolutionary Spain.

This point is brought out by Felix Morrow in his analysis of the May events in Barcelona in 1937, provoked, as is now well known, by the Catalonian nationalists, acting in collusion with the Stalinists. The CNT, according to our author, should have taken up the challenge of the Stalinist and bourgeois forces and made the ensuing struggle the starting point not only of a thoroughgoing social revolution in Spain itself, but of a revolutionary world conflagration triumphantly sweeping the major or countries of Europe. In other words, the CNT workers, upon whom rested the tremendous historic responsibility of holding the first line of defence against the fascists, should have thrown caution to the winds, indulged in a grandiloquent historic gesture, plunged recklessly into the adventure of breaking up the anti-fascist front, thus opening wide the gate to the fascist avalanche — and all in hope of immediately bringing about the world revolution.

For — much to the astonishment of all of us — we are assured that the European revolution was so palpably near during the May events that it was only the reformist degeneracy of the Spanish anarchists that stopped it from proceeding along the 'inevitable' stages of development envisioned by Felix Morrow and other revolutionary strategists.

It is interesting in this connection to trace the logical steps in the glib reasoning employed by the latter in order to conjure up the vision of a triumphant European revolution just waiting around the corner, ready to burst forth at the historic opportunity afforded by the May events, but hopelessly bungled up by the Catalonian anarchists.

Social Revolution via Breakdown of Military Fronts Against Fascism?

Had the anarchist and POUM workers of Barcelona kept up their resistance against Stalinist aggression during the May days — Mr Morrow assures us — the entire loyalist Spain would have been swept by a triumphant social revolution.

'Any attempt by the bourgeois–Stalinist bloc to gather a proletarian force would have simply precipitated the extension of the workers' state to all Loyalist Spain.'[9] But — the reader will ask — what of the well-armed Communist police and military units, the flying corps mainly controlled by the Stalinists, the Assault Guards, the Carabineros, the Civil Guards, many of the Socialist-controlled military units, the bourgeois sectors, the navy controlled by the right socialist Prieto? Would they give up without any fight? Would all those units, many of whom were drilled and trained for the specific purpose of exercising

---

9. Morrow, *Revolution and Counter-Revolution*, p 146.

a check upon the revolutionary workers, disintegrate at the first clash with the latter? And how about the International Brigades, the preponderant majority of whom were firmly controlled by the Stalinists?

That the workers supported by the CNT units stood a good chance of victory in the case of this new civil war, can be readily granted. But this would be a Pyrrhic victory at best, for it is clear that a civil war behind the front lines resulting in the demoralisation of the front and the withdrawal of the troops for the participation in this new civil war would open wide the gates to the triumphant sweep of the fascists.

This rather obvious contingency is pooh-poohed by the simple expedient of holding out before the reader the 'ominous' implications of a tactic based upon it. 'It is an argument against the working class taking power during the course of civil war.'[10] We readily grant the case as presented by the author, provided his point is that *taking power without being able to hold it*, is in itself a desirable thing, especially when it involves the fatal impairment of the chances to win in a civil war in the outcome of which the revolutionary forces are vitally interested.

Concrete situations have to be dealt with as such and cannot be conjured away by evoking sacred formulas or reduced by syllogistic reasoning. There was the concrete danger of immediate intervention by the foreign powers against the Barcelona workers. The CNT press cited facts, alarming to everyone with the least knowledge of the situation. Felix Morrow does not deny those facts, but again he parries them off with a syllogism: 'Every social revolution must face the danger of capitalist intervention.'[11] Ergo...

And wasn't the Russian revolution threatened by intervention? Didn't the European workers frustrate the interventionists in 1919-20? Couldn't the Spanish workers expect the same efforts on the part of the European proletariat on behalf of their revolution?

Fascist Intervention in Spain More Dangerous Than Intervention in Russia

What is generally ignored in those appeals to the historic precedent of the Russian revolution is the totally different kind of intervention carried out in Spain and the different kind or efforts required to check it. In 1919-20 an aroused proletariat stopped *its own democratic governments* from extending their intervention. In the case of the German intervention of 1918, the workers, although quite a power as compared to their present status in fascist countries, were quite powerless to prevent its dealing of heavy blows to the revolution.

But the Spanish situation demands on the part of the French and British workers a much more active effort than in 1919-20. They could easily stop

---

10. Morrow, *Revolution and Counter-Revolution*, p 148.
11. Morrow, *Revolution and Counter-Revolution*, p 150.

their own governments from intervening against the revolution, but they are powerless against the *indirect intervention* reverted to by their governments by way of encouraging the intervention of Mussolini and Hitler. Only a high degree of revolutionary fervour and the readiness to intervene actively on behalf of the Spanish revolution, *even at the price of provoking a war against the fascist powers*, would be adequate to meet the danger of fascist intervention.

Were the European workers ready to go to war for the sake of Spain, and, what is equally important, were the petty-bourgeoisie, peasantry and the liberal elements of the middle classes, without whose consent and willing cooperation Chamberlain–Mussolini's intervention plan could not be challenged in earnest, were they ready to go as far as to hazard an open break with the fascist powers for the sake of Spain?

French Workers Would Not Sympathise with Breaking Up of United Front in Spain

No one with the least knowledge of the situation will say that two years ago the French and British masses of people were ready to go to war for the sake of Spain. Nor will he readily concur with Felix Morrow that had the revolutionary forces of Catalonia ousted the bourgeois parties and Socialist and Stalinist elements, 'the French bourgeoisie would open its borders to Spain, not for intervention but for trade enabling the new regime to secure supplies — or face *immediately* a revolution at home'.[12] In order to do full justice to the profundity of such a statement, one has only to bear in mind that almost half of the French proletarian organisation are under the thumb of the Stalinists and the rest are swayed by the socialists. France is not Spain and unfortunately the anarchists are but a small, although growing, minority. (The same holds true of the Communist oppositionists.) How could a civil war waged against the socialists and the Stalinists of Spain, in the face of the terrific danger of a fascist breakthrough at that, fire the socialist and communist-minded workers of France to the extent of having them lay down an ultimatum to its own bourgeoisie demanding arms for the anarchist workers of Catalonia? And, of course, the ultimatum would have to be laid down in the face of the frenzied opposition of the trade-union leadership (socialist and communist), of both parties who would use all powerful means at their disposal to slander, vilify, distort the nature of the struggle waged by the revolutionary forces of Spain. That in the long run the truth would come out, that a successful social revolution in Spain would have a powerful effect in freeing the French workers from the hold exercised upon them by the parliamentary socialists and Stalinists is quite evident, especially in the light of the effect which the Russian revolution had in weakening the almost

12. Morrow, *Revolution and Counter-Revolution*, p 151, Schmidt's emphasis.

monopolistic power held by the old social-democracy. But in order to achieve this effect the Spanish revolution would have to *survive* and keep on struggling for quite a long time in an atmosphere of hostility and isolation while receiving aid… from the French bourgeoisie.

And this aid in armaments, without which the Spanish revolution could not hold out in the face of an intensified intervention of the fascist powers, who would be egged on for that purpose by Chamberlain and the Cliveden set, this aid would be extended by the very same French bourgeoisie in the face of the course confidently laid down for the Spanish revolution by Felix Morrow — that 'of preparing to resist imperialism by spreading the revolution to France and Belgium and then wage revolutionary war against Germany and Italy'.[13] Is there any wonder that the Spanish workers turned a deaf ear to the advice of those 'strategists' who in their eagerness to 'strike up a flame to light up the world' have overlooked the logic of plain ordinary common sense which warns about the impossibility of eating the cake and having it at the same time.

Camouflaged Defeatism

For the great masses of workers are realistic even in the highest moments of revolutionary daring. They will strike up a flame to light up the world, provided that flame also light up to some extent the immediate steps to be undertaken in order to survive in the terrific struggle against the old world. The workers are not defeatists, and too often, as the history of revolutionary struggles has shown, the *over-emphasis* upon gaining points of departure of world-historic importance, the aesthetic delight of high-towered historic observers at the torch kindled by a martyred generation of workers, camouflages an essentially defeatist attitude born out of a sterile romanticism.

Note: This article was written before the tragic climax of the Catalonian struggle. The collapse of Catalonian resistance will afford additional ammunition to those who maintain that the revolutionary force of Catalonia had nothing to lose by choosing an extreme course. It will be claimed that nothing worse could have happened to the revolutionists as compared to their present fate.

But it could have been worse. *The tragic end would have come two years earlier* had the revolutionists pursued the tactics advocated by the Trotskyites. Such tactics would have placed the Spanish workers in the same position of inferiority in point of armaments which proved deciding in the tragic climax of the Catalonian struggle.

And whatever one's opinion of the tactics of the Spanish struggle might be, there can be no dispute about the overwhelming historic significance of this struggle. It acted as a formidable breakwater to the sweeping fascist wave. That

---

13. Morrow, *Revolution and Counter-Revolution*, p 152.

it continued acting in this capacity for more than two years was due in no small measure to the realistic policy pursued by the revolutionary forces affording them some chances of survival as against the certainty of a total annihilation facing them two years ago.

TROTSKY AND SPAIN: THE POUM'S ASSESSMENT

Readers will be aware of the critical attitude taken by Trotsky towards the policies of the POUM, the Workers Party of Marxist Unification, which was formed in September 1935 with the fusion of the Workers and Peasants Bloc (BOC), led by Joaquín Maurín, and the Communist Left, which was led by Andreu Nin and Juan Andrade, and which had been the Spanish section of the International Left Opposition. Relations between the ILO and its Spanish affiliate had never been good, and had been broken off prior to the latter's fusion with the BOC. The disagreements between Nin and Trotsky continued in respect of the POUM's policies during the Civil War, and whilst Trotsky's criticisms have long been available, collected in *The Spanish Revolution (1931-39)* (Pathfinder, New York, 1973), the POUM's side of the dispute is much less known in the English-speaking world.

We present here two critiques of Trotsky's standpoint by Spanish historians who were members of the POUM during the Civil War. Both have been translated by Mike Jones from the website of the Fondación Andreu Nin.

The first, by Wilibaldo Solano, investigates the relationship between Trotsky and Nin, and is the text of Solano's contribution to the *Trotsky Today* events organised by the Nin Foundation in the Madrid Atheneum in February 1989. Wilebaldo Solano (1916-2010) joined the youth organisation of the Workers and Peasants Bloc (BOC) in 1932, and became a member of its Executive Committee. When the POUM was formed, Solano was elected General Secretary of its youth section, and edited its weekly paper, *Juventud Comunista*. He evaded the Stalinist crackdown upon the POUM which saw the arrest of most of its leadership and the murder of its Political Secretary, Andreu Nin, and he became a member of the POUM's Executive Committee, directing the clandestine weekly *Juventud Obrera*. He was arrested in April 1938, but the planned show trial was cancelled upon the collapse of the Spanish Republic, and he moved to France, where he was arrested and jailed. Rescued from prison by the French Resistance in July 1944, he joined the Maquis. After the war, Solano devoted the years in exile in France to the POUM, becoming its General Secretary in 1947, and ensuring that it remained a Marxist organisation. He wrote extensively on the history of the POUM and the Spanish Civil War, and helped to establish the Nin Foundation in the 1980s.

The second article is a section of Chapter VII of Ignacio Iglesias' book *Experiencias de la revolución española* (*Experiences of the Spanish Revolution*, Editorial Laertes, Barcelona, 2003). Ignacio Iglesias (1912-2005) was born into a left-wing, working-class family in Asturias. He was expelled from the Communist Youth as a Trotskyist, and subsequently joined the Communist Left and took part in the formation of the Workers Party of Marxist Unification (POUM) in September 1935. He helped edit the POUM's paper, *La Batalla*, during the civil war. He went into exile in France, and was sentenced by the collaborationist authorities in November 1941 to 12 years' hard labour. Released by US troops from Dachau, he helped produce *La Batalla* in France until his departure from the POUM in 1953. He subsequently wrote various historical works, including *Trotsky et la Révolution Espagnole* (*Trotsky and the Spanish Revolution*, Lausanne, 1974), *El proceso contra el POUM. Un episodio de la revolución española* (*The Trial of the POUM: An Episode of the Spanish Revolution*, Paris, 1974), and *León Trotsky y España (1930-1939)* (*Leon Trotsky and Spain (1930-1939)*, Gijón, 1977). Iglesias is far less generous to Trotsky than Solano, and the reader will notice that the former had distanced himself from the traditions of the POUM in that he dated the degeneration of the Russian Revolution back to the Bolsheviks' monopolisation of political power, and, as he put it in another article, considered that Stalinism was ultimately rooted in the Bolsheviks' concept of party organisation.[1] Nevertheless, despite this, Iglesias raises some points of criticism of Trotsky's standpoint on the Spanish Civil War which deserve consideration.

I: Wilebaldo Solano, *Andreu Nin and Leon Trotsky*

It is very moving for me that public meetings can be held in Madrid about Trotsky. I remember the years in which the conditions were such that it would have been impossible to render homage to Trotsky or Andreu Nin in Madrid.

In late 1936, the Juventud Comunista Ibégrica, the POUM's youth organisation, held a meeting in Madrid. We held it in the Infanta Isabel theatre, and, on the following day, the Stalinist press began a great offensive against our movement, an offensive that placed us in a very difficult situation within the overall defence of Madrid, when our youngsters were fighting and dying in the trenches of the Moncloa. Afterwards, many scandalous things took place in Madrid. Here, in July 1937, some of the best-known leaders of the POUM, such as Juan Andrade, Pedro Bonet and Julián Gorkin, were arrested and held captive in the so-called chekas of Atocha and la Castellano And, very near Madrid, in El

---

1. See his 'Apuntes para una anatomía del estalinismo' on the Nin Foundation website, which essentially relies upon the stock interpretation of Lenin's *What Is To Be Done?* — RH.

Pardo and Alcalá de Henares, Andreu Nin, the POUM Political Secretary and former Deputy General Secretary of the Red International of Labour Unions, was kidnapped and murdered, following an heroic resistance to torture. I do not know if Stalin's agents who tortured him knew that Nin had been one of the first people to raise the banner of October in Spain. Permit me to remind you that it was also in Madrid, in the famous congress of the Teatro de la Comedia, where Nin succeeded in persuading the CNT to confirm its adherence to the Russian Revolution.

Not everyone knows all this. But if so many people have been to the *Trotsky Today* events it is because the historic process that we are seeing in the USSR and Eastern Europe, apart from being a very profound revolutionary process, constitutes the most important event in today's world and poses huge problems for all those who claim to be socialists. The failure and collapse of Stalinism in the USSR cannot but make us reflect deeply upon it, and stimulates an especial interest in those who opposed Stalin and his reactionary politics, in Trotsky as a person and in Trotskyism, in the drama of Nin and the POUM, and in everything in the labour and socialist camp which opposed Stalinism.

We old revolutionary Marxist militants experience such feelings much more frequently these days. We experience them when the great figures of Bolshevism and the Russian revolutionary intellectuals are rehabilitated. We experience them when we take part, as we did some months ago in Barcelona, in some colloquiums about perestroika, in which representative figures of the continuing movement in the USSR participate. Not long ago, I was honoured to participate in a colloquium in Paris marking the fiftieth anniversary of the Fourth International, in which Trotskyist militants and former militants of various tendencies attempted to draw up a balance sheet of their experiences. That balance sheet was very critical and very interesting. Very surprisingly for me, I noted that various prominent militants returned to pose the old question of the relations and the conflicts between the Fourth International and the POUM. A distinguished Argentine author addressed himself particularly to the founders of the Fourth International who were present in the hall, Michel Pablo and Yvan Craipeau, both participants in the 1938 conference, in order to ask them why 'we did not come to an agreement with men like Andres Nin and with parties like the POUM', and why 'those who were in the leadership of the movement permitted a chasm to open up between revolutionaries faithful to the same fundamental ideas'. In the debate that followed, it was largely confirmed that Stalin's police, the GPU, through its agents, did everything it could to poison the relationship between Trotsky and Nin, between the movement for the Fourth International and the POUM, in the course of the Spanish revolution, when the Kremlin did its utmost to liquidate every trace of opposition to its plans, both in the USSR and in Spain.

Naturally, I intervened in that debate, which was more honest and more productive than the one we had in 1969, in Paris, with the active participation of Pierre Broué, and which was reproduced in a book entitled *La Révolution Espagnole*.[2] But today, although the theme is 'Trotsky and Spain', I do not think that it would be opportune to return to the question and, given that we do not have much time, I will say something more brief and of more interest about Leon Trotsky and Andres Nin, that is, about the men, their friendship, their common struggles, their divergences and their estrangement, and about the feelings which they had, each in respect to the other, in the last years of their lives.

A Long and Strong Friendship

I am convinced that Nin was one of Trotsky's most loyal friends, and a man whom Trotsky held in the highest esteem. The friendship between them lasted for some 15 years, between 1921 and 1935. As is known, Nin arrived in Moscow in the summer of 1921, being part of the delegation sent by the CNT to the founding congress of the Red International of Labour Unions. As Joaquín Maurín has explained, Nin immediately stood out in the congress debates. In September of the same year he wanted to return to Spain but was detained in Berlin as a result of a request by the Spanish government, which wanted to implicate him in the legal case it was pursuing over the assassination of Dato. Upon regaining his liberty when the German government refused his extradition, Nin returned to Moscow where he was appointed Deputy General Secretary of the RILU. Later he would be elected a deputy of the Moscow Soviet and the RILU representative in the Communist International. These functions meant that he would be dealing constantly with the most significant Russian leaders. In reality, one can say that no other Spanish Communist ever occupied such important posts and was so close to the leaders of the October Revolution and the Soviet state. In 1967, Maurín wrote in the New York *España Libre*: 'The Russian Communist leaders, from Lenin and Trotsky to Bukharin and Zinoviev, knew the worth of Nin and valued his cooperation in matters of significance.' And so he intervened in very important matters and took on tasks such as the clandestine reorganisation of the Italian trade unions in 1924 under fascism, and the construction of the Latin American trade-union movement. It was he who introduced to the Soviet authorities every Spaniard of any significance who visited the USSR between 1921 and 1927: Josep Pla, Rodolfo Llopis, Diego Hidalgo and, above all, Francesc Macià, the future President of the autonomous

2. *La Révolution Espagnole*, supplement to *Études Marxistes* (Paris), no 7-8, 1969. Notes provided by the Nin Foundation unless otherwise stated.

Catalan government, who was in Moscow to request support from the Soviet government for militant Catalanism.

Some, through ignorance or bad faith, have had the audacity to say that Nin was 'a high-ranking official' or 'a top bureaucrat'. His whole militant life gives the lie to such nonsense. It has also been said that at various times he was closer to Zinoviev and Bukharin than to Trotsky. The truth is that he was close to all of them until the factional struggle within the Bolshevik party became acute. He did not immediately join the Left Opposition, but he did not take too long to do so and he did not conceal himself nor capitulate as did so many others. Many officials, leading or not, bowed before the powerful in order to keep their privileges. Nin, as Victor Serge said, 'is with those who are demanding freedom of thought and speech in the Bolshevik party and thorough reform of the regime, with the aim of returning to a workers' democracy'.[3] In any case, when he joined the Opposition he was still the Deputy General Secretary of the RILU and lived in a supervised liberty in Moscow. When he was dismissed, his friend Lozovsky, the General Secretary of the RILU, maintained a relationship with him, and did not hesitate in consulting him about the problems which arose in the world trade-union movement.

According to Alfred Rosmer, Nin was neither arrested nor deported to Siberia because Stalin did not dare to persecute influential foreign militants. Nin took advantage of this circumstance in order to intensify his work in the Left Opposition and to organise, with Serge, assistance for prisoners and deportees. He was one of the leaders of the Opposition and with Radek, Kapitonov and Stepanov he energised the international section (a future agent of Stalin in Spain) and maintained a special relationship with Trotsky while that was still possible. Some of his letters to Trotsky when the latter found himself deported in Alma-Ata have been published in recent years and give an idea of the character of the relationship established at that time. On one occasion, Nin sent to Trotsky a volume of reproductions of paintings and sculptures by Diego Rivera.[4] Trotsky replied to thank him for sending the book and to let him know that he appreciated this artist who — in an irony of history — would open the doors of his house in Mexico to him in 1937.

3. 'Adiós a Andres Nin', first published in *La Révolution Prolétarienne*, no 253, 25 August 1937 [English text in David Cotterill (ed), *The Serge-Trotsky Papers* (London, 1994), p 145].
4. Diego Rivera (1886-1957) was one of the greatest exponents of the muralist school and one of the greatest Mexican painters of the century. Founder of the Communist Party of Mexico and Central Committee member from 1922 to 1927, when he declared his support for Trotsky. Helped gain his asylum in Mexico and he and his wife Frida Kahlo were his hosts. In 1939 broke with Trotsky.

Nin Sounded the First Alarm Call

At that time, Nin was not only preoccupied with Trotsky and the deported Russian oppositionists in Siberia. He also took an interest in his Spanish comrades who were confined in the Modelo prison (Pedro Bonet, David Rey and others) and in Montjuich castle (Maurín). With the help of Serge, he demanded that the International Red Aid mobilise itself to help them. During 1927-29, Nin kept up a fairly frequent correspondence with his friend Maurín, as much when the latter found himself in the military fortress that dominates Barcelona as when he was able to take refuge in Paris. That correspondence has a high political value. And, a curious thing, it circulated by the normal postal service and, in some cases, when it had to avoid the multiple censors, emissaries who travelled frequently between Moscow and Paris facilitated it. Two of them are fairly well known; Angelo Tasca and Palmiro Togliatti, leaders of the Communist Party of Italy. Well then, on 17 January 1929, Nin sent a letter by 'special post' to Maurín in which, among other things, he told him that he was taking advantage of the occasion in order to write to him at length and in full. In that letter he not only informed him about what happened in the recent plenum of the CPSU's Central Committee and the repressive measures adopted recently by Stalin, but he added the following:

> They want Moscow completely free of oppositionists. The situation of the deportees has worsened; it is now three months since Trotsky received letters from anyone... The Political Bureau has decided to expel Trotsky from the USSR... Everyone assumes that this decision is inspired by the aim of physically liquidating Trotsky. As it would not be convenient to do it here, it will be done in another country. Those people are resolved on everything. It is necessary to alert opinion everywhere. One can expect anything. There is the precedent of the death of Butov, Trotsky's secretary.

That is to say, Nin broadcast to the world, through Maurín, the first call in defence of the now endangered Trotsky. There's more to this letter, and it is of great political interest. It explains that Stalin negotiated with Turkey in order to remove him there and thus 'he will be able to eliminate him one way or another'. In the end, what Nin predicted did happen.

When Nin wrote this letter, the leading nucleus of the Left Opposition had been reduced to Trotsky's first wife Alexandra Bronstein, Serge in Leningrad and Nin in Moscow. Nin's warning was justified. The case of Butov — he died in prison after a 50-day hunger-strike — and others demonstrated that the situation had moved from repression to physical extermination. Well then, what I wanted to say is that one of the men who had a very close relationship with Trotsky, writing to him, informing him, sending him letters and books, was Andreu Nin. This was something therefore which counted in Trotsky's life and I believe that it counted and was valued in an extraordinary way.

Subsequently, when Nin succeeded in leaving the USSR and established himself in Spain, the two maintained a correspondence at least until 1933. For that reason, Trotsky once said to Serge that he had never written so continuously to anyone and that the letters written to Nin would constitute a volume of hundreds of pages.[5] We have some of the latter. Others were stolen by GPU agents when they broke into the premises of the International Institute of Social History in rue Michelet, Paris in the night of 6-7 November 1936. Therefore they must be in the Soviet archives. In order to explain the motives of his correspondence with Nin, Trotsky declared to Serge his passion for the Spanish revolution in the first place and his friendship with Nin, whom he wanted to help carry out the role that he believed he could play in the Spanish revolutionary process.

From the Break in 1933 to the Foundation of the POUM

This correspondence ceased at the beginning of 1933, due to a conflict between the Left Opposition and the Communist Left of Spain, which was a small organisation, but was made up of very valuable militants with much character, such as Andrade, Fersen, García Palacios and Molins i Fábrega. It was a political conflict over the perspective of the party in Spain and the role and methods of the International Secretariat of the Left Opposition. For that reason it ended with a very harsh letter by Trotsky and a reply by Nin telling him that in future he should address himself to the Communist Left and not to him, since the latter was 'a responsible, democratic organisation and not a group of friends'. From then on, the relations between Nin and Trotsky were interrupted. But Trotsky always regretted that Nin and Andrade did not travel to see him during his French exile, when he lived in Saint-Palais, near Royan, in July-September 1933, a place visited by plenty of militants of various working-class organisations from numerous countries.

It is not possible to sum up now the period between the crisis of 1933, which interrupted the relations of Nin and Trotsky, and the foundation of the POUM in October 1935, following intense joint activity of the Communist Left and the

---

5. In a letter of 3 June 1936 to Victor Serge, Trotsky wrote: 'For several years I corresponded with him [Nin] quite regularly. Some of my letters were veritable "treatises" on the subject of the living revolution, in which Nin could and should have played an active role. I think that my letters to Nin over a period of two or three years would make up a volume of several hundred pages: that should indicate how important I regarded Nin and friendly relations with him.' (Leon Trotsky, *La Revolución Española*, Volume 1 (Barcelona, 1977), p 346) [LD Trotsky, *The Spanish Revolution (1931-39)* (New York, 1973), p 215]

Workers and Peasants Bloc within the framework of the Workers Alliance and in the revolutionary upsurge of October 1934. But one can say that the Workers Alliance, which the BOC inspired and with which it provided a theoretical basis, opened up the road to the creation of a peninsula-wide revolutionary party with a mass basis in Catalonia. Well now, in this period, Trotsky recommended the so-called 'French turn', that is to say, the entrance of the Trotskyists into the socialist parties, with the aim of creating left-wing currents capable of playing a leading role in Europe, which was now threatened by Hitler. The Communist Left and the BOC had rejected the invitations of Largo Caballero and Carrillo to join the PSOE and the Socialist Youth because they had another perspective and did not believe in the consistency of the gyrations of the left Socialists nor in the 'Bolshevisation' of the Socialist Youth which in reality ended in Moscow in 1936 in a shameful manner.

According to what we know today, Trotsky passionately followed this process and, contrary to what has been said in certain publications, he did not have such a clear attitude as some imagine in relation to the creation of the POUM. The proof is that in a private letter sent to Jean Rous in 1935, he said more or less that 'the new party has been established; I have noted it'. But he manifested his disposition to collaborate with it.[6] Of course, then came the elections of February 1936, in which the POUM participated, forming part of the workers' republican electoral coalition which the Stalinists hastened to baptise the Popular Front. In reality, it was not the classical formula of the Popular Front. It did not constitute an organic coalition, but was an electoral front. Things developed in such a way in Madrid that there was never any joint meetings. Largo Caballero acted as liaison between the workers' organisations and the republican parties.

Trotsky, badly informed and believing that this was a repeat of the French Popular Front, wrote a very aggressive article against Nin and Andrade, which so surprised the French Trotskyist militants that they only published it in their internal bulletin. Trotsky demonstrated a total incomprehension of a wonderful mass phenomenon which radically modified the Spanish situation.[7] In effect, the

---

6. The letter from Trotsky (comrade Crux) is cited by Jean Rous in his report on the BOC and ICE fusion, October 1935 (included in *La Revolución Española*, Volume 2 (Barcelona, 1977), p 370) [Trotsky, *The Spanish Revolution (1931-39)*, pp 206-07].

7. The reason for this polemic might be found, apart from the intentions of the POUM in adhering to the coalition, in the preamble of the electoral manifesto which states that the signatories have managed to 'reach a common political plan which serves as a basis for and a promotion of the coalition of their respective forces in the immediate electoral contest, and as a model of the government which the left republican parties, with the support of the working-class forces, will need to develop in the case of victory' [Trotsky, *The Spanish Revolution (1931-39)*, pp 207-11].

electoral victory allowed the liberation of the 30 000 prisoners of the October revolution, the political defeat of the right and the rise of the mass movement. It was an extraordinary affirmation of the popular movement in a period in which Hitler was in full ascent and Europe was in obvious danger. Many of us continue to believe that it represented a success for the POUM, because, among other motives, the experience had demonstrated that revolutionaries, when they isolate themselves, end up marginalising themselves and fighting among themselves, and that, on the other hand, when they work in the real mass movement, they grow and strengthen themselves instead of splitting.

Trotsky and the 1936 Revolution

Without the electoral victory of the mass movement of 16 February 1936, which allowed the gaining of decisive positions, the reply of the working people to the military-fascist rising of July 1936, and the subsequent revolutionary process, would not have been possible. In Europe dominated by fascism, this armed resistance and the attempt to carry out a radical socialist transformation of Spanish society will remain in history as one of the principal events of the twentieth century. As is natural, Trotsky, in spite of the conditions of his exile in Norway having considerably worsened, and the hand of the Stalin–Yagoda clan, as he put it, having reached as far as his home, enthusiastically greeted the victory of the workers of Madrid and Barcelona, and proudly appreciated the role of the POUM in the struggle. In a letter to Jean Rous, written in early August, which was intercepted by Mussolini's police and only discovered many years later by the Italian historian Paolo Spriano, after expressing his concern at the disappearance of Maurín, whose value he appreciated rather more than some of his friends imagined, he wrote:

> As for Nin, Andrade and the others, it would be criminal to let ourselves to be guided now in this great struggle by memories of the preceding period. Even after the experiences we have had, if there are differences in programme and method, these divergences must in no way impede a *sincere and lasting rapprochement*. Further experience would do the rest. As for me personally, I would be entirely ready to aid *La Batalla*... My warmest greetings to all our friends, and also and especially for those who feel they have reason to be dissatisfied with me.[8]

Unfortunately, Nin never saw this letter. But in any case, Trotsky's state of mind was known by Jean Rous and other comrades and, as we know, the POUM

---

8. Trotsky, *La Revolución Española*, Volume 2, pp 65-67 [Trotsky, *The Spanish Revolution (1931-39)*, pp 239-41; the text there states 'I would be entirely ready to aid in the battle'].

claimed the right of asylum in Catalonia for the creator of the Red Army. A certain shameless opportunist places this deed among the errors of Nin and the POUM. But we are not ashamed of this error and the truth is that the POUM militants were ready to welcome and protect Trotsky, as they welcomed and protected many German, Italian and Romanian exiles who came to work and to fight alongside us.

It is probable that, had Trotsky been able to live in Catalonia, he would have better understood — without the necessity of intermediaries — the characteristics of the Spanish revolutionary process, and his relations with Nin and the POUM would have developed in much more healthy and interesting conditions, although, to be sure, the GPU was present in Spain and Stalin directed its actions, operating through his many agents, both Russians and Spaniards. But Trotsky first found himself in Norway, bound hand and foot, practically a prisoner, and then, having finally obtained a visa for Mexico (requested from Cárdenas by Nin),[9] he crossed the Atlantic in an oil tanker. And above all, at the beginning of August, came the first Moscow Trial (Zinoviev, Kamenev and Smirnov), which upset all his plans. Although he knew that the destiny of Europe would be decided for a long period in the great battle of Spain, Trotsky was fully conscious that life had imposed on him an essential mission: to denounce the terrible imposture of Stalin before the international labour movement and public opinion. It was therefore that he exacted from his associates and, in first place, his son Leon Sedov, a task without precedents.

On 9 January 1937, Trotsky disembarked in Tampico, Mexico. Scarcely installed in Coyoacán — where various POUM militants, headed by the famous David Rey, on a propaganda tour, but in reality searching for weapons, contributed to securing the protection of his house — on 19 January, TASS announced the second Moscow Trial (Radek and Pyatakov) for the 23rd. Such an event was foreseen by some, but nonetheless many people doubted that Stalin, after the painful impression of the Kamenev–Zinoviev trial, would proceed with a farce as criminal as it was absurd. Nevertheless, so it was, and Trotsky returned to the attack with more energy than ever. In *The Crimes of Stalin*,[10] a book less well known than *The Revolution Betrayed*,[11] Trotsky's struggle against

9. Costa Amic had been delegated by Nin, in his capacity as Justice Minister in the Catalan government, in October 1936, to request in his name political asylum for Trotsky from President Cárdenas (Victor Alba, *El marxismo en España (1919-1939)*, Volume 1 (Mexico, 1973), p 392). Lázaro Cárdenas (1895-1970), President of Mexico during 1934-40, followed left-wing policies regarding land distribution, the church and foreign capital. Furthermore he granted asylum to Trotsky and took in Spanish republican refugees with the end of the war.
10. L Trotsky, *Stalin y sus crímenes* (Madrid, 1947).
11. L Trotsky, *La revolución traicionada* (Barcelona, 1977).

the Kremlin's new imposture is splendidly recorded, a magisterial analysis of Stalinism as a monstrous degeneration of the peculiar dictatorship of the Russian bureaucracy.

Trotsky and the Murder of Nin

Between 25 August 1936, isolated in his Norwegian prison, and 9 January 1937, the date of his disembarkation in Mexico, Trotsky had very few possibilities of being informed about the Spanish revolution, which had been underway for six decisive months. The first serious information he received was from the POUM delegation led by David Rey and Costa Amic, which he received in a very cordial manner. These comrades confirmed that, in spite of all his preoccupations, he had great interest in the POUM. In those times, Mexico was much further away from Spain than it is today. Trotsky's information was very deficient and always late in arriving. At times the confusion was increased because the information came from the Trotskyist group which were engaged in internal disputes. We found the tone of some of his articles inexplicable, in that he rebuked us for having organised our own militias when all the organisations had done the same and we were in favour of the creation of a revolutionary army. Certain criticisms, such as that regarding Nin's participation in the autonomous Catalan government or his intervention in the Barcelona May events, could have been more favourably received — since they were also formulated within the POUM — but Trotsky's general tone was very much influenced by the crisis which had opened up in the movement for the Fourth International around the POUM and its policies. The Dutch party of Sneevliet, the Belgian tendency of Vereeken, his old friends Victor Serge and Alfred Rosmer, among others, had rebuked him over his new attitude towards the POUM, accusing him of sectarianism. In those circumstances this was too all much for Trotsky.

To be honest, the polemics that developed then were very painful for Nin, because he expected a different attitude from Trotsky. It is true that Trotsky, distanced from Europe in Coyoacán, found himself in one of the most dramatic moments of his life. Stalinist repression had penetrated into his own family, and his best Russian friends had capitulated or had been eliminated by Stalin. His solitude weighed on him more than ever and he knew that Stalin would do everything possible to eliminate him. Although he not did ignore the efforts of the GPU to infiltrate the Trotskyist movement, it is possible that he underestimated the importance of this infiltration. Today it is possible that, finally, we will get access to the Soviet archives and we will be able to verify with complete certainty that one of the GPU's tasks in that period consisted in opening up a chasm between the POUM and the Trotskyist movement, between Trotsky and Nin. We have said it many times and I repeat it today: it must have been very tempting for the Stalinists to isolate and discredit a revolutionary party which carried out an important role in the events in Spain and which represented hope for the revolutionary socialists of the entire world.

In the Paris colloquium to which I referred earlier in my intervention, we returned to the problem of the absence of the POUM from the founding conference of the Fourth International (it had been invited as an observer and our observer should have been Molins i Fábrega, the delegate of the POUM Executive in Paris). Well now, Yvan Craipeau and Michel Pablo explained, to my great amazement, that Molins was unable to participate as he missed the earlier appointment arranged by the person who should have taken him to the venue of the meeting. And this person was none other than *Comrade Étienne*, the member of the International Secretariat for the Fourth International, who in reality was Marc Zborowski, who was a GPU agent whose special task was to keep watch over Leon Sedov, Trotsky's son. In 1955, in a declaration before a US Senate commission, Zborowski admitted his role in stealing Trotsky's archives, in the suspicious death of Leon Sedov in a Paris clinic, and in the murder of Ignace Reiss. The US authorities pardoned him *for services rendered.*

The POUM, of course, had not considered adhering to the Fourth International because it held to another perspective and believed that it was premature to create a new International. But it collaborated with all the socialist and communist forces independent of the Kremlin and, at that juncture, it had a special interest in addressing every possible assembly in order to resist the Stalinist repression in Spain and its lamentable effect upon the military struggle against Francoism. So in spite of the attacks upon it by Trotsky and certain Trotskyist militants, it had decided to participate as an observer in the conference of the Fourth International. A document unpublished until quite recently — a report of the British delegates to the said conference in 1938 — states:

> It was a major error not to have been in contact with the POUM and the PSOP. Tomorrow we must set up a commission in order to meet them and inform them of what has taken place at the conference, etc, and to plan joint activity... We adopt the proposal of a commission for the meeting with the POUM: Lesoil, James, Cannon, Shachtman, Lebrun [Mario Pedrosa], Busson, Clart [Rous], Stefan.

These were the main leaders of the movement, and this statement indicates the importance that they placed upon establishing a relationship with the POUM.

The situation in Spain and in Europe had clearly deteriorated. The retreat of the revolution in Spain had facilitated Franco's offensives. The POUM was now in clandestinity. Stalin was preparing for his turn towards the alliance with Hitler and continued the repression of the Bolshevik old guard, with the purges, trials and deportations. The threat of war was clearer than ever following the annexation of Austria by Hitler. The European revolutionaries, in particular those of Spain and the USSR, found themselves in a truly dramatic situation and they began fully to recognise the utterly reactionary and terroristic nature of Stalinism.

I remember that in 1938, in the Barcelona state prison, where we POUM leaders, Andrade, Rey and other comrades, were confined, we wondered about 'Trotsky's silence' over the repression against the POUM and Nin's murder. In reality, we too were badly informed. On 8 August 1937, Trotsky had published a declaration in Mexico in which he stated:

> Nin is a veteran and incorruptible revolutionary. He defended the interests of the Spanish people and fought the agents of the Soviet bureaucracy... He strove to defend the independence of the Spanish proletariat, against the bureaucratic machinations of the gang in power in Moscow. He refused to collaborate with the GPU in order to ruin the interests of the Spanish proletariat. This is his only crime. And he paid for it with his life.[12]

The tone of this declaration makes us feel that he probably regretted the absence of any effective dialogue with Nin and the lack of any effective cooperation with the POUM, a party that fought in Spain for the truth about Stalinism and those who died in the USSR defending the fundamental principles of socialism against Stalin. Trotsky said on various occasions that Nin was 'his friend'[13] and this meant a lot to him, although he was not always fair to his friends and comrades. All men — and above all the most eminent — have their passions and their weaknesses. But allow me to finish also putting on record that Trotsky said, similarly, that the POUM 'was the most honest party in Spain'.[14]

12. L Trotsky, 'El asesinato de Andres Nin por los agentes de la GPU' (8 August 1937), *La Revolución Española*, Volume 2, pp 130-32 [Trotsky, *The Spanish Revolution (1931-39)*, pp 267-68].
13. In his declaration before the Dewey Commission on the Moscow Trials on 14 April 1937, Trotsky responded to Carleton Beals' question about who led the POUM, stating: 'Nin. He is my friend. I know him very well. But I criticise him very sharply.' (Leon Trotsky, *La Revolución Española*, Volume 2, p 93) [Trotsky, *The Spanish Revolution (1931-39)*, p 251]
14. In 'Lección de España última advertencia' (17 December 1937), Trotsky states: 'An excess of "caution" is the most baneful lack of caution. This is the chief lesson of the destruction of the most honest political organisation in Spain, namely, the centrist POUM.' (*La Revolución Española*, Volume 2, p 238) [Trotsky, *The Spanish Revolution (1931-39)*, p 251]

***

II: Ignacio Iglesias, *Trotsky and the POUM: A Balance Sheet*

Examining objectively, from the vantage point of today, Trotsky's extensive writings on the Spanish revolution and in particular the period of the Civil War, one gains the firm impression not only that did he not know how to hobble the poor nag of his illusions, but that he actually did not want to do so. These illusions were basically wanting to see everywhere a repeat of the Russian October Revolution. Not only did he always see and interpret events through the prism of the Bolshevik Revolution, but the positions or solutions which he proposed always turned out to be a perfect copy of those which he and Lenin elaborated in 1917. For Trotsky, therefore, the model presented by the Russian Revolution was both perfect and unique. And when it was argued that the conditions in Spain — to take one example — were different, he would respond disdainfully that 'this is the customary argument put to use by all opportunists',[15] and that 'abstract homilies of this kind make no serious impression'.[16] Andres Nin answered him in an indirect way at a conference in April 1937, at which he affirmed that 'the formulas of the Russian Revolution, mechanically applied, will only lead to failure', adding that 'from the Russian Revolution one must take the spirit, not the letter'.[17] But it seems that for Trotsky, the letter and the spirit were one and the same thing.

In some of his writings from the period of the Civil War, Trotsky considered some aspects of the conflict as if it were a copy of the Russian Civil War, talking to us of regiments and not of divisions, and placing on the same level the Red cavalry and Italo-German aircraft as regards their effectiveness. He actually claimed: 'If at the head of the armed workers and peasants, that is, at the head of so-called republican Spain, were revolutionists and not cowardly agents of the bourgeoisie, the problem of arming would never have been paramount.'[18] Was the revolutionary word sufficient when confronting a well-equipped modern army as the Francoist one was at that time? For him, without doubt, yes. And the word was obliged to correspond to a well-defined, detailed programme, written black on white, with no place for improvisation, since for Trotsky the revolution was something that could be expressed in an equation and which had to develop with the same implacable logic as an algebraic operation. Nevertheless, it has been shown in every revolution, as in life itself, each day and at times every hour requires improvisation, unexpected solutions in order

15. León Trotsky, *Escritos sobre España* (Paris, 1971), p 125 [LD Trotsky, *The Spanish Revolution (1931-39)* (New York, 1973), p 210].
16. Trotsky, *Escritos sobre España*, p 159 [Trotsky, *The Spanish Revolution (1931-39)*, p 278].
17. *La Batalla* (Barcelona), 26 April 1937.
18. Trotsky, *Escritos sobre España*, p 183 [Trotsky, *The Spanish Revolution (1931-39)*, p 320].

to be able to face the new problems which continually arise and which nobody can codify.

Therefore, according to Trotsky, what was lacking in the Spanish Civil War was not adequate weapons but a programme and the agency that could apply it, that is, a revolutionary party. And this meant a revolutionary party with a correct policy: in a word, a Bolshevik-Leninist party. This was at all times Trotsky's indefatigable rite: every page of his calls for the correct policy. Yet it remains a mystery precisely what this policy actually is. Is it one that will be successful through immediate action, as a marksman hits the bull's-eye? Or is it one that will enable previously proposed objectives to be achieved? Is it perhaps a matter of obtaining pure and simple success? If the correctness of a policy is determined by its practical results, then it is a matter of simple pragmatism and William James will have to replace Karl Marx. Whatever the case, one is forced to recognise that Trotsky, the tireless preacher of the so-called correct policy, never succeeded in practising it, given that at the final balancing of accounts he was the eternal loser, with power having slipped from his hands in the Soviet Union. Who had the correct policy then, Trotsky the conquered or Stalin the conqueror? And of what use to him then was his correct policy, since he proved incapable of creating a genuine revolutionary movement around it?

Trotsky's critical spirit was sharp, relentless, unflagging. He criticised everything and everyone. And yet that critical spirit suddenly stopped as soon as it became necessary to analyse his own political positions, his judgements or the accuracy of his abundant prophesies. Everything he said had to be accepted as both correct and infallible. He could not acknowledge his own failures or even his simplest errors, even though his own conduct proved that he was just as prone to failure and error as anyone else. He felt that his analyses and even simple statements were correct, and that those of other people were *a priori* wrong merely by their being different to his. His intransigence elevated him to the lofty heights of a true cult; even comrades in his own organisation comrades found themselves inexorably condemned for expressing the slightest difference in judgement. An indubitable inquisitorial attitude dwelled within him. And as it was not possible for him to tie the heretics to the stake, he contented himself with covering them with insults and branding them as traitors. We say it bluntly: Trotsky, just like Stalin, and just like Lenin before them, suffered from a very serious fault, a real perversion of the spirit, in that his intolerance would turn a political difference into heresy or even apostasy.

Towards the POUM and its leaders he behaved in an inquisitorial manner, firmly refusing to listen to the slightest opposing argument, presenting the facts at his whim, even attributing to the POUM political positions that it had never adopted. What were Trotsky's main accusations against the POUM?

We have already indicated them, but we will repeat them: having signed the electoral pact of February 1936, not having conquered power in July following the military uprising, having entered the government of Catalonia, not having implacably denounced the other organisations, and, above all, for having leaders who showed a generous spirit of conciliation, in particular towards the anarchists, and so on. To sum up: the POUM should have done everything that it did not do, and neglected to do what it should have done. As far as Trotsky was concerned, the POUM did nothing positive, suitable or correct in any of its actions. Born with the stigma of original sin, the POUM was condemned, undeserving of the slightest approval.

Amazing really, looking back, that attitude of Trotsky. But what is much more shocking is that, to this day, Trotskyists dauntlessly continue to make their own the errors and absurdities into which Trotsky fell, in judging the main events of the Spanish revolution and, above all, the POUM and its leaders. It must be said that these errors and absurdities are part of the inheritance that he bequeathed to them and which they have been unable to reject. A few years ago, the Communist League (the French section of the Fourth International) republished a pamphlet written in 1939 by a Trotskyist militant of Polish origin, who by the look of it was in Spain during the Civil War. What can one say of its content? Of course it repeats, if with less literary merit and less polemical talent, what Trotsky had already stated and repeated. *Qualis pater, talis filius.* Like father, like son, or, to use an old Castilian adage, a chip off the old block. In every way, the pamphlet's author glories in a greater insolence, which is always the case with neophytes eager to show their zeal.

Let us look at some specimens, eloquent enough, regarding the mentality of the Trotskyists both past and present:

> The Fourth International can thus rightly say: 'We foresaw all this — the tragic and unavoidable consequences of the policy of the Popular Front.'
>
> Nonetheless, only 'Trotskyism', the Bolshevik policy of the Fourth International in other words, could have saved the POUM and opened up great opportunities for it... The Fourth International proposed its programme to it.
>
> To vanquish Franco we needed a revolutionary leadership, that is to say a party.
>
> A revolutionary policy could have made the 'Bolshevik plague' penetrate even among the most backward and reactionary elements. Did we not see how even Cossack detachments passed over to the Red Army in the course of the Russian Revolution?

And to conclude, the constant *leitmotiv*:

After the defeats of the proletariat, the Fourth International will lead them to great victories.[19]

In spite of the enlightened bearing that the Trotskyist usually exhibits, he seems to us like a species of Neanderthal man, a prehistoric pithecanthropus, because of his anachronistic faith in the past. And in the name of that past, which they identify with a supposed Marxist-Leninist truth, they anathematise, condemn and excommunicate with summary ease.

What is most striking in Trotskyist literature is its mimicry. With respect to the Spanish revolution, in particular with reference to the POUM, each one of their accusations is the same as those of Trotsky, the arguments coincide exactly with those of Trotsky, even the expressions used are those of Trotsky. Trotsky, firstly from Norway and then from Mexico, criticised without knowing what he was talking about and without possessing genuine information. And his proxies who went to Barcelona, instead of studying the real situation in the country and drawing the necessary conclusions, repeated in the Catalan capital what Trotsky said thousands of kilometres away. That is to say, it was not they who informed Trotsky from Spain, but it was Trotsky who from afar informed those who were in Spain. What is strange about the matter — and it is worthy of psychological study — is that when Trotsky received some reports from his envoys in which they limited themselves to reproducing what he had said to them in his letters or articles, the old revolutionary believed that his points of view were confirmed and did not see that he was a victim of a lamentable mystification.

In this way, operating in a closed circuit without the slightest connection with daily reality, insisting that problems adapt themselves to their axioms and not the axioms to the problems, the Trotskyists performed in Spain, or with respect to Spain, a totally negative role. Not only did they not thoroughly address any problems, but they did not even study them; their role was to criticise, criticise and once again criticise. The truth is that they did nothing else but imitate Trotsky, who persisted in criticising, criticising everything even that which could not be criticised. For example, when he rebuked the POUM for possessing 'its own premises, its own radio station, its own printing plant, its own militias',[20] this only showed once more his lazy ignorance of Spanish reality, given that

---

19. M Casanova, 'La guerre d'Espagne', *Cahiers de la IVe Internationale* (Paris), January 1971 [Mieczysław Bortenstein (M Casanova), 'Spain Betrayed', *Revolutionary History*, Volume 4, no 1/2, 1992].
20. Léon Trotsky, *La révolution espagnole* (Paris, 1979), p 459 [Trotsky, *The Spanish Revolution (1931-39)*, p 303].

every organisation — even the smallest, such as the Syndicalist Party or the Federal Party — possessed premises, printing plants, etc. Moreover, Trotsky had forgotten that the same situation existed during the Russian revolution, until the Bolsheviks seized the lot by establishing their dictatorship.

More than once we have asked ourselves what motivated Trotsky's irascibility towards a party which, in every way, was closer to his ideas than any other and towards men who had struggled alongside him — such as Nin and Andrade — and who in spite of political differences continued to have great respect for him. Perhaps the fact that the POUM was created against the wishes of Trotsky — who then advocated entering the Socialist Party — can explain in part his attitude. But only in part and only up to certain limits.

I believe that the answer to our question came to us years later, when it was discovered that the GPU had succeeded in planting its agents in the International Secretariat of the Trotskyist organisation. During the Spanish revolution, the most active element of that Secretariat, the most intimate collaborator of Leon Sedov, Trotsky's son, was a certain Zborowski, a Russian-Pole known as Étienne; the latter came under suspicion from some Trotskyists, but Trotsky always defended him. In 1941, he emigrated to the United States, and there the police discovered his role as a GPU agent. There can be no doubt that he had received orders to poison the relations between Trotsky and the POUM, orders without doubt he successfully accomplished.[21]

We have never wanted to assert in commenting on Trotsky's attitude to the POUM that this organisation always had a suitable and irreproachable policy. It erred on occasions, just as throughout history all organisations have erred not a few times. In spite of all the mythology created around the Bolshevik party — established *a posteriori* by those who were its leaders in order to justify its supposed superiority to all the other parties — we know that it too had its vacillations and mistakes. It did not have a linear trajectory, nor were its tactical shifts calculated mathematically. Lenin admitted it in his book '*Left-Wing' Communism, An Infantile Disorder*: '... the entire history of Bolshevism, both before and after the October Revolution, is *full* of instances of changes of tack, conciliatory tactics and compromises.' Trotsky knew it, albeit with his individual dialectic revived to rude health against all criticism: 'Marx made mistakes, Lenin made mistakes, also the Bolshevik party as a whole. But these mistakes were corrected in time, thanks to the accuracy of the fundamental line.'[22]

There therefore exists a fundamental line which determines the so-called

21. On this subject, see Georges Vereeken, *The GPU in the Trotskyist Movement* (London, 1976); Elisabeth K Poretsky, *Our Own People* (London, 1969).
22. Trotsky, *Escritos sobre España*, p 153 [Trotsky, *The Spanish Revolution (1931-39)*, p 272].

correct policy. But according to what Trotsky repeatedly said, it is only within reach of Bolshevism-Leninism, which is a kind of universal executor. Every other party and organisation arises and exists merely in order to betray the proletariat, in whose name Bolshevism-Leninism acts exclusively. We insist that all this is pure mythology. There never existed, nor probably will ever exist, a unique type of ideal workers' party with a fundamental line and a correct policy capable of leading the workers to socialism, in the same way that the nursemaid leads the child by the hand, telling it what it may and may not do. It seems to me that it is time to finish once and for all with all that verbosity, which has caused not a little damage to all those groups and circles who believed and still believe themselves to be the repositories of absolute truth, and in consequence comport themselves like wretched pedagogues, passive revolutionaries incapable of any real participation in social struggles.

Yes, there is not the least doubt that the POUM made mistakes before and after 19 July 1936, although they do not correspond to those denounced by Trotsky and the Trotskyists. It was an error, I believe, not to have taken advantage of the reaffiliation of the 'treintista' unions to the CNT, agreed at that organisation's Zaragoza Congress in May 1936 — that is, almost on the eve of the Civil War — in order to attempt to do likewise with the FOUS unions, which were controlled by Poumist militants. In any case, it was necessary to attempt this immediately following 19 July, before compulsory union membership was established and before the CNT made a tacit agreement with the UGT which practically side-lined the FOUS. The precipitate entrance of the FOUS into the UGT only served to give the latter organisation the false impression of its having importance in Catalonia, of which Stalinism soon took advantage. The trade-union policy of the POUM was wrong and the party soon paid cruelly for it.

Neither was it wise, in my opinion, to appoint Andrés Nin as a minister in the Catalan government, since his presence was absolutely necessary in the POUM's Political Secretariat, in the same way that some of the party leaders were sent to the front to command the militiamen. The POUM, a small organisation, could not afford the luxury of having the best of its members distracted by a multitude of tasks. Similarly, the POUM erred in inadequately preparing for clandestinity following the Barcelona May Days of 1937; it let itself be deceived by the truce established by the Stalinists, underestimating their power. Finally, the POUM's original mistake was its intention from the very day of its foundation of being the real communist party, the continuation of the Bolshevik tradition, precisely at a time in which communism had discredited itself and in which the image of Bolshevism merely served to repel the anarcho-syndicalist masses. Trotsky rebuked the POUM for not being a Bolshevik party; its real defect consisted precisely in wanting to be a Bolshevik party. The language it always used in its press and its meetings, an imitation of Leninism, was hardly the best way of gaining a hearing from the CNT workers, as a means of extending the party's influence among the popular masses.

Nevertheless, the main error of the POUM — one shared by all the other organisations, starting with the Trotskyists — was that it judged the Soviet Union and the Communist Party according to criteria which had already been rendered obsolete. The predominant idea was that the Soviet Union continued being a workers' state which could be objectively criticised, but which first of all had to be defended. The POUM shared this false point of view. As a result, it judged the operation of the Communist Party of Spain superficially, and it considered its tactical changes to be mere errors. In reality, the error consisted in believing that the Stalinists were merely making mistakes, when undoubtedly their policy was consistent with that of the new social class that ruled in Moscow. During our war, it was judged that the Communists carried out the policy of the bourgeois republicans, but they were implementing their own policy; it was not the republicans who took advantage and made use of the Communists, but the Communists who took advantage and made use of the republicans.

As Trotsky never commented upon any of the errors of the POUM that we have outlined — with the exception of the last, which he would not have considered a problem as he shared that opinion — he must have considered them indeed paltry. His interest, his passion and his persistent obfuscation fell on other, more superficial and insignificant matters against which he could polemicise, and to which he could dauntlessly apply his schema of the Russian revolution without accepting the smallest modification. It is pertinent to ask if this obstinate intransigence did not ultimately conceal his incapacity to get to the root of the problem, that he himself was a member of the very leadership of the new social class which had arisen within the core of the Soviet state. It is for that reason that his criticism, although at times pertinent, in general did not offer any perspective, sometimes ending up as a fruitless discourse or a dead letter, and at other times transforming themselves into pure abstraction, a truly unworldly fantasy.

Unwilling or unable to look Soviet reality in the face, Trotsky considered that the problem of the communist movement was simply a crisis of leadership; it therefore sufficed merely to dislodge Stalin and his gang in order that international communists and the Soviet Union would revive the positive core of Bolshevism; the revolutionary flag would return to fly once more in the four winds. The problem thus consisted in ousting the bad elements and replacing them by good ones. Pure Manichaeism, inadmissible to those calling themselves Marxists. Jorge Semprún judged Trotsky's work absolutely correctly with these well-aimed lines:

In brief, Marxism does not serve Trotsky in order for him to investigate the concrete content of any new situation, but in order to seek in it the elements which confirm an *a priori* vision, thus confirming the orthodoxy not only of the church but also of its sects and chapels.

Thus, in fact Trotsky and the Trotskyists sought only confirmations, when, that is, they did not lose themselves in byzantine discussions.[23]

It is well known that although Trotsky paid great attention to political events in Spain from 1930 to 1934, he had almost entirely lost interest in them at the point when the revolutionary process in that country greatly intensified. How to explain this anomaly? The answer is simple: the disappearance of the Trotskyist group in Spain resulted in his feeling distanced from events that were either happening or considered likely to happen. Not being conversant in the Spanish language, he also lacked the necessary information that had previously been provided by Nin. So when on 19 July 1936 the Spanish workers launched themselves into a decisive struggle which stirred the whole world, and despite inspiring an international press which devoted much space to what was occurring in Spain, Trotsky himself felt almost alien to these events. He did not experience the Spanish revolution with that feeling of rejoicing with which it was embraced by broad masses around the world. It was the first revolution to take place for several years. Yet because he knew that Trotskyism was playing no part in these events, he did not devote the attention to them that they surely deserved.

In consequence, we are almost tempted to state that if the POUM had not existed, Trotsky would have written very little about the Spanish Revolution and Civil War. What he did write on the subject are merely polemics, dedicated to attacking the policy of the POUM. His isolation, his impotence in the face of the events, made him ever more deaf and blind both to the objections brought to him by his more generous comrades, and to all the lessons that reality presented to him day by day from a world that was in motion, being transformed, and whose centre of gravity was Spain. A foremost actor in the Russian Revolution of 1917, which ended by its devouring him, he possessed that very human tendency — one that is hardly political, and one which condemned him to failure — of wanting to give to it a universal significance, presenting it as a unique model to

---

23. A typical example was the exchange in September 1937, at a time when the POUM faced severe repression, between Trotsky and the North American Trotskyists, concerning whether, if the Spanish Trotskyists had been represented in the parliament, their deputy would have voted for Negrín's war credits [Trotsky, *The Spanish Revolution (1931-39)*, pp 282-89]. Firstly, it was common knowledge that Negrín never put his war credits to a vote of the deputies; secondly, had there actually been a Trotskyist deputy at this juncture, he would not have been in parliament but in prison.

imitate in every place and in any situation. In his time, Karl Marx pointed to the tendency of revolutionaries to imitate the personalities of the revolutions of the past. Trotsky, right to the end, persisted in imitating himself.

WORK IN PROGRESS

Frank Mintz and Michael Peciña's *Los Amigos de Durruti, los trotsquistas y los sucesos de Mayo* (1977) has been made available for download in PDF format at http://www.portaloaca.com/historia/ii-republica-y-guerra-civil/6445-los-amigos-de-durruti-los-trotsquistas-y-los-sucesos-de-mayo-libro.html. The authors and publishers describe this volume as containing the integral texts of the leaflets and manifesto of the Friends of Durruti.

* * *

Wolfgang and Petra Lubitz have with great generosity placed their *Leon Trotsky Bibliography: International Systematic Guide to Works about Trotsky and Trotskyism* on their Trotskyana website. For a number of years this valuable reference work has only been available in printed form. The Lubitzs have foregone sales of the print version of their work, and the movement should be grateful to them for making available a massive collection of bibliographical information that will benefit scholars for many years to come. It can be found at http://www.trotskyana.net/LubitzBibliographies/Trotsky_Bibliography/Leon_Trotsky_Bibliography.html.

* * *

Charles Wesley Ervin's *Tomorrow Is Ours: The Trotskyist Movement in India and Ceylon, 1935-48* is now available as a free download at < http://bookos.org/book/1060829/419598 >.

* * *

The Praxis Centre in Russia has recently published a Russian translation of the POUM veteran Wilebaldo Solano's book *The POUM: Revolution in the Spanish Civil War*. It contains a preface by Dan Gallin, 'The Party of the Last Chance', which has been translated by Ian Birchall and can be found on our website.

* * *

Lawrence and Wishart has recently republished some of its back catalogue in its 'Classics' series. These include:
* Marika Sherwood, *Claudia Jones: A Life in Exile*
* TA Jackson, *Ireland Her Own*

* Noreen Branson, *History of the Communist Party of Great Britain 1927-1941*
* Noreen Branson, *History of the Communist Party of Great Britain 1941-1951*
* John Callaghan, *Cold War, Crisis and Conflict: The CPGB 1951-1968*
* Geoff Andrews, *Endgames and New Times: The Final Years of British Communism 1964-1991*
* John Callaghan, *Rajani Palme Dutt: A Study in British Stalinism*

OBITUARIES

Hector Abaywardena (1919-2012)

Time is inexorably thinning the ranks of the great generation of Trotskyists who created the Lanka Sama Samaja Party (LSSP) of Ceylon/Sri Lanka. The excitable press in Sri Lanka has not been reluctant repeatedly to announce the end of the great generation in recent years. Hector Abaywardena's death is one of the most recent to have come to our attention. (In recent years his name has been rendered as Abhayavardhana in response to changing attitudes to languages. For the sake of consistency I have used Abaywardena throughout, with one exception.)

He was born in January 1919 in an Anglican vicarage in Kandy where his maternal grandfather, Reverend Amarasekera, was Minister. His father Hector Wilfred Abaywardena was the Chief Clerk in Regional Governor Reginald Stubbs' office. His middle-class Govigama Protestant heritage meant that he belonged to a privileged layer of society.

Abaywardena received an exclusive education, in English, at the élite Anglican Public School, St Thomas's College, Mount Lavinia. At the age of 15 he renounced Christianity and became an atheist. In his English class, he along with his fellow matriculation students were posed the following question by their teacher WT Keeble: 'Would you have been better off under your own king?' In responding to this question, Abaywardena began to address the issue of nationalism and his own status under British colonial rule. In 1935, while the LSSP was taking shape, he was still a student at St Thomas's. His views were also influenced by a relative, George Amerasinghe, who was an admirer of Gandhi and the Indian Congress. Through him Abaywardena began to follow events in the *Madras Hindu*, a newspaper he subscribed to for most of his life.

At about this time he also began to purchase publications of Harold Laski's Left Book Club through which he was introduced to critical views prevailing in Europe. These influences together fashioned a sense of nationalism which was strongly internalised and secular, looking to the Indian resistance movement and the Russian Revolution as models.

In 1936 he joined University College, Colombo where he read liberal arts and came under the influence of EFC Ludowyk and Doric de Souza, who introduced him to Marxist ideas. While seeking out the company of dissenters such as ERSR Coomaraswamy at the university, he also launched a discussion group, the Mount Lavinia Literary Society, which had among its guest speakers the Trotskyist Dr Colvin R de Silva and JR Jayewardene (later to be President). Thereafter he attended the Colombo Law College, where the Ceylonese élite were groomed for their places within British-ruled Ceylon. Abaywardena turned his back on this path, rejecting the very foundations of the system that offered position and privilege to aspiring young Ceylonese. He opposed British rule as well as capitalism.

Through the most radical political movement of his day, the LSSP, he threw in his lot with the under-privileged, the exploited and the marginalised. He committed himself to champion the cause of the voiceless, regardless of race, religion or caste. He identified not only with the resistance movement in his own country, but gave his best years in the service of the struggle in India.

His first exposure to radical politics was the Bracegirdle incident, in which the Colonial government sought to deport an Australian labour activist. He attended the mass meeting at Galle Face Green on 5 May 1937, organised by the LSSP, when the fugitive Bracegirdle made a dramatic appearance and a stirring speech before being whisked away into hiding. At the time, Abaywardena's father was the Chief Clerk in the office of Governor Stubbs, who sought the deportation of Bracegirdle and against whom the meeting was directed. Abaywardena was recruited to the LSSP in 1940 by Esmond Wickremesinghe, a leading party activist among university students (subsequently a leading journalist and publisher, and father to a Prime Minister).

Abaywardena became part of the clandestine section of the LSSP that was established to work underground in the event of the party being proscribed. His task was to maintain a safe house for Leslie Goonewardene, who headed the clandestine wing.

In June 1940 the colonial authorities proscribed the LSSP and arrested its leaders Dr NM Perera, Philip Gunawardena, Dr Colvin R de Silva and Edmund Samarakkody. In the wake of the Easter Sunday Japanese air raid in 1942, the imprisoned Sama Samajists escaped from Bogambara Prison, Kandy, and along with Leslie and Vivienne Goonewardene, who had been operating underground, made their way to India. Abaywardena joined them in India and worked with his fellow Sama Samaja exiles until July 1943 when he, Dr NM Perera and Philip Goonewardene were arrested in Bombay and deported to Colombo.

Released on bail, he disguised himself as an Anglican clergyman and took a ride on an RAF plane to Bangalore. He made his way to Baroda where he worked with a group of anti-British agitators who kept him under cover in a slum. Here, he contracted smallpox which nearly killed him. After he recovered, he went north to Calcutta from where most of the Sama Samajists operated until the end of the war.

He was among four Sama Samajists who remained in India after the war. He engaged in both party work and political journalism all over India. After some time in Bombay working on the fortnightly *New Spark*, he moved first to Madras where he became General Secretary of the Socialist Party which came out of the 1948 merger of the Bolshevik-Leninist Party of India, Ceylon and Burma (BLPI) and the Congress Socialist Party.

Then on to New Delhi, where he was editor of the *Socialist Appeal* and contributor to the *Hindustan Standard*. Later at the request of Ram Manohar Lohi (an important socialist leader of the Quit India movement), he spent two years in Hyderabad editing *Mankind*, separating himself from the Trotskyists. Next back to Delhi, where he began the critical journal *Maral*, named after the mythical Indian bird that was able to sift the milk from an admixture of water and milk. Each issue of *Maral* dealt with a different political theme, national or international. This practical internationalist work was recognised in August 1992 on the fiftieth anniversary of the Quit India movement; Abaywardena, Vivienne Goonewardene and Bernard Soysa were guests of honour in New Delhi.

In 1959 he married Kusala Fernando, a rich widow, and returned to Ceylon to begin a new chapter in his personal and political life, rejoining the LSSP and becoming its leading theoretician. This was a period of political ferment. Both the Sri Lanka Freedom Party (SLFP) and the United National Party seemed to be discredited and in decline. The LSSP entered the March 1960 General Election confident of being returned to power. Abaywardena is credited with formulating the classification of the SLFP as a 'weak petty-bourgeois party' and not a bourgeois party, which, once adopted by the LSSP, was the ideological and theoretical foundation of the Coalition with the SLFP in 1964, and for much of the coalition-seeking of the LSSP in subsequent years. It was a form of words that allowed the Trotskyists to overcome their innate objection to participation in a Popular Front. He also sought to convince the LSSP of the non-viability of pursuing a dual strategy that combined parliamentary work with revolution. After this, he promoted an alliance with the SLFP and the Communist Party, which finally emerged with the signing of the Common Programme of the United Front in 1968.

He considered that the LSSP had come to a fork in the political road. It could not continue indefinitely to operate simultaneously on both the parliamentary and revolutionary planes. Given the weakness of the working class, the party had to rethink its strategy. Hector had concluded that despite the LSSP having taken principled stands on all major issues, despite unequivocally championing every worthwhile cause, its inability to secure power stemmed from a long history of fragmentation and emasculation of the working class. This started in 1938 when Nehru visited Ceylon to report on the status of the plantation workers of Indian origin. The LSSP pleaded with Nehru against the formation of a communal organisation for them, fearing it would open the door for these workers becoming pawns in racial politics. They were prophetic: with the formation in 1939 of the Ceylon Indian Congress, the forerunner of the Ceylon Workers Congress, the stage was set for not only the injection of communalism into working-class politics, but also the cynical disenfranchisement of the workers of Indian origin in order to weaken the left-wing movement.

'It is alleged', wrote Abaywardena, 'that the presence of the Indian plantation workers on the electoral lists enabled them to return candidates of Indian descent to seven parliamentary seats and influence the verdict in another 20 parliamentary constituencies, such that left-minded opponents of the UNP were returned at the 1947 election.' The subsequent fragmentation of Sri Lankan politics along communal lines would proceed over the next half century. 'By expelling the Indians the UNP hoped to ensure its majority', explained Abaywardena: 'Bandaranaike saw no reason why he should not collect his votes by advancing the interests of the Sinhalese majority community of the country. Chelvannayakam saw the necessity of constitutional reforms to ensure that the interests of the Tamils were protected. All of them would be benefited by spreading communal attitudes for the purpose of collecting votes.'

The plantation workers comprised half of all organised labour in the country. By limiting them to trade-union activities and denying them a stake in mainstream politics, Sri Lanka's working class was mortally weakened and divided. Unlike the plantation workers, who were confined to their work environment and solely dependent for their livelihood on the sale of their labour, the urban worker was socially less homogenous. Many of them did not live in the towns but commuted from villages where they still had interests in small plots of agricultural land. Not only were they less dependent on the sale of their labour, but within rural society they could aspire to middle-class ambitions and status as small property owners.

Given the limited size of the urban working class, and given the weaknesses arising out of their social ambiguity, the doctrinaire policy of the left of seeking to advance reforms through a party of politically-conscious urban workers was in effect doomed. According to Abaywardena, the left failed because it 'persisted with the strategic line of mobilising the rural poor through a party based on the working class'. In effect his analysis was to overturn the theory of Permanent Revolution, concluding that the working class was incapable of the leadership role Trotsky's theory allotted to it. As Sri Lanka went through the tumultuous 1960s, Abaywardena realised the need to forge a united front with other progressive political forces in order to bring about changes that would improve the economic and political position of the weaker sections of society. Given the weak state of the economy, this required a major role on the part of the government, which needed to engage in the economy in order to deliver benefits to the people.

During the years the United Front was in opposition, Abaywardena launched the Socialist Study Circle where its future leaders were intellectually and politically groomed. It served as a forum for the development of the ideas behind the far-reaching political and economic reforms that would be introduced after 1970.

During the early 1970s, he also brought out and edited the English-language political weekly *The Nation*, to encourage discussion on current events. This publication involved a group of new younger figures in the LSSP: Jayantha Somasunderam, Ajith Samaranayake, Rajan Philips and Kumar David. When the United Front was in office during 1970-75, he served as Chairman of the Peoples' Bank, under NM Perera as Finance Minister, attempting to make available the finance that small enterprises needed for commerce, agriculture and industry. During this period the People's Bank launched its monthly journal *The Economic Review*.

The expulsion of the left from the Coalition by Mrs Bandaranaike and the exacerbation of the conflict between the LSSP leadership and the leftist Vama Samasamaja faction drew the curtain on *The Nation* and this phase.

After the front broke up in 1975, he founded the *Socialist Nation*. He also served on the Educational Bureau of the LSSP and was a long-standing member of the Politburo.

In 1999 some of his younger supporters — Paul Caspersz, Marshal Fernando, Silan Kadirgamar, Rajan Philips and Kumar David — organised the Hector Abhayavardhana felicitation symposium to celebrate his eightieth birthday. The proceedings came out as a book published by the Ecumenical Institute. In 2001 the Social Scientists Association published a collection of his speeches.

He died on 22 September 2012.
Corula Star

* * *

Ahmed Ben Bella (1918[1]-2012)

Ben Bella was one of the last survivors of the generation of Third World leaders so much admired by the left in the 1960s.[2] Ben Bella was born the son of a poor

1. Not 1916, as stated in some obituaries.
2. For the broader context of Ben Bella's life, see *Revolutionary History*, Volume 10, no 4, and Martin Evans, *Algeria: France's Undeclared War* (Oxford, 2012). The only biography

peasant in Marnia near Oran. But in one respect he was privileged — he went to school. At a time when 90 per cent of the Muslim population of Algeria were illiterate in French, he had secondary education. He could read, write and speak French — indeed, later when he was in Egypt he had to communicate in French because his Algerian dialect was unintelligible there. At school he also encountered the French regime's 'civilising mission' when a teacher launched a diatribe against Islam in the course of a lesson.

The French were quite happy to use Muslim soldiers to defend the French Empire. Ben Bella's eldest brother died fighting in the First World War, and his three other brothers died directly or indirectly as a consequence of the Second World War. Ben Bella served in the French army, fighting in Italy, notably at Monte Cassino, and was awarded the prestigious *médaille militaire*, which he received from de Gaulle personally. He could have remained in the French army and made a successful career there. But the massive repression of the Sétif rising in 1945 made him determined to devote all his energies to the pursuit of Algerian independence.

He became active in the MTLD (Movement for the Triumph of Democratic Freedoms) led by Messali Hadj. Municipal councils in Algeria were divided on racial lines: two-thirds of the councillors came from the settler minority, and one-third from the Muslim majority. Ben Bella became a councillor in Marnia and had responsibility for rationing and food supplies. But he was impatient with what he saw as Messali's excessive respect for constitutional action. He moved to clandestine work, becoming involved in the *Organisation spéciale*, the underground military wing of the MTLD. In 1950 he was jailed for his part in planning a hold-up of the Oran post office. He escaped and moved to Cairo, where he was a leader of what was to become the FLN (National Liberation Front), which launched the insurrection in November 1954.

In 1956, on the eve of the Suez invasion, a plane carrying Ben Bella and four other FLN leaders was diverted by the French and the five leaders were imprisoned. This was a totally illegal act, organised by the French air force without the knowledge of the Prime Minster, Guy Mollet — who was happy to accept the consequences. The French regime may have thought the rebellion had been beheaded — if so they understood nothing of the dynamics of a popular movement. The arrests also sabotaged some tentative peace talks in which Ben Bella had been involved — this undoubtedly pleased the more right-wing elements in the armed forces. The war in Algeria continued — though Ben Bella did not always agree with the strategy pursued, considering that launching urban guerrilla warfare in Algiers was a costly mistake.

is Robert Merle, *Ben Bella* (London, 1967), based on taped interviews. Omar Carlier is writing a full biography.

For over five years the Algerian leaders remained in prison. In the summer of 1961, when de Gaulle was preparing to relinquish Algeria and a far-right opposition was active in the army and among the settlers, the FLN were concerned that a right-wing takeover in France could lead to the summary execution of the FLN leaders — something already widely practised against rank-and-file activists. They approached activists linked to the *Voie communiste* — which had achieved some successful jail-breaks — and asked them to develop a plan to enable the FLN leaders to escape. The *Voie communiste* activists got support from local Communists who disagreed with their party's policy of refusing practical support to the FLN and developed two escape plans — one using underground tunnels from the cellars of the *château* where the prisoners were held, the other requiring cars with capacious boots in which the leaders could be concealed. But Ben Bella seems to have been unenthusiastic about the plans; perhaps as a result of his indiscretions additional riot police were brought in, meaning that no escape would have been possible without a shoot-out. They remained in jail till released in March 1962 at the time of the Évian agreements. Denis Berger, a leading *Voie communiste* activist, later said: 'Ben Bella was not that keen on escaping. His image as a statesman could have been damaged. And his image as a martyr.'[3]

By the time the FLN came to power it was deeply divided, by politics and personal ambition. As a result of an alliance with army leader Boumediène, Ben Bella became President in the autumn of 1962. A courageous and competent military organiser, he had little to prepare him for the totally fresh task of running a newly independent country. (The Bolsheviks in 1917 also faced totally unforeseen circumstances, but at least they had spent much time over two decades discussing the transition to socialism, even if often misguidedly.)

This was the golden age of the 'Third World'. Alongside Nasser, Castro and Nkrumah, Ben Bella became a hero to the European left, frustrated at the 'apathy' of their domestic working classes during the long postwar boom, and hopeful of finding an alternative road to socialism more attractive than those offered by Moscow and Beijing.

For some on the far left, Algeria was to be understood in terms of the theory of 'Permanent Revolution'. Trotsky's scenario, in which the working class took on the tasks of the bourgeois revolution and moved forward to socialism, had fitted Russia in 1917, where there was a well-organised and politically coherent working class. But permanent revolution was a theory of the possible, not of the inevitable. The Algerian working class was in no position to emulate its Russian counterparts. In fact the best organised and most politically developed

---

3. Quoted H Hamon and P Rotman, *Les Porteurs de valises* (Paris, 1979), p 362.

section of the Algerian working class was not in Algeria, but in the factories of mainland France. It had lost many of its best cadres in the fratricidal war between the FLN and Messali's Mouvement National Algérien. The tortuous history of the Algerian Communist Party disqualified it from playing any significant independent role.

And so, as in China, Cuba, Egypt and many other Third World countries liberated from colonialism (though concrete details varied considerably), the vacuum left by an absent working class had to be filled, and it was filled effectively by what could be called the intelligentsia — an educated layer who aspired to staff the state machine.[4]

Certainly there was much that seemed attractive about Ben Bella's rule. On taking office he declared that the new state was on the road to socialism. What exactly he meant by this was unclear. Probably the Russian model of state planning, with its recent triumphs in satellite technology, seemed to offer an example for a developing country, though Ben Bella was keen to develop small-scale enterprise rather than encourage heavy industry. He showed an appealing disdain for the niceties of diplomatic behaviour. On visiting the USA to attend the United Nations, he conspicuously refused to shake the hand of the South Vietnamese representative and caused consternation among the Americans by flying off to Cuba.

Because of his inexperience, Ben Bella surrounded himself with 'advisers', some of whom came from the revolutionary left. These included Michel Raptis (Pablo), formerly Secretary of the Fourth International, and Mohammed Harbi, one of the few FLN activists to have a solid knowledge of Marxism (he had been taught at school by Pierre Souyri, later to be a leading figure in *Socialisme ou barbarie*). Daniel Guérin, the French Marxist-anarchist writer, spent a month travelling in Algeria in November 1963, and submitted a report to Ben Bella personally.

Yet this influence should not be overstated. Ben Bella was erratic in the way he took advice; according to Harbi he tended to echo the last person he had spoken to.[5] And the influence of the far left waned quite quickly. According to Guérin, Pablo was considering packing his bags by March 1964, and later that year Guérin advised him not to return to Algeria after a trip abroad.[6] (To his credit, Pablo stayed to the bitter end; when Ben Bella was overthrown, he had to evade arrest and flee the country; some of his associates were imprisoned and

---

4. This analysis is based on Tony Cliff's article 'Deflected Permanent Revolution', http://www.marxists.org/archive/cliff/works/1963/xx/permrev.htm.
5. Cited by Omar Carlier, 'Ben Bella, L'homme, le mythe, l'histoire', *Jeune Afrique*, 22-28 April 2012.
6. D Guérin, *Ci-gît le colonialisme* (Paris and the Hague, 1973), pp 173, 384.

even tortured.)

The most original feature of Ben Bella's brief period in power was *autogestion* (a French term meaning 'self-management', sometimes, misleadingly, translated as 'workers' control'.) This arose from the chaotic circumstances of independence. In 1962, faced with an imminent handover to the FLN and the scorched earth tactics of the far right, 900 000 settlers (out of a total of a million) simply fled the country. Land and workplaces were abandoned; quite spontaneously workers and peasants took them over and ran them for themselves.

The government accepted the reality of *autogestion* and tried to regularise it. But the official decrees on *autogestion* fell far short of authentic workers' control. Seasonal workers — a large proportion of the Algerian labour force — were not represented, and the workers' councils coexisted with state-appointed directors. From 1963, Ben Bella's government transformed the trade-union movement into a wing of state power. Monique Laks, who later wrote a study of the Algerian experience, concluded that *autogestion* could not exist until the productive forces had been considerably developed.[7]

Some of the most acute comments on Ben Bella's rule came from Daniel Guérin, who was initially enthusiastic about the new regime. He described the first flowering of *autogestion* as a 'mongrel mixture of authoritarian conservatism and libertarian socialism'. But he also noted the 'authoritarian and arbitrary intrusion of the governmental bureaucracy stifling initiative from below'. When Ben Bella's rule came to an end, Guérin analysed his fall:

> He had thought it was clever to play a balancing game between his left and his right, which in the end benefitted only the right. Like Robespierre on the eve of 9 Thermidor, he had himself sawn off the branch on which he was dangerously perched. When the moment of truth came, the left, which was the only force that could have protected him against the machinations of the right, no longer had enough confidence in him to try to save him.[8]

The epitaph on Ben Bella's three years in power was the dog that did not bark — the absence of any significant opposition to the *coup* mounted by Boumediène in June 1965. The Algerian people were war-weary and tired of disputes between their leaders; but it seems clear that if workers had felt that the *coup* was stripping them of significant power, they would have shown rather more resistance. (A friend of mine was in a hairdresser's in Algiers on the day Boumediène took power. The barber, making conversation, mentioned in

7. M Laks, *Autogestion ouvrière et pouvoir politique en Algérie (1962-1965)* (Paris, 1970).
8. Guérin, *Ci-gît le colonialisme*, pp 346, 170, 175.

passing that there had been a *coup*.)

For Ben Bella it was back to jail. Boumediène kept him there more than twice as long as the French had held him. In 1980 he was released and went to France. But he remained unbroken. He now launched a new movement, the MDA (Movement for Democracy in Algeria), and returned to Algeria in 1990. He had now abandoned socialism (in terms of the Russian model), and instead stressed Islam: 'In my opinion, if socialism has failed, it is because it despised man and degraded him. As for Islam, it can organise society and establish equality between men.'[9]

But, as his biographer Omar Carlier points out, he needed the FIS (Islamic Salvation Front), but they didn't need him. He made little impact on the elections; for many in Algeria's youthful population, he already seemed a figure from the remote past. Now he devoted more time to his family (he and his wife had adopted three children, including a handicapped boy). But he had not deserted his principles. He reappeared in the anti-capitalist movement that blossomed at the turn of the century. He spoke at the European Social Forum held in London in 2004, saying: 'The fight then was for the liberation of Algeria from the French. Now it is for the liberation of the world from globalisation.'[10]

When he died in April 2012 he was buried alongside his old comrade and enemy Boumediène. Throughout his long life he had been a tireless fighter against imperialism. Whether he was ever a socialist is another question.

Ian Birchall

* * *

Bob Gould (1937-2011)

Bob Gould's revolutionary politics were based in his family background, from which he drew on his father's self-definition as a Marxist catholic. He had deep roots in the history of the labour movement and the workers of Irish origin. Father Steve, who lost an arm fighting in the First World War, was a supporter of the tempestuous JT 'Jack' Lang. His maternal grandfather had run as an anti-conscription candidate in the election of 1917. Bob was to call himself a catholic Marxist, and considered some of the high points of labour history happened when the political left found it possible to ally with the catholic forces — particularly the defeat of the Labor Party's conscription legislation in 1917-18.

He joined the Labor Party aged 17, migrating later into the Communist Party, and from there into the Trotskyist grouping led by the veteran Nick Origlass. This loose grouping lacked political dynamism, though Origlass' work within the Labor Party had some successes. In the first great crisis of the Fourth

9. A Ben Bella, *Ben Bella... Revient* (Paris, 1982), p 201.
10. *Socialist Worker*, 16 October 2004.

International Gould supported the positions of Michel Pablo at first, only later moving over towards an 'orthodox' position.

Gould's great political flowering came with the establishment of the 1965 Vietnam Action Campaign, of which he was the initiator and driving force. He organised the first street demonstrations against the war, on Friday evenings, and insisted that the main slogan had to be the immediate withdrawal of the troops, as against vague calls for peace talks or stop the bombing, which implied that US imperialism could have a role in determining the future of Vietnam. A culture of direct action on the streets flourished within the campaign and sharpened its political aims. He was arrested many times in the course of the anti-war campaign.

He became a leader of the 1960s 'counterculture', founding in 1967 the Third World Bookshop on Goulburn Street, importing records and books from the USA, and nurturing the independent filmmakers co-op that revitalised the Australian film industry. The bookshop had a series of conflicts with the censorship, over authors and artists such as Phillip Roth and Aubrey Beardsley and even, preposterously, Michelangelo's David. He put theory into practice setting up a collective household.

It was no idyllic life for Gould in the 1960s, however. He was one of the three people who pursued and restrained the man who tried to kill the Labor leader, Arthur Calwell, after an anti-conscription rally at Mosman Town Hall in 1966.

Also in 1967 he allied himself with the Percy brothers, Jim and John, to found the new socialist youth movement — initially called SCREW — Society for the Cultivation of Rebellion Everywhere – but soon adopting the name Resistance, which they regarded as a new start for Trotskyism in Australia, separate from the long tradition of the Origlass group. In 1969, Barry Shepherd of the US Socialist Workers Party visited Australia and won over the Percys, which led to a split in Resistance, the lines being led by the Percys on one side, and Gould on the other. The Percys followed the SWP along its Castroite trajectory. Gould conducted his activity within the Labor Party (apart from participation in the short-lived International Marxist League), and became an important advisor to trade unions in strikes and campaigns. One of the campaigns that he was most proud to be associated with was the campaign run by the rank and file in the wharf workers' union to save their building from being sold for a song to redevelopers, saving union members millions of dollars. He was also proud to be associated with the campaign run by the Nurses Association in the 1980s in opposition to the cuts to mental health funding. This was a campaign that the union ran among its members and took to the floor of the New South Wales ALP State Conference, achieving significant changes to the original proposals with a significantly better funding base than first proposed.

Late in his career he became prolific as a writer for the website he helped set up — OzLeft. He contributed numerous articles on the history of the labour movement in Australia, and other related topics. These can be found at http://members.optushome.com.au/spainter/Bobgould.html, and a Bob Gould archive section is being set up on the Marxists Internet Archive.

He became active in campaigns against the increasingly unpleasant anti-refugee policies of successive Australian governments, and was a founder of Labor for Refugees. His bookshop flourished and became one of the most noted second-hand book venues in Australia. It was while sorting books that he fell and sustained fatal injuries.

Corula Star

* * *

Ian David Kitson (1919-2010)

David Kitson's betrayal by the movement to which he gave his life is a miniature of the betrayal of the South African working class by the movement that held on to its leadership for decades, and which is only now, with the Manikana massacre, demonstrating its true nature to the world.

David Kitson was born in Cape Town on 25 August 1919. He qualified as a mechanical engineer at Howard College, Durban (now KwaZulu-Natal university), graduating in 1942. A period of military service with the South African forces provided him with technical skills, including the handling of explosives.

After the Second World War he moved to London, where his father had been born, and worked as a draughtsman for the De Havilland aeronautical engineering company. He worked, among other projects, on the landing gear for the famous Comet aircraft. He quickly became active in the TASS (Technical, Administrative and Supervisory Section) trade union, and as the Secretary of the Hornsey (North London) branch of the Communist Party of Great Britain. TASS funded him to study for two years at Ruskin College, Oxford. Then he found employment with the British Oxygen Company. He was offered promotion conditional upon abandoning political and trade-union activity — an offer he refused and which led to his sacking.

In London he married Norma Cranko, a Jewish South African Communist. In 1959, with their son Steven, they travelled to South Africa. The Sharpeville massacre, in which 69 unarmed demonstrators were killed, put an end to any thoughts of returning to Britain, and both of them put their energies into the work of the South African Communist Party (SACP), which together with the African National Congress (ANC) was operating underground. Kitson trained militants of the ANC's armed force Umkhonto we Sizwe (MK) — Spear of the

Nation — in the use of explosives for their sabotage campaign at the end of 1961.

The first High Command of MK was dismantled by the Rivonia arrests in 1963. Kitson and others were drafted into the second High Command. In the fierce repression of the times he was arrested in somewhat less than six months. He was interrogated but not tortured. He was sentenced to 20 years without remission, and held with other white political prisoners in Pretoria prisons. Norma had also been arrested, but was released after three weeks.

It took three years of campaigning before he and his comrades were permitted to undertake study. He took two degrees and had begun studying Russian when the prison authorities put a stop to it. He was considered a hard-liner among his fellow prisoners, many of whom were politically inexperienced students recruited straight into sabotage work. With his agreement, Norma divorced him and returned to Britain where she married again. In 1979 he was moved to death row, though not under sentence of death, as part of the collective punishment for an escape. The UK Foreign Office failed to intervene on his behalf, despite evidence of its serious impact on his health.

His son Steven was arrested while in South Africa to visit him in 1981. Norma organised a campaign in London aimed at embarrassing the South African government, and Steven was released. Clearly, a London-based campaign could serve to support and improve the conditions for political prisoners in South Africa. With supporters from the City Anti-Apartheid (CAA) group Norma organised the first continuous picket of the South African embassy in Trafalgar Square, with the slogan 'Free all South African political prisoners; Save David Kitson's life'. Almost immediately this caused problems with the ANC and the main body of the Anti-Apartheid Movement (AAM). The ANC would only tolerate a specific personal campaign for David Kitson, while the AAM would only support a campaign for all the political prisoners. The ANC circulated letters to their friends and supporters in Parliament and the unions, calling on them not to support the continuous picket.

Despite this the picket went ahead, and began developing the style and activity that characterised their work later — with continuous singing and visually attractive literature that began to recruit support from youthful passers-by. In November 1982, after 86 days of the picket, David Kitson and other prisoners were removed from death row. The CAA voted by a small majority to end the picket, but continued its campaigning work. (Several articles have erroneously reported that the picket continued until the release of Mandela in 1990; in fact it was resumed in 1986. The Revolutionary Communist Group became influential within CAA during this period, with its propaganda publication *Fight Racism! Fight Imperialism!*.)

On his release in 1984, David Kitson left South Africa to join Norma (who divorced her second husband amicably and remarried David), Steven and daughter Amandhla, in London. He had been adopted by the AAM as its 'Political Prisoner of the Year' and was expected to address the movement's Annual General Meeting. SACP General Secretary Joe Slovo instructed him to use his speech to denounce Norma, her supporters and her campaigning methods. At the AGM several leaders of SACP and AAM refused to applaud his speech. The Kitsons were expelled from the SACP and the AAM. The CAA was expelled from the AAM. TASS withdrew its promise of funding an emeritus professorship at Ruskin College. A key figure in all this was Solly Smith of the London ANC, who was subsequently exposed as being in the pay of South African military intelligence.

Norma's insistence on organising her own campaign in the face of the disapproval of the ANC, SACP and AAM undoubtedly contributed to the harshness of the Kitson's treatment. It has also been speculated that Slovo saw David Kitson as a rival to his position as the most prominent white member of SACP, and one with a more heroic record (Slovo left South Africa in 1963). The journalist RW Johnson has suggested a deeper reason. In his view there was an agreement between the ANC-SACP and MI5 such that they would be allowed to function in exile in England subject to strict limits, one of which was that there should be no demonstrations against apartheid. Norma's methods of campaigning would have put that agreement at risk. The ANC-SACP remembered how Peter Hain's 'Stop The 70 Tour' campaign outran all their attempts to contain it, and would not have wanted to see a campaign on that scale led by somebody associated with their movement.

Believing they would be unable to make any contribution to post-Apartheid South Africa under the ANC-SACP regime, the Kitsons went to live in Zimbabwe, where Norma continued to campaign with letters to the press about white racism. They were eventually readmitted into the ANC after interventions by Mandela and Sisulu, but David never received the recognition his heroism merited. Neither of them was invited to Mandela's inauguration. Norma died in 2002, after which David returned to South Africa and died in Johannesburg on 9 November 2010.

Even after his death, and an extensive account of his betrayal in Paul Trewhela's book *Inside Quatro*, efforts continue to marginalise his memory. The South African History Online website makes no mention of the Kitson's treatment by the ANC and the SACP. Graham Stevenson's website compendium of Communist biographies, which describes itself as an 'encyclopaedia', carries a précis of Denis Herbstein's *Guardian* obituary with an inserted section of his own describing the CAA as 'a range of exotic political animals'. Elsewhere in the post-colonial world he is beginning to be recognised, and *The Zimbabwean*

carried extensive extracts from Paul Trewhela's book.
Bridget St Ruth

***

George Leslie (1918-2012)[11]

At a funeral, often we learn about aspects of the lives of our friends that we were unaware of during their lives. I am going to speak on behalf of the Editorial Board of the journal *Revolutionary History*. Several members of the Board are here today. George was a founder member of our journal and was one of the longest-serving members of the Editorial Board. Probably there are many of you here today who don't know about this aspect of George's life so I should say a little by way of explanation. *Revolutionary History* researches and publishes material about socialist and communist movements of workers, their occasional successes, their more frequent defeats. Our motto is: 'Those who do not learn from history are doomed to repeat it.' Our aim is to help the activists in the working class to learn from history, and if possible, hopefully, not to be doomed to repeat it. We are Marxists, and most of us trace our personal and political histories to the trend within Marxism called Trotskyism, to the influence of the man we think spent his life as one of the most important thinkers and leaders of independent working-class politics. We are proud of the labels Marxist and Trotskyist, and equally we are proud of our political and intellectual independence. Whatever our individual affiliations, collectively we owe nothing to any other organisation. George was very much one of us. He was our comrade.

So I cannot talk about George's life as seen from our viewpoint without mentioning people and events that have been of great importance in our movement but are little known outside it. I will try as briefly as I can to make these things clear as I go through, and to show how they were eventually linked to great events.

Over the course of nearly 25 years of diligent work we have established a reputation for high quality of research. The academics give us grudging respect, but use our material regularly. We have relationships with groups doing the same kind of work in several parts of the world. George has been an important part of our team through the whole period of our collective life. He provided Al Richardson and Sam Bornstein, the authors of three books on the history of Trotskyism in Britain, with many insights and contacts. And, very valuably, he was the Chair of our Editorial Board meetings. He kept our meetings in order and ensured we got the business done efficiently. He had many years'

---

11. This is the text of an oration by John Plant at the funeral of our comrade on the Editorial Board, George Leslie, at the Islington Crematorium on 29 June 2012.

experience in the trade-union movement and he knew just how to balance democratic freedom of discussion with effective conduct of decision making. Before each meeting was finished and we adjourned to the bar, George would take a collection for the cost of the room, in the traditional manner of the working class by going round the room with his cap, paying for the room and booking it for the next meeting.

George was born in Islington on 15 June 1918. His name was George Richard Leslie Tiley, but because of difficult circumstances later in life he chose to be known by the surname Leslie.[12] The circumstances in which he grew up were very tough. His father suffered what was then called 'shell-shock' during military service in the First World War, what is these days called post-traumatic stress disorder. This meant he was to all intents and purposes unemployable. He became involved in the National Unemployed Workers' Movement, a very forceful and active organisation, to a large degree inspired by the Communist Party. With them he became involved in marches and demonstrations for the rights of the economic victims of the war and the failures of the capitalist system. George's earliest political experiences, as far as we know now, were accompanying his dad on the May Day marches, which in the 1920s and 1930s were immense shows of strength and determination on the part of the workers, when red flags and trade-union banners dominated the central London scene.

George was the only boy among six children. Because the family of an unemployed man could only afford a two-room flat, George spent much of his childhood sleeping in neighbour's houses, as there was no way one boy and five girls could be accommodated. Childhood in these hard conditions made him vulnerable to asthma and eczema and the various sicknesses of poverty. It is a credit to his toughness that he reached 93 after living through those hard decades. It is no surprise that he was to devote so much time later in life to defending the welfare state and the rights of pensioners.

George's education was limited to what was available at elementary schools in Islington up to the age of 14. His dad had had more education, and would often write letters for his neighbours, but in the hard conditions he grew up in, George had to find work at weekends and after school to help the family survive. This lack of formal education was an obstacle that George was aware of throughout his life. He gravitated to the great market area around Caledonian Road. Sheila tells me that he knew and was friends with several of the leading characters featured in the recent TV documentary on the Caledonian Road. One of his first full-time jobs after leaving school was delivering vegetables around the Somers Town area. While working around the market he obtained

---

12. We are now permitted to reveal that George found life in the army unbearable and went underground for a period.

some knowledge of antiques, a field he came to love, and was occasionally able to work in.

His first experience as a militant worker in his own right was during a national strike of market workers in the late 1940s. He showed himself capable and determined as an organiser and quickly became a member of the national strike committee. That was the beginning of a life-long relationship with the Transport and General Workers Union. He joined the permanent staff of the union in its Region 1, and supported its members in a series of jobs — paying out strike benefits, organising legal advice, supporting them in claims for state benefits and so on. It was there he met Sheila, who was already working for the T&G, and they were to be married and have four children — Georgina, Adelaide, Mark and Esther. Sheila was always willing to help George with the secretarial and administrative aspects of his work for which he felt his education had not fitted him.

George and Sheila joined the Revolutionary Communist Party, which was an attempt, sponsored by the Fourth International leadership, to unify the various combative Trotskyist groups in Britain, formed in 1944. Almost from its birth the RCP was stressed by disagreements, some of political principle, some about personalities in the leadership. Like most of the membership, George seriously wanted the RCP to work. Unlike some of the leading figures, he did not want to split the group on the basis of unnecessary differences. He was one of a small group that supported the theory of the American Max Shachtman, who described the Soviet Union not as a degenerated workers' state but as bureaucratic collectivism. George's friend Bert Atkinson was in effect the leader of this group. The other members were Charlie Sargeant (also a market worker) and Arthur Farragher.

But if George and Bert were willing to subject their own thoughts to the needs of the group, there were enough of the leadership who were willing to tear it apart. One of the central arguments was whether the Trotskyists should immerse themselves in the Labour Party. Many, many thousands of words have been devoted to the argument, at the time and subsequently. George and Sheila were among those who formed the Open Party Faction, not rejecting the idea of working in the Labour Party but insisting the Trotskyists themselves were not in a position at that time to achieve their objectives in the Labour Party. The RCP tore itself apart, with the resulting fragments laying the basis for the complicated pattern of Trotskyist groups that occupied the scene for six decades. The biggest share of the wreckage was grabbed by Gerry Healy, later to be the leader of the Workers Revolutionary Party. His purge of the RCP drove out many of the best members, including the founders of the groups that later became the Militant Tendency and the Socialist Workers Party — Ted Grant and Tony Cliff.

George gravitated towards Ted Grant's group, which had set up an office in Kings Cross, despite his political and personal criticisms of Grant's conduct during the crisis of the RCP. Later in fact Grant was to acknowledge that he should have supported the Open Party Faction, but at the crucial time he had not. George's experience in the trade-union movement was a valuable asset to the Grant group, and despite his worries about his education, he became a member of the group's Editorial Board. He never wrote articles, but he had a strong sense of the key issues that needed to be dealt with in each issue of the group's journal. Because he lived in Islington, near the group's centre, comrades from out of London would often stay overnight before or after meetings. One of these was Jimmy Deane, the leader of a group of Grant's supporters in Liverpool, out of which eventually was to grow the powerful Militant group that was able to lead the revolt of Liverpool Council.

George drifted away from Grant's group, and at present we don't know the reasons for that. Although he remained on friendly terms with many of them, he was still sufficiently motivated to attend the book launch for Grant's memoirs and raise all over again the story of the Open Party Faction, and Grant's failure to support it.

So from the 1960s George was not associated with any of the Trotskyist groups. Tony Cliff attempted to recruit him, without success. George focussed his energies on the work of the Transport and General Workers Union, and represented the union's own staff on the Hackney Trades Council. On one occasion he led a strike against the union by its own staff. The General Secretary of the T&G, Jack Jones, noticed how former members were living longer as a result of the welfare state, and developed the idea of a retired members' section of the union. He asked George to organise it. George hesitated in the face of such a major administrative task, but with the assurance of Sheila's support he took it on, building a large and effective organisation. He eventually became the secretary of the retired members' organisation for Region 1 of the T&G.

On his own retirement from work he found a whole new area of activity among pensioners, and was active in many campaigns and groups. His opinion was still valued by the union, and he was an observer and adviser on a number of its committees. He became a member of the National Executive of the National Pensioners Convention.

This cemetery can be called George's family plot. His parents and sisters had their ashes scattered here. It is proper and fitting for him to rest here in North London after a life so much involved with the struggles of the people of the area. Comrade George, on behalf of your friends and comrades in *Revolutionary History*, go well.

JJ Plant

***

Terry Liddle (1948-2012)
— Atheist, Republican, Socialist, Member X369799 IWW

Comrades, a great revolutionary libertarian socialist is no more. He was always full of hope, full of life.

I last met Terry in August last year in the *Great Harry*, a Wetherspoon's pub in Woolwich, we reminisced over past times, long-gone socialist groups and pubs now no more.

Although Terry was born and was brought up in Plumstead, for all his political life, until his mother died in the 1980s, he lived in his mother's council house at 83 Gregory Crescent, Middle Park Estate in Eltham. He was schooled at Bloomfield, a Secondary Modern school in Plumstead which had pretensions to be something it was not, and educated by the London socialist movement of all types and hues and by thousands of books and pamphlets.

I first met Terry when he turned up at my Stalinist parents' house for a Woolwich Young Communist League meeting. We were both 15-year-old schoolboys at the time. Shortly after this he went on public speaking lessons led by Joe Bent, an old Stalinist who had a Communist Party speaking-pitch in the East Lane market, Southwark. Terry said that Joe opened his meeting with these words: 'Morning! I am Bent.' It drew a crowd at least.

Terry quickly broke with Stalinism and joined the Healyites of the Socialist Labour League, but argued against their 'Stalinist' methods. He left the League and had to, so he said, leave his mother's council house in Eltham for a room in south-west London for a few months. This experience led Terry to abandon Leninism as well as Stalinism and to start researching the pre-First World War socialist and libertarian movement. But Terry still had Trotskyist drinking companions and Maoist friends like Mike Baker and Maureen Scott. Indeed he married a Stalinist.

At the Woolwich Marxist Discussion Group which met sometime in the mid-1960s two older socialists walked into the room of dissident young communists and assorted Woolwich young lefties. One of them was Bill, who was then known as Bill Turner, a middle-aged man in his early 40s, and an older man called Archie Armstrong. Both became Terry's drinking partners. Their favourite tipple was not beer but cider, or rather scrumpy, which was still sold in Woolwich pubs. Bill became his lifelong friend and political companion in several campaigns and bitter faction fights. Terry used to drink with Archie in the *Village Blacksmith* in the 1970s.

In 1967 the North-West Kent Vietnam Solidarity Campaign was formed composed of dissident Bexley YCLers and assorted Woolwich socialists, and of course Terry was an active member. It used to meet in Will Fancy's house.

From 1968 onwards, together with Bill, Terry worked within the dying Independent Labour Party. They tried to transform it into a revolutionary organisation and to preserve its magnificent library in the basement of its offices in Kings Cross Road. Unfortunately another group based in Leeds were trying to get their hands on its money, name and publications. The faction fight was long and bitter, and the Leeds faction won.

Outside the ILP offices Terry told me one early evening in 1970, 'I am going to be a dad', and of course we had a pint or two to wet the baby's head. Terry married Daphne, who I last heard of as a leading light in the New Communist Party. They called their son Owen and they had a stormy on-off relationship for many, many years. They soon separated and the state soon prosecuted Terry. As he was the 'liable relative' he was responsible for paying for Daphne and Owen's maintenance. When Terry told the judge, 'I have no money, I am unemployed', the judge said, 'Get a job', at which point Terry, or so he said, started reading from *Alice in Wonderland*. He was sentenced to six weeks in jail.

A few weeks before their marriage the London ILP were challenged to a debate by the National Front. Always willing to reject the dogmas of the left, whose line was and is 'No platform for fascists', Terry and Bill accepted the challenge. A date was set and a hall was booked, but the debate never took place due to the intervention by the Jewish anti-fascists of the 62 Group. This resulted in Terry and Bill as well as the fascists being physically assaulted by the group.

Anyone who picked up the *Evening Standard* on 7 May 1970 could not help seeing a large photo of Terry with the caption 'The Wildman of Abbey Wood' on the front page. The *Standard*'s headline was 'The Battle of Abbey Wood', and it was a report of local people resisting an eviction on the Abbey Wood council estate. Assorted revolutionary socialists from Bexley and Woolwich, supported by local council tenants, were resisting the eviction from their GLC council house of a former council caretaker and his family. The GLC was Tory-run at this time; its leader was Horace Cutler who implemented the tied cottage system of 'the house goes with the job'.

In the early 1970s Terry met Mike Mallet, who told him about a libertarian Ukrainian who had fought the Leninists, Nationalists and the Whites during the Russian civil war and the Red Army right up to the mid-1920s. Quickly Terry got the Makhno bug and researched and wrote about the struggles by libertarians, communists and socialists against the ruling Russian Communist Party. In the 1980s he continued this research on Makhno at the University of East London's Department of Independent Study, obtaining a degree for his work.

It was also in the 1970s that Terry became active in the atheist movement and tried to activate the moribund Republicans of the time. In the National

Secular Society with Bill Turner he soon became embroiled in a faction fight against Barbara Smoker, who was its leading member and who made money by being the vicar at atheist funerals. Terry and Bill finally left the NSS to form the Socialist Rational League.

In 1977 Terry with other libertarian communists set up the 1649 Committee to celebrate the 'shortening' of King Charles I. As Terry explained: 'Monarchy in Britain was abolished and the country was proclaimed a Republic.' For the Royal Jubilee they organised a 'Stuff the Jubilee' rally on Blackheath, the plan being to march to Buckingham Palace to proclaim the Republic. It was not a huge success as only five people turned up. In 1983 Terry was one of the founding members of Republic, which brought 1500 people on to the streets protesting against the 2012 Jubilee.

With the Tories winning the 1979 election and the resulting rise in unemployment to the three million mark, Terry became active in the unemployed workers' movement. This was an alternative to the SWP's sectarian 'Right to Work Campaign'; it was a broad, mostly unattached and anarcho-left organisation which tried to work with the official labour movement. Interestingly Frances O'Grady, the new General Secretary of the TUC, was one of its active members. This is Terry's view of the movement which he wrote for *The Commune* in January 2012:

> In the early 1980s there were three million unemployed, and students were moving straight from graduation to the dole queue. No exception, I went to sign on at Spray Street dole office in Woolwich. Outside a group of people were leafleting. They were Greenwich Action Group On Unemployment (GAGOU). As the factories which lined the river from Erith to Deptford closed down, it was set up by the newly unemployed and a community worker from Greenwich Council — shades of things to come!
>
> GAGOU spent a lot of time on individual cases, of which there were many. In this we enlisted the help of sympathetic staff at the dole office. And in turn, when they were in dispute, our banner would appear on their picket line. But we did not make links with local union branches, many of which would not let the unemployed join, or with the Trades Council.

The 1980s saw Terry join and become active in the Labour Party, becoming his local branch's Chair. He was also prominent in the council tenants' movement. By 1989 he was opposing the trend of the middle classes, who were becoming dominant in the Labour Party, to stop people from smoking at Labour movement meetings. He wrote a pamphlet on this called *The Right To Smoke: A Socialist View*. What some of his comrades thought strange was that he wrote it for Forest, a front for the tobacco industry, who published it as one of their pamphlets making the case that smoking does you no harm. What Forest did not say is that tobacco companies made millions out of people making, buying and smoking tobacco.

Terry was a prolific writer of pamphlets, introductions to larger works and compilations of poems and articles by living and long-dead comrades. He was a founding member of the Freethought History Research Group in 2003 and was its Secretary for several years. As the *History Workshop Journal* said in 2005:

> The FHRG aims to preserve and help make available to the interested public the history of free thought in Britain, a history which spans two centuries and includes such incredible characters as Dan Chatterton and John Gott. As old stalwart freethinkers die, their valuable and irreplaceable archives and libraries are frequently thrown away. FHRG member Bob Morrell has often rescued such material from rubbish skips!

In 1994, still in the Labour Party, Terry contributed to a Fabian report attacking Labour for being wedded to state collectivism in health care. No doubt Terry's collectivist and socialist ideology made him welcome to anyone from the left attacking the Labour Party's support of the British capitalist state.

From the late 1980s Terry worked for the Department of Social Security (DSS). His account of his times there appeared in *The Commune* for January 2012.

In the late 1990s Terry left the Labour Party and joined the Greens as a Green Socialist. He seems to have quickly made an impression on the Green Party as in 2000 he was their candidate for Greenwich and Lewisham in the first London Mayor and Assembly elections. He got 11 839 votes which was more than most other revolutionary socialists have polled in London. Although most of his voters did not have a clue as to Terry's politics, beyond being the Green Party candidate, Terry was such a well-known political character in the area that a fair number would have heard of him.

With Terry's health failing his GP told him to give up alcohol. Daphne also strongly advised him to stop drinking. Terry not only became a teetotaller but made a virtue out of necessity and developed a socialist argument against the demon drink. In a letter in the *Weekly Worker* on 13 April 2006, Terry wrote:

> It is true that people still smoke despite the health warnings on cigarette packets. But fewer people smoke now than did in my youth in the 1960s, and many who still do would like to give it up. It is now generally accepted that tobacco is unhealthy. Government information campaigns have played

a part in this. The same could be done for alcohol.

A socialist society would still bear the birthmarks of the bourgeois society from which it emerged. Even a workers' state, until the process of its self-abolition is complete, would be an authoritarian body. In the final analysis it would be bodies of armed workers imposing their will. The will of the proletariat should be imposed on the bourgeoisie, including those who have profited from the manufacture and sale of drink.

They should not be killed, except where there is no other choice, or fined, but set to hard labour repairing some of the damage they have done. In so doing they may become human; just as a society freed from the poisonous swill sold by profit-hungry capitalists will become both human and humanistic.

And on 7 February 2008 he wrote in the *Weekly Worker*:

How does Jim Dymond know he would not benefit from a lecture on the health and social dangers of alcohol (Letters, 31 January)? He is, I hope, a rational person and I may convince him my arguments are correct. A recent survey into the 20 most widely-used drugs has revealed that alcohol is more dangerous than ecstasy, so there is scientific evidence to substantiate my contentions.

No, I couldn't vote until I was 21, but at 18 I could drink myself into stupidity and, sad to say, I did. In some parts of the United States the legal drinking age is 21. All we have to do is see how it works there and adapt these measures to British conditions.

Prohibitionists have a big job convincing the majority that theirs is the only answer to the sea of alcohol in which Britain is drowning, but then socialists also have a big job in convincing people that socialism is the answer to all the horrors of capitalism. That doesn't mean we shouldn't do it.

If parents deprive their children in order to buy alcohol then it is time for social services to intervene. I doubt if society would let heroin addicts look after children, so why should alcohol addicts be allowed to do so?

The Red Army at one time banned its troops from drinking alcohol at any time. Banning some people for some of the time from drinking alcohol is not prohibition, but it is a step on the path to that end.

After his second heart attack he saw the light and rediscovered beer and cider and the Polish beer, Tyskie.

He kept his unflinching and uncompromising Socialist, Atheist and Republican faith to the end. In 2004 he debated at a CPGB conference entitled 'Headscarves, Secularism and the Battle of Democracy'. He spoke in favour of the ban (the French MPs banning by a massive majority to ban the Islamic headscarf and all other overt religious symbols from state schools). From the point of view of an intransigent militant socialist atheist, he called for the ban on ostentatious religious symbols in schools to be understood in the context of French history. He described socialism as a materialist science which demands an intransigent and unyielding struggle against superstition, obscurantism and idealism. Socialists should support anything which weakens the influence of religion in society as something to be welcomed, not opposed on the basis of a 'spurious libertarianism'.

And he replied to the debate by saying that 'CPGB comrades should put themselves in the position of Bolsheviks confronted with Muslims conducting a protracted guerrilla war against Soviet power in central Asia 80 years ago, and asked: "What would you have done — handed them a leaflet? Hopefully you would have shot them."'

In July 2012 the *Republican Communist Network* republished an article of Terry's. He had written it as a member of the South London Republican Forum where he compared the opposition to Victoria's 1897 Golden Jubilee celebrations with the opposition to the monarchy since then. It concluded:

> This time round the monarchist ardour is on the wane. A celebration of the life and work of the Red Republican, George Julian Harney, has already taken place. On 30 May, the Socialist Alliance will be holding an anti-Jubilee rock concert in Brixton. And there will be Thomas Paine and Charles Bradlaugh celebrations in June and a meeting on Bradlaugh in Bromley in April. On 25 May there will be a march and meeting to remember the heroic struggle of Bobby Sands. There will be a strong anti-monarchist element in the Socialist Alliance local election campaign in May. The war in Afghanistan is far from popular and the prospect of war in Iraq even less so. Mrs Windsor's jubilee could well be the last.

In many ways Terry's politics were those of William Morris, and here is the concluding paragraph of his article on Morris' politics published in the first issue of *The Commune* on 13 November 2008:

> The world is as ugly, squalid and impoverished as it was in the time of Morris. Capitalism, made psychotic by its werewolf lust for profit, has torn the heart out of much of humanity, turning it into a shadow of what free human beings could be. We have again to take up the fight of Morris but under the name he himself chose — Communism.

So Communists all: Raise a glass to Terry, for a true Revolutionary Socialist is no more.
Scott Reeve

* * *

Theodore Melville (1932-2010)[13]

Theodore Melville had in recent years become almost invisible to those who had previously been his comrades in components of the Trotskyist movement, and the announcement of his death by the Posadist Fourth International evoked several warm recollections but little factual information.

Melville's publicly-known life consisted to a large degree of organising exhibitions of surrealist visual art. His father John was one of the founders of surrealism in Britain (the unwary reader should be warned that surrealism is at least as fissiparous a movement as Trotskyism, and its historical documentation needs to be approached with considerable caution), and together with his brother Robert and Conroy Maddox established the 'Birmingham surrealists'.

Theodore was at Oxford University in the mid-1950s, and would appear to have been a member of the Communist Party before the crisis of 1956.

The earliest record we currently have of Theodore's involvement in the Trotskyist movement finds him serving as a member of the Editorial Board of *International Socialism* (listed in issues 7 to 10) in the period before that journal became the exclusive property of the International Socialists. He contributed articles and poetry, among which '114 Exciteable[14] Persons (Algeria)' — reproduced below — is widely regarded as the best. A note to *IS* issue 4, in which it appeared, says that he was at that time employed in the Walker Art Gallery, Liverpool. He was understood during this period to be a member of the 'Fourth International' and its British associate the Revolutionary Socialist League, as was John Fairhead (whose trajectory took him into the Monday Club).

Melville and Fairhead were associated with Pat Jordan and the Nottingham group at about that time, and Theodore was at least partly responsible for an especially heinous recruitment. In 1963, Melville and Fairhead associated themselves with the tendency directed by the Latin America Bureau which opposed itself to the International Secretariat, and which was led by Juan Posadas. They organised a faction among the London membership that was soon enough to designate itself the Revolutionary Workers Party, splitting away with 12 members. Later information on this organisation is both sparse and unreliable, but it appears unlikely that they ever achieved any larger membership. The political positions of the RWP defy parody, combining unconditional support

---

13. Thanks to Alun Morgan and Ian Birchall for contributions to research.
14. This is the spelling used throughout in the version on the Marxists Internet Archive.

for the USSR and its satellites with a conviction that atomic war launched by the capitalist states was inevitable. Posadas was later to consider that 'flying saucers' existed and revolutionary human progress depended on making an alliance with the alien organisms that used them.

Melville is praised in the Posadists' official obituary for his dedicated contribution to the production of their journal *Red Flag* until his sickness made him physically incapable of continuing the work. He died of cancer on 15 July 2010 aged 78 years. A funeral service was held at Lodge Hill Crematorium on Monday, 6 September at 1.30pm. It is impossible not to be saddened at the waste of a talented life in such a political blind alley.

114 Exciteable Persons (Algeria)

114 dead,
114 exciteable persons
reported
by the press,
spoken of
in connection
with liberty.

A mere 114 dead
in the morgue
of our time,
an infinitesimal number
of 114 dead.

Desert sands
and darkness over the Caspah
and tortured men
and 114 dead.

114 dead
and listening to music
and love affairs
and cold winds
and laughter
and writing
and getting up
and contemplating
and 114 dead.

114 exciteable persons,
departed
suddenly,
unexpectedly,
leaving no forwarding address.

114 unremarkable persons,
save that they died
between the 10 Dec & 13 Dec (inclusive),
in the year, 1960.

114 exciteable persons.

* * *

Akiva (Aki) Orr (1931-2013)

Akiva Orr was a revolutionary activist and writer, founding member of the Socialist Organisation in Israel (*Matzpen*), an enchanting raconteur and a unique larger-than-life character.

His parents emigrated with him, their only child, in 1934 from his birthplace, Berlin, to Palestine. In his youth, spent in Tel-Aviv in an apolitical petty-bourgeois milieu, he was a keen swimmer and won the 200m breast-stroke youth championship in 1946 and 1947. In 1948 he was conscripted to the Israeli navy, but was not involved in hostilities during his service. (The navy played a minor role in the 1947-49 war.) Demobilised in 1950, he joined the Israeli merchant navy as a deckhand (eventually rising to become third mate).

A major turning point in his life was the great seamen's strike of 1951, a seminal episode in Israel's class struggle. The strike was directed against the *Histadrut*, the Zionist trade-union federation, which refused to recognise the independent committee elected by an overwhelming majority of the seamen and rejected their demand to run their own union, free from bureaucratic diktat. The *Histadrut*, whose petty-bureaucrat nominees were crushingly defeated in the election, was also co-owner (together with the Jewish Agency) of the main Israeli shipping company Zim. Aki's ship, the *Tel-Aviv*, moored in Haifa harbour, was occupied by its striking crew. In a pitched battle with large forces of police and *Histadrut* thugs, Aki was threatened by a police officer wielding a drawn handgun. This set him thinking, and he became politicised.

In the autumn of 1953, Aki went up to Jerusalem to study Mathematics and Physics at the Hebrew University, where he and I were classmates as well as members of the Jerusalem branch of the Socialist Left Party, a short-lived split from MAPAM led by the demagogue Moshe Sneh, a blatant Stalinist and (temporarily) covert Zionist. We became close friends and remained in contact when Aki interrupted his studies after his first year and went back to sea for a couple of years. By the time he resumed his studies, the SLP had dissolved and most of its members joined the Israeli Communist Party. So Aki and I were now members of the student cell of the ICP's Jerusalem branch.

The two great simultaneous international crises in the autumn of 1956 affected us in contradictory ways. Like many in the international 'official' Communist movement, we were shocked by the brutal suppression of the Hungarian revolution, and our trust in the ICP leadership — already undermined earlier that year following Khrushchev's famous not-so-secret speech — was seriously eroded. At the same time, on the much closer issue of the tripartite (Israeli-French-British) aggression against Egypt, we fully supported the laudable anti-war position of the ICP, which of course echoed the policy of the USSR in this as in everything else.

Sometime after that war, Aki and I decided to write a book, based on publicly available material (mainly press reports), vindicating the ICP position and proving that the Suez war must have been planned in collusion between the three aggressors (which was officially denied for quite a long time). We also aimed to show that Israel's role in that war was a logical culmination of Israeli policy right from its foundation. In the event, most of the work on the book was done by Aki, assisted by his first wife, Lea, and by me. It was published in 1961 under the pen-name 'N Israeli' as *Shalom, Shalom v'eyn Shalom* (*Peace, Peace When There Is No Peace*).[15]

In the course of writing the book, we became convinced that the ICP's critique of Zionism was insufficiently radical. It focused on Zionism's ties with imperialism and Israel's hostility to the USSR in the Cold War; but — unlike the Palestine CP long before 1948 — it avoided confronting Zionism as a settler-colonising project. Accordingly, the book represented a shift from the ICP's stance. Yet, it was not a complete break: for example, we depicted British imperialism as the main culprit and instigator of the 1948 war, and Israel as part-victim. The book was in fact a half-way house between our old ICP orthodoxy and the more thorough analysis of Zionism we were to adopt in Matzpen in the mid-1960s.

Meantime, our criticism of the policies of the USSR and 'official' Communism grew in response to events. In 1958, following the revolution that overthrew the Iraqi monarchy, we witnessed how the Iraqi Communist Party, which emerged from years of illegality as an almost unrivalled mass party and could have pushed events in a radical left direction, was held back by 'advice' of the Soviet

---

15. English translation by Mark Marshall (with additional appendixes) online http://www.akiorrbooks.com/files/PEACE.pdf.

Union. Closer home, in 1959 poor immigrants, mostly from North Africa, in the Wadi Salib neighbourhood of downtown Haifa, demonstrated against their exploitation and discrimination. There were clashes with the police. The ICP, instead of supporting the protests, joined other parties in calling for calm. These and similar events persuaded us that the USSR, the 'official' Communist movement, and its local franchise, the ICP, were not revolutionary forces but concerned primarily with defending the interests of the USSR as a big power. Another object of our criticism was the ICP leadership's refusal to discuss the party's history, which was regarded as a great secret. Reading Trotsky's *My Life* and *History of the Russian Revolution* (in excellent Hebrew translation dating from the 1930s) also affected our thinking.

By 1962 we had made contact with two comrades in the Tel-Aviv ICP branch (Oded Pilavsky and Yirmiyahu Kaplan) and several ICP supporters and started regular discussions in a spirit critical of 'official' Communism. These discussions had to be held in secret, since the ICP did not allow unauthorised meetings, especially between members of different branches. We did not have immediate plans for forming a faction or a new organisation; but our hand was forced by a leak. We faced immediate expulsion. This is how the Israeli Socialist Organisation came into being. The first issue of our monthly journal, *Matzpen*, appeared in November 1962. Aki contributed to this first issue an article about the lessons of October 1917.

His articles, on diverse topics, continued to appear regularly in *Matzpen* even after he moved to London in the summer of 1964, intending to pursue postgraduate studies in the general theory of relativity at King's College. His contributions to Matzpen in Hebrew are being compiled at http://www.matzpen.org/.

In London he devoted much time and energy to educating the left on the true nature of Zionism. He also sought out and befriended several old-timers of the revolutionary socialist movement. Among his many friends were the Austrian-born poet Erich Fried (who later introduced him to the German student leader Rudi Dutschke), the veteran revolutionary Rosa Meyer-Leviné, and — a special friend — the West Indian Marxist CLR James. At the same time he took great interest in the youth counter-culture of the 1960s and formed many contacts with its representatives.

Following the June 1967 war, Aki intensified his activities in educating the far left about Zionism and the Israeli-Palestinian conflict. He was a much sought-after speaker and addressed numerous meetings.

In 1968 he joined the libertarian group Solidarity led by Chris Pallis (aka Maurice Brinton) and distanced himself from Marxism. He was then greatly influenced by Cornelius Castoriadis. At the same time he continued his intensive activity as speaker and writer on Zionism and Israel.

In 1990 Aki returned to Israel and continued to speak and write, devoting much energy to propagating a form of anarchism which he called 'Autonarchy', advocating entirely direct decision-making without mediation of any elected delegates or representatives.

His publications are too numerous to list here. They can be found on http://www.akiorrbooks.com and http://www.autonarchy.org.il.

Aki died suddenly at his home in the village Tenuvot, Israel. He is survived by his daughter, Sharon, and two grandsons, Max and Theo.
Moshé Machover

* * *

Dave Packer (1945-2012)

Some of Dave Packer's earliest political activity was in and around Southampton, where he was an active member of the Young Socialists and a little later of the Revolutionary Socialist League/Militant.

In January 1974, he was one of a group of 18 signatories to a letter of resignation from Militant. A 'secret faction' had been formed within Militant, around Ted Coxhead. The Militant leadership came into possession of a faction document and published it to the membership to initiate formal discussion. This was begun but for whatever reason it was broken off, and the faction's letter was published in *Red Weekly*, the paper of the International Marxist Group (IMG), which the faction soon joined. The faction's key criticism of Militant was that it failed to prepare the working class in practical terms for the implementation of its programme.

He was to continue in active, committed membership of the IMG and its various successor bodies, and the United Secretariat of the Fourth International (USec), for the rest of his life. He came to some prominence in the organisation as the Manchester organiser, at a time when the organisation was probably at its strongest following the Socialist Unity election campaigns.

In 1977 *Red Weekly* was superseded by *Socialist Challenge* and Packer worked on the new paper for a time, starting a long-term political alliance with Phil Hearse that lasted through the period of intense factional fragmentation that was to disrupt the IMG. Labour Party work was intensified in response to Tony Benn's campaign for the party leadership, and by 1982 the IMG was considering announcing its dissolution. Instead it renamed itself the Socialist League and remodelled its paper as *Socialist Action*. At this point the organisation was strong enough to maintain The Other Bookshop in Islington and its own printing company.

This was the beginning of a period of political defeats for the British working class. Benn's defeat in the leadership contest was followed by Kinnock's purge of Militant. The Socialist League responded by lowering its profile, closing the bookshop and taking other steps to become invisible within the Labour Party. The epoch-making defeats of steel workers and coal miners followed soon after. No part of the left was immune to the problems of rethinking and reworking strategy and tactics. For the Trotskyists in the USec currents things became more difficult with the US Socialist Workers Party's drawing the conclusions of its Castro admiration to propagate fundamentally revisionist politics.

The organisation's membership had halved by the mid-1980s, to about 500 members. It was to split three ways. Dave Packer, Phil Hearse, Jane Kelly, Stephanie Grant, Davy Jones, Bob Pennington, Terry Conway, Dave Sheppard, Grant Keir and others established 'Faction One' that sought to rescue the best of its past practice from the imminent wreck. They split away under the new name of the International Group (a calculated harking back to the days of Pat Jordan), which received a semi-recognition from the USec, acknowledging them as individual members while reserving its position on their organisation. The membership of the new organisation was reported to be 110. Of the rival factions, one was led by Brian Grogan and supporters of the US SWP, the 'Pathfinder' tendency, which pursued a Castroite line increasingly liberated from Trotskyism by Jack Barnes and the Carleton College Group, and the other led by John Ross retained the 'Socialist Action' name and progressed ever more deeply into a strategic alliance with Labour lefts, prominently Ken Livingstone.

It was Dave Packer who took the step of initiating contact with the Socialist Group, led by Alan Thornett, the surviving section of the former Workers Socialist League following the débâcle of a merger with a toxic North London sect. He argued that the two groups had already converged politically. They were both working in the Labour Party and had a common assessment of the impact of the miners' strike — which had been defeated. They had also taken the same view on the Malvinas/Falklands war.

This resulted in the 1987 fusion conference establishing the International Socialist Group as a new organisation with around 180 members. It was remarkable that such a fusion could be conducted at all between groups with roots in the incompatible 'International Committee' and USec tendencies. More remarkable still that the fused organisation has survived and functioned for more than two decades.

Dave Packer's political work had the additional dimension of representing his organisation in the USec. In that fevered and disaster-prone context he continued to seek practical and effective alliances. He is credited with 'brokering' alliances with the tendency in the Ligue Communiste led by Gérard Filoche and with Socialist Action in the United States. He and Phil Hearse stood by the positions developed by Ernest Mandel and supported by the USec only a few years earlier, which were being jettisoned.

The ISG's conviction that Trotskyists should relate to 'the traditional organisations of the working class' was strongly influenced by Peter Gowan; it set them somewhat at odds with the USec and its incessant chimera-hunting. Dave Packer and other ISG leaders participated in *Labour Briefing* and sought to establish good working relationships there.

In 1990 and for a time afterwards Dave Packer's political work was inhibited when his long-term partner Jane Kelly suffered a severe accident and he became her carer. He was influential in the discussions which brought the UK SWP into the Socialist Alliance in 2000 and the establishment of working relationships with the Scottish Socialist Party. The SWP, however, talent-spotted George Galloway and conducted the gymnastic manoeuvre of switching horses in mid-stream while stabbing the discarded horse to death. It was the death of the Socialist Alliance, while the rough beast of Respect shambled towards parturition.

While this sad charivari played itself out, Dave Packer was turning his thoughts and writing to the global environmental crisis, and the need for a revolutionary response to it. He was influenced by John Bellamy Foster's writings in particular, and was central in pushing the organisation towards a redefinition of itself as 'ecosocialist', a step that led to the group's re-establishment of itself in 2009 as Socialist Resistance, recognised as the British Section of the USec.

Responding to the financial crisis of 2008 and onwards, he worked with Raphie de Santos, to analyse the new situation and try to formulate strategy for the socialist movement. Part of his response was to become involved in the anti-cuts Coalition of Resistance to the extent which his health allowed

He died on 3 July 2012 suddenly of a brain haemorrhage at the age of 65. His funeral took place on Friday, 20 July, attended by 100 people and opened by his partner of almost 30 years, Jane Kelly.

Bridget St Ruth

* * *

Dave Spencer (1940-2012)[16]

Dave Spencer lived out the socialism he believed in, more completely than anybody I have known. Much of what he was rightly proud of was achieved outside the framework of organised left groups, and he became increasingly convinced that 'organisation from below' was the strategy for the working class

---

16. I am immensely grateful to Dave's friend and comrade Keith White for much of the information and most of the insights in this obituary, and for correcting some errors in my earlier draft. Keith in turn drew on numerous reminiscences on the internet and in print, too many to be acknowledged individually, but Pete McLaren, Socialist Alliance National Secretary, merits specific mention.

to adopt for its own emancipation. This was a theme running through his recent article in *The Commune*.

He was born into a working-class family — his father worked in the car industry in Coventry. Dave grew up in a Labour family, in a Labour city and, from 1945, under a reforming Labour government. He was educated at Bablake School.

When he was 16 the Suez crisis and the Hungarian uprising set the scene for a period of ferment and debate in the labour movement. The Cold War raged and nuclear war was a real fear. CND was born with mass demonstrations and the colonial peoples were demanding their right to freedom. Dave saw that our society was not free, not equal, was dominated by the super-rich whose profit drive laid waste to the natural resources and lives of millions of people. He wanted resources shared and used wisely, he wanted free and open discussion on an equal basis, people getting together to sort out their problems and needs.

He read English at Leeds University and Leicester, where he found exciting political discussion enriched by such stellar lecturers as EP Thompson, Cliff Slaughter and John Rex. He became a Marxist.

Dave was a member of the Labour Party Young Socialists in the 1960s, which the Socialist Labour League, working through their paper *Keep Left*, came quickly to dominate, trouncing the 'Young Guard' alliance of the Cliff and Grant groups. Dave wrote about the window of opportunity for action in the SLL in the aftermath of 1956, when an influx of members won from the Communist Party was taking some time to absorb. Later the SLL was to become monolithic and its sectarian blunders laid it open to mass expulsion in 1964.

But before that happened Dave participated in what was a politically formative period with the LPYS and SLL. At university the students were organised into Marxist Societies, which held open and creative discussion meetings. Young SLLers learned from the experience of their Wigan comrades, who had organised a weekly disco that attracted large numbers of youth and created opportunities for discussion and organisation. They adopted the same method, persuading students from the Marxist Society to turn out on to council estates to get support for the weekly discos, and drawing the new youth into self-organisation. Dave helped persuade his local Coventry Labour Party to open up its headquarters and a downstairs area was turned into a sort of youth club where young people could meet up without fear of intimidation. The notorious division between 'mods' and 'rockers' was overcome in some of these projects.

One blog poster has vividly described his first encounter with the SLL Trotskyists at this period:

I first met Dave 50 years ago on a 'Hands Off Cuba' Demo in Coventry (during the threatened USA invasion of Cuba) in 1962. It was down at the bottom of Hertford Street, Coventry, on an old bomb-site — they were still about then before the building of the precinct, near the Bull Yard and the Three Tuns Pub. It was a big demo of a few hundred and I was with a contingent of Communist Party youth — the Young Communist League — who were fine but a bit serious and a little humourless, and I remember looking over at a bigger contingent of the Young Socialists, who were Trotskyists I was fearfully and whisperingly told, who seemed full of life, singing songs, playing guitars and chanting socialist slogans. A fairly alluring sight in contrast. But anyway it was there that Dave approached me, from the Trots — spoke to me and got me — and later reeled me in with talk of real social change and revolution — not the peaceful coexistence of Soviet bureaucrats or the stale staid reformism of Labour.

The SLL leadership was cautious about the success of 'Wiganisation' (as Dave called it), and its heavy-handed purge of 'Pabloites' turned off nearly as many youth as the previous initiatives had won. The SLL's refusal to take part in the Vietnam Solidarity Campaign and its massively successful demonstrations was a major failing, and a symptomatic indication of its future spasms of self-isolation.

Increasingly dissatisfied with the SLL (in no small part in response to SLL leader Healy attempting to instruct him to 'get rid of' his wife Margaret, a devout catholic), Dave was a founder member in 1967 of Workers Fight (originating in a faction that removed itself from the Revolutionary Socialist League — as Militant was then known). In 1968 this group was the only one to accept Tony Cliff's 'unity' invitation, and established itself as the Trotskyist Tendency in the International Socialists. Dave described how IS branches in Manchester and Coventry adopted the method of factory bulletins pioneered by the French Lutte Ouvrière organisation. By 1970 the Coventry IS had built a membership of about 100, with a majority component of factory shop stewards. The bulletins were self-organised by groups in the factories. IS provided students and others to hand them out at the factory gate to reduce the risk of victimisation of key comrades inside the factories.

While at least some of the Workers Fight group operated in a completely cynical manner, Dave played an enthusiastic role in the IS. He personally sold hundreds of copies of Cliff's book *The Employers' Offensive*. He had no taste for narrow factional interests, he always revelled in broad movements, making real connections with wide layers of the workers' movement.

In 1971 Workers Fight was expelled, and a more centralised approach was adopted by IS, with nationally produced 'Rank and File' papers replacing the self-directed factory bulletins. He functioned as the Workers Fight organiser in the city. He argued persistently for the group to turn more vigorously towards the Labour Party and more generally into the broad activity of the masses.

Dave had become well known and well respected in the Coventry labour movement, and had been working as a teacher and later as a lecturer. He had sought for a way of applying radical socialist approaches in education and found inspiration in the work of Paulo Freire and his theory of critical pedagogy. The feminism of the Greenham Common peace camp was an equally powerful inspiration. Dave's vision was that through education people could develop strength and confidence and be better able to take charge of their lives. He struggled to test and prove this vision. It was his greatest achievement.

Dave lectured at Henley College, where he famously created the Primary School Project, in which he took the college into local schools to encourage adults who were normally excluded to get back into education. The Primary School Programme benefited thousands of adults in Coventry, and gave women in particular the chance to return to education, gain qualifications and then pursue careers or further studies at university. At its peak, more than 2000 adults were studying GCSEs and A-levels in various centres around the city each year, starting from very humble beginnings in a few spare classrooms in Eburne School. Many of these classes were based in the poorest areas of Coventry.

He encouraged people to write about their lives and emotions and what they produced exceeded his wildest hopes. Many women re-evaluated their future plans, even relationships, as a result of their studies. Though the scheme became widely known and eventually won a national prize, Dave never received the recognition he deserved from his employers — though his 1997 PhD was glowingly praised and in the hearts of his many students there was gratitude and deep affection.

In Dave's own words during a recent debate:

My way of teaching English was to discuss a controversial topic for an hour or so to get everybody thinking. The women would then go home and write down their thoughts or experiences. Grammar could come later. One of the favourite topics was: 'All men are bastards. Discuss.' One day the women of my class in Bell Green came in to discuss the proposed closure of their local Primary School. What to do? I seem to remember suggesting in an abstract way occupation and joining the local Labour Party to get rid of their councillors. Three days later, on the front page of the local paper there was an article, 'Parents Occupy Bell Green Primary School', and there in the picture were the smiling faces of my students!

Once the occupation began socialists from all over the city turned up 'to help'. Friends encouraged Dave to attend. He wouldn't. He said that if he was there they would see him as their teacher and look to him to tell them what to do. If he kept away then they would work things out for themselves.

When Henley College decided to host the first year of a De Montfort University degree in Computer Science, Law and Accountancy, an innovation in a time when degrees were all single-subject, Dave persuaded them to aim recruitment at those who were generally excluded. This offered chances to go further for many of the students who had gone through the Primary School Programme.

Dave became more prominent in the Labour Party during the leftward shift of the 1980s as a result of the fight against Thatcherism and her attacks on local government and the trade unions. There was the 'Benn for Deputy' campaign and the de-selection of right-wing MPs and local councillors. Dave was critical of the failure of Militant to open up and take full part in the movements and campaigns that emerged everywhere. He wrote:

> For example when I became a candidate to be a West Midlands County Councillor for Coventry South-East which Militant thought was 'their patch' their fury was unbounded and threats of violence were made. The Militant had voted for the right-wing candidate against me. Later they organised to knock me off the shortlist for MP for Coventry North-East by spreading rumours that I was a 'sexist womaniser' in order to get on their preferred candidate, their 'contact' Bob Ainsworth,[17] now Minister of Defence for the Armed Forces.

Workers Fight had undergone a series of transmutations and by this time was called the International-Communist League (not to be confused with the international organisation of the US Spartacists that now uses the same name). It had launched a paper, *Socialist Organiser*, to influence the newly-emerging movements in the Labour Party and elsewhere. London Labour Briefing was growing on a similar basis and the I-CL at first worked with it, before splitting over the question of whether raising the rates in Labour-controlled councils could be part of the strategy for the left (I-CL said no, Briefing yes).

Dave was an early and keen Briefing supporter, seeing it as a practical way

---

17. Former union activist in the Jaguar factory in Coventry, where he had some involvement with the International Marxist Group. Elected to Parliament for Coventry North-East in 1992 and had a rapidly advancing career as first party whip, culminating in appointment as Defence Secretary in 2009. In opposition was shadow Defence Secretary until demoted by Miliband. In December 2012 announced he would not contest the next election.

for socialists to collaborate effectively, and was enthusiastic about *Briefing*'s Streetlife supplement. He often quoted 'the personal is political'. He helped initiate West Midlands Labour Briefing, which tried to draw together the left throughout that vast area. It had huge potential, but the Metropolitan Counties and the GLC were abolished in 1986. Local Briefings such as Coventry and Warwickshire had more long-term success.

In the Labour Party he became a West Midlands County Councillor and was almost selected as the candidate in the Euro-constituency. Through *Socialist Organiser*, the Rank-and-File Mobilising Committee, the 'Benn for Deputy' campaign and Briefing, Dave was always pushing his comrades to think bigger, broader and become more open to debate and dialogue. In 1981 young YS members in his tendency played a significant role in the Coventry anti-racist/fascist movement, forging important links with bands like the Specials.

In 1981 the I-CL fused with the Workers Socialist League (of which I was a member at the time). Like Dave I was enthusiastic initially about this development, but it soon became clear it was going nowhere. Worse, our energies were being wasted on disagreements that were not capable of resolution. I resigned before it came to the split, feeling I had been unable to 'make the Left [that is, the old WSL leadership] fight'.

During this period Dave developed criticisms of the former I-CL leadership. These were not on the issues which were emerging between (broadly speaking) the leaderships of the pre-fusion WSL and I-CL. For example on the Falklands/Malvinas conflict where he supported the former I-CL's neutralist position. He was more concerned about the political culture of the fused organisation, the notions of Leninism espoused by both of the groupings. As the two factions moved more and more into sharp, tension-ridden conflict, Dave and others watched as members (from both traditions) dropped out and 'comradely' relations all but disappeared.

His emphasis was on building a party within which many differences could coexist happily together. Indeed it was during the faction fighting that he came to the conclusion that differences were not only healthy but necessary if a thriving mass party with a genuinely positive relationship with working people were to emerge. He was more concerned with what he had always considered the spirit of the fusion, focussing on what we had in common. He and others on the National Committee started to discuss working together to 'knock some sense into the old leaderships'. What started as 'the sensible faction' on the NC grew into a more formal grouping, the Democratic Centralist Faction which drew its membership from both of the pre-fusion organisations, including one member of the old WSL Executive Committee.

The full story of the fusion and how and why it went wrong remains to be written and no doubt there would be several contesting versions of that tale. However, Dave's role was pivotal. He was a (perhaps *the*) key mover and strategist of the DCF. He decided early on that Alan Thornett's grouping was less sectarian than Sean Matgamna's and that given a choice he preferred Thornett. After the Thornett group was expelled the DCF attempted to overturn the decision and then left to help set up the Socialist Group.

This was a small group of people (around 50) and within it the former DCF members played an important role in pushing forward the organisational norms they had sought to secure in the fused WSL. For three years there was, as far as Dave was concerned, a fruitful period of discussion about what sort of party was needed. This period included half the miners' strike and much of the Coventry Labour Briefing activity.

The Socialist Group fused with the International Group in 1987 to form the International Socialist Group, and Dave was elected to its National Committee. He was particularly keen to push for a lively open internal bulletin and much irritated by what he saw as a reluctance on the part of the ISG leadership. The ISG was for a time very successful in Coventry, but by 1990 Dave and most of the members had dropped out.

After the miners' strike and other defeats, when the Labour right became rampant, Dave eventually withdrew from the Labour Party after an increasingly difficult relationship. He had been suspended from office for two years after the 1992 election and his support for John Hughes[18] in Coventry North-East.

He was a founder of the Socialist Alliance and helped set up the very first Socialist Alliance in Coventry and Warwickshire in 1992 with, amongst others, Dave Nellist, after 127 left-wing members were expelled from the Labour Party — although Dave himself was still a member for a little longer. He did as much as anyone to build that local SA into a fighting force with over 300 supporters, sitting on its Organisation Committee and helping with its monthly newsletter — and hosting its editorial meetings at his house in Earlsdon to produce it every month. He helped build the SA nationally over the next six years, and attended all the national meetings. Dave continued to work tirelessly for and with the SA nationally as it became a large organisation and stood 98 candidates in the 2001 General Election. He helped those who tried to prevent the Socialist Workers Party from closing down the SA in 2005, and was a leading member of the Socialist Alliance Democracy Platform within it. When the SA was re-launched later that year, Dave did not agree with the direction it took and he did not rejoin locally or nationally. This is when he joined the Democratic Socialist Alliance, which had split from the re-launched SA.

18. Hughes was the Labour MP for Coventry North-East from 1987 to 1992, when he was de-selected and ran as an Independent Labour candidate.

When Arthur Scargill launched the Socialist Labour Party, Dave saw it as another opportunity to pull the left together, and worked hard to build it. In 1997 he organised the general election campaign in which Hanna Khamis was the SLP candidate for Coventry North-East and Dave ran in Coventry North-West, while Militant campaigned for their candidate Dave Nellist in Coventry South. By chance I was working temporarily in Coventry at that time and was able to assist a little with the campaign. As always Dave was conspicuous by his optimism, energy and dedication, and charismatically led what was admittedly a small band of followers. Some of us went to Militant's eve of poll rally, but they were totally silent about the SLP candidacy. It was left to their star guest speaker Ken Loach to remind them to call on their supporters in Coventry North-East to vote SLP, which they eventually grudgingly did. Like most SLP members, Dave left in disgust at the behaviour of the leaders.

For 20 years until his death, he worked with *New Interventions*, a magazine of open socialist discussion, where it was a great pleasure to meet him again on the Editorial Board. He organised our subscriptions and finances, and negotiated printing contracts, as well as taking part in our discussions and writing for the magazine. Here he found some allies (not myself) to take part in the Campaign for a Marxist Party, of which the DSA was one of the founders. Like the SA before it but on a small scale, the CMP was smashed up by the Communist Party of Great Britain in what was the most disreputable of their operations. Within days of the destruction Dave was back in action drafting and negotiating the basis for a new platform document.

More recently he was attracted to *The Commune*, which reflected his continuing emphasis on organisation from below, and on becoming embedded in the daily struggles of the class. He was also increasingly involved in local community campaigning. Locally, he and others organised discussions through the Coventry Radical Network.

The last thing he brought to success was through Gosford Park Residents' Group, which won the creation of a children's playground, which will be a permanent reminder of his concern for and contribution to the area. He trained in shiatsu massage and aromatherapy and as a qualified counsellor helped refugees on a voluntary basis.

Dave always loved music, and tried to incorporate it into his political life. In the mid-1960s after the YS discos had been stopped, a dissident Keep Left branch in Coventry of which he was a member ran a folk club, the Bandiera Rossa, in a local pub. In 1966 he and others organised a May Day celebration in the Belgrade Theatre with Dominic Behan, Ewan McColl and Peggy Seeker and a local Irish group playing. The SLL boycotted it, saying it was petty-bourgeois. They also ran a rhythm and blues club in a pub for a while with a resident band called the Edgar Broughton Band which had a few hits at the time. He enjoyed singing in a local choir and playing the piano.

He loved literature especially Tolstoy, Dickens, Shakespeare, Conan-Doyle's Sherlock Holmes, Raymond Chandler and Dashiell Hammett; he loved laughter, Sergeant Bilko, Al Reid and many, many others. He also loved the simple pleasures of good food — visiting cream-cake shops with his grandchildren against doctor's advice. To play with his grandchildren was one of his greatest joys.

Having reached the end of this sketch of such a full life, I am filled with admiration for his energy, sense of direction and resilience. Years ago I compiled my own funeral play list and included a song by Prince Buster. Dave deserves it far more than I.

> You pick him up, you lick him down
> Him bounce right back,
> What a hard man fe dead!

JJ Plant

* * *

Alan Woodward (1939-2012)

Alan Woodward, who died suddenly in October 2012, was a socialist activist and independent thinker for over 50 years. He never sought national prominence, but was always a 'rank-and-filer' in the best sense of that term.

I first met Alan at a meeting of the Tottenham International Socialists in Tottenham Trades Hall in September 1964. (At least four of us who were at that meeting were at Alan's funeral 48 years later.) Alan had been radicalised during National Service, and first made contact with the minute Socialist Review Group through Brian Lynam (who subsequently, in the ferment of the far left, became a Posadist). After military service he trained as a teacher. In 1964, at the time of the birth of his second child, he moved to Tottenham, which was to be the scene of his political activity for much of the next 50 years.

I had just arrived from Oxford, and though I had some scraps of Marxist theory in my head, I had little idea of how to operate politically in an area like Tottenham. Over the next few years I learned enormously from Alan, though we had a few rows along the way. IS had been largely built in the Young Socialists, but as Alan and I were both coming up to the age limit we began to work in the Labour Party.

Although we did not realise it, this was the end of an era for the postwar Labour Party. Coleraine ward of the Wood Green Labour Party was solidly working-class. There were 20 to 30 members at each meeting — I was the only graduate. By the end of the decade Harold Wilson and expanding higher education meant such Labour Party wards were a thing of the past.

Alan became ward literature secretary, trying to push *Union Voice* and *Labour Worker*. We moved resolutions on Vietnam and the imprisonment of Kuroń and Modzelewski to a largely uninterested membership. Alan became quite frustrated with the Labour Party — one of his favourite descriptions of some of the contacts we made there was 'thick as 17 lavatory seats nailed together'. On one occasion he and I were formally reprimanded for doing the *Evening Standard* crossword during a constituency meeting on the Common Market addressed by Ian Mikardo.

But in the end entry work paid off. In 1967 the Haringey Labour Council introduced steep rent rises for council tenants. The tiny IS branch (10 active members at most) had no council tenants in membership. We issued a press statement opposing the increases, then set up meetings on the estates as Labour Party members opposed to the increases. Tenants associations were set up on all the estates and there was a demonstration of some 500 outside the Civic Centre. And in all this Alan was the driving force.

At the same time the Tottenham IS met in Alan's front room. Often on a Saturday evening branch members and close contacts would be invited round for a few drinks and intense political discussion. For me it was an essential part of my political education.

Alan had been working as a teacher, concentrating on the bottom streams, but he became frustrated with this, and took various industrial jobs in the Enfield area, where he helped to build trade-union organisations. When he was sacked from one such job (I think around Christmas 1969), he organised a number of us to picket the home of one of the managers. We were rapidly chased off by police.

In 1968 a small group of us, including Alan, resigned from the Labour Party, and announced our commitment to building the International Socialists as an open organisation. In the aftermath of 1968 the IS tried to involve itself more in working-class struggles, and for a while Alan served as secretary of the Industrial Sub-Committee, the only time he was involved with the centre of the organisation.

In his 40 years in the IS/Socialist Workers Party, Alan was always a loyal activist. He did his share, and often more than his share, of mundane tasks like paper sales and factory leafleting. He was rarely if ever involved in internal disputes or factionalising. But at the same time there were always reservations. Those of us who came to revolutionary politics around 1960 were a suspicious bunch. We lived in the aftermath of the Khrushchev speech; we knew revolutions could go wrong, and that there was no guarantee that ours would not go wrong too. Alan was more suspicious than most; he always made it clear that he could not be counted on to follow the party line blindly or to act as a party hack.

In the early 1970s Alan took a course in trade-union studies at Enfield College of Technology, then moved to Coventry where he took an MA. This marked the beginning of a career as a trade-union tutor, something he continued to do for the rest of his working life, educating and inspiring large numbers of shop stewards and union activists.

In the 1980s he returned to Tottenham, where he spent the rest of his life. In 1987 he was diagnosed with stage four cancer; it was spotted early and his spleen and half his liver were removed. Those who visited him were required to inspect the large scar across his stomach. His intellectual curiosity did not forsake him. He acquired a large volume on cancer which he studied, anxious to discover what exactly was happening to him. Happily he recovered completely and until quite recently was still riding a bike. Not surprisingly, defence of the NHS was one of his favourite causes for the rest of his life.

Alan had a deep and visceral hatred of racism and fascism in all their manifestations. In the early 1990s the British National Party began appearing at Brick Lane in East London; Alan took a vigorous part in the counter-demonstrations. As one younger comrade said to me: 'This man is old enough to be my father, he's had chemotherapy, and he's leading us across the road to attack the BNP.'

Throughout the 1990s Alan continued to be active in SWP branches in Tottenham and Enfield. He did the required jobs and turned up for paper sales, more regularly and punctually than many of the more hackish branch members. But there was also scepticism — if you stood next to him on a paper sale you would hear murmured, not the officially endorsed slogans, but something along the lines of '*Socialist Worker* — cheap at half the price'.

Yet in support of workers' struggles he was serious and showed an amazing attention to detail. In the 1990s he and I did a *Socialist Worker* sale outside one of the few remaining well-organised furniture factories in the Lee Valley. We also did collections for a strike at University College Hospital. Each week Alan would take the money to UCH, and get a receipt which he would hand to one of the stewards. One week a steward handed to Alan over a hundred pounds which had been collected inside the factory. It was a striking indication of the trust which Alan's scrupulous approach had inspired.

At some point after 2000 Alan left the SWP. It is hard to be sure of the date because there was no dramatic departure or denunciation of former comrades. Alan stood as a Socialist Alliance candidate for Haringey Council in 2002, which meant working closely with SWP members, although he later told me he had left the SWP by that point. It was certainly testimony to his critical intelligence that at an age when most of us tend to be rather set in our ways, he was prepared to make such a break with his circle of acquaintances and his previous beliefs. Though there was no personal antagonism, he now had less contact with his old SWP comrades and became a supporter (though not a member) of the libertarian/anarchist Haringey Solidarity Group. He became the driving force in the Radical History Network, organising scores of meetings (see http://radicalhistorynetwork.blogspot.co.uk).

The essential cause for the break was the question of revolutionary strategy and organisation. He had now become sharply critical of Leninism and was suspicious of any sort of party that sought to impose its leadership; he was often highly critical of his old party, the SWP , which he accused of being 'obsessed with its central priority to build The Revolutionary Party — over all other considerations'. When I wrote a little pamphlet on Lenin in 2004 he sent me a page-by-page critique, attempting to demolish my arguments. Yet at the same time he rejected the anarchist position — as he put it to me a few years ago: 'I believe in the party, but not the party that you believe in.'

Alan had always been a writer (I commissioned some of his earliest pieces for *Labour Worker* — forerunner of *Socialist Worker*). But it was particularly in his last decade that he began to write copiously — a whole string of pamphlets on various aspects of working-class history, and also an autobiography. Many related to the question of workers' councils, which Alan with some justice saw as absolutely central to the socialist cause.

Alan's fierce concern to defend his independence meant that most of his writings were self-published — he was not prepared to compromise with any editor or publisher. Even his bibliographies were composed in his own style which diverged from standard practice (giving the number of pages in a book, but not its place of publication). Hopefully as much as possible of his work will be reprinted or made available on the Marxists Internet Archive.

But he always remained an activist. He was the Industrial Organiser of Haringey Trades Union Council, for which he edited news bulletins, and there were few picket lines or local campaigns in his area where he did not make his presence felt. In 2009 workers at the Visteon factory in Enfield occupied after being summarily dismissed. Alan, aged 69, was there from the beginning and spent a week in the factory, sleeping on the floor. His account of this struggle can be read at http://libcom.org/history/ford-visteon-enfield-workers-occupation-alan-woodward.

Alan's contribution to a discussion was always distinctive and instantly recognisable. He was clear and concrete, but he made no concessions whatsoever to the conventions of formal debating. One thing that immediately identified Alan was the way that almost every sentence ended with the word 'etc'. Maybe this was just a meaningless verbal habit, but I suspect there was more to it. In contrast to the party hacks who had everything neatly sown up in a dogmatic formulation, Alan seemed to be insisting that nothing was definitive, that there was always more to be said. (Perhaps there is a parallel with the way Victor Serge, whom Alan admired, so often ended sentences with three dots… to mark incompleteness.)

In 2008 I interviewed Alan as part of the research for my biography of Tony Cliff. He still spoke very positively of the International Socialists of the 1960s. He recalled that Cliff's 'capacity to build an organisation was absolutely magnificent', but thought that 'as time developed he began to be obsessive and he began to dominate and began to insist on his own perspective more or less at any price'. (A full transcript of this interview is available on the London Socialist Historians Group website at http://londonsocialisthistorians.blogspot.co.uk/2012/12/alan-woodward-interviewed-by-ian.html.)

One of Alan's last documents was entitled: 'What Is Socialist Libertarianism?'. Here he argued that: 'A libertarian society can therefore only be built from below, and that for us means workers' councils in workplace and neighbourhoods.' He concluded:

> This is not yet another leadership party, and we decline to build such a leadership. In its place, we propose setting up a party or organisation — the wording does not matter — that develops our own supporters' skill, knowledge and initiative, for a body that guides those actively engaged in the job in hand.

Personally, I do not find much to disagree with here, and would suggest that it expressed quite a lot of what Alan and I learned in the International Socialists in the 1960s. Of course, when it came to putting it into practice, we should have disagreed sharply. But then that was what we expected from Alan — someone who constantly called our ideas into question. He will be greatly missed.

The last time I saw him — a few months before he died — he was handing out leaflets at Seven Sisters tube station for a meeting in defence of the NHS. It was typical of Alan that he explained to me at some length reasons why I might not want to go to the meeting he was publicising.

A commemoration meeting held after his funeral brought together many of Alan's old friends and comrades, several from the early 1960s, and those he had worked with in the SWP, Haringey Solidarity and the Radical History Network, comrades with many differences but united by the principles that had animated Alan's life.

Ian Birchall

James D Young (1931-2012)

THE prolific and distinguished socialist historian James D Young died aged 81 on 24 June 2012, the anniversary of the battle of Bannockburn, one of the decisive battles of the First War of Scottish Independence as several of his obituarists have pointed out.[19] He was born on 3 April 1931, in Falkirk into a working-class family of Independent Labour Party and later Labour Party sympathies, and died in Polmont, not far from the town of his birth. His middle name, seemingly always abbreviated, was Douglas.

As outlined in his autobiography *Making Trouble*, he left school at 14 years of age, working as a labourer in a sawmill, then as a checker on the railways. Here he became involved with trade unionism, and at the age of 19 he was elected Secretary of the Trades and Labour Council in Grangemouth. He has described how he was won over to socialism by a veteran rank-and-file radical, James Dick, who introduced him to the literature of socialism and conveyed to him a rich oral history. This was to be the root inspiration of his best-known book *The Rousing of the Scottish Working Class*. It was through the unions that he achieved a scholarship to Newbattle Abbey College to study under the famous poet Edwin Muir. Newbattle must have been an interesting place to study, with a good proportion of students from trade-union and socialist backgrounds seeking to understand economics and politics, as well as a long tradition as a centre for poetry and literature. The poet George Mackay Brown was a student at the same time as Young. It was here that the basis was built for Young's love of literature which was to be reflected in many of his later writings.

After Newbattle he found a place at Ruskin College, Oxford, where he studied English Literature and working-class history under GDH Cole. He was working for the Oxford University Press and part-time lecturing for the NCLC. He was active in the Communist Party of Great Britain and chaired a meeting at which John Gollan (of the *Daily Worker* editorial board) denounced Michael Kidron as a Trotskyist. Young had no idea what Trotskyism was at that time, but defended Kidron's right to speak. Kidron was at that time the editor of *Socialist Review*, the journal of Tony Cliff's group. This incident sparked Young's curiosity about Trotsky and Trotskyism. He read Trotsky's *History of the Russian Revolution*, the only work by Trotsky in the Ruskin library. Kidron provided him with a copy of Cliff's *Stalinist Russia*. Young joined the Socialist Review Group in 1955, though his reading of Trotsky's *Revolution Betrayed* immunised him against full

---

19. Some obits have stated 23 June as the date of death. We rely on that from Young's son at http://seanblackbooks.blogspot.co.uk/2012/06/goodbye-dad-james-d-young-1931-2012.html.

acceptance of Cliff's theory of 'state capitalism'. He has claimed that about 1955 he struck up a friendship with EP Thompson, and sold his journal *The New Reasoner*.

After completing his studies he moved to London with a job on the *New Statesman* and wrote regularly for *Socialist Review*. Some differences with Cliff emerged at this stage and were to develop over time. Young described what he called the 'utter cultural alienation from everything "British" or Scottish or Irish' among most of his comrades. Cliff reproved him for taking his (Cliff's) daughter to a football match. A serious socialist would have nothing to do with football. Younger members of the leadership ridiculed Cliff on the matter, Young reported, and were proud of their independence, which was in contrast with the ethos of the Healy group (the Socialist Labour League). Ian Birchall has pointed out that Cliff's daughter, who does not remember the incident, could have been no older than 11, and Cliff's concern could as likely have been to do with her safety. Veterans of the SRG vigorously dispute Young's version of the cultural level of their colleagues.

Young came to be thought of as part of an 'ultra-left' tendency. They succeeded in winning the SRG to join the first Aldermaston march for unilateral nuclear disarmament (far from an 'ultra-left' position) but in very little else. (Just how this happened is far from clear, and there does not seem to be any record of a major debate on Aldermaston.) Young claims that most members of the SRG favoured the Shachtmanite 'bureaucratic collectivism' theory against Cliff's 'state capitalism' at this stage (though this claim has not been verified in other research and is disputed). The admirably open quality of the SRG at this time meant that Young was able to write about topics such as Lewis Grassic Gibbon, or Scottish nationalism, in the *Socialist Review*, even after having left the SRG in 1960. Young and other SRG members and ex-members were active in the Labour League of Youth, and the Young Socialists organisation of the Labour Party, and often collaborated with the SLL members there, and even on the SLL's *Labour Review*. He maintained contact via Seymour Papert (later to become a distinguished computer scientist) with Socialisme ou Barbarie in France, and met Raya Dunayevskaya in London. He treasured memories from this London period of street-fighting against fascists. He was later to write about the value of the political experience of the SRG, and how he learned much that helped him to form his 'Marxist-humanist' approach. He and his friends met and discussed with CLR James, who was then living in London. He developed a great admiration for James, which he was later to express at length in his 1999 book *The World of CLR James: The Unfragmented Vision*.

He left London and returned to Scotland, taking a PhD with the title *Working-Class and Radical Movements in Scotland and the Revolt from Liberalism, 1866-*

1900 in 1974 at Strathclyde before achieving a Readership in history at Stirling, a position he held until 1990 when health problems force him to abandon it. Before then he had made a name for himself by being the only faculty member to support the students' opposition and occupation of the campus buildings in protest at a visit by the Queen.

His first published book was *Totalitarianism, Democracy and the British Labour Movement Before 1917*, which appeared in 1974. Research financed by the Social Science Research Council into the project 'British Workers' Culture and Attitudes to State Intervention' provided him with rich material that was incorporated into *The Rousing of the Scottish Working Class*, which was published in 1979.

This title clearly responded to EP Thompson's *The Making of the English Working Class*, and set out in the most coherent and convincing way yet achieved that the Scottish workers had a history and tradition quite distinct from that of England. He was to update it with two subsequent editions as new information came to light. It is a work that opens eyes to the richness and breadth of the Scottish working-class tradition and its rootedness in a specific Scottish culture. It blends Young's loves of literature and the workers. In the course of this work he became increasingly convinced of the arguments for Scottish Socialist Republicanism and worked with the John MacLean Society, which published his pamphlet *The Life and Work of Karl Marx* in 1983. He became an optimistic exponent of Scottish independence from England. Will that optimism be justified in the end? The Scottish devolved assembly has been able to pass social legislation on issues such as university tuition fees and social care costs for the elderly far in advance of those in England. Reciprocating Young's support for the nationalist cause, Bill Kidd MSP recorded a short obituary in the proceedings of Holyrood, including positive comments on Young's republicanism.

The Scottish Republican Socialist Movement published his 1986 lecture *John MacLean: Educator of the Working Class* in pamphlet form,[20] and he won himself few friends south of the border by his rejection of the view that MacLean was 'mad' when he adopted the Scottish workers' republic line.

In 1987, he published a splendid speech, *Culture and Socialism: Working-Class Glasgow, 1778-1978*, to mark the opening of a mural on the history of rebellious labour in Glasgow. This can be recommended as an example of his work, and is available online at http://citystrolls.com/workers-city/young.htm.

He was very productive in the late 1980s, with *Socialism Since 1889: A Biographical History* in 1988, and *Socialism and the English Working Class: A History of English Labour, 1883-1939* in 1989. Sadly it was in 1990 that the first

20. Download available at http://www.scottishrepublicansocialistmovement.org/Documents/JM%20Educator%20of%20the%20Working%20Class%20PDF%201-10.PDF

signs of cancer and heart disease appeared.

The Very Bastards of Creation: Scottish International Radicalism, 1707-1995: A Biographical Study (1996) took its title from an outburst by John Wilkes, a radical defender of liberty in England. Young's point was that the 'left' in England was blind to the problems of national oppression and of intensive industrial exploitation in Scotland. He deployed a series of biographies of radicals and socialists in Scotland to assert the existence of an independent radical tradition that deserved the chance to govern itself.

The World of CLR James: The Unfragmented Vision appeared in 1999. Young tried to tear away the smothering and obscuring layers of academic studies of James, and to reinstate his revolutionary vision in the tradition of 'classic' European socialism, closer, he claimed, to the Second International than to Trotskyism. He found in James a confidence in the workers' ability to self-organise, which was at odds with Trotskyism as he saw it.

He wrote often for *The Scotsman* and *The Herald Scotland* as well as numerous small socialist and republican magazines, and it will be some considerable time before a full bibliography can be proffered. Always keen to combat attempts at distorting and depoliticising history, he produced voluminous disputes and rebuttals in respect of book reviews and academic presentations. This attitude failed to endear him to other academics, and their reviews were often critical of his inclination to sweeping statements and sharp criticisms.

His *The Two Falkirks: A History* (2004) expresses his love of the working class of that town and the surrounding region, where he had spent most of his life. His last book, on which he was working until a few weeks before his death, as yet unpublished, is a study of how James Connolly, the great leader of Irish Republican Socialism, learned his socialism during his early years in Scotland. It has been reported that he sent a corrupted disc of the text to Clydeside Press and we can only hope they succeed in rescuing it.

He was cremated on 2 July at Falkirk Crematorium. At the end of his review of *The Very Bastards of Creation* (http://nova.wpunj.edu/newpolitics/issue23/challi23.htm) in the American socialist magazine *New Politics*, Ray Challinor, aware of Young's health problems, concluded: 'Though it is unclear how long he will be able to continue, one thing is certain — James D Young will die with a pen in one hand, his other raised in a clenched-fist salute.' Challinor was right, though it was a keyboard not a pen.

Ron Heisler

HIGH THEORY FOR THE MARXIAN CHATTERING CLASSES

Philip Bounds, a self-styled 'libertarian Marxist' and sometime defender of Sean Matgamna, has scraped from the barrel of the Communist Party of Great Britain's intellectual life in the 1930s a substantial, imperfect, thankfully provocative book.[1] In it, he has given us clear, ample descriptions of the literary theories and positions of the main protagonists. This is to the advantage of the general reader: several of the key texts have become difficult to obtain in second-hand bookshops of late, and Bounds convinces us that these precursors — of a major succession of Marxist literary theorists, of whom the dominant figures have been Raymond Williams and, to a lesser degree, Terry Eagleton — are an interesting phenomenon in their own right. Some were vivid personalities. The *echt* Stalinist TA Jackson is worth disinterring, alas. A working-class autodidact steeped in English literature and capable of writing beautifully on a good day, he had strong aversions to washing regularly and Trotskyism in equal measure. It would be good to know why he was sidelined by the Party leadership and why they prevented publication of a further instalment of his memoirs (the manuscript hides in the Marx Memorial Library apparently). But such questions seem not to have occurred to Bounds. In compensation, Christopher Caudwell, the most original of the bunch, is at last rescued from the deadening fog cast over him by the soporific prose of David Margolies.

That the CPGB actually produced some interesting theorists at all is quite remarkable. After years of pursuing a policy of dedicated ineffectuality, it had managed to whittle membership down to 2350 by August 1930. By then it had no more than a few prominent intellectuals.

Third Period Communism, whose dismantling only properly set in during 1933, had been conducive to a strictly workerist ethos, one sublimely sectarian. Charlotte Haldane, wife of the Marxist scientist JBS Haldane, who went through the Stalinist mill, recalls the incident of a Party 'professional', a former

---

1. Philip Bounds, *British Communism and the Politics of Literature, 1928-1939* (Merlin Press, London, 2012, pp 320, £18.95).

elementary school teacher, visiting her home and seeing on the wall a Cezanne lithograph — *The Bathers*. The woman 'burst out into an amazing tirade of invective and abuse', wrote Charlotte:

> The vehemence with which she... reproached me for finding pleasure in owning it, was hardly short of hysterical, and having relieved herself of a series of almost incoherent allegations against the painter, the picture's owner, the 'highbrows', the bourgeoisie, past, present and future, and all their works; having pronounced this sweeping anathema, the good lady swept out.

Charlotte added:

> Time and time again the Party professionals indulged themselves in such... pronunciamentos; or else forced upon their reluctant artist comrades the acceptance of the most trashy or trivial works produced by politically orthodox and impeccable Party colleagues.[2]

Ralph Fox is one of Bounds' trinity of key literary thinkers. Like with Caudwell, it was his fate to die in the war in Spain — and perhaps unnecessarily. According to AL Rowse, who knew him well, the Communist Party sent him 'to Spain, against his will, to be a martyr'.[3] As for Caudwell, he initially drove an ambulance to the war front, then enlisted in the International Brigade. His brother Theo argued with Harry Pollitt in London to get Christopher recalled. Pollitt protested that Caudwell had only been instructed to drive the ambulance, certainly not to enlist. Caudwell died at Jarama on either 12 or 13 February 1937. A letter of his, dated 7 February, reveals that in enlisting he was not in violation of Party discipline.[4] Did Pollitt knowingly lie to Theo? Whatever the truth, the Party reaped a reward through the two martyrdoms — considerable prestige and respect came its way. The dead heroes were invaluable icons, assets to CPGB propaganda. Living, they had been merely minor players in a congested literary scene.

Fox was stationed in Moscow between 1930 and 1933, the English Librarian at the Marx-Engels Institute. Its head, Ryazanov, had been keen in 1930 to appoint Reg Groves as an English translator attached to the Marx and Engels *Collected Works* project. The move was stopped by British Party objections.

---

2. Charlotte Haldane, *Truth Will Out* (London, 1949), p 308.
3. James Whetter, *A British Hero: Christopher St John Sprigg aka Christopher Caudwell* (Gorran, 2011), p 168.
4. Christopher Pawling, *Christopher Caudwell: Towards a Dialectical Theory of Literature* (Basingstoke, 1989), pp 22-23.

Was Fox the channel through which they came? Possibly — some would say probably.[5]

A very fluent writer, Fox could be intelligent at times in matters literary, with spurts of real insight. Consistent in following a political 'line', he failed to be so, however, in his attempts at elaborating a Marxist literary theory. Quite rightly, he took FD Klingender to task on one occasion for his crude sociologism and moralism (derived from Ruskin and Arnold), but — as Bounds points out — *The Novel and the People*, for which Fox is best remembered, is the most *prescriptive* Marxist work of literary criticism of the decade; in other words, fell into the same trap as Klingender had done earlier. Bounds notes how seriously adrift Fox was in defending the base/superstructure metaphor against charges of reductionism (reductionism leaves out — in its purest form — the dialectical interplay between writer and society; cannot explain, for instance, how Balzac the ultra-reactionary could be so profound in analysing the workings of French capitalism in his novels — to Marx's joy). Fox had another problem: ever the good 'Moscow' man, he found himself yoked to the credo of 'socialist realism' — a view of 'reality' that insisted it be peopled with heroic-worker types. Yet Engels' stern warnings against the pitfalls of tendency [*tendenzen*] literature made explicit the need to avoid Party-oriented propagandist fiction.[6]

For Fox, the writer was someone who 'on the fringe of his own inner consciousness' proceeded to 'hammer out reality' and beat 'it out madly by the violences of thought'.[7] Most awkward for Fox was the fact that the writers in the recent past who fitted this job description most brilliantly, James Joyce and DH Lawrence, were the kind of modern literary pioneers whom he loathed and despised as decadent — symptoms of capitalistic decadence. And yet, amazingly, Fox was enormously sympathetic to the quasi-fascistic figure of TE Lawrence (the great portrait by William Roberts in the Ashmolean Museum makes this quality of the man unmistakeable). Fox saw Lawrence as a radically divided individual, on the one hand loyally serving British imperialist interests, on the other enthusiastically promoting pan-Arabism. There is an interesting parallel in the case of Robert Bolt, who wrote that most insightful screenplay for David Lean's film *Lawrence of Arabia*. Bolt had been a CPGB member in the 1940s before graduating to Maoism.

5. Bounds, *British Communism and the Politics of Literature*, p 137. There is a relevant draft letter to Riazanov from Stewart Purkis in the Archives at the Warwick Modern Records Centre among the Groves papers.
6. *Left Review*, November 1935; Bounds, *British Communism and the Politics of Literature*, p 134. On Fox on tendentiousness, see Bounds, *British Communism and the Politics of Literature*, pp 150, 155.
7. Bounds, *British Communism and the Politics of Literature*, p 159. Fox's lively metaphor on 'consciousness' was borrowed from Naomi Mitchinson.

Alick West, the second of Bounds' trinity, is far more substantial than Fox as a literary critic. Going by his autobiography, *One Man and His Time*,[8] he was a rum cove indeed. In it he confesses to having had Rightist inclinations: he had gone through a social credit phase (although, to be fair, there had been a trickle of social credit Leftists) as well as having been heavily influenced by an utterly dark book, *The Decline of the West*, by the extreme conservative Oswald Spengler. West admits he had often been strongly drawn to the doctrine of group identity at the heart of fascist ideology; yet we find it puzzling that he makes no mention at all of Martin Heidegger, whose brilliant work *Being and Time* had been published in Germany in 1927 to instant universal acclaim, his fame expanding rather more dramatically in 1933 when he became the Nazi Rector of Freiburg University. West was a fluent German speaker and had taught English at Basle University for a decade until returning to England in 1935. We suspect strong congruities between Heidegger's irrationalist anti-capitalist world-view and West's inner mind-set around 1930. Perhaps he feared that mentioning the noxious German would have invited the wrath of the furies — or of his CPGB critics. His very odd rendition of his own life-story remains tantalisingly full of question-begging blanks and silences. Far more dialectically sensitive than Fox to the problematic of literary creation, he still disappoints in the end, lacking any fresh big insights of his own as regards method.

We turn from the pale imaginations of Fox and West to Caudwell with some relief, for Caudwell is the one true star illuminating the CPGB's pallid 1930s firmament. Yet his Party existence was remarkably short-lived: not joining till after 21 November 1935, he died within 15 months. Despite his enthusiasm for the Moscow road, we doubt he would have stayed a Party epigone if he had survived — his penchant for facts and scientific truth would have eventually opened up an unbridgeable cleavage. Caudwell's wide background reading for *Illusion and Reality* (1937) — there are close to 300 works listed — is instructive. Here was a man steeped in anthropology, myth, magic, as well as the physical sciences, striving to capture all the infinite contents of man's world in a meaningful whole as perceived from the vantage point of the 1930s with its massive advances in the sciences (including the emergence of psychoanalysis) compared with Marx's day.

Too little attention has been given in the past to the fact that Caudwell is arguably the greatest rhetorician in the Marxist tradition springing from English-speaking soil. His writings are chock-full with brilliant passages that seem to glow with the white heat of the ecstatic moments in which they were conceived. His facility was buoyed up by an endless stream of scientific metaphors, as when

8. Alick West, *One Man and His Time: An Autobiography* (London, 1969).

excavating the nexus between the practitioners of literature and a latter-day capitalism whose 'effect' is 'to explode the whole field of consciousness into fragments'.

> This unendurable tension [writes Caudwell] is shown in the chaotic and intoxicated confusion of all *sincere* modern bourgeois art, decomposing and whirling about in a flux of perplexed agony. It is expressed by the cries of the Lawrences [DH and TE] and their followers, demanding a release from the torments of modern intellectual consciousness; and the schizophrenic vision of Joyce, condensing the whole Witches' Sabbath of bourgeois experience.

Elsewhere, Caudwell chides Joyce, who 'reflects the decline of bourgeois culture, the abandonment of its exploded certainties, and as yet no new understanding to take their place'. An accomplished science journalist, Caudwell was capable of seizing Marx's thoughts and rejigging them with added insight. There 'were periods', he asserts, 'when the whole superstructure, as if with explosive force, was rapidly shattered and transformed'. It was 'involved in one stupendous explosion, lasting for one or two centuries, like the slow-motion film of a bursting bomb'. He talks of how 'by virtue of the warp and woof of manifold relations engendered by social relations, which intersect in nodes, the 'nodes or individuals are individualised and become more than specimens of a species'.[9]

Caudwell is most famous for one phrase, 'the bourgeois illusion of freedom', from which he spun a web of criticism of the English novel, going back to its sixteenth-century proto-bourgeois origins. He was paralleling, of course, Marx's tracing of mystification among the political economists. But whilst remaining a fierce critic of British fiction, finding a continuing ideological tendency to depict individuals as if they were operating as free agents in society (a sound reading of Thomas Hardy would have soon put him right on that point!), Caudwell can still surprise us with the thought that 'art is no more propaganda than science'.[10] For him, ideology was to be found everywhere, corrupting every aspect of society, obstructing the individual's ability properly to recognise 'necessity' in the world, which constitutes true 'freedom'.

That Caudwell was eclectic and intellectually untidy is beyond dispute. However, his innate intelligence led him to realise that a meaningful Marxist

9. Bounds, *British Communism and the Politics of Literature*, pp 158, 160; Christopher Caudwell, *Illusion and Reality: A Study of the Sources of Poetry* (London, 1937), p 281; Christopher Caudwell, *Scenes and Actions: Unpublished Manuscripts* (selected, edited and introduced by Jean Duparc and David Margolies, London, 1986), p 217; Christopher Caudwell, *Further Studies in a Dying Culture* (London, 1949), pp 126, 149.
10. Caudwell, *Illusion and Reality*, p 155.

approach to literature would have to accord as much respect to matters of form as was given to content. He was perhaps at his best discussing poetry (he was a forgettable poet). And he was drawn to dialectics — he had read Hegel. He explains: 'The external world does not impose dialectic on thought, nor does thought impose it on the external world. The relation between subject and object, ego and Universe, is itself dialectic.'[11]

At times, Caudwell comes close to the young heretic Lukács. Thus there was a Caudwell 'crisis' in the making, but whose outcome was put on hold for over a decade. It was triggered when London's Muscovite bureaucracy initiated an offensive aimed at reining in the mob of scruffy brain workers, who were assuming intellectual pretensions above their station. Maurice Cornforth, who had studied under Wittgenstein, was the manager of Lawrence & Wishart. His *idée fixe*, be it noted, was that Wittgenstein provided useful materials to support the brilliant discoveries of J Stalin in the philosophy of language. Cornforth, in 1950, launched a broadside against Caudwell's 'idealism'.[12] The idiosyncratic scientist, JD Bernal, focussing on the writings on physics, declared Caudwell's dialectic to be 'more Hegelian than Marxist'. Even Lukács, eager to distance himself from reminders of his own youthful unorthodoxy, attacked *Illusion and Reality* for its idealism and 'irrationalism'.[13] Posthumously, Caudwell had become the subject of a bitter CPGB factional fight. His intellectual legacy, however, nourished an embryonic 'New Left', which eventually sped away from the CPGB after the trauma of 1956.

The history of the British Left over two centuries and more can be seen — to a large extent — as an endless stream of factional struggles. And the tanks and Kalashnikovs with which this perpetual warfare has been conducted are to be found essentially in the movement's newspapers and journals. Bounds' decision to ignore periodical literature misses out on much of the blood and guts — the gladiatorial aspect — of theoretical debate. And he seems not to realise that his theoretical protagonists were contending not merely with Muscovite orthodoxy, but also with a home-grown school of Marxism, which flourished within the National Council of Labour Colleges and the left of the Independent Labour Party. Criticism of the arts had been maintained in the Social Democratic

---

11. Caudwell, *Further Studies in a Dying Culture*, p 227.
12. Maurice Cornforth, 'Caudwell and Marxism', *Modern Quarterly*, Volume 6, no 1, Winter 1950-51.
13. Bounds, *British Communism and the Politics of Literature*, p 167; Christopher Pawling, 'Revisiting the Thirties in the Twenty-First Century', in Antony Shuttleworth (ed), *And In Our Time: Vision, Revision and British Writing of the 1930s* (Cranbury, 2003), pp 62-63; György Lukács, Werke, Volume 10 (*Probleme der Ästhetik*) (Luchterhand, 1969), pp 701, 768, 769, 785; Werke, Volume 11 (*Die Eigenart des Ästhetischen*), Halbband 1 (Luchterhand, 1969), pp 98, 267ff, 276, 598, 636, 785.

Federation's *Social Democrat* (which ran till 1913), in Christian socialist journals, in the ILP's *New Leader*, especially under the editorship of HN Brailsford from 1922 to 1926. Then there is the cultural emphasis of James Leatham (who'd been in the SDF) as expressed for so many years in the *Gateway* and numerous pamphlets. Not to forget that lively booklet by John S Clarke, *Marxism and History* (NCLC, November 1927), with its chapters 'The Material Basis of Art' and 'The Arts and Social Development'. It was prompted, we should say, by some juvenile remarks by one of Bounds' subjects, John Strachey.

Above all, Bounds inexplicably overlooks the challenge of the *Adelphi* magazine to the Moscow orientation. Under the charismatic leadership of John Middleton Murry, the *Adelphi* escalated at the start of the 1930s into an electrically-charged Marxist voice of a kind not encountered before in Britain: a pleasure to read, it thrived on controversy, established weekly debates at its Strand offices, and launched a hugely popular annual summer school. The audience apparently was a mix of workers and middle classes. As for JMM, he came of working-class stock, was the husband of the New Zealand short-story writer Katherine Mansfield, and had been a close friend of DH Lawrence. In 1930, he came out as a Marxist and communist, and threw himself into ILP activity. A brilliant writer, he commanded good writing from his contributors — and he had a good nose for talent. In his columns we find names such as WH Auden, the American critic and author of *To the Finland Station* Edmund Wilson, George Orwell (using his real name, Eric Blair), John Lewis, who eventually abandoned creative Marxism for a platitudinous existence in the CPGB, and our old friend FA Ridley.

JMM captured the *Zeitgeist* of radical middle-class England in the early 1930s whilst the CPGB was serving up the turgid Muscovite nostrums of Palme Dutt's *Labour Monthly* and *Communist Review*. It was as if he was the witty ring-master of a Marxist circus; and the CPGB had its allotted place as a butt of humour, given an occasional walk-on part — like a performing seal barking on cue whenever JMM cracked his whip, as with the luckless Pat Sloan. But praise was not denied Stalinists when praise was deserved. The review of Christopher Caudwell's *Illusion and Reality* — the most original work by Bounds' chosen few — was warm beyond measure. The reviewer (presumably JMM, June 1937) called Caudwell 'a genuine Marxist philosopher':

> The category 'bourgeois society' is employed by him as Marx meant it to be employed — which is extremely rare. In other words, Mr Caudwell has experienced Marxism as a real revolution in thought.

No opportunity was missed by the *Adelphi* to tweak the CPGB's nose. Trotsky's *My Life* was favourably reviewed (December 1930), and Frank Ridley contributed 'Marxism, History and a Fourth International' in May 1932. JT Murphy, who had been kicked out of the CPGB (his moral crimes included sending his son to a private school, Bedales, however), was a welcome contributor. Rosa Luxemburg, whose memory was under attack in Stalinist circles, was honoured with eight pages given over to her 'Letter from Prison' (November 1932). We also note Ellis Hillman's old confidant, Jon Kimche, of the ILP Youth Section, who wrote 'The ILP and Revolutionary Policy' (November 1932). The *Adelphi*'s debunking of Popular Frontism could be cruel. In July 1937, it pointed out that the 'solid substance of the Popular Front in France consists of peasant-proprietors' or 'French Kulaks'. The editor recalled how the Secretary of the French Communist Party had recently ended a speech with the revolutionary cry: '*Et vive le petit rentier!*' FA Lea (May 1938) reviewed Waldemar Gurian's *The Rise and Decline of Marxism*, commenting of the 'Marxist-Leninists': 'No wonder they hate "Trotskyism". It is the nemesis of their own duplicity.'

The *Adelphi*—whilst not offering blanket endorsement—had a clear spiritual affinity with Trotsky, one the Communist Party could neither countenance nor ignore. JMM's reply to a letter from Pat Sloan (April 1933) revels in the Party's discomfort — he was a deft stirrer. To 'do him [Sloan] justice', wrote JMM, 'he too has been civil. He has neither recommended his friends to spit upon us, like Mr Palme Dutt, nor has he, like the *Daily Worker*, tried to cover up his lack of argument by calling us "scurvy".' JMM (July 1936) reported with glee that 'Comrade Gallacher once disposed of me completely in the *Daily Worker* by referring to me "as the gentleman who wrote a life of Jesus". *Actum erat*; it was all up with me. And I dared to call myself a Communist!' Ralph Fox was reduced to paroxysms of loathing by the thought of JMM. In *Communist Review* (April 1932) he declared: 'We are inclined simply to laugh when charlatans like Middleton Murry and Ethel Mannin appear in the *New Leader* as saviours of the British workers.' But in *The Novel and the People* (1937), a curate's egg of good writing and ugly sectarian politics, Fox implicitly admitted Middleton Murry's stature as an obstacle to CPGB expansionism. Wrote Fox: 'We have had important writers who have sprung from the working class in our own country — HG Wells, Middleton Murry and DH Lawrence.' 'All three of these men tried to make their way into "society"', he lamented. But he found solace in the thought that:

> ... young writers are renouncing the path taken by Wells, Lawrence and Middleton Murry. They are not going to allow this degenerate social clique

to monopolise the intellectual life of our country.[14]

Perhaps Fox had rather more than a normal healthy Marxist complex about class, being the son of a partner in a large Halifax engineering firm.

As regards culture, the *Adelphi* had much to say. It was integral to its Marxist *Weltanschauung*. JMM discussed 'Communism and Art: or Bolshevism and Ballyhoo' (January 1933), showing his usual relish for the jugular. He assailed:

> ... negative and reductive Communism, which is the antithesis and counterpart of capitalism, inasmuch as it regards the human body solely as the creature of economic interest... Proletarian art is a mere chimaera, which if it has reality and value, has reality and value of the same kind as the commercial 'art' of the age of advertisements.

The word JMM was groping for here was not yet in English usage; but in Germany 'kitsch' was to be anatomised memorably by Adorno. The *Adelphi* was to promote the short stories of the worker writers Jack Common and Fred Urquhart, it should be said — but on the basis of the intrinsic quality of their writing. Outraged by the predominance of 'egotism' in society — the capitalist spirit of greed — JMM concluded that: 'Art *cannot* realise its implicit purpose:... it is now merely an abnormality... Proust, Joyce, Eliot — what are all the works of these men but the evidence of the impossibility of art? ... If they are decadent they are decadent in relation to some perfection' unobtainable under current conditions. JMM made the imaginative leap to the conclusion that 'Communism is itself an art' — '*the* art: ars artium'. Bounds' heroes — Fox, West and Caudwell — fed voraciously, if without acknowledgement, off his intellectual largesse.

JMM reviewed Reuben Osborn's *Freud and Marx* (April 1937). C Day Lewis, on a career path that would extend from CPGB membership to the Poet Laureateship, contributed 'The Poet and Revolution' (August 1932). There was Edmund Wilson with 'Art, the Proletariat and Marx' (October and November 1933); Waldo Frank with 'The Writer's Part in Communism' (August 1935); and Leslie Greener asking 'Is Art Dead?' (April 1936).

JMM dissected John Strachey's *The Coming Struggle for Power* (February 1933), neatly deflating the fellow-traveller's posturing as a serious literary theoretician. He noted that:

---

14. Ralph Fox, *The Novel and the People* (London, 1937), p 162.

... as for TS Eliot, Mr Strachey sees him as a kind of stock-market indicator. He directly relates the fluctuations of weariness and hope in Eliot's poetry to the slumps and booms of Capitalism! Perhaps it was a prophetic vision of 'Marxian Literary Criticism' that made Marx say: 'Thank God I am not a Marxist.'

But such reprimands could not hold back a career that encompassed membership of Mosley's New Party, crude defaming of Trotskyists whilst writing for the *Daily Worker*, serving as a feeble minister in the Attlee government — and eventually becoming an apologist for the British Empire. Bounds, however, repays Strachey's literary scrawlings with too much reverence.

And what was the fate of JMM? His personal failings loomed large; he seemed to cherish antagonising people. Rayner Heppenstall described him *circa* 1933 as 'the best-hated man of letters in the country'.[15] A slave to fluctuating intellectual passions, he moved on from Marxism to pacifism in the late 1930s. By the time he died, he seemed already a ghost from another era.

The fresh blood Communist intellectuals on the Party's cocktail circuit, once firmly shooed away from the allures of the *Adelphi*, found a congenial haven in the pages of the Party-approved *Left Review*. Founded in 1934, *Left Review* aimed at dislodging the *Adelphi* from its hegemony in the ILP-*marxisant* niche. But even when it was in rapid decline, in 1936, the *Adelphi* could boast of a 700-strong subscription list. We rather doubt *Left Review*'s claim of 1000 subscribers (October 1937). Amidst financial straits, it closed down in 1938; the *Adelphi* survived into the postwar period.

What were the Left-inclining readers of *Left Review* like? There is anecdotal evidence. James Boswell, a brilliant Party cartoonist, contributed a devastating sketch to the *Eye* (December 1935). We see two suavely-dressed literary types, wine-glasses in their hands, one remarking: 'Of course, he is not really class conscious like ourselves.' Valentine Ackland, who sifted out poetry submissions for the *Left Review*, complained that most of these authors were at Oxford or Cambridge, or lived in Chelsea or Bloomsbury; and described them as 'time-servers, toadies... desperately imitating Auden and Day Lewis'. William Coldstream, the leader of the Euston Road school of painters, supported the Popular Front and joined the Artists International Association. During the General Strike, he had driven a lorry for the strike-breaking side.[16]

Glyn Jones reviewed Day Lewis' *Noah and the Waters* (*Adelphi*, June 1936). He went for the heart of the problem:

15. Quoted in FA Lea, *The Life of John Middleton Murry* (London, 1959), p 213.
16. Christopher Hilliard, *To Exercise Our Talents: The Democratisation of Writing* (Cambridge, 2006), p 135; Coldstream exhibited at AIA exhibitions.

I wonder how many working-class cruets have supported a book of verse by a Marxist poet. My impression... is that... workers who care for poetry at all... prefer Hardy or [WH] Davies to writers with professed proletarian sympathies. And the reason is I think that a good deal of 'communist' verse has the air of deriving so little from any vital contact with the lives of the workers themselves, of implying too often the common-room rather than the [miners'] lodge and the coal-face.

Jones found Day Lewis' play 'quite irrelevant and unreal'. But there were Popular Frontists who understood the realities. William Empson, who had belonged to the Cambridge Labour Club, was an anti-fascist with no illusions about the great proletarian leader. He wrote: '... tell a Durham miner that Marx has something to tell him, and so he may, but don't pretend Stalin has.'[17]

WH Auden was the natural leader of the Marxist poetry pack, and whilst never a CPer, came close to the Party for a while. As close, that is, as one who ejaculated insincerity with such frequency could come to any cause. In 1935, Auden, at the behest of the CPGB film-maker Ivor Montagu, did translations from the Russian of two songs for the London screening of Vertov's *Three Songs of Lenin*.[18] More significantly, after returning from the war in Spain, he published the poem *Spain* in March 1937. Three months later, in June, Stalin's thugs began arresting and shooting leading Spanish anarchists. Auden's piece was to become infamous for its advocacy of 'the conscious acceptance of guilt in the necessary murder'. This putrid thought is not a million miles away from the sentiments expressed in 'Perfectionism and the Moscow Trials', an anonymous article — probably by John Lewis — appearing in the news sheet of the Christian Left in February 1937.[19] Here the Christian's 'call to community' entails that he 'freely' shares in 'the collective sin inseparable from human existence'. The Christian has to risk sharing 'in the responsibility for blunder, suffering and crime'. In other words, his religious call was to back up the Moscow Trials — and, a few months later, to whitewash the Spanish purges.

Auden's apologists such as James Fenton have been eager to deconstruct his tell-tale line as being merely a reference to the inevitability of taking life in war conditions.[20] But Auden's contemporaries — Orwell was particularly scathing

---

17. John Haffenden, *William Empson: Among the Mandarins*, Volume 1 (Oxford, 2005), p 435, letter of September 1938.
18. These poems have only recently been rediscovered: see *Times Literary Supplement*, 21 May 2009.
19. *The Christian Left*, no 6, 28 February 1937. This essay is reproduced in this issue of *Revolutionary History*.
20. James Fenton, 'Auden's Enchantment', *New York Review of Books*, 13 April 2000, pp 64-65. A skilled casuist, Fenton resorts to bland, academic-style obfuscation: 'Auden, it

— had a sharper insight into his alignment. Orwell restrainedly described Auden's key stanza as being:

> ... intended as a sort of thumbnail sketch of a day in the life of a 'good party man'. In the morning a couple of political murders... [then] a ten-minutes' interlude to stifle 'bourgeois' remorse... All very edifying. But notice the phrase 'necessary murder'. It could only be written by a person to whom murder is at most a *word*.

Orwell judged that:

> Mr Auden's brand of amoralism is only possible if you are the kind of person who is always somewhere else when the trigger is pulled. So much of left-wing thought is a kind of playing with fire by people who don't even know that fire is hot.[21]

Auden for many years tried to suppress his poem. When he allowed it into his *Collected Poetry*, the odious line was rephrased as 'the fact of murder'. Julian Symons noted the poet's determination to rewrite his own poetic past. Bounds is unjust to Symons, it should be said, in asserting that:

> The claim that British communists were little better than Stalin's cultural stooges is usually made by writers who are experts in Literary Studies rather than the history of communism... It can be found... in such important works as Julian Symons' *The Thirties: A Dream Resolved* (1960)...

Symons was politically engaged, being a member of a Trotskyist group for several months (probably in 1937) then adhering to theoretical Trotskyism for several years from 1938 onwards. He was a keen observer of the Stalinist phenomenon.[22]

Among the CPGB's élite intellectuals — the stratum of hardened, proven

---

seems clear to me, had used the word "murder" as an intensifier, not in any casual sense: to kill, even in defence of the Spanish republic, is murder, and we have to accept this.' No, we don't have to, Mr Fenton! As soon as we contextualise the moment of the penning of Auden's poem, with the Moscow Trials just having taken place and tensions rising between the Communist Party and anarchists in Spain, Auden's echoing of the Party's interior thinking is apparent.

21. George Orwell, *Inside the Whale and Other Essays* (London, 1940), pp 169-70.
22. Symons quoted in Katharine Bail Hoskins, *Today the Struggle: Literature and Politics in England During the Spanish Civil War* (Austin, 1969), p 124; Bounds, *British Communism and the Politics of Literature*, p 8; Bonnie Allen and John Walsdorf, *Julian Symons: A Bibliography* (Newcastle, 1996), p xxvi.

Moscow men — there was obvious concern and resentment at the latitude extended to writers on the cultural wing, even if that latitude was authorised. Shortly before the Party switched line to a 'United Front' policy, in August 1932, Palme Dutt, the fountainhead of intellectual terrorism, had circulated an infamous internal memorandum. Disdaining the proposal that the Party set up a 'society for intellectual workers', Dutt warned that intellectuals were ideologically treacherous and hence 'the first role of intellectuals who have joined the Party is to forget they are intellectuals and act as Communists, that is, enter fully into the Party fight', that is, do (and think) as they were told. Dutt was an innately unpleasant piece of work: the same year as he wrote the memo he advised Harry Pollitt on how to tackle a forthcoming debate with Fenner Brockway of the ILP: '*No politeness*', he instructed: 'Treatment as *class enemies* throughout. You speak for holy anger of whole international working class against the foulness that is Brockway. Make the whole audience *hate* him.'[23]

Palme Dutt was sulking at the fruits of the Popular Front, going by his response to the *Modern Quarterly*. Published by Lawrence & Wishart in conjunction with Gollancz, and launched in 1938, it targeted the intelligentsia of the academic and scientific world. The editorial board had a majority of open Stalinists and *sub rosa* Stalinists. The great catch was the presence of Labour's Professor Harold Laski. In March 1938, *Modern Quarterly* dutifully reported the severe criticism it had received from *Labour Monthly* (Palme Dutt, in other words). What was found objectionable was:

> ... the absence of any attempt to relate the basis of the journal to Marxism, the lack of forces in England for authoritative theoretical discussion of scientific and philosophical forces from the standpoint of Marxism, and the failure shown by writers in the first number to use the work already accomplished by Marxists in the fields dealt with.

Which is all quite odd, Palme Dutt being a member of the *Modern Quarterly* editorial board.

As surefooted as it was in formulating political 'lines' and imposing them on affiliated Parties abroad, when it came to giving direction in matters of literary policy and the arts, the Stalinist regime was uncertain and fumbling. But in any case the field of aesthetics had a rather low ranking in the scale of things. The Soviet cultural commissars were trying to straddle more than one horse: the holy writ of the writings of Marx and Engels on the arts, which could not be disputed; the mythology and ideal of the heroic-worker, which was absorbed

---

23. Bounds, *British Communism and the Politics of Literature*, pp 41-42; Kevin Morgan, *Harry Pollitt* (Manchester, 1994), p 82.

into the approved schema of 'Socialist Realism'; and the need, or natural wish, to claim a continuity between the great legacy of nineteenth-century Russian literature and writing in the Soviet era. Hence, in the latter case, the toleration of Lukács's theory of 'critical realism'. Inevitably, literary modernism was the main casualty of the overall policy, exemplified in the comments of Karl Radek on James Joyce's *Ulysses*, which he condemned as 'a heap of dung, crawling with worms, photographed by a cinema apparatus through a microscope'. In better times, Eisenstein had toyed with the idea of making a film of the novel.[24]

Bounds correctly points out that the English translation, *Problems of Soviet Literature* (1935), based on the proceedings of the Congress of the Union of Soviet Writers in 1934, at which Radek made his infamous attack, was 'the only substantive document on Soviet policy that British communists were able to consult during the 1930s'. Of the Kharkov congress declaration of November 1930 that 'proletarian literature should be national in form and socialist in content', Max Eastman had tartly observed that it was a 'meaningless profundity'.[25] William Empson, writing in 1935, commented: 'What seems clear from the varying accounts of the position of the author in Russia is that no one definition is generally accepted.'[26] FD Klingender, who was to produce some creditable work in the 1940s, complained in *Left Review* (December 1935) about 'the chaotic state of existing art theory' and the fact that 'any systematic body of Marxian thought on art does not as yet exist (at any rate outside the USSR)'. Nor did it exist even within the USSR for that matter. Caudwell could never come to terms with the great achievements of literary 'modernism', which these days are rarely disputed; and Bounds concedes that Caudwell's explanation of the so-called 'artistic poverty' of his age was 'clearly aimed to impose a measure of intellectual coherence on the more diffuse doctrine of cultural crisis which had been enunciated by Zhdanov, Radek and other Soviet communists'.[27] Bounds' gentle phrase 'more diffuse' covers a multitude of sins of confusion and contradiction within the Soviet theorising community. But such heaven-blessed sins allowed a space to emerge in Britain in which was born a rich school of Marxist aesthetics, whose maturity, however, was to be reserved for the 1950s and 1960s.

There were two influential voices in particular that helped mould contemporary thinking on Marxist aesthetics, and whom Bounds ignores: Max Eastman and William Empson. Eastman was Trotsky's loyal, but far from

24. Bounds, *British Communism and the Politics of Literature*, p 76.
25. Bounds, *British Communism and the Politics of Literature*, p 63; Max Eastman, *Artists in Uniform* (London, 1934), p 9.
26. William Empson, *Some Versions of Pastoral* (London, 1935), p 17.
27. Bounds, *British Communism and the Politics of Literature*, p 175.

uncritical friend. In 1934, Allen & Unwin published a London edition, with corrections to the New York edition, of Eastman's *Artists in Uniform*. This is a book that was widely read, presenting a knowledgeable perspective on Soviet cultural policy by a Russian speaker. Eastman states that Stalin 'cared little one way or the other about the Marxo-Leninist aesthetics concocted by the *Napostovtzi*, or the pillory and guillotine of lyric art set up by the RAPP' (the Russian Association of Proletarian Writers). The 'truth' is that 'Stalin *used* this monstrous growth of bigotry, this "Marxo-Leninist" aesthetic *Inquisition*, to purge the literary world of "Trotskyism", of honest and courageous revolutionary critics'. Eastman then reminds us that Stalin eventually had the RAPP organisation summarily 'liquidated'.

Eastman quotes Rosa Luxemburg in *Vorwärts* (14 March 1903) as saying: 'The working class cannot create its own art and science until after it is completely emancipated from its position as an actual class.' Trotsky is brought in: 'Art has its own laws... the Marxian methods are not the same as the artistic.' And Lenin is raided for the thoughts that:

We must preserve the beautiful... There is nothing better than the *Appassionata*... the proletarian culture must appear as a natural development... Every artist, everybody who wishes to, can claim the right to create freely according to his ideal...

To the chagrin of the *Daily Workerists*, no doubt, Eastman included a substantial supplement that could not be impugned: 'Lenin's Views of Art and Culture' by Vyacheslav Polonsky, the founder editor of the Soviet periodical *Press and Revolution*. We are indebted to Andy Croft for publishing the internal report of the 'Ralph Fox (Writers') Group of the CPGB' (*circa* 1938), which bitterly blamed the antagonism of British writers to the Soviet Union on the 'works of André Gide and Max Eastman'.[28]

Empson's *Some Versions of Pastoral* (1935) contains the best critique of the day of the cult of proletarian writing. All of Bounds' main characters would have known it. The brilliant Empson's career was wrecked when he was found with a girl in his room, and condoms among his belongings, at Magdalene College, Cambridge. He was expelled and, become unemployable in Britain because of the scandal, was forced to work abroad for several years. His Leftism remained undiminished.

'Pastoral' is a word descriptive of a convention in English poetry of the sixteenth and seventeenth centuries in which aristocratic versifiers, or their

28. Eastman, *Artists in Uniform*, pp 127, 132, 165, 168; Andy Croft, 'The Ralph Fox (Writers') Group', in Shuttleworth, *And In Our Time*, p 167.

hangers-on, would adopt the guise of a lowly shepherd for their poetic *personae*. At its worst, the trick assumes a repulsive phoniness. Think of Martin Amis doing 'working class' in his novels. Empson regarded 'good proletarian art' as 'usually Covert Pastoral'. And he denied the possibility of a 'pure proletarian art'. He cited the views of the painter George Bissill, a former miner, who had refused a cartoonist's job at the ILP's *New Leader* because he did not want to be a 'proletarian artist'. Empson reported that Bissill 'dislikes proletarian art because he feels that it is like pastoral, and that it is either patronising or "romantic"'. *Romantic* here seems to relate to the depiction of heroic-worker types.[29]

Soviet orthodoxy, however, had moved on from 'proletarian' art to 'Socialist Realism'. And even the ever loyal Ralph Fox was struggling, admitting of the new genre that it 'was still in its infancy and that no writer (with the partial exceptions of Mikhail Sholokhov, André Malraux and Ralph Bates) had so far managed to apply its principles with complete success'.[30]

The celebrated Orwellophobe, Andy Croft, is rather reproachful of the Party for a perceived laxity in matters cultural. He asserts that 'relative to other communist parties, the British Communist Party was slow to recognise the importance of the arts'. This is true enough, the ethos having been, as Irvine Welsh would say, 'fucking philistine'. Croft goes on:

> The Party did not express a view on cultural issues until 1945, when it established a National Arts Advisory Collective. It did not possess a literary magazine until 1952. In other words, before the Second World War, the Party's cultural organisation was extremely haphazard and *ad hoc*.[31]

Charlotte Haldane would have taken exception to this statement: she recalled distinctly 'various compulsory Party educational groups or classes for artists, musicians or writers'.[32] Moreover, Croft seems oblivious to the thought that was invested in the institutions of the Popular Front strategy. John Lehman, when launching New Writing — a commercial enterprise for Penguin Books — understood the strategy perfectly. 'I think LR [*Left Review*]', he wrote, 'should undoubtedly have a party member as editor, and be advised by anti-fascist fellow-travellers. My show [*New Writing*] the other way round.'[33] The outsourced cultural managers had been well instructed. In any case, Croft disregards the fact that *Left Review* had been specifically founded as the British

29. Empson, *Some Versions of Pastoral*, p 8. Bissill's reputation, after years of neglect, has risen sharply recently.
30. Bounds, *British Communism and the Politics of Literature*, p 149.
31. Croft, 'The Ralph Fox (Writers') Group', in Shuttleworth, *And In Our Time*, p 165.
32. Haldane, *Truth Will Out*, p 309.
33. Hilliard, *To Exercise Our Talents*, pp 136-37.

voice of the Writers' International.

Party control tightened as the 1940s progressed — centralisation became pronounced as Party membership substantially increased from the 17 500 it stood at in January 1939. In 1947, following Andrei Zhdanov's speeches on Soviet cultural policy, which had viciously heaped Kremlin displeasure on Prokofiev and Shostakovich, the CPGB formed a National Cultural Committee. On it sat Party hacks as disagreeable as Sam Aaronovitch (who lacked the finesse of his son, David Aaronovitch).[34] When Jack Lindsay set up a fine cultural magazine titled *Arena*, the NCC called him in for a chat; it was proposed that the Party nominate a majority of the editorial board. Lindsay refusing, the line was broadcast that Party members were not to read the magazine, and it soon died through want of sales.

Clearly, cultural-artistic policy had assumed an elevated importance in the minds of the Party leadership by the 1940s. Alison Macleod recalls going with Brian Pearce to a major meeting on Party arts policy in the early 1950s. John Berger, who later acquired star status as a television art presenter — and who has always denied that he ever joined the Party — delivered a long talk. The chairman then announced that there would be no questions and no discussion, and closed the meeting.[35]

Rather worse, however, were tactics on the cultural front during the period of the Hitler–Stalin Pact. The nadir of this phase was perhaps reached with the publication in 1940 of *Socialist Review*, edited by one 'Georg Noble', which incorporated the Stalinist *Young Worker and Youth Review*. Claiming to reflect 'all shades of left-wing opinion' and publishing 'work by progressive writers and artists', it issued a 'Special Peace Number'. Contributors on this occasion included Aldous Huxley, Louis MacNeice and John Middleton Murry. There was also a featured article that had been solicited from Hugh Ross Williamson. The editor explained that this presented:

> ... a viewpoint with which we do not entirely agree. His arguments closely resemble those of the BUF [Mosley's movement]... At present the BUF is campaigning against this war but only because a war against Germany is in its opinion the wrong one.

But Williamson must be allowed to speak for himself. His argument was that the Labour Party 'volte-face' on the issue of war 'was due to the success of a new form of socialism in Germany, which was achieved by dispensing with Trade Union Organisation, Marxist doctrine and Jewish capital'. He emphasised that

---

34. Bounds, *British Communism and the Politics of Literature*, p 128.
35. Personal communications from Alison Macleod, 2009, 2010.

'*The Daily Herald* (... whose chairman is Lord Southwood, née Elias), the Left Book Club (Gollancz), the *Tribune* (Strauss), the *Daily Worker* (Communist) have all relentlessly attacked National Socialism' for a five-year period. However, conceded Williamson:

> The Russo-German Pact dramatically restored a proper perspective in certain quarters and — though too late to save peace — sent the Communists back to the position they never should have deserted — 'for peace and socialism'.

Socialist Review's promotion of an all-inclusive peace front extending to self-righteous moral lectures from fascists is dumbfounding even by the standards of Stalinist cynicism.

Literary theorists of a Marxist persuasion have to work with strong assumptions and theories about the relationship the writer has with society. Necessarily, they have to engage with some notion of dialectics unless they are crass empiricists or structuralists — total reductionists. Back in 1977, Terry Eagleton — still, we would guess, in the throes of an Althusserian phase — complained bitterly that 'one has only to look at the best of the English Marxist aestheticians — Christopher Caudwell — to see how a *melange* of bourgeois empiricism, Romanticism and vulgar Marxism has been made to do the work of a scientific literary method' (that is, a structuralist approach).[36] There is some truth in the point, although one could quibble that, years later, when Eagleton began flirting with the sirens of postmodernism, one looked in vain for evidence of a credible 'Marxist' method flowing from *his* pen.

Bounds rarely gets to grips with the issue of 'dialectics' in his chosen writers. On one occasion, however, he finds fault in Alick West's *Crisis and Criticism* (1937), questioning 'why a thinker of West's subtlety should have adopted such an undialectical approach'. West's 'theory of cultural crisis' had been posited in terms of 'the opposition between individualism and communitarianism'. Bounds shows how feeble was West's definition of 'communitarianism' (it would be acceptable even to the Tory David Cameron), how lacking in substance; and how inflexibly he handled the contradiction between individualism and the communitarian impulse.[37]

Dialectics were taken seriously in Communist circles. Ralph Fox attacked FD Klingender (*Left Review*, November 1935), who had been moralising on 'Revolutionary Art Criticism'. Fox wrote:

---

36. Eagleton quoted in Pawling, 'Revisiting the Thirties in the Twenty-First Century', in Shuttleworth, *And In Our Time*, p 46.
37. Bounds, *British Communism and the Politics of Literature*, p 97.

Where in all this conception is dialectic? In this horrible jumble of rigid moral and sociological assumption, where is the idea of inner development, where is the real connection between form and content?

Kitty Cornforth (wife of Maurice) assailed Mark Graubard for a lack of the 'slightest understanding of the Marxist method' (*Student Vanguard*, June-July 1933). 'DR' lambasted Fred Casey in *Communist Review* (September 1931) for having 'us believe that the work of Marx and Engels in the sphere of dialectics was an unfinished work… until Dietzgen came along with the final touches…'. Actually, Casey had a bit of a point: Marx promised Engels for some years that he would write a brief tract on dialectics, but such a piece was never found. The best substitute that Stalinist Moscow could come up with was Adoratsky's small volume, *Dialectical Materialism*, which Martin Lawrence published in 1934.

'Dialectics' had early on been given a hallowed role in the internal educational work of the CPGB. We recall Councillor Bertie Cohen of Hackney, back in the 1960s, telling how when in the Young Communist League in the 1920s, attendance at educational classes had been compulsory. He had been obliged to attend one such on the subject of dialectics. 'I was completely lost!', he explained: 'What did dialectics have to do with a working-class chap like me?'[38]

The writings of Fred Casey — who admired the worker-philosopher Dietzgen — such as *Thinking* (1931), were widely studied in the network of Labour Colleges. And the Communist Party, which loathed the 'pseudo-Marxist NCLC' (that is, not under Party control), made its due response. Casey organised two classes for a 12-week course called 'Thinking' in Liverpool. He naively gave over one of the classes to a CPGB member to teach — one S Knight. Knight found Casey guilty of 'idealism' for writing that 'Thought can be primary', whereas the classic Marxist writers stated that: 'Matter is primary. Thought is secondary.' A campaign amongst the students aimed at ousting Casey, seemingly fomented by Knight, was finally suppressed by intervention from above.[39]

Problematic for the Party, too, was Ryan Worrall's *The Outlook of Science: Modern Materialism* (1933). This attempt to integrate advanced scientific thinking with a dialectical approach was a very credible effort for the period. However, Worrall was distinctly a non-person, having been expelled from the CPGB for unreliability (he was smeared as a police agent) before joining the

38. Personal communication from Bertie Cohen, *circa* 1968.
39. Our account is biased in favour of the CPGB since we rely on two articles in *Communist Review*: one by S Knight (August 1931) and the other by 'DR' (September 1931). We are grateful to Alan Spence for copies of lecture notes/courses run up by Knight at Wigan *circa* 1930. Based on Casey's *Method in Thinking*, they show that whilst Casey was bringing students to Marxism, Knight was intent on bringing them into the Communist Party.

Marxian League with Ridley and Dewar. His book was difficult to fault for the physics since one chapter was read and approved by Albert Einstein, another being vetted by Max Planck. There is a five-page section entitled 'Science, Art and Religion', which relies on Bukharin and Trotsky's *Literature and Revolution*. Worrall is pithy:

> Art is not fixed rigidly as a form of class oppression. Certainly art has a class content — reflects the class struggle of society, but not in an entirely one-sided fashion… it is also a means of expression of revolutionary thought.[40]

August Thalheimer, a leading German Communist, gave a lecture course on dialectics in 1927 at the Sun Yat-Sen University in Moscow. This eventually led to the book *Introduction to Dialectical Materialism: The Marxist World-View*. Containing sections on Chinese and Indian dialectics, it is possibly the most readable presentation of 'Diamat' — official Soviet dialectical materialism — of the time, with its clarity, lively examples and good humour. One's intelligence is not insulted. The work, unfortunately, was fated. Thalheimer was unceremoniously booted out of the Communist Party in 1928, to become a Brandlerite heretic. The New York translation of early 1936 seems excellently done and, according to the ILP magazine *Controversy* (June 1937), the Left Book Club had announced it was to bring out the British edition. Then suddenly this was withdrawn despite many orders being received. The Club's selection panel had consisted of three individuals: the publisher Victor Gollancz, Professor Harold Laski and Pat Sloan, Moscow's man. Gollancz and Laski happening to be travelling abroad at the same time, Sloan was left in sole charge: thus publication was killed. Notoriously, the Left Book Club also turned down the chance to publish Orwell's *Homage to Catalonia*, although in this case Gollancz's decision was primary. Eager to placate the CPGB, his *de facto* business associates, at any cost, Gollancz had rejected the best-written work ever offered to the Club. A consummate humbug, he was to publish the novels of the Irish writer Francis Stuart, from 1948 onwards; this despite knowing that Stuart, a gross anti-Semite, was infamous as an enthusiastic regular broadcaster on the Nazis' Berlin radio service during the War years.[41]

Sloan was symptomatic of Communist Party machinations in sections of the

---

40. RL Worrall, *The Outlook of Science: Modern Materialism* (London, 1933), pp 146-51.
41. 'Censorship of the Left' (editorial), *Controversy*, June 1937. Stuart, in his last TV interview (BBC, as I recall), described Jews as the 'canker in the rose'. Gollancz commissioned Louis W Bondy to write *Racketeers of Hatred* on fascism, paying a £200 advance. He rejected the MS, stating that 'we shouldn't be so nasty to the Germans'. It was published by Newman, Wolsey & Leicester (London, 1946), personal communication from Louis Bondy, *circa* 1980.

publishing world. Orwell was probably exaggerating only a little with his opinion that 'for about three years, in fact, the central stream of English Literature was more or less directly under Communist control'.[42] FA Ridley was lucky to get two books published by Ernest Wishart in 1935. A year later, Wishart had merged his firm with Martin Lawrence to form Lawrence & Wishart. Henceforth critical Marxist minds like Ridley's were not to be countenanced. Wishart had published the black writer George Padmore's *How Britain Rules Africa* just before the merger. Padmore, who had a not insignificant role in Moscow at one time, fell out with the CPGB when he began to question Moscow's approach to 'black' issues. Now something extraordinary happened. The 'house organ' of the merged publisher, the *Eye*, printed an anonymous review rubbishing Padmore's work, even though he remained on the publisher's list. Party loyalists were thus warned to steer clear of it.[43]

Andy Croft, an NCO in the army of the 'revisionist' school of CPGB historians, to this day is adamant that:

> ... if the Communist Party did try to use the Left Book Club as an instrument of control over British literary life, it was not very successful. In fact it is extremely difficult to identify any Communist control in literary London in the 1930s.[44]

These seem the imprecisions of a football-besotted soul who has been somewhat overtaxed by the endless chanting of his own doggerel verse.

The Stalinist injunction in the arts world might be summed up as 'control or kill'. Even music was not exempt. Benjamin Britten was attracted to Popular Frontism. His reward was, according to Michael Tippett, writing in July 1936, that Emile Burns, 'official of the party here, attacks Ben as counter-revolutionary because he hasn't joined the L of N [League of Nations] Union'. Alan Bush, a Stalinist till the end of a long life, was a classical music producer at the BBC radio service. He and Tippett had quarrelled, Tippett having gone through a Trotskyist phase before reverting to his natural pacifism. Bush managed to block the broadcasting of Tippett's *A Child of Our Time* for a period, according to John Amis. Few today bother with Bush's dull, academic compositions; but Tippett's anti-fascist oratorio has won its place as a concert hall classic.[45]

42. Orwell, *Inside the Whale and Other Essays*, p 163. On pages 173-74, Orwell writes, 'communists and near-communists had a disproportionately large influence in the literary reviews'.
43. Article by Reg Reynolds, *Controversy*, July 1937.
44. Croft, 'The Ralph Fox (Writers') Group', in Shuttleworth, *And In Our Time*, p 165.
45. Thomas Schuttenhelm, *Selected Letters of Michael Tippett* (London, 2005), p 125. John Amis has told the story of the blocking of the oratorio on at least two occasions on Radio

But to return to dialectics — and the often dire writings of Edward Conze on that subject. London born, he spent 10 years in the German Communist Party. Returning to England in 1933, he joined the Labour Party and enrolled in the ILP. He produced a dialectics pamphlet for the NCLC and a book, *The Scientific Method of Thinking: An Introduction to Dialectical Materialism* (1935). The latter received a drubbing at the hands of NA Holdaway, one of JMM's expert lieutenants at the *Adelphi* (November 1935), who found traces of mysticism, pragmatism and Platonic logic. Holdaway went for the panpsychic fallacy — whose roots lie in the sometimes embarrassing miscellany of Engels' unfinished notes, the *Dialectics of Nature*. He deplored that implicit in Conze's book was 'the assumption that there can be a generally applicable scientific method... a universal tool equally capable of use on society and nature'. Holdaway points out that dialectical materialism is 'the subjective aspect of capitalism, and its laws are the reflection of the material nature of capitalism, and its contradictions'.

TA Jackson published 'The Conzological Method of Twisting' in the *Eye* (October 1935). In his most effluent style, he homes in on some obvious defects in Conze's book before proceeding to raw abuse. Conze's 'real purpose', he alleges, is to 'give utterance to a whole string of malignant Trotskyite slanders upon Communists and Communism'; Jackson arraigns the 'Trotskyist' Conze on the charge of having 'Trotskyist purposes'. Gratuitously, he also mentions two works Conze had co-written with Ellen Wilkinson (an ex-CPGB member), thus associating her with the devil's work. It is all rather excessive considering that Conze was never a Trotskyist.

Conze was hit, but not out. In the ILP's *Controversy* (February 1937), in 'The Menace of Anti-Fascism', he rounded on 'the communists', who have 'invented a world conspiracy of "Trotzkyites"'. He pointed out that:

Their evidence is as flimsy as that of Hitler... the word 'Trotzkyist' is as elastic as the word 'Jew'. It is arbitrarily applied to any socialist who refuses to subordinate the struggle for socialism to the needs of Moscow's foreign policy.

A month later he replied to Pat Sloan's article 'The Menace of Edward Conze' (*Controversy*, March 1937). Here he launched a damaging missile at his erstwhile foe, TA Jackson. He quoted from the latter's piece in *Plebs* that January, in which Jackson had demonstrated his mastery of Stalinist dialectics. Claiming he was totally opposed to letting 'fascism' get control of any of the British colonies, Jackson then explained he 'would fight in the same way, and

---

3. It was finally broadcast on 10 January 1945 on the insistence of Arthur Bliss.

urge others to fight to preserve the British Empire — and with it the proletarian power of the working class of Britain to some day return to these Africans, Asiatics, Polynesians, etc, the power of self-determination which is theirs by right'. Clearly Jackson was having no truck with any ultra-leftist conceptions of colonial freedom struggles. As for Conze, who became obsessed with Buddhist dialectics, his life was to take a strange dialectical turn. Decades later he moved to East Germany and, it is reported, acted as a Stasi informant. Perhaps he had been a Stalinist agent all along!

In 1936 Jackson had published his big book, *Dialectics*. And *big* book it is, running to several hundred pages, the small content stretching a long way with countless examples. We recall reading somewhere the review by FA Ridley, who made the point that whilst dialectics were supposed to demonstrate the transformation of quantity into quality, Jackson had demonstrated the complete reverse. NA Holdaway tore into the book in the *Adelphi*. A furious Jackson replied (August 1936), incensed by Holdaway's waspish remark that he seemed to agree with Sidney Hook that 'Pragmatism is Marxism and Marxism Pragmatism'. Holdaway responded effectively in the same issue; and added for good measure that 'Comrade Jackson from his beginning, has to affirm the "mirror-image" nature of thought (or mechanistic materialism). Lenin, of course, explicitly denies this mirror-image theory.' The same month (*Left Review*, August 1936), Jackson had conceded that since both Marxism and pragmatism employ 'the criterion of Practice as the test of Truth, both are apt to seem the same to a superficial scrutiny'. He attacked Sidney Hook for denying 'all possibility of an objective dialectic of Nature *or* (except in a subjective-relative sense) of Human Society'. And he also used the article as cover to blast away at Max Eastman, proclaiming that 'Eastman's fundamental Utopian-Anarchism is avowed and — by means of his Pragmatism — lands him continually in objective activities indistinguishable from Fascism'. Eastman's association with Trotsky was, of course, Jackson's real target. We can only take pity on such half-crazed sectarianism; and confess we are puzzled by Bounds unaccountably deeming Jackson 'great'.

Even Moscow found Jackson's book a bit of a trial. The *Modern Quarterly* (July 1938) republished a review from *Under the Banner of Marxism*, which discerned a 'good literacy style' emanating from one who was 'not a theoretician of the Bloomsbury academic, "highbrow" type'. However, the book 'fails to explain the nature of the Leninist stage in the development of dialectical materialism'. The reviewer sought the reason for the weakness, suggesting it was due in part 'to the absence of English translations of a number of writings and speeches of Lenin and Stalin'. Poor Jackson — he wasn't Stalinist enough! After a listing of several other failings, he was let off lightly with a pat on the back, for making 'the butt of his wit' figures such as Professor John MacMurray, Raymond Postgate, Max Eastman and the 'neo-Dietzgenian' Fred Casey, who were guilty of 'theoretical poverty and political harmfulness'. The *Adelphi* probably had Jackson in mind when it published a fine parody of Stalinist dogma in 'The Doctorate of Dialectics' by H John Edwards (August 1937).

But already a fresh strand of dialectics was starting to grow shoots in Britain. Hungarians familiar with the work of George Lukács — Karl Polanyi and the art historian Frederick Antal — had emigrated to England; and in 1937 a Christian Left Group organised a week's study conference on the early writings of Karl Marx. Lukács's *History and Class Consciousness* was discussed, despite no English translation being available as far as we can tell.[46] Lenin had denounced the work, and the conference report noted that: 'It is only fair to add that as far as we know the author would repudiate part at least of the position outlined above.' This classic remains the key text of the 'Western Marxism' school. Far more accessible to the Anglophone world was a 1938 New York translation of a work by Lukács's disciple, Mikhail Lifshitz. *The Philosophy of Art of Karl Marx* was a masterly short survey, which points to a Hegelian Marx. Distributed through Collet's in London, it left its imprint on Jack Lindsay, Alick West and a new generation of thinkers on aesthetics. Four decades ago, we recall, we persuaded Richard Kuper at Pluto Press to republish it.[47]

We have detected a few factual errors in Bounds' book which call for correction or heavy qualification. The British Communist Party did not 'unilaterally' abandon its sectarian approach to trade unionism in 1931. The fostering of split-away unions was abandoned in that year, true enough, occasioned by the obvious abject failure of the policy; and this commonsensical step forward received the approval of Otto Kuusinen, acting on behalf of the Comintern.[48] We cannot, by the way, object to Bounds' statement that 'in no sense was George Orwell justified in claiming that Party intellectuals took their opinions from Moscow'.[49] It was Moscow's policies that they were in the habit of swallowing, despite some grumbles from time to time. Bounds emphasises Alick West's unhappiness with the Popular Front strategy. But West, in his 1969

---

46. For the trumpeting of Jackson, see Bounds, *British Communism and the Politics of Literature*, p 144. The British Library has a copy of the post-conference report: 'Notes of a Week's Study of the Early Writings of Karl Marx and Summary of Discussions on British Working-Class Consciousness' (1 January 1938)', 'Prepared by a Christian Left Group', *Bulletin*, no 2.
47. We are grateful to Ian Birchall for backing our suggestion. It was published by the New York Critics Group, which issued the magazine *Dialectics*.
48. Kuusinen approved the move to prioritise working in reformist trade unions in June 1932.
49. Bounds, *British Communism and the Politics of Literature*, p 5.

autobiography, fails to cite a single instance where he argued over that policy with the Party bureaucracy. He was a prime example of the tame intellectual type so beloved by the Party leadership — so loyal, so malleable, the 'inner doubts' as audible as the squeaks of a bat.

Bounds seems to labour under a misapprehension about John Lewis: he writes of a 1935 symposium that 'a number of Marxist intellectuals (for example, John Lewis and WH Auden) joined with their Christian counterparts (for example, John MacMurray and Karl Polanyi) to assess the relationship between their respective creeds'. John Lewis was always a committed Christian — a Unitarian minister, in fact, until he resigned his post to teach philosophy at Morley College.[50] Questionable in the extreme also is Bounds' description of Jonathan Swift as 'a Protestant cleric of solidly aristocratic background, who served the Tory government of Lord Oxford as a propagandist...'.[51] That he received Tory aristocratic patronage is beyond dispute — political patronage in those days was normally aristocratic. But the *Oxford Dictionary of National Biography* makes Swift's non-aristocratic family background clear. His father was steward of the King's Inns at Dublin (a lawyer, in other words). Two of his uncles were also lawyers. On his mother's side, his grandfather was the vicar of Thornton, Leicestershire — and had been accused at one time of holding an unlawful non-conformist conventicle. So there is a strong streak of dissent among the skeletons in the family cupboard.

Some reservations regarding Bounds' work were inevitable considering its ambitious nature. But its attractive elements should not be overlooked. We pray, however, that it does not end up merely as the career fodder of the hustlers and dominatrices who frolic so abundantly in university literature departments. For such a fate would indeed signal the extinction of Marxist aesthetics as a living cultural force. Stalinism may have all but destroyed Marxism, but academia destroys the soul.

50. Bounds, *British Communism and the Politics of Literature*, pp 117-18.
51. Bounds, *British Communism and the Politics of Literature*, p 214.

Paul Le Blanc

MAKING SENSE OF TROTSKYISM IN THE UNITED STATES: TWO MEMOIRS

The Socialist Workers Party (SWP) of the United States was for a number of years the largest and strongest section of the Fourth International — both of which were formally established in 1938, both representing the revolutionary socialist perspectives associated with Leon Trotsky. Rooted in opposition to Stalinism in the early Communist movement, the US Trotskyists worked closely with Trotsky in building the Fourth International, the global network of small revolutionary groups adhering to the original 'Bolshevik-Leninist' perspectives. They also played an heroic role in US class struggles of the 1930s, and their reputation among many was as unyielding partisans of workers' democracy and Trotsky's revolutionary Marxist orientation. Yet in the non-revolutionary aridity of 1950s America, their ranks dwindled down to handfuls of stalwarts, perhaps 400 ageing members, in a handful of cities.

The memoirs of Peter Camejo and Leslie Evans[1] were produced by two of the most talented of the '1960s generation' rebels who flowed into and revitalised the SWP. Camejo (joining in 1959) was perhaps the best-known activist leader of the party in the 1960s and 1970s, and Evans (who joined in 1961) was perhaps its most capable writer, editor and educator of that same 'youth' layer. Both basically turned away from Trotskyism, quite consciously, during the 1980s. What is strange is that the SWP as a whole absolutely did the same thing — expelling or driving out all those not inclined to go along with the transition to its own esoteric variety of Castroism. Yet to their credit, neither Camejo nor Evans were able to remain inside the newly-revised version of the SWP, and their stories each in its own way reveal much about the 'how' and the 'why' of this development. What each has to say, however, goes beyond the specifics of that experience. Larger questions emerge regarding the nature of activism and social change, the validity of Marxism, the possibility and/or need of socialism.

Camejo was writing his autobiography in a race with terminal cancer —

1. Peter Camejo, *North Star: A Memoir* (Haymarket Books, Chicago, 2010, pp 364, $18.00); Leslie Evans, *Outsider's Reverie: A Memoir* (Boryana Books, Los Angeles, 2010, pp 438, $18.95).

which he almost won. Evans helped edit this book and prepare it for publication, and he was consequently inspired to write his own autobiography. But the two books are dramatically different in more than one way. Camejo focuses much more on social movements and struggles, all motivated by a never-ending opposition to the injustices of capitalism. Evans focuses much, much more on political ideas as well as internal life and conflicts within the SWP — and far more than Camejo he has made his peace with the status quo, settling into a niche very much to the right of his fellow memoirist. Camejo rejects the old Trotskyism because he sees it as an obstacle to revolution — Evans rejects it in large measure because he has decided that revolution itself is a bad thing, although this break was neither simple nor easy for him:

> In 1983 I may have begun to have doubts about Lenin and Marxism, but a lifetime of personal and political loyalties didn't die easily or quickly. Part of it was habit, part loyalty to my fellow expellees. Then there were the dead to whom you had to answer. Trotskyism, like most religions, had its many martyrs, who inspired belief and dedication by their example. There was Trotsky himself, assassinated by Stalin's agent in Mexico in 1940. His son, Leon Sedov, was murdered in a Swiss hospital in 1938 by Russian doctors secretly working for the KGB. There were the Old Bolsheviks, most of Lenin's Central Committee, shot in the back of the head in the basements of Moscow's Lubianka Prison, where the cells were conveniently supplied with floor drains. And the countless anonymous victims I had become familiar with from the movement's literature: the Trotskyist prisoners at the Vorkuta labor camp in Siberia, marched in groups to the firing squads in 1937 singing the *Internationale*, and the hundreds of Chinese Trotskyists shot by the Maoists in 1952, it was said after having their tongues cut out so they couldn't shout any last protests. A few of them were jailed instead and remained there until after Mao's death. (Evans, p 312)

In his own fashion, Evans seeks to remain true to this tradition — by writing as honest an account as he can, and certainly respectful of the finest in the old traditions from which he has turned away. As such, his memoir is a treasure-trove for those seeking to understand at least some of the dynamics of the SWP in its years of growth and decline while Evans was a member. Yet it is hardly the kind of book one would hand to a young activist to help her or him carry on the revolutionary struggle for a better world, a struggle Evans now rejects.

Camejo also seeks to remain true to his earlier commitments — in his own fashion. But its thrust and spirit make it an ideal volume for young activists. He tells us:

The battles in which small groups of Trotskyists fought against Stalinism will go down in history as heroic. Trotskyists were murdered in tremendous numbers in Russia and were persecuted in other countries as well. They faced enormous hostility from the huge mass base of the Communist parties, but also endured attacks from pro-capitalist forces.

As an instrument to revive the mass world movement for social justice, however, I think that Trotskyism had historical, internal, sectarian limits that blocked it from being able to become a critical force for social change. But during the early 1970s I can see in my diary that I still thought it was possible that the Trotskyist movement would gradually, and with occasional opportunities for explosive growth, come to replace the influence of the Stalinists and social democrats. (Camejo, pp 115-16)

Both books give a vibrant sense of the perceptions and realities that made 'believers' of Evans, Camejo and many other activists of that time.

Glory Days

An almost 'glowing' chapter in Evans' memoir deals with the amazing year of 1968. His focus is global, involving a blend of triumph and tragedy: the dramatic surge in the Vietnamese liberation struggle; the decision of President Johnson not to seek re-election due to anti-war pressure; the quest for 'socialism with a human face' in Czechoslovakia associated with the 'Prague Spring' — and the repressive Soviet invasion a few months later; the assassination of Martin Luther King, Jr, as he was coming to the aid of striking sanitation workers, followed by enraged urban uprisings in black communities throughout the nation; militant student strikes throughout the United States; the May-June student and workers' upsurge in France that almost toppled the De Gaulle regime; the mass student struggles in Mexico, violently repressed by the regime; and the militant protests in Chicago during the Democratic Party convention. All of this gave life to what had often been abstract assertions of revolutionary internationalism. 'The afterglow of 1968', he writes, 'radiated for several years, raising spirits and hopes.' (Evans, p 194)

Camejo's account puts us in the thick of the battle. He tells us about tactics and strategy of the late 1960s and early 1970s — the remarkable 'Battle for Telegraph Avenue' in the radicalising Berkeley of 1968, the People's Park confrontation, defence campaigns and electoral campaigns, all in the context of a sustained analysis of capitalism, state repression, imperialism, etc, that he held as much at the time of writing as at the earlier time of doing. A richly-detailed chapter is devoted to the movement to end the Vietnam war, in which Camejo describes and defends the basic SWP strategy.

Although less detailed, Evans's account is also positive. He describes the National Peace Action Coalition (NPAC) in which the SWP was a leading force — in competition with the seemingly more radical People's Coalition for Peace and Justice (PCPJ, backed by diverse elements that included the Communist Party, an increasingly ultra-left SDS, some radical pacifists, etc). He notes that what 'NPAC had going for it... [was] a clear focus on the war, based on mass peaceful legal demonstrations, and the SWP cadres, who were generally tough dedicated people embedded in the leadership of real anti-war groups in a dozen major cities'. When NPAC 'called for national demonstrations in Washington and San Francisco for 24 April 1971, PCPJ backed a week of civil disobedience and disruptions in Washington beginning 1 May'.

Far more than the May Day actions, 24 April was building all over the country, and then came under attack from conservative newspaper columnists Rowland Evans and Robert Novak, who published an attack warning of 'Trotskyite Communists ... [who] were running NPAC', and lamenting that 'what makes all this significant is that the Trotskyists are not the few bedraggled malcontents of a generation ago but the most dynamic, most effective organization on the American far left'. Les Evans comments: 'I cite this to show how the government and much of the mainstream press viewed us in those years, and how we viewed ourselves. We had come from the few hundred "bedraggled malcontents" I had joined in 1961 to become generals of the anti-war army.' Indeed, 800 000 in Washington and at least 250 000 in San Francisco mobilised — in contrast to the 16 000 drawn to PCPJ's more 'radical' but disparate action on 1 May (Evans, pp 209-10).

The fact that both Evans and Camejo are quite prepared critically to examine and reject much of what they and the SWP did gives weight to the fact that both present a very positive account of the US Trotskyists' role in helping build the mass movement that contributed to ending the US war in Vietnam — peaceful, legal, broad-based mass actions focused on a central demand: *bring the troops home now*. Their great respect for certain figures in the older generation is also enhanced by the fact that they now disagree with much of what these figures stood for.

Among the electoral campaigns run by the SWP — which were always educational campaigns to get out socialist ideas and help build social movements and struggles — the most dynamic by far was the Presidential candidacy of Peter Camejo and his running-mate Willie Mae Reid. More than most other candidates, Camejo was able to generate energy and enthusiasm, sometimes to break into the mass media, and to get out the socialist message. The SWP membership, he suggests:

... sensed that, unlike the other party speakers, there was something unique in my presentations that attracted new people to the SWP. However, most people did not realize that it was the non-sectarian manner of my approach — they just thought it was because I was a good speaker, a sort of political stand-up comic who used a lot of humor to illustrate points and keep the audience entertained. (Camejo, pp 129-30)

The combined size of the SWP and its youth group the Young Socialist Alliance, by 1976, exceeded 2000 people — mostly in their twenties and thirties, with tremendous energy and commitment. There was a substantial weekly newspaper, *The Militant*, a monthly theoretical/political magazine, the *International Socialist Review* (which Evans edited in its most successful phase), plus the international weekly *Intercontinental Press* edited by Trotsky's former secretary Joe Hansen. There was also Pathfinder Press, a publishing house producing a remarkable array of books and popular pamphlets, largely overseen by George Breitman, another veteran of the movement, whose *Malcolm X Speaks* made the speeches of Malcolm X available to millions, and who made excellent editions of Trotsky's writings available throughout the English-speaking world. The SWP also boasted a substantial three-story national headquarters, a chain of combined offices/book stores/forum halls (with weekly forums) in a growing number of cities, maintained by an impressive corps of paid staff and many, many more hardworking volunteer activists.

What Happened?

How could something so good go so wrong? Looming large in both accounts is the figure of Jack Barnes. The rise of Barnes cannot be understood without reviewing some history about, and tracing some tensions within, the US Trotskyist 'old guard'. Evans gives considerable attention to such matters.

Back in 1953, the semi-retired founder of American Trotskyism, James P Cannon — now living on the West Coast, surrounded by like-minded comrades there, and in touch with veteran comrades around the country — pressured the new national leadership of union veterans Farrell Dobbs and Tom Kerry into a brutal factional dispute with a significant layer of comrades, led by Bert Cochran. The Cochran group, favouring a dramatic curtailment of open SWP activities in the McCarthyite anti-communist atmosphere generated by the Cold War, had aligned itself with the leadership of the Fourth International headed by Michel Pablo, who was calling for Trotskyists around the world to fold their banners in order to carry out a 'deep entry' into Communist and social democratic movements and organisations. Cannon would have none of this — pressuring a reluctant Dobbs and Kerry onto a course of struggle and split. Working closely with Cannon in this were a dynamic husband and wife team, Murray Weiss and Myra Tanner Weiss. Once the integrity of the SWP was preserved, and particularly with Stalinism's crisis generated by the Khrushchev revelations of Stalin's crimes, the couple pushed forward (with apparent support from Cannon) in outward-reaching regroupment efforts on the left. In the process, they developed a substantial influence among recently-recruited younger comrades who were involved in forming a new youth group in the late 1950s, the Young Socialist Alliance (YSA).

Believing that they were the rightful leaders of the SWP, Dobbs and Kerry deeply resented Cannon's interventions, and had a profound antipathy toward the 'Weissites' (Murray, Myra and anyone associated with them). But 'Weissites' were not the only forces involved in building up the YSA. Clusters of young comrades around Tim Wohlforth and James Robertson and new recruits Peter Camejo and Barry Sheppard were also helping lead the newly-formed YSA. Dobbs and Kerry, seeking to 'tighten up' the party regime, increasingly worked to side-line and marginalise the 'Weissites' — and when Wohlforth and Robertson moved into increasingly vociferous opposition (around the issues of the Cuban Revolution and the reunification of the Fourth International), they found themselves marginalised and finally expelled (going on to form, respectively, the Workers League associated with Gerry Healy's Socialist Labour League in Britain, and the Spartacist League). This left Camejo and Sheppard, but in the radical stirrings of the early 1960s new forces were increasingly drawn in. 'The real standout was Jack Barnes, a Carleton College graduate who joined the YSA and SWP in Minneapolis', according to Camejo:

> Jack helped recruit a group of very capable leaders into the YSA, including Carleton classmates Larry Seigle, Dan Styron, and Mary-Alice Waters; while at graduate school at Northwestern, Jack brought in brothers Joel and Jon Britton, Lew Jones, and several more from the Chicago area. (Camejo, p 37)

Evans adds nuance and detail. Initially, Barnes was not an impressive speaker:

> When I first heard him in 1963 he was halting and difficult to follow. Oscar Coover [an older party veteran], who had heard him give a talk in Los Angeles after I had moved to San Francisco, said to me afterwards, 'How can the national office send us somebody like that? He has no idea how to speak, and the way he waves that stump of his around would put anybody off.' Jack did have the habit when speaking of slapping his left elbow where the arm ended [due to a birth defect] with his right hand for emphasis. (Evans, p 178)

While he never lost that mannerism, Barnes soon matured as a speaker. By the 1965 YSA convention:

> Barnes emerged as the central leader of the YSA, the most authoritative and assured speaker on the major resolutions on the floor. When it was over, a brief plenum of the newly-elected National Committee was called before we all left for home. It was held in a small unheated room. Outside, snow was falling and the temperature inside was near freezing. We were all standing, wearing our overcoats and breathing out white clouds of chill vapor. It made me think of the Bolshevik high command at the Smolny Institute in St Petersburg during the October Revolution. It was in this setting that Barnes — nominating himself — was overwhelmingly selected as national chairman of the YSA. (Evans, p 157)

By this time, Evans notes:

> Jack's standing had risen enormously, from a branch leader in Chicago to the effective head of the party. Farrell Dobbs didn't hand over the post of National Secretary until 1972 but it was already clear that Jack and his inner circle were the heirs of the generation of the 1930s. The handful of middle-generation recruits from the late 1940s and the 1950s, such as Fred Halstead, Dick Garza, Ed Shaw, and Bob Himmel, were subordinate. (Evans, p 178)

Yet there were disturbing early signs. An angry dissident from the Bloomington, Indiana YSA told Evans and his then-wife Kipp Dawson about Barnes's heavy-handedness toward those differing with him, adding:

> Jack Barnes is the Stalin of the SWP... The older comrades are desperate for successors so they blind themselves to it but Barnes is building a machine just like Stalin did. He undermines anyone who isn't part of his clique and gets them out of the way. He doesn't want recruits who know anything, nobody who was ever in any other socialist organization. All he wants is empty vessels he can fill up with his picture of himself as another Lenin. (Evans, p 151)

Evans and Dawson decided to reserve judgement. By the late 1960s, Evans observed:

> Barnes himself adapted publicly to the standards of conduct of the older generation of party leaders, tough but fair. Still, there were differences and warning signs in private. Unlike any of the older group, Jack routinely said

vicious things about people to anyone who happened to be around, which I took as a technique to keep people in line as you knew he would pillory you out of your hearing if you displeased him. (Evans, p 227)

The national party leadership — in the minds of some of the new comrades — tended to be ranked in a particular way: 'Joseph Hansen and George Breitman were theoreticians, the highest superlative, while Tom Kerry and Farrell Dobbs were at best politicians, able to carry out policy but not to formulate it. George Novack ranked lower still, an educator.' (Evans, p 158) All were in their sixties, more or less. There was the need for… a Barnes. Even the way he wielded his half-arm:

… was something of a defiant pose, saying to the world that he was unyielding and wouldn't concede an inch to a physical obstacle. He was the same in politics, hard, ruthless, and unyielding. That was what attracted us to him. The SWP as it existed at the 1963 convention seemed an impossibly weak instrument to rouse and mobilize the millions it would take to turn out the men of property who owned the country. Barnes meant to build a different kind of organization, as hard and mean as himself. (Evans, p 143)

More than this:

… there was a clear strong intelligence that rarely sounded like sloganeering or the tendency in many of the older comrades to approach every new situation with a set of fixed dead categories into which everything had to be shoveled. He looked always at the places where a small group could intervene in a situation to shape it. He was hard, which is what attracted us to him, but he seemed to also be fair. I was surprised at his patience in waiting five more years to assume the title of National Secretary when he already carried its authority. He would wait seven years after that, until most of the older generation were dead, before making a decisive move to impose his own vision on the party.

It was clear to those who were watching that there was a Barnes machine, 'a group within the younger leadership, most importantly the Carleton people and a few he had picked up in Chicago, who were his base and who were almost always favored in the distribution of important assignments' (Evans, pp 178-79).
The new leadership layer worked hand-in-glove with the old, in the 1969-74 transition period, around a fierce dispute within the Fourth International

which began over whether Trotskyists in Latin America should support a continental strategy of guerrilla warfare or adhere to the traditional 'Leninist strategy of party building' rooted in the struggles of the working class — but soon encompassing a multiplicity of related issues. By the mid-1970s, SWPers felt, with some justification, that they had more or less won this dispute — but the taste of victory, and the certainty that theirs was the correct understanding of global reality, soured by 1979-80 as the Iranian Revolution that they had supported took an unexpected turn to reactionary Islamic fundamentalism, and as the Sandinista struggle in Nicaragua, which they insisted was about to collapse because it followed the wrong strategy, was swept to victory.

Disorientation and Disaster

The SWP actually began to flounder after the end of the Vietnam war. The question of questions was how to integrate the work of the party with the realities of the US working class. With Barnes and his machine firmly in place, and the old guard moving (or being moved) increasingly to the sidelines, there was a decision to break up large SWP branches and create smaller community branches — which badly flopped. The decision to shift to working-class struggles was hardly unreasonable, however, although neither Camejo nor Evans give attention to dramatic stirrings in the United Mine Workers (the struggles and triumph of Miners for Democracy), the United Steel Workers (the militant campaign of dissident Ed Sadlowski), the International Brotherhood of Teamsters (where Teamsters for Democracy was making headway), the Oil, Chemical and Atomic Workers (where a militant Tony Mazzocchi was becoming a force in the national leadership and beginning to agitate for a labour party), or the dramatic upsurge in organising and struggle among service workers and government employees. What they are alert to, however, is how the 'turn to industry' was increasingly bungled. Camejo puts it this way:

> The SWP gradually separated itself from all political activity, rendering the membership passive. Finding union jobs in auto, steel, or another industry allowed some members to maintain the illusion they were doing something political. But the SWP leadership went so far as to dictate that members should not be teachers, work for a library, or take any sort of 'middle-class' job, and there was not to be any more student movement work. This disconnect from reality led to internal conflict, factionalism and expulsions, until the SWP was reduced to a sect, a cult around Barnes. (Camejo, p 176)

While comrades were deployed in industrial jobs, the new party leadership seemed to have little understanding about how the SWP could relate to the actual problems and struggles of workers in the industrial workplaces. Evans along with some other comrades took a job as an iron ore miner on the desolate Minnesota iron range — which was hit badly in the 1980s by lay-offs brought on by an economic restructuring that led to what some economists called the 'de-industrialisation of America'. A party branch meeting was set to discuss what the comrades' response should be. The branch organiser — in touch with the national office — 'proposed that the party members at the next meeting of Local 1938... call for having a Nicaragua slide show'. A loyal comrade named Anne Teasdale, 'still disbelieving that this could really be the whole of the party's anti-layoff strategy, spoke up. "Don't we have something to say about what is happening here on the Range, the unemployment, what people are supposed to do about it?" She was met with rage.' One leading member accused her of 'lowering our international banner' and failing to support revolutions in Central America and the Caribbean. 'Others chimed in.' (Evans, p 289)

This relates to another key factor that Evans emphasises, coming into play beginning in 1978. 'Jack had had a revelation about Fidel Castro hardly less searing than Saint Paul's on the road to Damascus... Barnes said he was electrified by suddenly understanding that the Cubans had a strategy to intervene to promote revolutions.' Struggles in Nicaragua, El Salvador, Grenada, etc, provided proof that Cuba was becoming the fount of world revolution. He adds: 'It was clear that Jack was determined to make a turn toward Havana and that Joe Hansen was on the outs with the party's younger inner circle.' Hansen died at the beginning of 1979 — but Michael Baumann, who had been working closely with Hansen on *Intercontinental Press*, told Evans that 'Joe didn't agree with Jack on anything by the time he died'. Camejo reported to Evans shortly before his own death in 2008 that Hansen had approached him in the late 1970s with a proposal to form a bloc against Barnes, saying: 'Barnes is completely unacceptable. You can't treat people like that.' Evans continues: 'Peter added that he was frightened and quickly ended the discussion.' (Evans, pp 253-54, 256)

Evans was disturbed by the 'whispering campaign without a vote or documents', utilised by the Barnes machine to 'overturn 40 or 50 years and turn the orthodox into outcasts', recognising: 'This was going to be bad.' His next comment is revealing: 'It was clear that Jack's basic motivation in his whole current political shift was to seek the approval of Havana, which had close ties with Moscow, where Trotsky was a demonic figure. But I was still reluctant to break with the party's favorable assessment of the Cuban government on its home turf.' Aside from hoping that Barnes might be right, there was another reason for not challenging the reorientation:

There were two small opposition groups in the party that had done that, and become very isolated as a result. One was composed of Tom Kerry's supporters, led by Nat Weinstein in San Francisco and Lynn Henderson in Minneapolis. The other was based in New York, led by George Breitman, trade unionist Frank Lovell, and Steve Bloom. I thought Weinstein was hopelessly dogmatic and sterile. I was friends with Breitman and held him in high esteem, but didn't agree with him that the Cuban state was an undemocratic dictatorship though with an anti-imperialist and anti-capitalist character. (Evans, p 279)

A new party leadership school was established, with the students handpicked and the classes taught by Barnes and trusted lieutenants. 'The first graduates began giving classes and internal speeches saying Trotsky's theory of Permanent Revolution was an ultra-left mistake and that his claim to have reached agreement with Lenin in April 1917 on the aims of the Russian Revolution was not true', according to Evans. At the 1981 SWP convention, 42 per cent of the National Committee, mostly seasoned and somewhat critical-minded comrades in their thirties and forties, were replaced by little-known younger 'hards'. He comments:

The purge list included Dick Roberts, the party's only economist; Jeff Mackler, a leader of the teachers' union; Ray Markey, President of the New York librarians' union; Kipp Dawson, Syd Stapleton and Lew Jones, all important leaders in the anti-war work; and myself... Most of us concluded that the change of line being hinted at in the corridors was going public soon and the New York leadership wanted to strip potential critics of the status as National Committee members before any discussion began. We still thought there would be a discussion. (Evans, pp 277-278, 303)

In fact, the regularly scheduled national convention which was to occur in 1983 was cancelled in order to block the discussion, with expulsions already in full-swing.[2]

Over the next several years, Barnes' SWP engineered splits in other sections

2. For details and documentation on the struggle in the SWP and the expulsion campaign, and an analysis of its background, context and meaning, see *In Defense of American Trotskyism: The Struggle Inside the Socialist Workers Party, 1979-1983*, edited by Sarah Lovell (with an essay by Frank Lovell) in 1991, available at http://www.marxists.org/history/etol/document/fit.htm; and *In Defense of American Trotskyism: Revolutionary Principles and Working-Class Democracy*, edited (with a major essay) by the present author in 1992, available at http://www.marxists.org/history/etol/document/fit/revprinindex.htm.

of the Fourth International, creating small groups of co-thinkers who would sell *The Militant* in their respective countries, uncritically praising Fidel, Cuba and (for a time) the Nicaraguan Sandinistas. By 1990, they formally announced what had been true for several years — their abandonment of the Fourth International, in preparation for a new 'communist international' that would be created (they were sure) by Cuban and Central American revolutionaries. Camejo, who had little problem with supporting Fidelistas and Sandinistas, was too opposed to sectarianism, and too popular among activists, to be trusted by the Barnes machine — and special, quite successful efforts were made in 1982 to put him outside of the SWP. He comments:

> The Barnes cult added a distinctive twist. They decided to refer to themselves publicly as 'communist', which they do to this day. In the world of political sects this is a conscious effort to remain isolated. It assures their few followers that they stand alone, that they will prove right and everyone else wrong. The cult leader has mystical inherent knowledge that no one else is able to attain except by becoming a follower. (Camejo, p 176)

In the course of the 1980s and 1990s, the SWP devolved into a small and isolated entity — with little connection to the social struggles of its time. Its international collaborators fared no better. But the sad tale cries out for explanations. How could this have happened? What explains the degeneration? It cannot be laid simply at the feet of Jack Barnes. For Marxists, the 'evil genius' theory just won't do.

Original Sin?

For Camejo, the methodology of Barnes was rooted in a sectarian quality inherent in Trotskyism itself — which then caused him to carry out the quest for relevance in a hopelessly sectarian manner — changing one rigid 'orthodoxy' (a Trotskyism distinct from the revolutionary Trotsky) for another (a Castroism distinct from the revolutionary Fidel). The crisis arose in the organisation as early as 1970, in Camejo's opinion, with the choice facing the SWP being either to go 'forward, evolving into an organisation connected with the realities of the national and international living struggles of real people; or inward, self-isolating from realities because those realities did not correspond to a preconceived idea ordained as the unchangeable truth'. (Camejo, pp 114, 115)

Camejo was transformed by the international work he did in Latin America in the late 1970s. Sent by the SWP to Nicaragua in 1979, he was able to see a mass, popular revolution up close and personal. He describes a young militant of the newly-victorious FSLN (Sandinista National Liberation Front), addressing the labouring poor in a Managua barrio:

As he spoke it dawned on me. The way he communicated, the message he gave, was what I had always tried to say; but he used only clear, understandable words about his message built on the living history of Nicaragua and the consciousness of the workers and their families who were listening.

He explained how Nicaragua belongs to its own people. How rich foreigners had come and taken their country from them but that they were the people who worked and created the wealth of their nation. They had the right to run it and to decide what should be done. He spoke about the homeless children in the streets and how under the US-backed dictatorship nothing was done for them. He described in detail how the FSLN was trying to solve each problem. That it would take time. That Nicaragua was still in danger of foreign intervention. To never forget those who gave their lives so that Nicaragua could be a free nation. At each mention of the departed, the crowd shouted, '*Presente*', to affirm that the missing ones were still with them, here. At every meeting of the Sandinistas, regardless where it was held, someone would read off the names of people from that block, school, or union who had given their lives for freedom. Everyone at the meeting would shout '*Presente*'.

My mind began to race. Of course this young man was not going to use terms that would lead to confusion; he would place these issues in the culture, history, and language of his people. It dawned on me — that is why this movement had won. They didn't name their newspaper after some term from European history; they didn't speak of 'socialism' or 'Marxism'. While the rest of the left of the 1960s and 1970s was in decline throughout Latin America, caught up in the rhetoric of European Marxism and the influence of Stalinism, the FSLN had delivered a great victory for freedom. (Camejo, pp 170-71)

Camejo describes this experience as a 'tipping point' for him, and while the SWP leadership was willing to place Fidelista and Sandinista certainties into its 'programme' (chucking out the erstwhile Trotskyist certainties), it seemed incapable of emulating the example of being connected with living struggle. In one of the book's few glaring errors, however, Camejo incorrectly characterises the position of the Fourth International majority, led by Ernest Mandel, as being hyper-critical and even hostile to the Sandinistas — which might strengthen his point, if true, but whose inaccuracy throws the overarching point into question. (There are some who would criticise the pro-Sandinista attitude of both the Fourth International majority and of Camejo as a betrayal of the Trotskyist programme — which might cause him to say: 'See, *that's* what I'm talking about.')

The approach that Camejo criticises is reflected in a comment Farrell Dobbs made to him: 'The programme has been developed. Our job is to implement it.' Evans reports a similar comment from Barnes (before his Fidelista revelation):

One day Jack and I were talking in the headquarters and he told me his opinion that all serious theoretical work had been completed by Marx, Engels, Lenin and Trotsky and there was nothing for future generations to do but apply the existing theory to specific political situations. (Evans, p 226)

Camejo appropriately notes that this is:

... contrary to the essence of Marx's writings about the materialist basis of science and how it applies to economic and social relations. Science is a process, not a discovery or revelation by a genius. Not only is a political programme an evolving concept, but it also requires continuous discussion and debate in order for it to be effective. And it must, most important of all, be tested against reality. (Camejo, p 115)

Such an open and critical-minded approach can also be found — explicitly stated — in the writings of George Breitman and Joe Hansen, regardless of whether one agrees with some of their conclusions. But Evans reports on some similar stirrings from US Trotskyist patriarch James P Cannon in 1964-65:

The party is too ingrown [he said]. It has become intolerant of differences of opinion. It doesn't work with real people in the world. All of its activities are self-generated — *Militant* sales drives, election campaigns for our own candidates, forums in our own hall of ourselves talking to ourselves. This isn't a way to build a live organisation. If this goes on much longer the party will cease to exist. [He went on] I haven't said anything publicly in the party because I haven't seen an issue where these sectarian tendencies could be corrected and I didn't want to undermine Farrell and Tom. But now there is one.

Evans continues:

Here Jim produced a pamphlet called *The Triple Revolution* written by the futurist Robert Theobald and published by the Center for the Study of Democratic Institutions in Santa Barbara. The three revolutions supposed to be taking place in the world were in the growth of atomic weaponry, in struggles for human rights, but mainly in automation, leading, Theobald argued, to massive structural unemployment in the near term. (Evans, p 154)

Cannon asked Evans to take up these issues and to write about them in the party on his behalf.

When it became known to Barnes that Evans was moving in this direction, he let it be known that such a thing would not be welcome — but also Evans concluded, after some investigation, that Theobald and Cannon were wrong, and he dropped the matter. Cannon himself — satisfied that the SWP's energetic engagement with building the anti-war movement was shifting the party in an outward-moving direction — set the *Triple Revolution* discussion aside, without repudiating its importance.

What is clear is that the 'original sin' that Camejo perceives — while identifying a genuine problem — is overstated and by itself inadequate in explaining the SWP disaster.

Les Evans reaches for a different variant of 'original sin' to help explain the SWP disaster — Leninism. To make this case, he offers a set of authoritarian quotations from Lenin's *Collected Works* from the Civil War period of 1918-20 and concludes: 'Lenin, as his published works showed, was committed to an extreme Jacobin dictatorship over the whole of society to remold it to his vision.' (Evans, p 285) He goes on to assert:

> The general pattern internationally was that most of the FI sections that had sided with Cannon and the SWP in the 1953 split were of the hard party type, while those led by the Europeans were looser, as a legacy of having been committed to deep entry in larger left parties in the 1950s. The hard parties with their super centralist structures more often than not ended up with a mad captain at the helm, sailing ahead with seeming unanimity among the ranks until they hit the iceberg. Witness Healy in England, Moreno in Argentina, or the still long surviving cult around Pierre Lambert in France. This centralist and ideologically intolerant structure seemed to produce the same result not only for little parties but for national states both great and small, as witness Stalinist Russia, Enver Hoxha's Albania, Mao's China, and Ceauşescu's Romania to name a few. In the case of the state rulers the Trotskyists attributed everything to the virus of Stalinism, which in turn they explained by the economic privileges of the party bureaucracy in an economy of scarcity. This neatly exempted them from any charge of similarity. Yet the same totalitarian virus decimated the various Trotskyist parties in the 1970s and 1980s, at least those of the hard Leninist sort. Draw your own conclusion. (Evans, p 294)

There is much scholarship that would need to be confronted and refuted (or reinterpreted) to make this interpretation of Lenin stick. The desperate and often disastrous 'emergency measures' of the Bolsheviks during the Civil War period and its immediate aftermath do not provide a fair characterisation of Leninist organisational principles as they actually developed from 1902 to 1917. What passed for good 'Leninism' under Stalin and his disciples (or under Barnes and other sectarian cultists) is another matter. The fact remains, what Evans tells us about the organisational perspectives of Cannon, and of the SWP during the period of Cannon's leadership, does not harmonise well with his generalisation — or with any notion of Leninism à la Cannon leading to the Barnes disaster.

In a conversation in Cannon's home in the early 1960s, Evans commented on a dissident in the YSA, suggesting 'we would be better off if we could get him out'. Cannon asked: 'Does he do anything for the movement?' Evans conceded that, yes, he 'read French and had presented a talk on Ernest Mandel's *Marxist Economic Theory,* which was not yet available in an English translation'. Cannon responded sternly, 'Well, that is something. The party is a voluntary organization. You can't hire and fire in the party. If you lose an experienced person you can't go out on the street and hire a replacement. You have to conserve what you have.' (Evans, p 162) Or consider his description of the 1963 national convention of the SWP:

> I now had my first chance to observe how party discussions and internal democracy worked. Mimeographed internal bulletins began to arrive from New York. All party members were permitted to write their views, to be printed in the bulletin during the preconvention period and, if it involved a resolution, to be put up for a vote at the coming convention. This was an internal discussion, however; all party members were expected to present the majority line when speaking to non-members.
>
> There were some factions that were spread as minorities within several branches, and two that controlled their branches outright. The first type included a group around Jim Robertson and Tim Wohlforth, who dismissed the Cuban Revolution as an authoritarian nationalist event and who were opposed to the reunification with the International Secretariat. Another faction supported Arne Swabeck, one of the original founders of the movement, who lived in Los Angeles and had become convinced that Mao Zedong represented a true socialist tendency.
>
> There was a small group in Detroit who thought the Soviet Union was some kind of new capitalist state as contrasted with the party majority position that it was defined by the nationalized property and only the bureaucratic government needed to be removed. The two factions that had their whole branch behind them were in Seattle, led by Dick Fraser and Clara Kaye, who

championed 'revolutionary integration' for the black movement and opposed any support of black nationalism, and in Milwaukee, led by James Bolton, who had a pro-Maoist position similar to that of Swabeck. Articles defending and opposing these variegated viewpoints filled many thick mimeographed bulletins. Also there were a few very long, almost incomprehensible, articles larded with abstruse organic and early computer analogies signed by a single individual, Lynn Marcus. When I asked about him I was told his real name was Lyndon La Rouche and his party name was an immodest contraction based on Lenin and Marx… I had spoken before the branch that spring to propose that the militant black nationalism of the Muslims was a progressive force that should be supported despite their strident anti-white rhetoric. This was met with general skepticism. I felt vindicated when the main party resolution, titled 'Freedom Now', written by George Breitman in Detroit, called for support to black nationalism and the Nation of Islam. (Evans, pp 130-31)

At the same time, Evans was struck by 'the heat of the majority supporters' hostility to all the minority tendencies', and this would culminate — finally — in an organisational tightening under the Dobbs/Kerry regime as part of the leadership transition to the Barnes regime. Yet he notes that Cannon had disagreements with 'the tightening up process that Jack Barnes had been shepherding through the national structure' (Evans, pp 131, 234). After Cannon's death, Evans was assigned to go through his papers in order to help compose and edit new volumes of his writings. His comments, again, give the sense of a different Leninism than is described in the sweeping generalisation:

Reading over 50 years of Cannon's letters several things struck me. In the early 1960s in Los Angeles I had seen that he held meetings of the local National Committee members and outraged New York by sending in policy proposals in the name of the Los Angeles NC group, like a dual Political Committee. I always assumed that dated only from his somewhat early retirement to Los Angeles in 1950. Not so. In 1936 the Trotskyists had dissolved their organization to join the Socialist Party with the aim of connecting with a developing left wing. During most of 1937 Cannon lived in California, and from there he repeatedly upstaged the elected leadership of his group in New York, mailing out counterproposals to theirs to the faction national committee. This wouldn't have been tolerated for a minute in the Barnes-led SWP. Sharp exchanges took place openly between leaders of the Cannon faction without hiding them from other tendencies in the Trotskyist group. Another thing that struck me was Cannon's attitude toward former factional opponents. A surprising number of his close associates and even friends had earlier been bitter enemies: Sylvia Bleeker and Morris Lewitt, Joseph Hansen and Art Sharon were all members of the Shachtman faction or, worse yet, part of the clique around Martin Abern, one of the three original Trotskyist leaders, infamous for his onionskin copies of leadership documents that went out regularly to his select list.

Cannon's two closest friends seemed to be Ray Dunne in Minneapolis, who had always been a Cannonite, but the other was Joseph Vanzler, party name John G Wright, who was described in a May 1933 letter to Cannon from George Clarke as 'the vanguard of the freaks' and a supporter of the BJ Field minority... All of these people became part of the party's central leadership without prejudice over their former alignments. No such thing ever happened under Barnes. Anyone who opposed him was forever marked and generally quickly expelled. (Evans, p 233)

At one point, a Barnes loyalist threatened Evans around pursuing the *Triple Revolution* thesis with the comment: 'The Political Committee has had a meeting about that and has ruled that it is prohibited to discuss it. Cannon is completely out of line to try to raise it and if he pursues it any further he will be expelled. You had better shut up about it.' While Evans learned from a more seasoned comrade that 'no one was going to expel Jim Cannon from the SWP', he concluded that this meant 'Barnes didn't have the power to do everything he might want to do' (Evans, p 156). More, it suggests a qualitative difference between the Leninism of Cannon's party and that of the Barnes regime.

Digging Deeper

If 'the inherent sectarianism of the Trotskyist program' and 'the inherent authoritarianism of Leninist organizational principles' do not provide the answer to the question of the qualitative change in the SWP, where can we look?

For any Marxist group that wishes to bring about revolutionary change, one obvious question — if one is a Marxist — is: 'What is its relationship with the organised working class?' Camejo comments:

> Unions, which at one point had organized 33 per cent of American labor, had shrunk to just 12 per cent. No major political opposition appeared. Yes, there were many defensive struggles as the industrial unions were weakened by corporate and governmental attacks, which had stepped up under Reagan. But labor had no labor party or any kind of effective defense strategy. By the early 1980s the industrial working class and its unions had been in a sharp decline for two obvious, interconnected reasons. First was the growth

of globalization; second was the union capitulation to the Democratic Party. At every level the unions, pushed by the Democratic Party, were capitulating, supposedly a necessary step for US corporations to be competitive in the global economy. (Camejo, p 173)

The world had changed in important ways, and the SWP leadership — with few and marginal exceptions — didn't see it coming. Indeed, it might have made sense if the SWP *had* actually looked more carefully and thoughtfully at the dynamics of *Triple Revolution* that Jim Cannon vainly pointed to. The automation and computerisation discussed in that document did not bring mass unemployment in the immediate term, but they did contribute to the steady erosion of the industrial working-class base that had been the source of traditional union power — and these developing technologies were very much related to what came to be tagged 'globalisation'. (The so-called 'revolutions' in human rights and in weaponry also moved in slower and more complex — but no less transformative — ways.)

One must also give attention to the 'great divide' represented by the Second World War, which brought into being a very different world than the one framing the perspectives of Lenin, Trotsky and their comrades. Young SWP and YSA members — reading the 'classic' texts that had been written in qualitatively different contexts, and themselves having come into adulthood and consciousness in very different social-cultural contexts — could not easily grasp the actual meaning of what Lenin or Trotsky might be saying. But they did not know that. This naturally contributed to a stilted understanding of the texts, contributing to flattened and simplistic applications, and to growing disorientation.

Related to this, the vanguard layers of the working class — at least in the United States — had been nurtured by a *labour radical subculture* from the post-Civil War era of the 1860s down to the 1940s. The cadres of the early SWP had been shaped by and were an integral part of that labour radical subculture. But the class-conscious working-class layers were fragmented and eroded by the profound economic, political, cultural, social and economic changes of the post-Second World War period — whose components included a fierce and stultifying Cold War anti-communism, an unprecedented relative prosperity, working-class suburbanisation, transformations in an increasingly conformist mass popular culture, and more. The sub-culture of the radicalised sections of the labour movement, and those radicalised sections of the labour movement themselves, were no longer a vibrant reality as young members flowed into the SWP and YSA in the 1960s and early 1970s.

In *'Left-Wing' Communism: An Infantile Disorder,* Lenin emphasises that efforts by would-be revolutionaries to maintain 'iron discipline' if their Marxism and organisation are not actually rooted in vanguard layers of the working class and intimately connected with mass struggles, 'inevitably fall flat and end up in phrase-mongering and clowning'. One might say that this is precisely the essence of the 'Barnesism' emerging from the accounts of Camejo and Evans.

Some left critics may be inclined to see Barnes' adaptation to the Cuban and Nicaraguan revolutionaries as the opposite of 'ultra-leftism' (instead reflecting a submission to 'the conservative elements of those national programmes'), which gets into analyses of the Cuban and Nicaraguan revolutions that are beyond the scope of this review. But Lenin's decisive point — that no 'Leninism' is possible if there is a disconnect between would-be revolutionaries and the actualities of working-class life and struggle — points up the fatal problem that faced and finally overwhelmed the SWP. The lack of possibility for democratic correction, due to the deepening authoritarianism and cultism represented by the Barnes regime, sealed its fate. Perhaps all this was not inevitable — but that is the way it happened.[3]

Aftermath

In reaction to their experiences in the Trotskyist movement, the two authors went down different pathways.

Evans participated in two efforts to pick up some of the political pieces after the mass expulsions from the SWP — helping to found, in turn, Socialist Action and Solidarity, both of which still exist as fairly small groups. Before the end of the 1980s, he had given up on socialist activism and — essentially — on socialism and Marxism altogether. Acquiring additional skills and knowledge upon returning to university life, he went on to play an impressive role as a web journalist for the International Institute associated with University of California Los Angeles, as well as a staff member with the World Health Organisation and the World Bank (of all things). Also he and his wife have been quite active in their local neighbourhood committee's highly-focused efforts

3. Among other books shedding light on the story of the US SWP explored in Camejo and Evans are the following: Fred Halstead, *Out Now! A Participant's Account of the American Movement Against the Vietnam War* (Monad/Pathfinder, New York, 1978); Tim Wohlforth, *The Prophet's Children: Travels on the American Left* (Humanities Press, Atlantic Highlands, NJ, 1994); George Breitman, Paul Le Blanc and Alan Wald, *Trotskyism in the United States: Historical Essays and Reconsiderations* (Humanities Press, Atlantic Highlands, NJ, 1996); Paul Le Blanc and Thomas Barrett (eds), *Revolutionary Labor Socialist: The Life, Ideas, and Comrades of Frank Lovell* (Smyrna Press, Union City, NJ, 2000); Anthony Marcus (ed), *Malcolm X and the Third American Revolutions: The Writings of George Breitman* (Humanity Books, Amherst, NY, 2005); Barry Sheppard, *The Party, A Political Memoir: The Socialist Workers Party, 1960-1988*, Volume 1 (Resistance Books, Chippendale, Australia, 2005). Sheppard is currently working on the concluding volume of his important memoir.

to protect their own community in South Los Angeles, contending with 'gang crime, illegal dumping, graffiti vandals, drug houses and abandoned buildings'. Evans seems defensive about this, and goes on the offensive: 'For Trotskyists all politics is global. If it doesn't involve a foreign war for which imperialism can be excoriated, or a union-busting multinational corporation, it is hardly worth talking about.' (Evans, p 399) There is an element of truth to this — but it is not totally true, in my opinion.

Camejo was unable to give up on the radical activism that animated most of his life. He joined together in the mid-1980s with a short-lived 'non-sectarian' left-wing group called the North Star Network, made up of former SWPers and other radicals. The group ended up getting involved in Jesse Jackson's Rainbow Coalition — which he considers 'a major political mistake' since it became 'just another name for keeping progressives in the Democratic Party' (Camejo, pp 180-81). One of the appendices of his book contains an analytical critique entitled 'The Origins of the Two-Party System'. He also established ties with a break-away from the Communist Party, Committees of Correspondence, and with a Maoist-influenced group called Line of March — but concluded that intertwined vestiges of Stalinism and reformism hindered both from becoming effective left-wing forces.

For a time, thanks to considerable expertise on the capitalist economy, he worked very successfully for the investment firm of Merrill Lynch. From there he branched out into helping left-leaning people make 'socially responsible' investments, and also with raising substantial amounts of money — through his business and financial contacts — for such things as fighting AIDS, job creation, immigrant rights, unionisation and protection of the environment. He became perhaps the most dynamic — and one of the most radical — figures in the Green Party of California, running for Governor and then becoming Ralph Nader's Vice-Presidential running-mate in 2004. While raising questions about using the word socialism, and insisting that Marx should not be treated uncritically as a deity, he continued to embrace the socialist goal (preferring the term 'economic democracy') and a broadly Marxist analytical framework.

Both Camejo and Evans appear to have ended up with wives whom they have loved and who love them, children, grandchildren and interesting personal experiences, some of which are discussed or alluded to in their books. And both felt a need to share their reflections about US Trotskyism with readers whom they knew would be mostly on the left — which is our good fortune.

Thanks to various friends for feedback and help in making corrections, especially those around the on-line journal *Labor Standard* — http://www.laborstandard.org.

REVIEWS

Éric Aunoble, *Le communisme, tout de suite! Le mouvement des communes en Ukraine soviétique (1919-1920)*, Les nuits rouges, Paris, 2008, pp 288

In line with all the libertarian historians of the Russian Revolution, René Berthier stated in a recent book that, unlike the anarchists, the Bolsheviks never attempted to encourage land collectivisation.[1] This is exactly the opposite of the argument that Eric Aunoble defends in this study on the collectivisation movement in Soviet Ukraine, the result of painstaking academic research based on the study of unpublished archives. The Bolsheviks, he tells us, expressed a true radicalism in this area, while the Socialist-Revolutionaries (SRs) and the anarchists stuck to very moderate positions. And Aunoble adds that the small number of collectives claimed by the Makhnovists were in fact very few compared to the number set up by the Bolsheviks.

Independently of the thesis that underlies it, and to our surprise, the main merit of Aunoble's study is that it both looks at and teaches us about a phenomenon generally ignored by Western scholars and those from the former Soviet Union working on the subject: namely, the thousands of peasants who organised some 300 collectives in Ukraine alone. Aunoble is not wrong to point out that the 'profession of historian' often leads academics to 'underestimate the innovative capacity of utopias produced in revolutionary times'. For Aunoble, the Ukrainian collectives — these 'laboratories of Soviet society in the course of construction' — are 'the most complete evidence of the revolutionary creativity' of the time.

Supported by poor peasants, this 'world of plebeians in revolt', the collectivisation movement can only be understood, says Aunoble, through its own words and publications. So it is from a patient and attentive reading of the verbatim records of their general meetings and correspondence with the Soviet administration that the historian has attempted to paint this picture of the communist universe, focused on a clearly defined area: Izium district, located in the Kharkov region,[2] which offered the astonishing feature of comprising in

---

1. René Berthier, *Octobre 1917, le Thermidor de la révolution russe* (Paris, 2003). This work was mentioned by Peter Sommermeyer in *À contretemps*, no 21, October 2005, pp 13-17.
2. After being occupied by Austro-German troops, the Kharkov region came under the control of supporters of the nationalist Petlyura before falling into the hands of the Reds

the spring of 1919 15 per cent of all the Ukrainian collectives — 32 in number — while the district accounted for only 1.4 per cent of Ukraine's population.

Founded in the midst of civil war — the first one being established in February 1919 — the setting up of these collective farms followed on from the establishment of the new Soviet government, established a month earlier in the region. They did not survive its fall. Six months after the proclamation, in Kharkov, of the Ukrainian Soviet Socialist Republic, Denikin's troops retook the region in June 1919 and organised a hunt for communists. The collectives were suppressed, having experienced only a short period of hope. When the Bolsheviks replaced the Whites in December 1919, the context, as we shall see, was not at all the same.

The particular structure that characterised the rural community of pre-Soviet Russia — the *obshchina* or *mir* — intensely interested the social theorists of the nineteenth century. Bakunin saw it as the expression of a negation of property, Herzen detected a form of 'embryonic communism', and Marx, though somewhat belatedly, awarded it a major role in a future revolutionary process.[3] Nevertheless, Aunoble states that despite this tradition, the idea itself is more Western than Slavic. Directly inherited from Fourierism and Saint-Simon, it is prominent in the mid-nineteenth century, in many writings of Western social theorists, before being taken up and popularised in Russia by the intelligentsia. This enthusiasm had the effect of encouraging the formation of some student communes which would also serve as 'logistical bases' for various nihilist groups.[4]

As we know, the Russian Populists accorded a privileged place to the peasant commune. Yet, says Aunoble, they gradually moved away from this communitarian socialism to invent a kind of 'pragmatic individualism'. Understanding by socialisation the 'mere redistribution of land' and not its 'collective cultivation', they eventually ended up encouraging private property to the detriment of collective ownership. Similarly, Aunoble continues, these increasingly moderate populists no longer questioned the fundamental inequality of social relations within the villages. He says that at this point in early 1919 which saw the emergence of the collectivisation movement in Ukraine,

> in January 1919. Because of its peripheral position in the east, however, it remained relatively unscathed by the civil war. Moreover, its mixed ethnicity made it less sensitive than other regions to Ukrainian nationalism.

3. On this aspect of Marx's thought, his correspondence with Vera Zasulich, a prominent Narodnaya Volya (People's Will), activist, remains an essential document. You can read about this in Maximilien Rubel's 'Karl Marx et le socialisme populiste russe' < http//plusloin.org / text / veraz.htm >.
4. Daniel Brower, *Training the Nihilists: Education and Radicalism in Tsarist Russia* (Ithaca and London, 1975), quoted by Aunoble.

the Left SRs — the direct descendants of the populists — had definitively abandoned the original collectivist claims of their predecessors and argued that 'all income from the land must remain in the hands of the peasants'.[5]

The enthusiasm of the intelligentsia for collectivist radicalism no longer being what it was, and the populists, as we have seen, having put a lot of water in their vodka, the term for commune — *kommuna* — became popular among anarchist currents in the early twentieth century and in the aftermath of 1905, especially under the influence of Kropotkin, for whom: 'The Commune of tomorrow will know that it cannot admit any higher authority; above it there can only be the interests of the Federation, freely accepted by itself as well as the other communes.'[6] Thus, the word 'commune', Aunoble says, entered the Russian anarchist vocabulary, with its derivative 'communist'. Thus the expression 'anarkhist-kommunist' finally established itself among both supporters and detractors of libertarian ideas. The Bolsheviks, meanwhile, were not yet communists.

It was not until the spring of 1917 that in his *April Theses* Lenin proposed building a commune-state — of which the Paris Commune was merely a forerunner — and changing the name of the party from Social-Democratic to Communist. This became effective in March 1918. The word 'commune' became synonymous with 'Soviet', and the 'family of words was reconstituted: commune, communist, communism… united by meaning and assonance'. However, judging by Lenin himself, the meaning of the term remained largely libertarian because he warned his own comrades of the risk of confusion between the Bolsheviks and communist-anarchists that might arise as a result of this new name.[7] Aunoble says the advantage of this adoption of the anarchist vocabulary was that it offered a 'guarantee of radicalism' to the Bolsheviks who wished to break from the 'social-democratic compromise'.

After October 1917, the use of words 'commune' and 'communist' increased. Referring to an administrative district, Petrograd became the Workers' Petrograd Commune, member of the Union of Communes of the Northern Region. Nevertheless, at this juncture, the concept of 'commune' had nothing to do with any approach to collectivist work and life, especially in rural areas, at least officially.[8] Advocates of the proletariat and of industrial modernisation,

5. UPSR, *Proletariat i socializatsia zemli* (Kiev, 1917), quoted by Aunoble.
6. Peter Kropotkin, *Paroles d'un révolté* (Paris, 1978, originally 1885), quoted by Aunoble. Note that an entire chapter of *Paroles d'un révolté* is devoted to the concept of collectives. In *L'Entraide*, Kropotkin is particularly interested in forms of solidarity in rural village communes.
7. VI Lenin, *Selected Works*, Volume 2 (Moscow, 1968), quoted by Aunoble.
8. The people, however, did not wait for the green light from above to expropriate land and *farm it* collectively — Paul Avrich dates the first 'real' collectives from the first months

the Bolsheviks — for whom the rural population would remain in the service of the working class, the sole carrier of the historical project — in fact only belatedly and timidly showed any interest in rural collectives. Nevertheless, it must be said that they had moved a considerable distance, bearing in mind that their perception of the peasantry had long been a caricature.[9]

Despite special aid of 10 million roubles released in July 1918 for the creation of collectives, political distrust of this form of social organisation persisted until early 1919. Then, in a reversal of policy of the type of which they were experts, the Bolsheviks made the *kommuna* a main focus of their propaganda, to the extent that they soon held a virtual monopoly of collectivist rhetoric.[10] Thus, various publications aimed at Ukrainian peasants urged them to adopt collective farming of the land.[11] And the new programme of the RCP(b), adopted in March 1919, made the collective the new universal form of the organisation of social life.

To explain this reversal, Aunoble stresses — rightly we believe — the influence that the theses of Pyotr Nikitich Tkachev exerted on Lenin.[12] Elsewhere Aunoble indicates that by adopting the collectivist propaganda abandoned by the anarchists, the Bolsheviks moved to the left of them. Aunoble substantiates his argument by citing various resolutions adopted at two anarchist conferences that met at the beginning of 1919,[13] and concludes that the anarchists, who

following the Bolshevik coup. The same author has even identified the existence of anarchist collectives, as early as 1905, in the Gulyai-Polye region, see Paul Avrich, *Les Anarchistes russes* (Paris, 1979).

9. 'Uncivilised, turgid, stupid people... almost total lack of social consciousness' (Gorky), the peasantry is composed of 'barbarian tillers of the soil... cruel and merciless' (Plekhanov), showing 'unsociability and savagery' (Lenin) — quotes from Robert Conquest, *Sanglantes moissons* (*The Harvest of Sorrow*, Paris, 1995). In 1905, the same Lenin still speaks of the egoistic tendencies of the peasant owner, tendencies which make certain 'its hostility to the rural proletariat' ('The Proletariat and Peasantry', *Vpered,* no 12, 23 March 1905, in *The Alliance of the Working Class and Peasantry* (Moscow, 1957), quoted by Aunoble.

10. In 1918, however, according to Zhigur, one of the first Bolsheviks to have addressed this question, the collectives were 'semi-anarchist' — with 'almost nothing in common with Marxist communism'. In the Bolshevik imagination collectives were associated at that time with anarchist-communism. See A Zhigur, *Organizatsia kommunisticheskikh khoziaistv v zemledelii* (*The Organisation of Communist Operations in Agriculture*, Moscow, 1918), quoted by Aunoble.

11. Several of the texts published in these propaganda sheets are signed by the most influential leaders of the Bolshevik Party.

12. An iconic figure of the revolutionary movement of the years 1860-70, Tkachev regarded the *kommuna* as a social institution which would transform Russia from top to bottom, but should be subordinate to state policy. We can understand how this thesis must have appealed to Lenin.

13. These are the first congress of Ukrainian anarchist organisations, held in Elizabetgrad in April 1919, and the second congress of insurgent soldiers', workers' and peasants' Soviets

did not wish to break with the peasant mentality, had put a definite brake on the development of collectives. He even adds that the positions of the Makhnovshchina on collectives differed little from those — very moderate, as we have seen — of the Left SRs.

Thus, without being by any means the originators of collectivist propaganda, the Bolsheviks took advantage of the procrastination of the populists and anarchists to graft it conveniently into their speeches. In doing so, Bolshevism was the only movement to engage resolutely in the collectivist experiment.[14] Concluding his bold thesis, Aunoble argues that if by encouraging the creation of collectives, the Bolsheviks had, as he thinks, adopted the anarchist programme, the subsequent condemnation of these Bolshevik collectives by the anarchists would therefore have amounted to a self-criticism. The question remains of what we mean by the term 'collectives' and what exactly they were, in terms of both propaganda and reality.

The Bolshevik propagandist discourse on collectives appears in many publications sent from Kharkov to the provincial administration. The creation of collectives — profoundly egalitarian structures, according to the propaganda — aimed at emancipating the peasants from the old exploitative rules, enabling them to escape poverty, and eradicating any hint of a return to private ownership. To convince the peasant — a fundamentally backward individual in the Bolshevik imagination, let us remember — various devious arguments were used. For example, the revolutionary character of the proposed changes was played down; the patriarchal family was not to be disrupted. The religious card was to be played, invoking a supposed convergence between communist and Christian ideals.[15]

Who were these collectivists who responded to the call of Bolshevik propaganda? The quantitative study carefully conducted by Aunoble draws an accurate picture, which shows that most were very poor and dispossessed peasants, often illiterate, who, according to the author, constituted the vanguard of the rural proletariat, adhering to the idea that they were an integral part of that inherently revolutionary class — the proletariat — and determined to gain a hearing in the countryside through the establishment of collectives.[16] But apart

---

of the Military Staff of the Region of Gulyai-Polye, held in February 1919.
14. Once again it is necessary to oppose this vision to that of Berthier, for whom 'in the Bolshevik mentality any voluntary grouping of workers intending to work in common, uncontrolled by the state, is counter-revolutionary' (Berthier, *Octobre 1917*).
15. Aunoble, who denies the relevance of such propaganda, points out that, written in Russian, it could hardly touch the peasantry who spoke only surzhik, a rural mix of Russian and Ukrainian, but he adds that local Bolshevik commissars were specifically employed to translate them.
16. Note, however, that there are many books — usually less than forthcoming, it is true,

from their membership of the communist utopia, the 'revenge of the starved dead',[17] such a form of social organisation offered them the advantage of being able, finally, to dispose collectively of the fruit of their labour. Assuming that 'everything belonged to everyone' and that 'nobody could describe something as his own', the collective was primarily a space where work was actually organised in common according to the ability of each person.

Regarding the internal functioning of these bodies, Aunoble sees it as a variant of a 'fairly libertarian democracy'. Although it was statutorily decreed, for example, that general meetings would meet at least twice a year, these meetings, which could be convened at the request of one-fifth of the members of the collective, were usually much more frequent. The author acknowledges, however, that attendance at meetings was sometimes inadequate. Regarding the right to vote — 'a real test', he writes, 'of communal democracy' — he notes that it did not always apply to women, the aged and adolescents. In some collectives it was even reserved solely for the heads of households. The principle of job rotation was generally respected, even if the literate members, by assuming several responsibilities at the same time, risked developing a trend towards professionalisation. Aunoble emphasises that these elected officials nevertheless remained under the direct control of the members of the collective.

Despite their limitations, the author continues to believe that these collectives allowed the peasantry, or at least a portion of it, to act as a force for a radical social transformation that could attack those pillars of society: property and the family. As regards the role of women, despite the evidence provided by the author on the undeniable revolution in the field of manners and the questioning of power relations between the sexes that these collectives encouraged, we must acknowledge that this 'unprecedented real movement' toward human liberation did not realise all that was hoped for. It did not prevent the retention of women in a state of inferiority, which saw them restricted to household chores, often deprived of the right to vote and prevented from regularly assuming responsibilities. Aunoble does not deny any of this. However, he maintains

---

about these Soviet collectives — which have a much less clear idea of these communards than our author. Take, for example, Alexander Skirda, who in his *Nestor Makhno, le Cosaque libertaire, 1888-1934. La guerre civile en Ukraine, 1917-1921* (Paris, 2005), sees a 'malleable and disposable mass' of 'rootless' people 'dubbed as "poor peasants"', to whom the Bolsheviks would give 'the great landed estates that had been confiscated' and who would constitute 'the new power-base in the countryside'. Conquest reports, meanwhile, that these poor farmers would be reinforced by the massive influx of communists from the cities and perceives that the regime 'succeeded in building up some sort of base in the countryside', responsible, *inter alia*, for disarming the kulaks (Conquest, *Sanglantes moissons*).

17. A paraphrase of a line of the French Communist Youth song 'La Jeune Garde': 'C'est la revanche de tous les meurt-de-faim.' [*RH*]

that overall the collectivisation movement was firmly based upon an egalitarian perspective aimed at the 'dissolution of patriarchy'.

Aunoble considers that although the challenge to the traditional family and the practice of equality between men and women remained incomplete, they nevertheless constituted one of the two fundamental differences between this type of collective and the *obshchina*,[18] the other being the collective exploitation of the land.[19]

Reading the idyllic description given by Aunoble of this utopia in action, one wonders why libertarian historiography has consistently criticised this movement, from Voline — who, when retracing Makhno's epic story, contrasted the 'artificial collectives' thrown up by the 'communist' authorities who claimed them to be exemplary, with those 'freely created by the spontaneous initiative of the peasants' of Gulyai-Polye — through to Berthier.[20]

For Aunoble, this reading — as well as the charge of *commissarocracy* laid in respect of these collectives — stems from a purely Manichean approach. This is conceivable, but it needs to be demonstrated. On this point, Aunoble's reasoning seems sometimes hesitant, if not contradictory. For example, if the commitment (almost 'identification') of the collectivists with communism and the Bolshevik Party seems, indeed, unquestionable, it does not explain why adherence to this type of collective demanded of applicants — in addition to their being sober and conscientious — that they had the 'point of view of a communist or a sympathiser' and belonged to 'one of the existing communist organisations'. Despite the author insisting that these conditions — as a 'moral imperative' — came from the members themselves, the fact remains that they can equally be seen as directives emanating from elsewhere, and more specifically 'from above'.

Similarly, the names given to the collectives by their members — or their

18. Aunoble does not appear to have the same affection for these ancient autonomous structures of the Russian peasantry as other authors, including Skirda and Anatole Leroy-Beaulieu. The former sees in them a foreshadowing of communal democracy and a form of 'collective self-government' — see his *Les anarchistes russes, les soviets et la révolution de 1917* (Paris, 2000) — and the latter is quoted from *L'Empire des tsars et les Russes* (Paris, 1991, originally 1898) by Skirda, describing the *obshchina* as the 'democratic regime in its simplest and purest form, without intermediaries and without representation, a system of direct democracy where everyone personally participates in all deliberations, all decisions'.
19. According to Aunoble, by creating their own collectives, the communards were seeking precisely to separate themselves from their villages, which were still constituted as *obshchinas*. Over time, however, the revolution — or what was left of it — would paradoxically strengthen the *obshchina*, long regarded by the Bolsheviks as the main cause of the retarded political, cultural and economic development of the peasantry (Berthier, *Octobre 1917*).
20. Voline, *La Révolution inconnue* (Paris, 1947).

inspiration — confirmed the inclusion of these bodies in an exclusive frame of reference: *Marx, Lenin, Trotsky, Rakovsky, Rosa Luxemburg, Karl Liebknecht, October, International, Red Flag, Victory over Capital* (which became *Victory of Capital* under the unfortunate pen of an ignorant secretary), *Kronstadt* and *Paris Commune*. Other names, *Evangelical, Ray of Light*, etc — very exceptional, it is true — were inspired by religious faith.

As for the anarchist criticism that party bodies exercised systematic control over these collectives, Aunoble dodges it rather awkwardly, even going so far as to claim, against all probability, that they were created outside of any political patronage. This is a curious assertion as it is contradicted a few pages later, when the author informs us that the creation of any collective had to be endorsed by the party apparatus, even when it emanated from a decision taken by a cell meeting; this, incidentally, was already a blatant departure from the principle of autonomy. Moreover, the procedure for registration of collectives was fully within the bureaucratic channels of the Bolshevik system.[21] The statutes of each collective, drawn up according to a template, stated that 'the general assembly and the council direct all business', including 'the election of council members'. Aunoble states that the election should be confirmed by the party district. Finally, to be validated, the minutes of a general meeting required to be countersigned by the village Soviet. The rural district finance section retained the power to cut funding to any particular collective which did not give an account of its activities to the authorities.[22] Aunoble is forced to acknowledge this instance of *dirigisme* by the Bolshevik apparatus, albeit only by way of a euphemism. Thus he writes: 'One cannot discover any tendency towards decentralisation...' This, to put it mildly, is nonetheless annoying when one considers how elsewhere he has vaunted the 'autonomy' of these collectives.

21. To be registered, the collective was obliged to comply with very specific rules: filing a declaration of intent, a list of families making up the future collective, and its future statutes. Once these provisions were met, the registration dossier had to be endorsed by the Land Section — the centrepiece of the Bolshevik administration — which gave its verdict. If favourable, two of the three members of the Bureau of Collectives went on site and established an inventory of the confiscated area on which the collective was to be established.
22. On the question of relations with the central government, Aunoble bases himself on a careful reading of the correspondence sent by the collectives to the Land Section, where he discovers a profound disruption of the peasant mentality. Where their ancestors were content to give without receiving in return, he notes, the members of the collectives adopted a demanding attitude towards the state, which generally acceded to their demands by providing money, food and clothing to the poorest of them. We must add, however, that this generosity also had a price, the collectives being obliged to hand over their surpluses to the requisitioning organs and to produce according to a centrally-prepared plan. Thus, at the approach of the Whites, their cattle and horses were reserved for the Red Army, at a time when supplies were desperately short.

One can probably, as does the author, cite the extreme variety of situations that accompanied the creation of these collectives in order to avoid making generalisations about their degree of dependence.[23] But it seems risky to stick to the general line of the arguments of the Bolshevik era as evidence of the essentially spontaneous nature of this collectivist experience. As to concluding that this process had nothing to do with the Stalinist collectivisation of 1930 — 'the forced and terrorising nature' of which is common knowledge, says Aunoble — we can easily agree, for no sensible person has ever made that comparison. From there to consider that the events of 1919 were free of any Bolshevik attempt to control the rural regions of Ukraine is a step that Aunoble himself has been unable to take, even if, once again, he resorts to a euphemism. In short, he writes, it is absurd to deny the existence of questions of power in the formation of collectives since there was hardly any action in which these questions were not a factor. We can therefore conclude that there were such questions of power — and severe ones at that.

This experience, as we have seen, lasted only for the end of a winter and a full spring, six months in all. Falling under the control of the Whites from June 1919, the Kharkov region was retaken by the Reds in December. Of the 79 collectives identified before the arrival of the Whites, only two remained when the Reds returned. But in addition to this bloodbath caused by the White terror,[24] the returning Bolsheviks were confronted by widespread animosity on the part of the peasants towards the collectives. From then on the collectivisation movement, gradually abandoned by its originators, was doomed to disappear.

For Aunoble, this hostility of the peasants towards the collectives explains, in large part, their failure. It showed itself from the start,[25] increased over time and became dominant with the arrival of the Whites. The author himself acknowledges that without the effective collaboration of the peasants, the hunt for communists undertaken by Denikin's men would certainly not have been so successful. By becoming 'a village matter amongst people who know each other all too well', the terror, based on the peasants' rancour and dislike of the

23. Thus, Aunoble acknowledges that the *Karl Liebknecht* collective was sponsored by the party and would have by its huge size — 226 members, instead of the average 54 — met the Bolsheviks' criteria for the organisation of large social agricultural farms. But this was an exception. The collectives, he insists, were formed on the basis of affinity amongst or proximity between people, and not by a 'deliberate intervention of the apparatus'.
24. To survive the terror that was exercised directly against them, the collectivists had no choice except death, exile or enlistment in the Red Army — or among the partisans.
25. Aunoble notes that the reports of the general assemblies of the collectives often report slanders against their members and obstacles to their operation. They emanate, most often, from 'narrow-minded' villagers or those hostile to the communist regime, but reveal a very widespread mind-set. This constant pressure by the villages against the collectives was eventually to embarrass the Soviet administration.

communists, had its full effect. Aunoble — who notes in passing that the hatred of the collectives was not purely confined to the Whites[26] — considers it more appropriate to speak of local counter-revolutionary outbursts rather than one general counter-revolution.

It remains clear that the resentment — apparently the norm — of the villagers towards the collectives could never be completely explained by simplistic and vaguely ideological references to the degree of 'political backwardness' and the 'civil war mentality' of envious peasants under the influence of White propaganda.[27] If the author sometimes uses these explanations, we must admit that they do not constitute the core of his analysis. The real reason for this antagonism, he says, lies in the question of land — and more precisely its distribution. It was this which instilled the poison and aroused the hatred. Aunoble stresses that the sharing out of land, favoured by the October Revolution and warmly welcomed by peasants, mainly affected the poorest of them; explaining, for example, that each plot joining a collective consisted on average of ten times more land than the regional average. Which, after all, might actually inflame envy.[28]

There is, no doubt, another explanation for the anger felt by the villagers towards these collectives. It is that put forward by Skirda and Berthier. The former tries to understand the motivations of the peasantry 'wanting to parcel out the large expropriated estates in order to expand their cramped bits of land', and clashing with the collectivists whom the Bolsheviks encouraged 'to confiscate their property and their products'.[29] Berthier confirms this. He says these collectives gave 'their support to the requisitioning squads, in order to force the peasants to surrender their surplus grain'.[30] It is a pity that Aunoble

---

26. True to *his* line of argument, Aunoble insists that this hostility *vis-à-vis* the *collectives* was shared *equally* by all the opponents of the Bolsheviks: SRs, nationalists, followers of Makhno, Tambov rebels and Kronstadt insurgents, who denounced the communist 'scarecrows' and 'the rotten commune' (*Izvestiya Kronshtatskogo VRK*, 8 March 1921, quoted by Aunoble).
27. Thus, the author believes that the collectives had the knack of fanning the hatred of villagers terrified by these 'women with too much freedom', these 'too proud poor', and these 'too independent youths' who inhabited them.
28. On this point, Aunoble makes an original comparison: like Jews, he writes, the poor peasants suffered permanent humiliation under the former regime. Despised, confined to certain areas, deprived of land, reduced to the rank of sub-humans, they owed their salvation to the arrival of the Red Army in Ukraine. The Socialist Republic of Kharkov, he wrote, tried to build a society where it was 'impossible to distinguish between a Jew and a Christian, or between a pauper and a head of a household'. Following this line of argument, Aunoble naturally sees a parallel between the hunt for communists and pogroms, which seemed to follow the same logic.
29. Skirda, *Nestor Makhno*.
30. Berthier, *Octobre 1917*.

does not mention this explanation — radically contrary to his thesis, it is true — because, when taken into consideration, the hostility in the villages towards the collectives suddenly becomes more explicable.

Aunoble tells us that 'not being conducive to gathering a community around a minimum consensus that could facilitate a move towards a new society' and being radically opposed to peasant traditions, the collectivist movement could not but fail. The Bolsheviks reached the same conclusion in December 1919, when, anxious to defuse peasant discontent, they decided to go with the flow,[31] by totally reversing their line. Suddenly receptive to the plight of peasants dissatisfied by the initial land redistribution, the new land law altered this distribution by dismantling the greatest possible number of Soviet farms. Clearly, this was a restoration of the traditional village community to the detriment of collectives.

Aunoble tells us that with this policy change 'the social revolution was sacrificed on the altar of politics'. Gradually replaced by *sovkhozes*, economic units that were fully dependent on the state, the collectives were to decline until they disappeared and with went them any prospect of 'radical egalitarianism and direct democracy'.

As noted above, this study tends greatly to underestimate the revolutionary impact of the Makhnovist movement. Aunoble warns: 'Contrary to popular belief, Makhno did not encourage the establishment of agricultural communes.' Without questioning Makhno's influence in the creation of communes, he emphasises the very low numbers — 'two or three' in an area of 70 000 square kilometres — a figure that he compares to the 32 collectives set up in a district of 1500 square kilometres by the Izium communists.

Apart from the fact that these reduced figures are inconsistent with those advanced by other historians of the *Makhnovshchina* (including Skirda), they have the effect of spectacularly justifying Aunoble's oft-repeated assertion that the Makhnovists did not demonstrate 'any radicalism in the field of agriculture'. Moreover, having rallied to the moderate positions of the SRs, they had in a sense anticipated the turnaround effected by the Bolsheviks in December 1919, that is, the abandonment of any revolutionary perspective.

Obeying a certain logic, Aunoble's desire to denigrate the Makhnovist movement may well provoke the inquisitive reader towards further investigation, because, irrespective of one's particular viewpoint, the facts are all that really matter. However, it is unreasonable, to say the least, to equate two diametrically

---

31. Thus, pragmatic as hell, Lenin concedes *vis-à-vis* the 'small commodity producers': '… they *cannot be ousted* or crushed; we *must learn to live* with them…' ('La Maladie infantile du communisme (le "gauchisme"')', May 1920, *Selected Works*, Volume 3, cited by Aunoble)

opposed types of organisations: the Soviet ones, favoured by Aunoble, whose actual independence can be doubted; and the free and non-party ones that the *Makhnovshchina* claimed to promote. If Makhno and his supporters condemned the former, it was not due to a sudden burst of moderation on their part, but because they seemed to them to be the exact opposite of the organisations which they supported, ones which they thought would outline the basis of a society emancipated from all control from above.

As for libertarian historiography, it has naturally played its part in this 'anarchist re-reading of the Russian Revolution' which Aunoble seems to mock. Despite its shortcomings and weaknesses, it has the merit of not confusing a sovietised collective with a free one. For in January 1919, the Bolsheviks did not, as Aunoble claims, merely adopt in an unchanged form the anarchist's collectivist programme, they added their own ingredients — bureaucratic logic, interventionism, political manipulation — that were deeply incompatible with libertarian ideals. To assert this is not to fall into any apologetics for Makhnovism (not that this is necessarily the case with libertarian histories), but merely to stick to specific categories.

Pondering at the end of the book on a possible legacy of the Ukrainian experience, Aunoble thinks he has found a trace — 'truly... remarkable', he says — in the Spanish 'short summer' of 1936. He sees similarities — civil war, the flight of large landowners, the spread of revolutionary troops — but also profound differences. One of them is that the process of collectivisation in Spain, unlike the Ukrainian one, saw the coexistence within villages of a majority of collectivists and a minority of advocates of a simple division of the land. However, taking up the ideas of Carlos Semprún Maura on the conservatism of the Spanish collectivists as regards family structure, Aunoble concludes that on this issue the Ukrainian collectives went much further than those in Spain and that Iberian collectivism had more in common with the *obshchina* self-managed by the heads of family than with the *kommuna* of beggars. This is one point of view... But the parallel — discreet but real — that he seems to want to see between some leaders of the CNT-FAI, anxious from October 1936 to curb the movement towards self-management, and the Bolshevik leaders reducing to nought Ukrainian communism tends, as we have already noted, towards complete confusion.

Nevertheless, despite its limitations, this methodically documented study is certainly useful to those interested in the Russian Revolution. Primarily, it is because it rescues from historical oblivion a very revealing indication of the utopian aspects that Bolshevism contained from its earliest days. Reading Aunoble, one understands that what became a means to dominate and oppress those within it was also once for them a source of dreams. The dream of the

collectivists of Izium was trampled underfoot by those whose commitment to *realpolitik* always led them to choose power over revolution, but one should never forget that the dream had the merit of actually existing. The questions it raises still remain, including their relevance for those who do not dream.
Sarah Gruszka

Eric Aunoble replies:
It is not for me to return to our obvious ideological differences that are based on experiences and reflections that we do not share. Rather, I'm embarrassed by your approach: if you claim to have used the form of an academic review, you have fundamentally moved away from it by a questionable use of both concepts and facts. In terms of analytical tools, you find in my work an array of contradictions and euphemisms and say that you need 'merely to stick to specific categories'. I see only two that you use: the 'true collective' on the one hand, and the 'Sovietised collective' on the other. That is to say, you have adopted a strictly bipolar reading, and one that is highly partisan. Besides, when you start your presuppositions about what I am saying, you use the indicative tense to quote me, while you use the conditional to discuss the points of divergence… This reading in black and white leads to easily demonstrable misinterpretations. Feel free to detect a euphemism in the expression of 'questions of power'. It comes from reading historians and sociologists influenced by Foucault, although they are more distant from my ideological world than yours. It is not used to euphemise, but suggests equality as a social relationship that is to be built, and not as an idle dream, an immanent goal that is never realised. That's useful for revolutionaries, is it not? Then there is formalism, when, convinced *a priori* of a Bolshevik monopoly, you see in the names of collectives the reflection of an 'exclusive frame of reference'. However, apart from the names of Lenin, Trotsky, Sverdlov and Rakovsky, the collectivists shared their pandemonium with other revolutionaries (Labour, Victory over Capital…), and some as much SR as anarchist (Red Flag, International). One of the Makhnovist collectives called itself 'Rosa Luxemburg'.[32]

Assuming that political cultures are already strongly and deeply cleaved, you omit what I say about the concrete factors of the revolutionary process. When you consider the collectivists' attachment to communism, you quote texts and

32. Rosa Luxemburg and Karl Liebknecht did not appear as totems for the Russian Communists during the first few weeks following their murder. The same type of error occurs with the cultural analysis. 'Ray of Light' does not refer to religion, but to the imagination of the Enlightenment imported since 1905 and that of science fiction (Leonid Heller and Michel Niqueux, *Histoire de l'utopie en Russie* (Paris, 1995); O Figes and B Kolonitskii, *Interpreting the Russian Revolution: The Language and Symbols of 1917* (New Haven and London, 1999).

procedures that easily appear as bureaucratic, without telling your reader that the roles of collectivist, communist and functionary were often simultaneously taken by the same people.[33] Need I remind you that the two main leaders of the canton's administration, far from being bureaucrats cut off from the real world, lived in collectives (p 81)? Need I remind you that they did not hold executive positions (p 114)? Need I remind you that they had been involved in revolutionary activity in the vicinity for several years (p 102)? Similarly, the notion of the Communist Party is particularly unclear at this time. It overlaps with that of the collectives not only in the minds of naive communists, but also in the administrative and institutional reality of the first half of 1919 (pp 101, 106). In this confusion there is no control from above as you continue to believe, but a series of horizontal controls, already described by Marc Ferro[34] as a characteristic of the Russian Revolution. This period of revolution and civil war was full of 'hesitation' and 'contradictions', and not only in the discourse of the historian. This period saw both centralist and rank-and-filist Bolsheviks, and the emergence of an insurrectionary anarchist army wearing outlandish and gaudy uniforms whose leader, after whom the movement was named, was formally called 'Father'… To account for such a situation, one cannot content oneself with hasty conflations, however 'likely' they seem. I shall show two of them in your review. You repeat Berthier, who accuses the collectivists of aiding the requisitioning of grain from small farmers. Where? When? This does not appear in my sources, where there are many complaints by villagers against the collectivists. Contemporary Ukrainian history — very anti-Bolshevik — says not a word about this… It describes the confiscations carried out in 1919 by detachments of Russian workers, which had poor results. The picture changes a year later — in 1920 — precisely when the collectives have almost disappeared in favour of poor peasants' committees, which have requisitioning as part of their functions.[35]

Having misjudged this by a year, you then manage to be out by a few thousand kilometres. In footnote 16, you explain that the collectivists are in many cases uprooted city dwellers. You may have missed the fact that, having shown that

33. 'Functionary', that is to say, someone occupying an administrative post, not 'Commissar', that is to say, a 'person given a temporary assignment by the state' (Larousse). Your use of the term is misleading and false: the Bolsheviks certainly appointed many commissars, but the appointment process that I describe in contrast follows criteria for participation in collectives (p 81) and applies to local activists (p 102).
34. Marc Ferro, *La Révolution de 1917* (Paris, 1992, originally 1967); Marc Ferro, *Des soviets au communisme bureaucratique* (Paris, 1980); Marc Ferro, 'Y a-t-il trop de démocratie en URSS?', *Annales ESC*, Volume 40, no 4, 1985.
35. Stanislav Kulchytskyi, *Komunizm v Ukraine: Persha desiatyrichchia (1919-1928)* (Kiev, 1996), p 111; *Istoria ukraïns'koho selanstva*, Volume 1 (Kiev, 2006), p 571.

this is factually wrong in respect of Ukraine (p 90), I discuss this issue on page 193. It seems clear that Rosa Luxemburg had noticed this in respect of Russia,[36] long before Skirda or Conquest. However, I will refrain from being too assertive on this matter because the only 'scientific' study on the subject, written in the USSR,[37] is based on scattered sources without a guarantee of their being representative. In addition, it is broadly acknowledged that this thesis about the uprooted is invariably accepted without its ever being subjected to a critique. It corresponds to the Soviet Vulgate outlined in 1920 (p 193), subsequently converted to Stalinist dogma (p 231). The theme of the collective as a 'leftist deviation' and thus essentially anarchist in nature, was invented — or, rather, reinvented — by the old Bolsheviks in the mid-1920s (p 233), before Makhno or Voline had written on the subject. This same argument also finds favour from a school of historians (whose existence you obviously ignore) who see in 1919 a dress rehearsal for 1930-33.[38] For opposite reasons, it has also become a commonplace among libertarians, whose appraisal of the collectives differs little from that of the anarchists.

Let's talk about Makhno! I had no serious preconceptions on the subject. When I chose to concentrate my work on the red areas the closeness of ideas certainly was a factor, but my prime interest was in studying continuities and discontinuities of the USSR as it formed. I find it more interesting to see how the worm has entered the fruit than to declare that the apple is rotten because it has fallen into the wrong hands. Contrary to what you imply in footnote 8 of your article, I do mention the existence of many, mostly anarchist, collectives during 1917-18 (pp 52-53). The persistent flourishing of Makhnovist collectives in 1919 does not invalidate my thesis (which concerns itself not with the respective revolutionism of Bolsheviks and anarchists, but with the capacity of the poor classes to carry out social transformations). Moreover, in the academic version of my work, I merely note Nabat's lack of enthusiasm for collectives. The many questions raised by historians as well as by libertarian and Marxist friends finally pushed me to resume the work on the basis of published documents. So I write at second-hand — as do Skirda and Avrich. And if nobody sees more than a few Makhnovist collectives in 1919,[39] it certainly does not prove they did not exist,

36. Rosa Luxemburg, *La Révolution russe* (Pantin, 2000, originally 1918), p 57.
37. VV Grishaev, *Sel'skokhoziaistvennye kommuny Sovetskoi Rossii 1917-1929* (Moscow, 1976).
38. I refer you to the contemporary Ukrainian historiography already cited; and Andrea Graziosi, *The Great Soviet Peasant War: Bolsheviks and Peasants, 1918-1933* (Cambridge, 1996); and Stéphane Courtois, *The Black Book of Communism* (Cambridge, 1999). Truly, 'no sensible person ever made the comparison' between 1919 and 1930?
39. Where do you get the 'figures' — which are not 'reduced' — 'advanced' by other historians of the *Makhnovshchina*, including Skirda? When Skirda described a flowering

but it strongly inclines one to think that this is the case. To be sure, it would require some extensive historical research on Makhno, starting off by checking whether original archival material actually exists. Nevertheless, the Makhnovist position in favour of the individual distribution of the land is known.[40] And it explains the popularity of Makhno in the spring of 1919. Therefore, one could ask a number of new and interesting questions about social relations in the Makhnovist camp. More broadly, one could extend the work of Marc Ferro, one of the few writers whom I think are useful for revolutionaries, by comparing the 'anarchic' tendencies in the Russian revolution and how they were shaped by political currents. Because it is basically the same story that was played out in the factories, regiments, towns and villages — the flourishing of competing independent organisations exacerbated the power struggles (and not only political ones), which led to their being reconstituted at local, regional and national levels. The decision to favour a particular social group or a particular level of organisation has consequences that must be detailed. I believe that I have shown the resulting contradictions in the Bolsheviks' policy — emancipation alienating the peasantry from the Reds and, consequently, a return to order. I made assumptions about Makhnovism — free villages based on respect for the community and for ownership to the detriment of the dominated groups — which it would also be useful either to confirm or refute.[41]

One must not read just to reinforce one's existing views, nor write to repeat dogmatic truths and to fling them in someone's face, as has been customary for decades among both libertarians and Marxists. Judging by some reactions to my book, these customs die hard: symmetrically to your criticism, that of Jean-Jacques Marie praises my approach, but picks out of it only the wisdom of the Bolsheviks in putting an end to the collectives in 1920...[42] Rather than

of communes around Gulyai-Polye, he was speaking of 1917-18, not 1919 — I have consulted the Russian translation, made by the author: *Nestor Makhno, Kazak Svobody (1888-1934), Grazhdanskaia Vojna i Bor'ba za vol'nye sovety v Ukraine 1917-1921* (Paris, 2001), Chapter VI, pp 34-38. Decidedly, chronological precision is not your forte...

40. VF Verstiuk, in *Istoria ukraïns'koho selianstva*, Volume 1, pp 577-78. The Ukrainian Wikipedia — http://uk.wikipedia.org/wiki/maxnovci — summarises the work of the historian VF Verstiuk: the *Makhnovshchina* was the 'means for the peasantry to chart its own path in the revolution, to represent a force that tended towards democratic development based on the peasants' economic independence.

41. Incidentally, it would perhaps rescue Makhno from the revival that he is currently experiencing on the part of Ukrainian nationalists. Thus, the rock festival 'Independence Day with Makhno' held each summer in Gulyai-Polye since the 'Orange Revolution' is (according to its initiator — see http://www.ostbar.com.ua/project/1) 'the commemoration of the most genuinely democratic celebration of Independence Day; a state festival that ideologically unites the overwhelming majority of Ukrainian citizens'.

42. CERMTRI, *Cahiers du mouvement ouvrier*, no 38, April-June 2008, pp 108-10. By the same token, I recognise that my words on the Spanish revolution are fleeting, but I

leave the legacy of the revolutions of the twentieth century to be lost in the hands of serious bourgeois historians, one could make the Russian Revolution fruitful for revolutionaries today, by studying the original documents and then presenting a series of questions 'in the context of the real situation'.

Editorial Note: This review and the author's reply were published in *A contretemps: Bulletin de critique bibliographique*, no 32, October 2008. We have removed the section headings from the original. We received considerable assistance with the translation from Harry Ratner, who points out that the French word 'commune' can have several meanings; it can denote a political entity such as the Paris Commune, a commune of squatters, or an administrative unit such as a parish council in England or a local authority in France. Given the context of Aunoble's book, 'communes' has been rendered as 'collectives' or 'collective farms' or 'collectivists'. The word has been translated depending on context.

* * *

David Austin (ed), *You Don't Play With Revolution: The Montreal Lectures of CLR James*, AK Press, Edinburgh, 2009, pp 334, £14

'Never play with insurrection unless you are fully prepared to face the consequences of your play', Engels famously warned in 1852 in the aftermath of the defeat of the wave of revolutions across Europe in 1848. The recent democratic revolutionary processes unfolding across the Middle East and North Africa have seen many people rightly returning to the writings of Marx and Engels to help them try and make sense of 'the Arab 1848'. Similarly, amidst the victory of many democratic nationalist movements in the colonial Caribbean and the wider tumult of decolonisation during the 1950s and 1960s, the Trinidadian Marxist historian and activist CLR James also seems to have been struck by such historic parallels. Though he didn't explicitly use the term 'Caribbean 1848', in a 1967 lecture, 'Marx's *The Eighteenth Brumaire of Louis Bonaparte* and the Caribbean', James noted that:

> ... in 1848 and 1851, France, a backward country — underdeveloped, so-to-speak — was making the transition to the modern state. We in the Caribbean are making the same transition, so that what he [Marx] writes here has an extraordinary application to what is happening to us and you cannot understand what is taking place in the Caribbean in particular, and in various other underdeveloped countries, unless you have a proper view of economics, historical analysis, and political developments. (pp 139-40)

do emphasise the secondary status of my sources and the hypothetical nature of my assertions.

This lecture was just one of those given by James when he voyaged to Canada for a three-month sojourn from December 1966 on the invitation of a little group of Jamesian Caribbean radical student activists based in Canada — 'The CLR James Study Circle' — and its sister group based in Montreal, the Caribbean Conference Committee. The 'Montreal lectures' of James have now been collected together by David Austin — a young black scholar who has, among other things, produced a great audio profile of CLR James, 'The Black Jacobin', for CBC Radio in Canada —under the title *You Don't Play With Revolution*. This title — with its nod to Engels' warning about the dangers of playing with insurrection quoted above — comes from a line in James' *Party Politics in the West Indies* (1962) where he stressed: 'I am a Marxist, I have studied revolution for many years, and among other things you learn not to play with it.' James came to Canada from London, to which he had returned from Trinidad after the recent electoral defeat and subsequent collapse of the Workers' and Farmers' Party (WFP) which he had founded in 1965 to try — in vain — to challenge the political conservatism represented by Eric William's People's National Movement (PNM). In Canada, which Austin notes had become 'the most active site of exile Anglophone Caribbean *political* activity in this period' (p 11), James gave a series of characteristically stimulating public lectures on a range of subjects including 'The Making of the Caribbean People', 'The Haitian Revolution in the Making of the Modern World', 'Shakespeare's *King Lear*', 'Slavery in the New World' and 'The Origins and Significance of Negritude'. Yet the veteran theorist also took the opportunity to give a series of private educationals in revolutionary history and political theory to his young supporters alongside his public formal lectures, on topics including not only Marx's *Eighteenth Brumaire* but also 'Existentialism and Marxism' (a surprisingly generous discussion of Heidegger which concludes by recommending *La Phénoménologie* by JF Lyotard, 'one of our comrades in France'), 'Rousseau and the Idea of the General Will', 'Marx's *Capital*, the Working Day, and Capitalist Production' (in which James stressed 'the history of the working day is one of the greatest battles that have been fought for democratic rights for working people') and an extended series 'Lenin and the Trade Union Debate in Russia' of 1920-21 (which James describes as 'one of the finest political discussions that I know of — anywhere', comparable to the Putney Debates 'at the high pitch of the English Revolution' (p 161)). Apart from James' lecture 'The Making of the Caribbean People', the lectures collected together here have never been published before, and so we are therefore indebted to the work of Austin for gathering together this incredibly valuable collection of material. Transcribed from recordings made at the time, these lectures gives us a unique insight into James' political and intellectual thinking at a critical juncture — between the disappointment of the failure of the WFP and the eruption of what he would later hail as 'the world revolution' of 1968 — and also the impact and impression he made on a younger generation of Caribbean radical activists in the Canadian New Left.

Austin, who himself stands in this black radical tradition hailing from the Caribbean in Canada, in his illuminating introduction rightly highlights the importance of the impact the young Jamesian activists would also make on James in the course of these discussions in what Austin calls 'a kind of Aristotelian lyceum' in Montreal (p 10). Many of these students were already outstanding 'organic intellectuals' of the emerging Caribbean radical movements of the 1960s and 1970s, including the Vincentian activist Alfie Roberts, Grenadian Franklyn Harvey, Antiguan Tim Hector, Jamaica-born Robert A Hill — and had their own agenda and ideas — see for example, David Austin (ed), *A View for Freedom: Alfie Roberts Speaks on the Caribbean, Cricket, Montreal and CLR James* (Alfie Roberts Institute, Montreal, 2005). For these young Caribbean socialists, James symbolised the hope and vision of real social change and liberation from below for the post-independence Caribbean which James saw as drifting 'towards reaction internally and neo-colonialist relations with the Great Power' — the US — externally and with a political system that was 'only the old colonial system writ large' (p 18). As Robert A Hill had put it to a conference of Jamesians in Detroit in September 1966, just before James' tour (a speech included in the appendix), 'the ideas of James' were 'the only hope of Caribbean transformation' and James' 'exemplification of method' was 'the only certain basis on which we could drive ourselves into the antagonism of Caribbean society' (p 296). Accordingly, as Austin notes — and as one can get a sense from the serious nature of the questions and contributions in the discussion after James' lectures which are also included in the volume — 'James was so struck by their sense of purpose that on one occasion he is said to have turned to them and asked, "Who are you people?"' (p 16) The volume usefully includes correspondence from the period between James and these activists and other key Jamesians such as American labour historian Martin Glaberman, together with other relevant items in an appendix (including a lecture by Glaberman, 'CLR James: The Man and His Work' given in Canada in 1965, which would be useful for those readers new to James).

Overall, the lectures are, as one would expect from James — a public intellectual *par excellence* — incredibly wide-ranging, full of off-the-cuff recommendations of works of political theory that revolutionaries should read, and witty in the allusions James makes to contemporary politics and politicians. Here is a sample, from James' lecture on Marx's discussion of the working day in *Capital*, when James breaks off to imagine what Marx might have to say about a national independence in Trinidad that leaves the routine business of capitalist exploitation unchallenged:

> Marx would say Independence in Trinidad... what independence? There are six banks there that are masters of the country: Tate and Lyle who have the sugar estates there; Texaco, BP, and Shell — they have the oil and they have the gas stations. Lord Thompson owns the paper, the *Trinidad Guardian*, owns the radio station. He has large shares in television. Everything that matters in the country, they own. But the British still tell you about independence, freedom, liberty, equality, constitution, etc. That is what Marx is talking about. He says the working-day, that battle — the day begins at 7.00 and ends at 3.30 — that is one of the greatest victories for human life and human development that has ever been won... it takes some time to get that in your head, the habit of looking at things that way. Independence or African independence — independence, my eye! (p 147)

Perhaps one thing that may come as something of a surprise for admirers of James coming from an anarchist or autonomist perspective, which presumably includes the publishers of this volume — AK Press — is James' strident defence of the tradition of classical Bolshevism and Lenin in his three-part series lectures 'Lenin and the Trade Union Debate in Russia'. As James puts it, 'there is, in the minds of many people today, and even some of us that are sympathetic, some feeling that Stalinism was in reality a continuation of Leninism; that the distinction between Leninism and Stalinism was not sharp... I want to read certain passages [from Lenin's contribution to the trade-union debate] which show you that, objectively, it was not so, and in theory, analytically, it most certainly was not so.' (p 187) Indeed, as James remarks at one point after quoting one such passage from Lenin with respect to the open party debates that took place around the question of the necessity for trade-union independence — even under and from a 'workers' state' — 'all talk about the dictatorship and Lenin in the Bolshevik Party is a lot of nonsense. Isn't that clear? Isn't it obvious? Where could you get a more serious, democratic personality? You cannot anywhere. The British Labour Party did not carry on discussions like that.' (p 174) For James, the Bolshevik Party was 'the finest political party ever heard of', and 'what Stalin introduced into it afterwards had nothing to do with Bolshevism' (p 175).

James concludes his educational series to his young disciples by surveying matters from a great theoretical height with his deep, cultured historical vision: 'I recommend to you *Lear* — Shakespeare in the seventeenth century. Rousseau in the eighteenth century. Marx in the nineteenth century. And Lenin in the twentieth century. Then you have to master and tackle the West Indian problem.' (p 204) I would, however, dispute ever so slightly Austin's contention that James' Marxist educationals and lectures in Canada in this period 'represent James at the height of his political maturity' (p 17). Certainly, James' renewed stress on the importance of Marxist theory which comes through so strongly in these lectures is refreshing — and, as Austin rightly notes, reminiscent of his classic 1960 lecture series in Trinidad, *Modern Politics*. In the Montreal lectures, however, perhaps understandably shaken by his recent experiences with the PNM and WFP and in the aftermath of the various splits in what was once the Johnson-Forest Tendency during the 1950s and 1960s, James seems distinctly reluctant to engage at any deep theoretical level whenever the discussion seems to move towards concrete questions relating to organisation, strategy and tactics with respect to the class struggle in the Caribbean itself. Though James strongly defends the idea that the working class in the Caribbean region exists as a 'class-in-itself', we hear little about it acting as a 'class-for-itself' except in the very abstract — indicative perhaps of some of the limitations that remained with James' strategic vision for Caribbean transformation throughout the 1960s, which resulted in part from the fact that James himself had long tried to go beyond the boundaries of the tradition of Lenin and classical Bolshevism on the question of how best to build up independent working-class revolutionary organisation. That said, when the 'Caribbean Spring' against the dominance of the American Empire in the region does finally erupt, with the working class undoubtedly playing a central role within it, this series of 'Montreal lectures' by CLR James will deserve a special place alongside his other writings on the reading lists of those making it (and those inspired by it internationally). As for those who will be leading such struggles, it is to be hoped that many of them will have long already got their copy.

Christian Høgsbjerg

* * *

Nikolai Bukharin, Valerian Ossinsky, Karl Radek, Vladimir Smirnov, *Les communistes de gauche contre le capitalisme d'État: La Revue 'Kommunist' (Moscou, 1918)*, Smolny Collective, Toulouse, 2011, pp 408, €20[43]

The discussion about the Brest-Litovsk peace led to a serious crisis in the Bolshevik Party. The supporters of the 'revolutionary war' against Germany opposed Lenin and the (very weak) majority of the leading elements. The Moscow Regional Committee refused to recognise the authority of the Central Committee. Bukharin, Piatakov, Bubnov, Safarov and Inessa Armand formed

43. Translated by Harry Ratner. This book is available from Smolny, 43 rue de Bayard, 31 000, Toulouse, France. See also the website http://www.collectif-smolny.org/.

a public factional bureau. On 5 March 1918, Bukharin published the first issue of an opposition journal, *Kommunist*, on behalf of the Bolshevik committees of the city of Petrograd and its region. Together with the 'left communists', they published four issues which the Smolny collective has published for the first time in a French translation by Julia Guseva — an excellent idea!

The left communists opposed Lenin on two issues: on what Lenin called the introduction of 'state capitalism', that is, the centralisation of a disintegrating economy, and the introduction of a form of labour discipline necessary for its reconstruction.

At the Fourth Soviet Congress on 15 March, Lenin got a motion adopted which defined 'the main, immediate and urgent task of the moment — the improvement of the discipline and self-discipline of the working people…, a ruthless struggle against the chaos, disorganisation and economic ruin which are historically inevitable as the legacy of a most agonising war'.

A decree of 23 March, signed by Lenin, introducing the first practical measures on these lines, provoked numerous protests. The leadership of the railway workers' union saw in it the beginning of the commissars' personal dictatorship. According to Bukharin, the decree contradicted *State and Revolution* in which Lenin asserted that under socialism every cook will know how to run the state. Bukharin sarcastically declared that if one appointed a commissar over the 'cook' she would never learn how to run the state! But for Lenin there was no question of waiting until the cook had learnt to run the state before putting the economy back on the rails.

The railways — subject to all sorts of rogues and speculators — were paralysed. In a brief note of 18 March, aimed at combating the chaos which blocked the transport of wheat and coal, Lenin called for ruthless and draconian measures, the strengthening of centralisation and dictatorial rights for the military detachments tasked with the maintenance of order — a situation which would worsen until the end of the Civil War. That same evening the government discussed regulations along those lines, and these were adopted on 21 March. Responding to protests by the railway union (led by the Mensheviks and Left SRs) against a decree which, according to them, subordinated the trade union to the Transport Commissar, Lenin strengthened its power of compulsion. He argued for the general application of the measures called for in the decree on the railways adopted at his insistence on 23 March and published in the press on 26 March.

Lenin returned ceaselessly to this — in his view — crucial point. In a note of mid-April he emphasised: 'The most ruthless measures to combat chaos, disorder and idleness, and the most vigorous and severe measures for raising the discipline and self-discipline of the workers and peasants, are to be regarded as absolutely essential and urgent.' To this end he called for 'completion of the nationalisation of all factories, railways, means of production and exchange…, persistent carrying out of centralisation of economic life on a nationwide scale'. He substituted compulsion for the disorderly initiative of committees and declared: 'The dictatorship over layers of the bourgeoisie must also be dictatorship over the layers of the proletariat and the peasantry which do not act in the interests of the state.'

Lenin expounded his new orientation in *The Immediate Tasks of the Soviets*, published on 28 April. He insisted on the control and recording of all production, especially of wheat, to the extent of repeating these two words three times in the same sentence. But in the general dislocation of society and the spread of hunger, 'the mass of working people', to whom Lenin wanted to give the task of the recording, and control and distribution of all products, tended to disintegrate into individuals seeking all sorts of means to feed themselves and their families. From then on Lenin replaced the people's initiative with the party apparatus and various organisations.

Next, he wrote, 'the Russian is a bad worker compared with people in advanced countries'; we must therefore 'learn to work', 'introducing compulsory labour service immediately, but… very gradually and circumspectly' and introduce piecework to raise the productivity of labour above that of the advanced capitalist countries. It was always to remain below that.

Finally Lenin, for the first time, spoke of the need for personal dictatorship, which 'in the history of revolutionary movements… was very often the expression, the vehicle, the channel of the revolutionary classes'.

Moreover, large-scale manufacturing industry, which constitutes the material productive base of socialism, 'calls for absolute and strict *unity of will*', which can be assured only by the submission of the will of thousands of individuals to a single will:

> Given ideal class-consciousness and discipline on the part of those participating in the common work, this subordination would be something like the mild leadership of a conductor of an orchestra. It may assume the sharp forms of a dictatorship if ideal discipline and class-consciousness are lacking.

The latter was the case in Soviet Russia in that period. The development of the revolution required 'that the people *unquestioningly obey the single will* of the leaders of labour'.

It was these policies that the *Kommunist* harshly criticised in its support of working-class initiative. At the same time, the *Kommunist* writers affirmed in their theses on the current situation that 'the decisive majority of the working class, soldiers and peasants... and particularly the mass of exhausted, declassed, soldiers' (p 70) rejected revolutionary war and supported the Brest-Litovsk peace; and that this had harmful effects on Petrograd: 'stoppage of production, increase in unemployment, declassing of the proletariat and loss of class militancy' (p 75). We shall return to examine these articles in detail to help us better understand what was at stake in these discussions.

Jean-Jacques Marie

* * *

Michel Cordillot, *Aux origines du socialisme moderne. La Première Internationale, la Commune de Paris, l'Exil. Recherches et travaux*, Éditions de l'atelier, Ivry-sur-Seine, 2010, pp 254, €22

Mathieu Léonard, *L'émancipation des travailleurs. Une histoire de la Première Internationale*, La Fabrique éditions, Paris, 2011, pp 414, €16[44]

The founding in London on 28 September 1864 of the International Workingmen's Association (IWA), subsequently called the First International, opened a new period in human history. Marx and Engels had proclaimed in the *Communist Manifesto* in late 1847: 'The history of all hitherto existing society is the history of class struggles.'[45] But until 1864, this class struggle, except for localised and short-lived episodes, had never taken a conscious or organised form. With the foundation of the IWA it began to take on this conscious organised form, today more than ever the target of innumerable attempts at distortion and dislocation, but which transformed the fragmented and scattered labour movement into an international force able to confront not only individual employers but capital and its state nearly everywhere.

Annie Kriegel noted in the bibliography of her *Que Sais Je? Les Internationales Ouvrières*, published in 1964: 'There still is no history of the IWA.' Indeed one cannot consider as such the 90 pages of the last chapter of Edouard Dolleans' *Histoire du mouvement ouvrier* (1947) nor the 50-odd pages that Franz Mehring devoted to it in his excellent biography of Marx (French edition, 1983), nor other similar works. Though numerous partial studies have since been published, such as Jacques Rougerie's work in 1968 on the IWA's French sections, they cannot take the place of an overall view.

This neglect could be surprising but those who Franz Mehring ironically called

---

44. Translated by Harry Ratner.
45. I don't know why the recent editions of the *Manifesto* include the translation by Marx's daughter Laura Lafargue, who added a sentence which does not appear in the German text: 'The history of all society up to our days has been nothing but the history of class struggles.' This is quite superfluous and parasitical, and it uselessly schematises the thought of Marx and Engels.

'devotees of Marx' in the social democracy of his time and their twin brothers of the Stalinised Communist International could hardly get excited about a First International that was, right up to its break-up, open to all working-class currents. Also, however important was Marx's role as animator and political leader, he attended only one congress of the International, that at La Haye in 1872 just before its disappearance. And these good people, reducing Marx to a cipher endorsing their turpitude, had no incentive to examine the real nature of this International. It was in fact really and profoundly internationalist as was shown by its organisation of militant and effective solidarity between the workers of different countries (France and England) during the strike of bronze-workers in 1867, as described by both Cordillot and Léonard. The internationalism of the Second International sank to the level of formal proclamations as the support of the majority of its parties for their own national states grew apace. As for the internationalism of the Stalinised Third International, it only grotesquely masked its subordination to the Kremlin which dissolved it in 1943.

The two works under review complement each other to provide a comprehensive and well-argued view of the subject. Léonard's is a chronological account covering the existence of the IWA from its foundation to its dissolution and even beyond. Cordillot's collection of articles throws light on certain key events: the role of its French section in the strikes of leather-workers, tailors and other workers in 1867, the activities of the workers' commission of 1867, the political itinerary of the communard Zéphyrin Camélinat, the historian of the Commune Benoît Malon, the exiled Blanquists in New York, etc.

Léonard's panoramic account is more complete and confirms Cordillot's observation at the beginning of his study of the workers' commission set up in 1867:

> At the start of 1867, two years after the foundation of the first section in Paris (rue des Gravilliers), the IWA had not succeeded in implanting itself deeply in France. Several months later, in the wake of imperial prosecutions, but also because of internal dissensions, it seemed moribund. However, within less than two years it had not only avoided purely and simply disappearing, but had become a social force which shook the empire and seemed to be developing irresistibly. Meanwhile a profound change had taken place as the mutualist leaders of Proudhonist passivity had been replaced by revolutionary elements, claiming to be collectivists, whose best-known spokesmen were Eugène Varlin and Benoît Malon.

The subject of both books is already well — or, rather, badly — known. Nonetheless, these two works, Cordillot's in its fragmented way and in particular Léonard's continuous narrative, present a real history of the IWA, taking in its changes in direction, internal conflicts, difficulties, partial victories and disintegration.

Both show that the working-class movement had begun to establish itself, above all in England, by the time the First International was created. But from the start the International came up against many obstacles: from the outside in the form of repression, and internally in the form of fundamental differences amongst the various currents within it: Proudhonists, syndicalists of the British trade unions, Marxists, Blanquists, anti-authoritarian anarchists, etc, whose coexistence was rarely peaceful. Léonard gives an accurate and detailed account of these differences and the conflicts which flowed from them and which, after the crushing of the Commune, became very severe, and of the shifting alliances that formed and broke up as events developed.

One can gauge the scope of these differences if one recalls that the French section of the IWA was at first dominated by the very reactionary disciples of Proudhon — whose photograph Mauras[46] was to display in his office. Reactionary in what way? Proudhon opposed strikes, political action by workers and the employment of women, whom he thought should remain at home producing and nursing children. He saw strikes as a crime: 'There is no more a right to coalition [his way of describing a strike] than there is a right to brigandage, rape, adultery.' Léonard recalls — quoting the anarchist Kropotkin — that Proudhon was trying 'to make capitalism less offensive'. One might as well wish to turn La Fontaine's wolf into a lamb.

Proudhon replied to Marx's critique of *The Philosophy of Misery* by declaring: 'The real meaning of Marx's work is that he regrets that everywhere I have thought like him and said it before him.' One can gauge the legitimacy of this reproach of Marx by reading what Proudhon wrote to justify his condemnation of strikes in pursuit of wage increases: 'Any increase in wages can have no other effect than a rise in the price of wheat, wine, etc.' And he supported this traditional bosses' argument with this astonishing explanation which denied the extraction of surplus value from the worker — that is, the labour-time not paid for by the capitalist who is trying to accrue the maximum possible — by asserting: 'What is a wage? It is the cost price of wheat, etc, it is the integral price of everything.' In this way Proudhon quite simply denied capitalist exploitation. He really did understand everything...

Léonard shows how the IWA became the rallying point for thousands of workers in France and elsewhere. Involved in active support of the strikes

---

46. Charles-Marie-Photius Mauras (1868-1952) — an extreme right-wing Catholic, nationalist and anti-Semitic ideologue, founder of the proto-fascist Action Française, supporter of the Vichy regime during the Second World War [*RH*].

launched from 1867 onwards, it raised to its leadership militants who were committed to the class struggle in place of the Proudhonist mutualists who ignored it or wished to bypass it.

The external obstacles multiplied as soon as the IWA introduced an organising force into the strikes that it seldom initiated, but in which it intervened to organise political support. The bosses reacted with extreme brutality to the attempts of the workers to organise themselves. Léonard writes in detail of the strike of the miners of the Creusot, at the heart of the fiefdom of the ultra-Catholic leading employer, Eugène Schneider, Senator of the Empire, beloved of this regime and of the priesthood to whom he donated a truly massive tithe: in fact he diverted to the Church 10 per cent of the contributions to the workers' social insurance fund — without asking their permission. The Church, though largely financed by the regime, pocketed this tithe without hesitation and never reimbursed the contributors. Christian charity has its limits. On the day following the last legislative elections of the regime, Schneider sacked 200 workers suspected of not having voted for him. In January 1870 the miners went on strike. The Empire dispatched 3000 soldiers to the rescue of the imperial senator. Two leaders of the IWA were involved in supporting the strike; Varlin, who established a branch of the IWA in the Creusot, and Malon.[47] Six strikers were struck down by the military, 25 condemned to prison terms ranging from 18 months to three years, and hundreds more sacked. But the strike committee, announcing the end of the movement, declared: 'We loudly proclaim our support for the great International Workingmen's Association, this superb free-masonry of the proletarians of the world.' Thus are defeat and victory were combined. During the suppression of the Commune it was, quite logically, a priest who denounced Varlin, to the military, who shot him on the spot...

The bloody crushing of the Commune started the death throes of the First International. Even though it had not initiated the Commune and Marx had expressed great reservations about the rising of the people of Paris, fearing for the fate it was to suffer, the bourgeoisie of France and beyond denounced the International as the organiser of the revolt and unleashed an international campaign of calumny. The movement in France was decimated: in England the trade unions moved increasingly towards a nationalist reformism. The dispute between Marx and Bakunin was only the most acute instance of the split into groups and factions which paralysed and then dislocated the First International. Léonard provides a clear and on the whole fair account of the successive phases of this development, which saw many — including Marx and Engels — produce their least convincing texts.

47. Benoît Malon's articles on the Creusot strike can be found in numbers 11, 12, 15 and 16 of the *Cahiers du Mouvement Ouvrier*.

A new period now opened: that of the formation of workers' parties in the countries in which the development of capitalism produced a vigorous impulse to the growth of the working class. The German Social Democratic Party, born of the fusion of the supporters of Ferdinand Lassalle (killed in a duel in 1863) and of Marx and Engels, was the motor force of this development, which differed widely from one country to another and which never managed to establish itself in the country which proclaimed itself the Eldorado of capitalism — the United States — whose bourgeoisie succeeded in preventing the construction of a workers' party. This gave a somewhat ironical flavour to Marx's decision to transfer the headquarters of the International to... New York. This certainly allowed it to distance itself from the settling of accounts amongst the European sections, but from then on it could only decline rapidly as it had obviously outlived its time.

In his conclusion, Léonard writes:

Founded in 1889, the Second International was composed of the social democratic parties, and which despite its Marxist rhetoric remained strictly political with the creation of a bureaucratic apparatus which was supposed to represent and instruct the working class but which increasingly became separated from social realities. It ended up by using its power against it [that is, the working class].

What does 'political' mean here? The wish to engage in the political struggle or an ensemble of compromise and accommodation? The least cavalier explanation reduces the evolution of the social democracy to the realisation of a pre-established schema since one does not know from whence this 'bureaucratic apparatus' mentioned by Léonard originated. The German social democracy that was banned for 10 years by Bismarck is conflated with this same social democracy which, 30 years later (and by then having been gradually integrated into the monarchic state) supported this German monarchy's war. This explanation also fails to differentiate the different currents of social democracy from each other: Jaurès, soon becoming hostile to colonialism before being assassinated for his opposition to the First World War, is thrown in with the Dutch social democrat Van Kol, a supporter of colonialism; Rosa Luxemburg and Karl Liebknecht, engaged in the struggle to bring down the bourgeois order and the bourgeois state, are put in the same camp as Ebert and Noske, who had them assassinated in order to defend this very order and state; Lenin, who opposed the war, is assimilated with Plekhanov, who supported it with all his might. One could lengthen this list.

Moreover, 'strictly political' is wrong. With the exception of France — not to mention the United States, where it never existed — the social democracy was mainly involved in the construction of the trade-union movement.

After recalling the various splits among the anarchists — the majority of whom were to support the war-like 'sacred union' in 1914 — Léonard adds:

> Bolshevism and its avatars imposed the unique model of the party-state on the whole of the working-class movement: a regime which would combine and in turn impose political terror, barrack-room communism, cannibalistic bureaucracy, state capitalism, discipline of production, nationalistic militarism, personality cult and the universal concentration camp.

Here again this mixing up of history and its convulsions puts the Bolshevism of 1917, of 1929 and (excruciatingly!) of 1938 on the same plane, or, in other words, puts Lenin, Trotsky and their comrades who expropriated capital, annulled debts to the banks and nationalised the banks, etc, on the same plane as Stalin and his *nomenklatura* who, after having liquidated yesterday's revolutionaries and imposed the horrors of the gulag, looted the state's property and re-established private property.

These shallow analyses allow Léonard to avoid studying the real conditions under which a bureaucracy grew like a canker on the body of the workers' parties and unions and subordinated them to the defence of the bourgeois state — and permits him to avoid discussing how to combat it. They suggest that all political activity inevitably leads to bureaucracy. They substitute metaphysics for the real movement of history, thus leading one to replace action with a critical contemplation that becomes ever more contemplative as it becomes ever more critical, reminding us of Péguy's words about Kant, that he has clean hands but has no hands. It all feels more like a political pamphlet than a history. But the three controversial pages in which these arguments appear should not detract for one instant from the rich and living history that Léonard unfolds in the 400 pages of his *L'émancipation des travailleurs*.

Jean Jacques Marie

* * *

Alain Cuénot, *Pierre Naville (1904-1993): Biographie d'un révolutionnaire marxiste*, Éditions Bénévent, Nice, 2007, pp 686, €26

Pierre Naville is not a well-known name today. But during eight decades his writing and activity were intertwined with the fortunes of the French left. Alain Cuénot's biography — 648 pages of carefully documented text — provides an opportunity to assess his contribution and evaluate his strengths and limitations.

Naville's initial involvement was with the surrealist group. They challenged artistic convention radically, but the political implications they drew were erratic and idealist. It was during his military service (from which began a lifelong interest in military questions) that Naville developed a critique of surrealism which urged his erstwhile comrades to look to the material forces in society that could bring about change.

He joined the Communist Party (PCF), and became joint editor of the review *Clarté*; he commissioned Victor Serge to write on the failed Chinese Revolution (Serge's articles were published in English in *Revolutionary History*, Volume 5, no 3). In 1927, he visited Moscow, where he met Serge and Trotsky and became a firm supporter of the Left Opposition. He was expelled from the PCF, but the party was not fully Stalinised and his local section spent two whole Sundays discussing the issues.

In France he worked closely with Alfred Rosmer and was a protégé of Rosmer's remarkable wife Marguerite Thévenet (of whom we learn disappointingly little — 'Discreet Marguerite' left few clues for historical researchers). But in 1930 French Trotskyism suffered its first major split, with the dispute between the Rosmers and Raymond Molinier. Faced with the great gulf between the tasks of the movement and its actual capabilities, Trotsky was attracted by the young Molinier, who was perhaps unscrupulous but seemed to promise quicker growth. (It was a scenario repeated many times in the history of the movement.)

For the Rosmers it was the end of the road. Though their friendship with Trotsky was renewed, they played no further part in the Trotskyist movement. But Naville did not quit. He remained an active member of the French Trotskyist movement, accepting discipline even though he disagreed with the line on entry into the SFIO. And in 1938 Naville played a central role in organising the founding conference of the Fourth International (again it is disappointing that Cuénot devotes only a footnote to this event).

In June 1939, James P Cannon came to Paris to instruct the French Trotskyists to enter Pivert's PSOP; when Naville refused he was expelled from the Fourth International. Naville now came to the conclusion that organised Trotskyism was finished, although he always retained a great admiration for Trotsky as an individual. During the Occupation he devoted himself to writing books on behaviourism and the materialist philosophy of d'Holbach. He considered the Trotskyists' activity during the war to be futile.

But at the Liberation he resumed activity. For the next 48 years he pursued the twin aims of increasing understanding of the world he lived in and building an independent socialist organisation.

In the years 1948-54 Naville played a leading role in the Parti Socialiste Unitaire — often known as the 'first PSU' to distinguish it from the PSU of the 1960s and 1970s. While presenting itself as independent of both the Communist and Socialist Parties, in fact the PSU had a very ambiguous relationship to the Communist Party, and at times functioned almost as one of its satellite organisations. Whatever his record as a critic of Stalinism at other times, Naville can be legitimately criticised for keeping relatively silent about his differences with the PCF in this period.

More significant was his role as the leading figure in the editorial team of the *Revue internationale*. The Liberation was a period of intellectual ferment. *Les Temps modernes*, the journal launched by Sartre, had considerable influence. Naville's aim was to produce a rival journal that would be explicitly Marxist (something Sartre himself later described as a 'better' option). Though the journal was irregular because of financial problems, it maintained a consistently high standard, carrying for example David Rousset's writings on his experiences in a German concentration camp and some of the early writings of Charles Bettelheim.

When the PSU collapsed Naville continued with his efforts to regroup the left in a period in which the mainstream working-class parties were playing an appalling role. He was involved with the short-lived Parti Socialiste de Gauche and contributed to numerous left publications. In particular he was sharply critical of Mendès-France, who was highly regarded by sections of the left. Yet though he was a professional researcher and a prolific writer, Naville was distrustful of 'intellectuals' (though Cuénot is perhaps wrong to stress his antagonism to Sartre; while Naville polemicised sharply against Sartre, he seems to have recognised him as a worthy opponent). Yet in some ways Naville was a moderate — while critical of the government's Algerian policy, he did not support full independence for Algeria and rejected illegal activity, refusing to sign the Manifesto of 121 which defended desertion and practical support to the FLN.

In 1960 the New Left merged with a sizeable group of Socialist Party members who could no longer stomach their party's Algerian policy, and the Parti Socialiste Unifié (PSU) was founded. Naville helped to draft the founding statement and was a member of the party leadership, twice standing as a parliamentary candidate. In some ways Naville represented a left current in the party. He was among those who tried to block the membership of Mendès-France, and he polemicised against the theorists of the 'new working class'. But though he used Marxist concepts, he seems to have regarded the revolutionary tradition as obsolete and on occasion he was quite happy to work within the framework of the Gaullist state, as when — in 1968! — he lectured on military theory to a gathering of generals at an event organised by the ministry of the armed forces.

At the same time Naville continued to write copiously. Unlike many of his contemporaries he was tempted by neither Third Worldism nor epistemological speculation (he insisted that the eighteenth-century materialists were more important for Marxism than Hegel), and concentrated on Marx's theory of exploitation, regarding this as more significant than the young Marx's focus on alienation; he insisted that Marx was a scientific sociologist, not a philosopher. (Cuénot's claim that he was a precursor of Althusser is perhaps not quite the compliment it was intended to be.) Hence his interest in wages and working hours, and his insistence that workers' control must be at the very centre of the socialist project.

Naville also wrote extensively on the Stalinist states, especially in his five-volume work *Le Nouveau Léviathan*. Drawing on the work of Bruno Rizzi, he condemned the regime in Russia as imperialist and an obstacle to socialist renewal. Yet by the time of his death in 1993 the main points of his analysis were crumbling. He had claimed that private capitalism could not be restored in Russia, and he had had high hopes in Gorbachev.

Yet whatever criticisms can be made — and there are many — Naville's life was devoted to a quest for Marxist understanding and socialist organisation. Cuénot's book is a significant addition to our knowledge of the French left in the twentieth century.

Ian Birchall

* * *

Neil Davidson, *How Revolutionary Were the Bourgeois Revolutions?*, Haymarket Books, Chicago, 2012, pp 812

No concept is more central to the Marxist theory of history than the idea of 'bourgeois revolution'. It informs the opening passages of the *Communist Manifesto*: 'The bourgeoisie, historically, has played a most revolutionary part...' For obvious reasons, the transition from feudalism to capitalism is of all the 'transitions' the one best explained by Marx and by Marxists. In so far as we can explain the transition, we historicise capitalism and convey its limits. Bourgeois revolution forms a link between the past and the future; in particular the insistence that there were bourgeois revolutions in history validates the idea of a socialist revolution. If revolution was how capitalism arrived, it must also be how we depart from here.

Yet the notion of bourgeois revolution has barely been touched by serious enquiry. Of all the many generations of Marxists perhaps only the Communist Party historians of the 1940s and their counterparts in France even began to appreciate how much was at stake. For the PCF (Lefebvre, Soboul), this was straightforward; in order for the party to appear as the heir of all republican virtue, as the Popular Front required, it was necessary that its historians wrote about the revolution, and did so in a simple, celebratory tone. In Britain, the initial task, starting with Christopher Hill's *1640*, was to remind everyone (in a country which had long forgotten King Charles I's execution) that there had ever been a bourgeois revolution here. That task accomplished, the first difficulty was in working out how and why it had taken place. Readers will be more than familiar with the collections *The Transition from Feudalism to Capitalism* and *The Brenner Debate*, which were long treated as authoritative.

Not in these collections and nowhere in postwar Marxism can be found a book which treats the concept of bourgeois revolution with as much care as Davidson gives it. This is simply an extraordinarily ambitious book, in which every relevant authority on the subject of bourgeois revolutions, from the immediate participants and the first generation of commentators, right up to the academic Marxists of the present (with every strand of activist voice in between) gets heard and none of the 800 pages is wasted. Significantly, Davidson takes the idea of bourgeois revolution far beyond its usual end-date of 1917, analysing the colonial revolutions of the 1950s and 1960s as the last revolutions to be capable of belonging to this category.

The earliest chapters refute in passing the common non-Marxist argument that there is no need for a theory of bourgeois revolution as it is anachronistic and in no way reflects the language of contemporaries. Davidson shows that figures such as Harrington or Milton, writing in the immediate aftermath of the Commonwealth, were concerned with exactly how revolutions happen and who gained from them. This example gives a flavour of Davidson's essential method, which is to find a narrative source in (Marxist or pre-Marxist) political philosophy, to study that writer carefully, to re-contextualise some of the most familiar passages of his writings, and to show that they had a meaning often far different from that often ascribed to them.

Davidson's huge book shows that several of the shared assumptions on which the postwar literature was based were false. Crucially, Davidson confronts directly the main problem with the conventional notion of bourgeois revolution. If, as Hill, Hilton and everyone else in their generation assumed, a revolution was necessary for *every nation* to pass from feudalism to capitalism, then what do we say about the 200 or so contemporary states (that is, everywhere save Holland, France, Britain and the US) in which the transition was unaccompanied by a popular insurrection?

Davidson chooses the simplest answer, which he terms 'consequentialism': a bourgeois revolution is any process whatsoever (may it be under conditions of political revolution or the blackest counter-revolution) which achieves the consequence of a transformation from feudalism to capitalism. Davidson finds ample authority for this position in writers from Marx and Engels to Trotsky, Deutscher and Tony Cliff (Davidson is a member of the British Socialist

Workers Party as, of course, I am).

One obvious influence on Davidson's writing is an article by Alex Callinicos from the bicentenary of the French revolution (*International Socialism*, no 43), in which it was argued that 'bourgeois revolutions must be understood, not as revolutions consciously made by capitalists, but as revolutions which promote capitalism'. Davidson develops this insight, arguing in effect that bourgeois revolutions should not be defined in terms of agency, structure or ideology, but simply in terms of their outcome, that is, the establishment of an independent, national centre of capital accumulation.

Davidson's answer is vastly superior to the mere assumption that the classic bourgeois revolutions required (or, in some formulations still require) repetition in every country. Yet it raises troubling political questions. For if a bourgeois revolution can be defined as *any process*, however insurrectionary, then why should we not extend the same grace to proletarian revolutions, and allow them to have happened wherever property was collectivised, even under the tracks of Stalinist tanks? Davidson's short answer is that prior to the socialist revolution the working class will not be a class which owns property, in contrast to the bourgeoisie which was economically dominant even before its political ascendancy. Our generation needs a popular insurrection to make the change happen, theirs only needed it sometimes.

To my mind, this subtly exaggerates the difference between bourgeois and proletarian revolutions: part of the point of the bourgeoisie's thirst for political power was to convert its long but impermanent economic ascendancy into durable rule. There is another difficulty: in each of the Dutch, English and French revolutions and in the American war of independence, the class microfractions that challenged the old regimes (that is, a 'middling sort' of teachers, doctors, lawyers, journalists, junior officers, low-level bureaucrats, unemployed students, etc) were visibly the same, even though the movements were spread over 150 years and two continents. A pure consequentialism would leave no explanation for this pattern other than coincidence.

In two of the most interesting chapters of the book (21 and 22), Davidson attempts to generalise away from the national towards the international, portraying capitalism not as a series of national paths but as a global mode of production, in which breakthrough societies required genuine insurrections, and later developers (in which all possessing classes could see the promise offered by the new order) were able to develop in the same direction by emulation, without requiring the same assault on classes based on older kinds of property. It follows that there were two types of bourgeois revolution, one (from below) requiring a revolutionary assault, and the other (from above — for example, Germany, Japan, Italy), in which capitalism triumphed through élite action.

These two types of transition are distinguished as two acts within a single, global drama broken in the middle by a moment of 'systemic irreversibility', between 1740 and 1760, after which the ultimate global domination of capitalism was assured, making the transitions 'from above' possible, indeed typical.

For this reader, the confidence with which Davidson feels able to describe, using normative, sociological language, the way in which bourgeois revolutions occurred in different, national states, undermines the persuasiveness of his polemical term 'consequentialism'. It becomes clear that, even for Davidson, the 'how' of the bourgeois revolution is not a matter of mere happenstance at all.

As Davidson comes closer to the present, his focus shifts towards the remaining set of societies for which bourgeois revolution has still had any political meaning; that is, the former colonies of the Global South. Davidson treats his reader to a summary of the main theorists of Third Worldism, comparing their ideas to those found in Trotsky's theory of permanent revolution, and then in Tony Cliff's 1957 article on deflected permanent revolution. Davidson summarises Trotsky, and then Cliff's refinement of Trotsky, before transcending each. The basis on which he does so is essentially this: Trotsky was right to see the possibilities (in conditions of global capitalism) for a national transition, under conditions of combined and uneven development, from feudalism to socialism. Cliff was correct also to insist that a benign outcome was not inevitable, and that national revolutions might result only in the ascendancy of a local bourgeoisie. But both writers in any event belong to an epoch when we could speak of capitalism and pre-capitalist societies, and that stage has since passed. Trotsky's approach is therefore criticised for a tendency to portray the going over from underdevelopment to socialist politics as inevitable, which in retrospect it clearly was not, and for a residual association of democratic tasks with a bourgeoisie (in Davidson's account, by contrast, the democratic aspects of bourgeois revolutions was generally the work of quasi-proletarians — that is, the Levellers, Babeuf, etc — the losing fractions of the bourgeois revolutions, not the winners).

Davidson sees little contemporary value in Trotsky's theory of permanent revolution, deflected or otherwise. To my mind, Davidson, despite having ably summarised Trotsky, under-emphasises the most interesting part of Trotsky's theory. As long ago as *Results and Prospects*, Trotsky portrayed the victory of the Russian revolution not as a question of regional and global politics:

> Left to its own resources, the working class of Russia will inevitably be crushed by the counter-revolution the moment the peasantry turns its back on it. It will have no alternative but to link the fate of its political rule, and, hence, the

fate of the whole Russian revolution, with the fate of the socialist revolution in Europe. That colossal state-political power given it by a temporary conjuncture of circumstances in the Russian bourgeois revolution it will cast into the scales of the class struggle of the entire capitalist world. With state power in its hands, with counter-revolution behind it and European reaction in front of it, it will send forth to its comrades the world over the old rallying cry, which this time will be a call for the last attack: Workers of all countries, unite!

This insight that the true significance of a national revolution may rest in the capacity it creates for a regional or global challenge to capitalism was of course vindicated by 1917, and something similar could be said (if on a more modest scale) for both 1968 and the Tunisian and Egyptian revolutions of 2010-11.

It might be objected that Trotsky barely developed his idea of a revolution as a regional or global process, and that his mode of expression is literary or latent rather than analytical or historical. All this is true, but the mode of Marx's *Manifesto* is no less literary; and we can speak with confidence of Marx's views of the working class, even bearing in mind his failure ever to continue his magnum opus beyond *Capital*.

It might alternatively be objected that you do not need the theory of permanent revolution to justify a focus of the internationalisation of protest. Davidson himself cites passages from Rosa Luxemburg which acknowledge the necessity (if not the opportunity) of internationalisation; and there have been plenty of others in the tradition who have insisted on this, going back to Marx and Engels themselves.

But where I think Davidson undermines himself is in paradoxically providing a vocabulary for those who disagree with him to explain what the international aspect of permanent revolution is for. Early in his book, in a discussion of the American War of Independence, Davidson distinguishes between social revolutions (that is, revolutions achieving a transition from one kind of class society to another, or to the abolition of classes) and political revolutions (for example, revolutions to topple a particular regime).

My view is that there is still something significant in Trotsky's intuition that the crossing of national borders adds depth to a revolutionary upheaval (that is, makes possible a social as opposed to a mere political revolution) which survives Davidson's assault. This insight is not relevant merely to 'underdeveloped' countries, but is part of the process of internationalisation itself and the challenge that international upheaval represents to nation-states (that is, it ceases to make them the arbiter of a successful outcome; for while a political revolution can succeed in toppling a regime even while leaving that regime's social basis intact, that outcome is harder once the revolt is regional or global). Until the revolution succeeds, it follows, the last word on permanent revolution will not be spoken.

Finally, while I disagree with some of the book's formulations, there is a grandeur of ambition to this work, matched by calibre of insight and authority of tone, which I have not found in any other Marxist writing for decades. It reminds me of the politics of which the British left used to be capable, in an epoch of shop stewards and unofficial strikes, when there was a mass audience for revolutionary ideas, and the best Marxists did not hide their impotence by writing merely for students. It is written as if by understanding one or two simple ideas well, socialists can yet grasp *everything*. I really would encourage all readers of *Revolutionary History* to read Davidson's book.

David Renton

* * *

Bob Dent, *Hungary 1930 and the Forgotten History of a Mass Movement*, Merlin Press, Pontypool, 2012, pp 178, £13.95[48]

Bob Dent, residing in Hungary since 1986 and author of several works on Hungary, has completed an historical work, based on truly thorough research, on the fate of a commemorative plaque. This plaque (which has since disappeared) was installed in 1955 on the façade of the Museum of Fine Arts near the Heroes' Square and the Budapest municipal park at the spot where the most important workers' demonstration in interwar Hungary had taken place. It carried the inscription: 'In memory of the heroic struggle of the working class. On the twenty-fifth anniversary of the great mass demonstration of 1 September 1930. The organised Hungarian workers, 1 September 1955.' (p 143)

Following on the detailed description of the event and its consequences (pp 61-87), Dent's investigation revolves around two questions: firstly, the appropriation by the Communist Party of an action organised by the Hungarian Social-Democratic Party (SDP) and its trade-union organisations; and secondly, the changes in the Communists' description of these events during the controversy between the two workers' parties and the rule of the Communist Party between 1945 and 1990 (pp 129-68). To locate the events in space and time the author describes the urban and class topography of the Hungarian capital (pp 58-60) and outlines the historical background (pp 13-28) by reminding us of the principal aspects of the social and political evolution of Hungary from the close of the nineteenth century. He dwells on the policies of the SDP and in particular the Bethlen–Peyer pact agreed between Horthy's Prime Minister and the workers' leader in 1921 (after the crushing of the

48. Translated by Harry Ratner.

workers' council republic and the White terror) which was to provide the legal framework for the Hungarian workers' movement up till 1944.

The day's action of 1 September 1930 occurred in the context of the crisis following the 'Black Thursday' on Wall Street, and its aims were well defined by the slogan 'Bread and Work'.

In order to establish the facts, Dent reconstitutes the chronology of the social movements which shook Hungary from August 1929. Thus more than 50 strikes, meetings and demonstrations are noted at which the question of unemployment was the main concern. In competition with the tiny illegal Communist Party, the SDP and its trade unions — which previously had in practice consisted only of organised employed workers — now took up the grievances of the unemployed so that the demands became very varied: 'Work or passports' in order to survive or to emigrate, voting and democratic rights, wage rises, public works, unemployment insurance and benefits, the eight-hour day, help with transport, etc. Often the demonstrations took place in front of public buildings (town halls, ministries, Parliament) and were nearly always repressed by the police. In many places conflicts broke out between unemployed and employed workers, between trade unionists and non-unionists and between locals and outsiders. The movements culminated in two vigorous appeals to workers of all grades launched on 1 and 17 August 1930 by the principal leaders of the SDP, Peyer and Garami, for a mass demonstration on 1st September. 'There is no time to waste', Peyer declared. 'To the streets!' Garami exhorted in *Népszava* (*People's Voice*), his party's paper (pp 47-48). The analyses of their motivations are no less interesting; particularly those of Peyer, as he typified 'the classic European labour bureaucrat' (p 20), always concerned about his political respectability.

On the day, despite the banning of the demonstration by the authorities, while the police patrolled the adjacent streets and boulevards, workers converged from all directions on the municipal park, the venue of the demonstration. The numbers were all the greater as many employers had shut their factories. Though the marshals of the SDP tried to guarantee the peaceful character of the movement, skirmishes and violence soon broke out in various places. According to the *Magyar Hírlap* (*Hungarian News*), one person was killed, five were in danger of dying, 22 seriously wounded and many more lightly wounded (p 67).

Dent provides a very detailed account of the confrontations and the behaviour of the demonstrators and of the police. He uses the reports by three Hungarian papers as well as the explanations given subsequently by various protagonists; he critically examines the testimony of the future Communist politician, János Kádár, and draws attention to the traces left by this day in the poetry of Attila Jószef and the graphic art of Gyula Derkovits, whose testimony is also used.

According to the leaders of the SDP, the banning of the demonstration and the presence of the police were mainly responsible for these incidents. But one notes the similarity between the explanations given by Peyer and those of the conservative papers. *Pesti Hírlap* (*Pest News*) emphasised the role of 'subversive Communist elements', *Magyar Hírlap* claimed that 'several hundred Communist riff-raff... had infiltrated the demonstration', and Peyer declared that the disorders were caused by 'youths and lumpen proletarians with whom we have nothing in common and whose actions we most sharply condemn' (pp 64, 67, 91). In a way these views were confirmed by the *Kommunista* of 8 September 1930 which wrote:

> We gave the slogans to the masses. We led the struggle against the police. It was against us that the most vicious hatred was churned out by the bourgeois press and by the "People's Strumpet". We acknowledge and we are proud that 100 000 proletarians demonstrated on the street under our leadership. (p 129)

The juxtaposition Népszava–Népszajha (People's Voice–People's Strumpet) says a lot about the Communists' attitudes towards the SDP. János Darnyik, the building worker killed on 1 September, was also claimed by the Communists to be a party member. Bob Dent devotes much study to this claim.

A discussion of Darnyik's identity is included in the chapter in which the author examines the description of the events of 1 September as it has evolved since the consolidation of Stalinist power in 1948-49. Relating to the celebrations of the anniversaries of the event he shows that the evolution of this 'biased history' has been far from having been a smooth progression. It reflects both the resurgence of the Communist International's policy of 'social-fascism' and the evolution of Hungary as a result of the changes in the USSR; especially after Stalin's death in March 1953. In the course of this history the reader is given a chilling description of the moral and social environment of Hungary during the dictatorships of Mátyás Rákosi and János Kádár. One notes that it is during Kádár's period that the events of 1 September begin to benefit from a more moderate and more objective treatment, to the extent that the old sectarian line is abandoned in favour of a more popular frontist approach: the description of the event becomes more neutral, the slogan 'Bread and Work' is no longer claimed to be exclusive to the Communist Party, and János Darnyik who lost his life is no longer described as a Communist but simply as a building worker.

In 1990, the sixtieth anniversary coincided with what the Magyar euphemism described as 'a regime change'. Lips are sealed about 1 September 1930; not a word – even in the dailies which continue to call themselves *Népszabadság*

(*People's Freedom* — paper of the former United Party) and *Népszava* (paper of the Hungarian Trade Unions. In 2000 the silence was as total.[49] Dent reckons that this silence is both understandable and regrettable. In fact in East Europe the history of the working-class movement and that of the Communist Party have been conflated and this ideology continues to be detrimental to a real history of the working class.

This leads the author to return to the country's history from the 1920s, through the Second World War and up to the uprising of 1956, whose aims would supposedly have been achieved by the 'regime change' of 1990. He reminds us of the importance of the workers' councils which were simultaneously for freedom of expression, multi-partyism and free elections, but also for the defence of social ownership under their control. Dent affirms that no participant in 1956 wanted privatisation or the dominance of the market, and that this was forgotten in the course of the mentioned regime change. He hopes that knowledge of events such as the great workers' demonstration of 1 September 1930 will help to revive interest in the general history of the workers' movement.

Julien Papp

* * *

David Fernbach (ed), *In The Steps of Rosa Luxemburg: Selected Writings of Paul Levi*, Haymarket, Chicago, 2012, pp 349, £20.00

To have a selection of Paul Levi's writings in English is to be welcomed, not simply out of historical interest, but as a contribution to a critical assessment of the failed Communist movement, in the hope that key lessons can be learnt. Levi was precisely one of those who foresaw a number of the early roadblocks to success and attempted to combat them. This volume, assembled in four sections, contains some key Levi texts when he headed the Communist Party of Germany (KPD), his materials on the March Action, some analyses looking at the Soviet Union, and various items commenting on the beginnings of the slow death of the Weimar Republic.

The editor, and in part translator, has provided the texts with a 32-page introduction, which appears to be a word-for-word repeat of his essay in *New Left Review*, no 238 (November-December 1999), and which contains many factual errors. The literature referenced omits not only the classic German studies of the KPD by the likes of Hermann Weber and Ossip K Flechtheim, but also more recent studies which could utilise the Berlin and Moscow archives. During the 1990s, Luxemburg scholars and researchers of the quality of Ottokar

---

49. Note also that such words as worker, labourer, wage-earner, employee, not to mention proletarian, have dropped out of the vocabulary of the Hungarian papers. They now speak of '*munkaadő*' and '*munkavallalo*', he who provides jobs and he who works.

Luban and Feliks Tych published materials in *Internationale wissenschaftliche Korrespondenz zur Geschichte der deutschen Arbeiterbewegung* on Spartakus and its prominent figures which, had they been consulted, could have backed up statements regarding criticism of the Bolsheviks' practice and opposition to an International dominated by them and run on their lines, but also helped to avoid simple errors.

Not only was Luxemburg's 'The Russian Tragedy' published anonymously, but so were all items in the *Spartakusbriefe*. It was not merely the 'prevalence of the ultra-left' that caused Jogiches to oppose the KPD's formation, this was the tactic he and his comrades had followed in the SPD and then in the USPD, in order to win the leadership or as many adherents as possible. Rosa was apparently swayed by Liebknecht's great optimism. Clara Zetkin stayed in the USPD until its next congress, 'as we agreed'. Jogiches was not a 'Pole' but a Lithuanian. Meanwhile Radek, doing Lenin's bidding, was breaking off individuals and groups from the USPD and had succeeded in setting up a separate party out of the Bremen and Hamburg ultra-left elements.

The ultra-left elements who fused with the Spartakusbund to set up the KPD(S) were a mixed bag holding syndicalist, council communist, etc, positions, with a range of theoreticians such as Anton Pannekoek, Karl Schröder and Otto Rühle, plus 'National Bolshevists' (Laufenberg and Wolffheim), although Johann Knief, the leading figure in Bremen, was out of step with the Bremen people as he favoured participation in the elections. He died, however, in January 1919 of appendicitis. That month the utopians involved the KPD(S) in the disastrous Berlin events which led to the murders of its brains (Luxemburg and Jogiches) and its public face (Liebknecht). Levi took on the responsibility of leadership. He 'and his Marxist friends recognised' that one would have to 'separate from the adventurous and lumpen-proletarian elements', as Arthur Rosenberg put it in his classic *Geschichte der Weimarer Republik* (Frankfurt/Main, 1961), p 66.

The KPD(S) national conference of August 1919, in Frankfurt, was unable to deal with that problem, but, as Fernbach relates, Levi did present his analysis denoting the end of the revolutionary epoch which created the republic and consequently requiring a new approach. Levi was a great deal more farsighted than the Bolsheviks in recognising this situation. The decisive move to separate from the bombers, saboteurs, utopians, lumpen-proletarians and desperadoes was undertaken at the Heidelberg KPD(S) congress. Levi's speech and the theses whose acceptance determined who was, or was not, a party member are included in the volume. But the editor saw fit to omit Levi's analysis of the international economic and political situation. He also does the same with Levi's speech at the Fourth Congress in Berlin. This seems to me to be a major error, as Levi's analyses were superior to any others including those emanating from Moscow, and with his departure the KPD became dependent upon the latter, the economics and social situation often being determined by politics, not the reverse as it should be.

Fernbach says that 'almost half of the party's membership' were expelled at Heidelberg. Only the delegates who rejected the theses were expelled, after walking out. A struggle went on in the districts to win over the better elements of the ultra-left. Only at the KPD(S)'s Third Congress in Karlsruhe and Durlach were those opposed to the theses expelled. Neither did Radek support Levi in his 'drastic pruning of the KPD'. Doing Lenin's bidding and perhaps having his own ambitions, he sent a letter to Heidelberg opposing the 'pruning'. In fact, he was already then seeking out replacements for Levi. When founded in April 1920, the KAPD counted approximately 30 000 members, but it would soon break up due to its heterogeneity. Later one of the KAPD leaders wrote a novel which depicted a typical member as a sort of bumpkin who went into industry but, during the war, dropped out of the SPD and his union and became an outlaw. Max Hölz, who led his own armed group in Saxony which raided police stations, jails and public buildings, often blowing them up, was such an outlaw who, after expulsion from the KPD, joined the KAPD.

The Kapp Putsch, the impressive general strike, and the proposal for a workers' government with a far-reaching democratic programme presented by Karl Legien, was not just the key missed opportunity post-November 1918, but could have 'changed the fate of Germany' as Borkenau's quote points out. The USPD lefts scuppered it; Pieck and Walcher gave it support and offered 'loyal opposition'. It is unclear what Fernbach means by describing Walcher as expressing himself 'in clumsy terms more pertinent to a trade-unionist'. The declaration was suitable, its critics bemoaned the lack of insults attacking the SPD and USPD leaders, in the Bolshevik fashion, which actually often had a negative impact. Walcher came from the Stuttgart revolutionary circle around Fritz Westmeyer, Clara Zetkin *et al*, and although a metalworker had been an editor of the *Schwäbische Tagwacht* and was an able speaker and writer.

Levi's objections to the 18 — then 21 — conditions, drafted by Zinoviev but later credited to Lenin, for being an organisational, not a political, method of determining membership, were far-sighted. Rules and resolutions replaced deeds. Luxemburg had long before — in 1904 — criticised Lenin for this fault (opposing opportunism with a rule when it reflects a material pressure faced by all involved in the class struggle). Levi criticised the over-centralism of the ECCI, as well as the KAPD's invitation to the Second Comintern Congress. However, Fernbach errs regarding Levi's response to Lenin over the disastrous march on Warsaw. Lenin asked whether the German masses would rise up as the Red Army reached East Prussia. He replied that it was a largely rural and conservative province so he doubted it. Moves were set afoot to oust Levi. The ECCI began promoting a 'left' inside the KPD Zentrale of Ernst Meyer and Paul Frölich. While Levi was working to bring the revolutionaries of the USPD into the KPD, the ECCI was already promoting an anti-Levi group within the USPD, which following the fusion would cooperate with the corresponding elements within the KPD. The editor Wilhelm Herzog 'left Moscow with a mandate to prepare an anti-Levi group' (see Richard Löwenthal, 'The Bolshevisation of the Spartacus League', *St Anthony's Papers*, no 9 (London, 1960), p 44).

Levi had grasped that Europe's post-First World War revolutionary situation was over and that a new phase had commenced. Yet Lenin had not seen this. Hence his Polish adventure. When Lenin first drafted the theses 'The Fundamental Tasks of the Comintern' for the Second Congress, Thesis V read 'the task of the moment for the Communist Parties is not to accelerate revolution, but to accelerate the work of preparing the proletariat'; however, he changed it to: '… the task of the moment… consists in accelerating the revolution, without provoking it artificially, until sufficient preparation has been made. The preparedness of the proletariat for the revolution must be advanced by deeds.' Levi opposed the change.

Fernbach errs again in claiming that the majority of the USPD accepted the Twenty-One Conditions and joined the United KPD. A majority of delegates voted in favour, but only about 280 000 actually joined; 340 000 stayed in the USPD, but about 350 000 dropped out in disgust. Between the national conference in September and the Halle Congress six weeks later a membership ballot over the Twenty-One Conditions was held, but only 26 per cent of the membership participated: 235 000. As the USPD had constantly shifted towards Communism many members saw no point in a split, in particular the older ones who had been in the prewar SPD and only recently seen the need to break with it. Many trade-union officials and activists were alienated by the plan to split the international movement by founding a Communist-led one. Though 500 000 was claimed for some time following the fusion congress in Berlin, later on a figure of 350 000 was given.

While Levi was credited with the successful fusion and remained party Chairman at the insistence of the revolutionary shop stewards, a manoeuvre was underway against him. Levi's manifesto, in tune with the tone of the congress, was substituted by one from Radek which had not been debated nor seen by the leadership. It stated, among other things:

> But while a party to which only tens of thousands listen, recruits its followers primarily through propaganda, a party whose organisation comprises hundreds of thousands, to which millions listen, must recruit primarily

by deeds, by action... The United Communist Party has strength enough, whenever events allow it or demand it, to go into action on its own. (*Dokumente und Materialen zur Geschichte der deutschen Arbeiterbewegung*, Volume 7, part 1 (Berlin, 1965), p 134)

This was a sign of the impending adventurism of the March Action.

Moving to the Stuttgart Demands and the KPD Zentrale's *Open Letter* of January 1921, interviewed by KH Tjaden in the 1960s, for his dissertation *Struktur und Funktion der KPD-Opposition (KPO)* (published in 1964), Hans Tittel, then Württemberg KPD district political secretary, said that the Stuttgart Demands originated in a discussion of the District Committee at which Brandler and Walcher were present. KPD member Erich Melcher was chairman of the local metalworkers' union. In his memoir, freely used in the biography by Ernst Stock and Karl Walcher, *Jacob Walcher (1887-1970). Gewerkschafter und Revolutionär zwischen Berlin, Paris und New York* (Berlin, 1996), Walcher relates that Radek noted the pile of resolutions supporting the Stuttgart Demands on his desk in the KPD Trade Union Department, and got the idea for the *Open Letter*. Walcher thought its tone 'unsuitably crude and exaggeratedly conceited', and besides it 'bears an "ultimative character"' (p 59). A bit 'clumsy' then?

Levi's concerns about the Twenty-One Conditions and the operation of the ECCI were proved correct in the way that the majority of Italian Comintern adherents were removed at the Livorno Congress of the PSI and a small, sectarian Communist Party set up. Gramsci later described it as 'the greatest single victory won by these reactionary forces'. The PSI split into a handful of parties, and fascism came to power. Levi's speech on this affair before the VKPD Zentralausschuss is given almost in full. It is possible that Radek set Levi up for 'exposure' using the Livorno events.

In November 1923, it was the turn of the Norwegian Workers Party to be split. Though affiliated to the Comintern, there were disputes over the Twenty-One Conditions. Radek had been ready to compromise but was overruled. Again, a Communist Party was set up which did not contain the majority of revolutionaries. In negotiations with Zinoviev in Levi's presence during the Halle Congress, the Norwegians were told that: 'When it doesn't concern questions of principle, the Executive Committee will show tolerance.' Zinoviev wrote in the German organ of the Comintern that 'questions which are international shall be regarded as binding', but there are 'of course a whole series of questions where the parties in the individual countries can also act on their own' (Einhart Lorenz, *Arbeiderbevegelsens Historie*, Volume 1 (1789-1930) (Oslo, 1972), p 136). Recognising the error in 1927, the Comintern promoted a Labour Party for Norway, encompassing the Workers Party, the Communist

Party, social democrats and the trade unions. The tactic failed.

The Swedish Communist Party too had disputes over the Twenty-One Conditions, and in August 1924 it led to Zeth Höglund, Frederik Ström and the leadership majority and their supporters being expelled, but that is another story. It is worth noting, however, that these comrades had actually run the Comintern's financial side from Stockholm during the Civil War in Russia — and accounted for every penny.

To return to 1921 and the March Action, obviously elements in the RCP(b) Politbureau had been pushing for more action from the KPD, though we do not know whether Lenin approved of the March Action and only dropped it once it was seen to fail, as some authors claim. Levi's pamphlet criticising it and his subsequent speech in defence are both given in full so one can judge who had right on his side here.

To cover up responsibility for the March Action and divert attention from those culpable, Levi was scapegoated for 'indiscipline' (note: politics is secondary!). The Third Comintern Congress was all about 'deals', hailing the March Action as 'a step forward', 'a struggle forced on the VKPD by the government's attack on the proletariat of central Germany'. Levi's expulsion by the KPD was confirmed, and it was deemed 'impermissible for any member of the CI to collaborate with him', though Lenin sent him letters to invite him back after some months as long as he toed the line. Levi would not play the game. One hundred thousand KPD members left the party with Levi, including most of the revolutionary shop stewards, union officials and Reichstag deputies.

Meanwhile Levi and his followers were analysing the Third Comintern Congress, to see if it matched up to its duties. It was noted that Trotsky and Varga had tried to show that capitalism had by then stabilised itself, particularly in Germany, so new tactics were called for. In presenting the Theses on Tactics, Radek was pushing Trotsky and Varga's analysis to the left to accommodate the KPD delegation. Both Lenin and Trotsky admitted that the theses were a compromise which favoured the left. Analysing all this in *Unser Weg*, Levi and his comrades were not impressed. They were even less so when analysing the results of the KPD's Seventh Congress in Jena in late August 1921. The leftism still dominant meant that the compromises made in Moscow in July were pushed even further to the left and were not 'ambiguous and capable of being interpreted', as in Moscow, but 'absolutely unambiguous and definite' (Curt Geyer in *Unser Weg*, no 10, September 1921). An anonymous comrade, presumably still a KPD member, writing in this issue devoted to the Jena Congress, sees the dominance of the left, 'Maslow people' etc, and in his item Bernhard Düwell also refers to 'Maslow people'. The Levites presented their analysis to the congress in the form of a resolution, but it was ignored. It must have been kept off the agenda. It can be found in the same issue of *Unser Weg*. Just as it would have illustrated the ability of Levi to have included the omitted parts of his analyses from the Second and Fourth KPD congresses, the inclusion of some sections of the analyses from *Unser Weg*, no 10, in the introduction would have given the readers an understanding of why he and his comrades gave up on the Comintern/KPD.

Fernbach errs in stating that Levi 'privately' described the Twenty-One Conditions as 'legalese'; he said so at the Second Comintern Congress. Neither did 'Bolshevisation' arrive from Moscow in the period following the March Action, but only in 1924. While the KPD did not adopt adventurist policies after the Jena Congress, and under Ernst Meyer's chairmanship turned to sensible united front tactics, and Frölich and Meyer became 'rightists', at the end of 1921 another group of leading KPD figures around Reuter-Friesland, also now an ex-leftist, were excluded for opposing the freelance activities of the ECCI plenipotentiaries. Levi realised, or had confirmed for him, that the real KPD leadership resided in Moscow.

It was sensible for Levi's KAG to join the USPD, as it was still a sizeable party with a significant working-class following. Unfortunately, things went downhill. The USPD discovered that it could not maintain all its newspapers, positions were suddenly threatened, and its Reichstag deputies doubted they could win their seats in the coming elections. Hence the defeatism and the collapse into the SPD. Again, things turned out worse than expected, as prominent USPD figures did not get the influence they had envisaged, and they were actually sidelined. Levi's arguments for being in the SPD are unconvincing. He had to make the best of it. He threw in his lot with the Klassenkampf left wing, he became a leading figure on the left, but by the time most of the current had been expelled and became the Socialist Workers Party (SAP), he had died. It is worth relating that when the USPD joined the SPD, it had 290 762 members, of which 84 697 rejected the fusion. Of these between 30 000 and 40 000 stayed with the rump USPD. Later it dissolved into the SAP.

Levi published Rosa Luxemburg's critical manuscript on the Russian Revolution and provided it with a substantial introduction, which is 36 pages of this volume. He upset many old comrades, but Luxemburg would have wanted it so. She identified unhealthy developments already in 1918, and these would only get worse with time. As scholars such as Ottokar Luban and Feliks Tych have established, Rosa's views were shared by the Spartakus leadership; they only wanted to hold back the criticism due to the Bolsheviks having their backs to the wall at the time. Too many left-wingers kept quiet about such negative features, and too many fooled themselves. The 'Workers' Fatherland' was a myth, but it took Khrushchev's 'Secret Speech' at the CPSU's Twentieth

Congress before many would accept that fact.

Fernbach asks what Luxemburg, had she lived, would have done in Levi's shoes. In Brandler's postwar correspondence with Isaac Deutscher, he talks of Rosa's 'depression' after the foundation KPD(S) congress due to the triumph of the ultra-leftists, so, had she lived, she would have broken with them. Brandler states besides that 'it was precisely Rosa who turned the whole Central Committee against the Comintern... It will be a Russian *Krämerei* [shop] with which we shall be unable to cope.' In *IWK*, no 3, September 1991, Feliks Tych wrote a piece on Leo Jogiches' criticism of the Bolshevik Party, where he assembles the argument, such as: 'He feared the new International would be built by the Bolsheviki on a very narrow, sectarian basis.' (p 312) In *IWK*, no 1, 1997, Feliks Tych and Ottokar Luban introduce a letter by Jogiches smuggled out of prison in September 1918 (I translated it in *New Interventions*, Autumn 1999), entitling their essay 'The Spartakus Leadership on the Politics of the Bolsheviks'. It states: 'Jogiches in no way wanted (hence also his later resistance to the founding of the Communist International precisely in Moscow) a transference of the Bolshevik model onto the Western European movement and onto the eventual Western European revolution.' (p 99) All this was known to the surviving Spartacus leaders, unfortunately the younger ones had illusions in Lenin & Co. Brandler admitted to Deutscher in 1948 that 'he was too naive to understand Rosa's fears' (see Isaac Deutscher, *Marxism, Wars and Revolutions* (London, 1984)). Fernbach asks whether Luxemburg would have 'sought to maintain a separate Spartakus organisation', or have rejoined the SPD'. The original error was to have left the USPD too early, compounded by fusing with the North German ultra-left rag-bag. It is difficult to see her being ousted from the KPD like Levi, despite the fact that she was opposed to a Bolshevik-run International, but it is equally unlikely that she would have collapsed into the SPD, which was a known quantity by then.

Levi surely did sound parliamentary work and used his power of analysis to warn of what was happening to Weimar Germany, and he undertook, and usually won, legal cases, one of which helped to expose the murderers of Luxemburg and Liebknecht and the resulting cover-up, which prompted congratulations from Albert Einstein. But when analysing events in the Soviet Union, due to his opposition to the New Economic Policy, he saw at one stage the peasants as being the dominant class. Concessions to capitalism were the only possibility in 1921 without a European revolution. Judging by the items included in the volume on the matter it is difficult to discern a coherent analysis in Levi's texts. Fernbach errs again in note 1 of 'The Needs of the Hour', when he describes the gathering of the Socialist International, the Vienna Union and the Comintern, in April 1922 in Berlin, as 'to discuss the possibilities of unification'. Its aim was to build a united front to defend the conditions of the European working class. The proposal for this to the ECCI came from the KPD Zentrale on 21 December 1921 (see *Dok u Mat*, Volume 7, part 1, p 633).

The tragedy of Levi's death for the German working class is stated by his former ultra-left opponent Arthur Rosenberg, by then presenting more sensible and thoughtful analyses. He wrote:

> In recent years Levi had continually grown as a proletarian statesman. He represented a policy as realistic as it was resolute. He demanded that the socialist working class had to return once more to ruthless class struggle if it not only wanted to save its own existence, but also the democratic republic in Germany… In the approaching crisis decisive sections of the German proletariat would have listened to Levi… (*Geschichte der Weimarer Republik*, p 196)

Readers not knowing German would be advised to supplement the editor's introduction with Ben Fowkes' excellent *Communism in Germany Under the Weimar Republic* (London, 1984), to correct many of its errors. The translated texts themselves can fill in some gaps in the knowledge of the readers about this historical period and hopefully provoke some thought.

Mike Jones

* * *

François Ferrette, *La Véritable Histoire du Parti Communiste Français*, Éditions Demopolis, Paris, 2011, pp 226, €14

The French Communist Party (PCF) is not what it used to be. It no longer has the loyalty of five million voters or exercises an iron grip on France's main trade-union confederation — though it played a significant role in Jean-Luc Mélenchon's impressive 2012 presidential election campaign. But its history remains a passionately contested topic.

So a volume that purports to offer the 'True History of the French Communist Party' has a certain whiff of titillation about it. Unfortunately the title is somewhat misleading. The 'true history' of the PCF's achievements and crimes would require several bulky volumes. This slim book of less than 60 000 words offers something much more modest, though of considerable interest all the same. It is a collection of three essays on aspects of the PCF's history.

The first section, the most scholarly and coherent of the three, deals with the foundation of the PCF and attempts to strip away some of the myths that have accumulated in both pro- and anti-Communist accounts. It has long been a source of embarrassment to those trying to show a direct line of continuity between the PCF of 1920 and its later Stalinist manifestation that so many of the party's founders rapidly disappeared from the PCF, to be replaced by a new generation of more pliable bureaucrats.

In particular Ferrette stresses the role of the 'Comité de la Troisième Internationale' (Committee of the Third International). Where historians do not ignore it entirely, they sometimes misname it the 'Comité *pour* la Troisième Internationale' (Committee *for* the Third International). This is not much ado about a preposition. The Committee was, before the founding of the PCF, the official section of the Comintern in France.

The PCF was founded at Tours at Christmas 1920. The founding congress was a dramatic affair — Clara Zetkin's illegal appearance, the young Ho Chi Minh's denunciation of French colonialism — but as is usual with such affairs, delegates were mandated and everything had been settled in advance. And the Committee's role in winning the arguments in the Socialist Party's local organisations was enormous.

The PCF was born — as advocates of entrism like to remind us — of a split in the mass working-class party in France, the Socialist Party (SFIO). But that is a slight oversimplification. Much of the work done to win over the majority of the SFIO was done by the Committee — not all of whose members were in the SFIO and some of whom were revolutionary syndicalists. In any case, in the rather feverish aftermath of the First World War, organisational loyalties were rather fluid. Jacques Duclos recalled that in the period before the founding of the PCF he attended SFIO meetings and even spoke at them — though he never held a party card.

Ferrette draws out the particularly important role in the foundation of the party played by Boris Souvarine, a member of the SFIO. Some historians have played down his significance. But though he was in prison in the period prior to the founding of the PCF, the conditions in prison posed no significant obstacles to communicating with his comrades; indeed he even managed to read proofs of articles while in jail.

Instead Communist historians have stressed the role of Marcel Cachin, who remained a PCF member till his death in 1958. Cachin was a deeply unattractive figure, who was voting for war credits as late as December 1917; but in 1920 he travelled to Russia — whether he was genuinely impressed by Soviet power or merely jumping on a bandwagon it is impossible to say. For Ferrette his importance is overstated.

The second section is devoted to an overview of histories of the PCF. Ferrette describes some of the early histories of the party and shows how they were influenced by political preoccupations of the time. He examines the monumental doctoral thesis on the origins of the PCF by Annie Kriegel — written in a brief period of lucidity between the frenetic Stalinism of her youth and the equally frenetic anti-Communism of her later years.

Finally he makes a lengthy analysis of the most recent major academic study — the widely praised *Camarades!* by Romain Ducoulombier (Paris, 2010), which Ferrette attacks vigorously as essentially conservative and anti-Communist.[50]

It is a pity that Ferrette confines himself to French histories of the PCF. There is no mention of the excellent *French Communism in the Making 1914-1924* (Stanford, 1966) by Robert Wohl, which avoids many of the pitfalls identified by Ferrette, and remains a valuable contribution. Wohl conducted interviews with Souvarine, Rosmer and others as well as doing archival research. Though not innocent of the Cold War, Wohl had no axe to grind in the disputes of the French left.

The third section, aptly titled 'the Communist Kaleidoscope', is the most fragmentary, consisting of a number of short chapters dealing with aspects of PCF history. Unlike the defenders of Lenin–Stalin continuity, Ferrette gives due attention to the 'Bolshevisation' begun in 1924 and instigated by Zinoviev. He defines Zinoviev's central error as putting party organisation before politics, and sees the origins of this in 1917, when Zinoviev opposed insurrection because the party apparatus was insufficiently prepared.

He also has some interesting comments on Trotskyism, suggesting that Zinovievite methods have had substantial influence in the Trotskyist movement.[51] He has some interesting comments to make on the role of Raymond Molinier, and gives what is to my knowledge one of the fullest accounts of Molinier's life. The young Molinier had been a founder member of the PCF at the age of 16.

Ferrette is an active member of the PCF, and believed that his research on the party's origins is relevant to a possible strategy for the party's future. He is a supporter of the French journal *Le Militant* (http://www.le-militant.org/Militant/English/English.html). One of his comrades is Vincent Présumey, author of the biographical sketch of Pierre Broué published in *Revolutionary History*, Volume 9, no 4.

Ferrette has merely scratched the surface — there is so much more to be said, especially about the early years, before we have a 'true history' of the PCF. Even the best histories tend to focus on the divisions in the leadership rather than on the party's day-to-day activity. Yet a perusal of the party's daily, *L'Humanité*, from 1921 or 1922 gives a fascinating picture of many-sided activity. In

50. Ducoulombier has replied at some length to Ferrette's critique at http://tempspresents.wordpress.com/2011/11/08/romain-ducoulombier-francois-ferrette/. My own review of Ducoulombier's rather mediocre volume will appear in a forthcoming issue of *Historical Materialism*.
51. A similar point was argued by Al Richardson in his preface to *Trotsky and the Origins of Trotskyism* (London, 2002).

particular the party's anti-colonial work and its campaigning for women's rights deserve further study. If Ferrette's little book inspires other researchers it will have served its purpose.

Ian Birchall

* * *

VN Gelis (ed), *Pandelis Pouliopoulos, First Secretary of the KKE: In His Own Words*, Createspace, np, 2012, pp 243

Pantelis Pouliopoulos (1900-1943) was a prominent Greek Marxist socialist who became one of Leon Trotsky's principal supporters in Greece. Born at Theva (Thebes), he went to Athens university to study law in 1919, and joined the Greek Socialist Labour Party (Sosialistiko Ergatiko Komma tis Ellados). Conscripted to fight against Turkey in the 1919-22 invasion of that country by Greece, he was arrested for voicing opposition to the war, being released once it had ended. From 1923 to 1925 he played a prominent role in the War Veterans' Movement, which the war had brought into being.

Pouliopoulos was a delegate to the Fifth Congress of the Communist International in 1924, becoming General Secretary of the Greek Communist Party (KKE, Kommounistiko Komma tis Ellados) later that same year. The editor states:

> On 24 August 1925 Pouliopoulos, along with 23 others, was tried in Athens on charges of promoting the autonomy of Macedonia and Thrace. He gave a five-hour speech in his defence and the trial was adjourned. On 22 February 1926, the trial of the 'autonomists' resumed. The charges were dropped, but instead of being released, the men were exiled to Anafi, Amorgos and Folegandros islands.
>
> Pouliopoulos was taken to Folegandros island. He was freed in 1926 with the fall of the Pangalos dictatorship.' (p 4 — I have given the page numbers; the book is not paginated.)

Pouliopoulos resigned as General Secretary of the KKE in 1926, but the Comintern reinstated him. He was then removed from the Central Committee along with Pastias Giatsopoulos in March 1927. Pouliopoulos and Giatsopoulos then issued a pamphlet entitled *Neo Xekinima* (*New Beginning*) and were promptly expelled from the party. They then formed an opposition group aligned with the Trotskyist Left Opposition, publishing a journal called *Spartakos*.

Forced into hiding under the Metaxas dictatorship (1936 onwards), Pouliopoulos was eventually arrested and imprisoned in Akronavplia:

In 1943, along with over a hundred other militants, he was executed by the Italian occupation forces in Nezero, near Larissa, in retaliation for the destruction by partisans of the Gorgopotamos bridge. Speaking in Italian to the squad of soldiers given the job of executing him, he exhorted them not to commit such a crime against the anti-fascist resisters and their adversaries in the war. When the soldiers refused to be executioners, it was the Carabinieri who were given the task. (p 6; another report says it was an Italian army officer who shot him.)

Pouliopoulos wrote extensively. His major work is *Demokratiki i Sosialistiki Epanastasis stin Ellada?* (*Democratic or Socialist Revolution in Greece?*). He translated Marx's *Capital* and *Critique of Political Economy* into Greek, also Trotsky's *The Revolution Betrayed*, Karl Kautsky's *Economic Doctrines of Karl Marx* and *Kant*, and Nikolai Bukharin on historical materialism.

His style is lively and direct. For example, he writes that:

A class of bankers, big ship-owners, industrialists, big merchants, big landlords and arms suppliers, after accumulating much easy riches during the wars and taking advantage of every internal abnormality in order to profit by the needs of the population, now holds in its hands huge concentrations of economic power (stock-market capital, land, factories, ships, building estates, etc), that is, it holds in its hands almost completely the lives of the people...

The military officer class, despite the blow sustained in the defeat in Asia Minor, not only did not lose its power, but, after being dominant in the so-called 'Revolution of 1922', has been stabilised and developed, has received big privileges, has activated a thorough militarisation of the land and, most importantly, has enthroned itself on our backs for good, becoming a decisive factor in the political life of the country, bringing in the methods of bestial stratocratic [military] violence from the barracks and the military schools in the service of the various tyrants and exploiters of the people. ('What the Veterans and Army Victims Demand', pp 29-30)

Pouliopoulos' capacity for independent thought is shown by his comments on the Macedonian question. In the 1927 'Open Letter to the KKE', Pouliopoulos declares that the party:

... without ceasing to support the self-determination of the Macedonian people up until their secession and to fight the concrete forms of national oppression over them by the Greek, Bulgarian and Serbian bourgeoisie[s], must abandon the tactical slogans of 'a united and independent Macedonia' and 'a united and independent Thrace', as they have proved mistaken, and have created confusion among the workers, refugees and peasants, thwarting their internationalist education, which is one of the tasks of the party. The Communists from the Balkans must be able to demonstrate before the Macedonian masses their autonomist slogans independent of the Bulgarian bourgeoisie and its Fascist organs inside the Macedonian organisations, and to defend the national liberation movement of the Macedonians wherever and whenever it manifests itself among the masses themselves, declaring at the same time that the only way for the Macedonian people to acquire their national freedoms and the basis of an independent state, if they want it themselves, is a joint struggle with the workers and peasants of the Balkans against the common enemy, the Balkan bourgeoisie and the dynastic cliques, for a Balkan federation of workers' and peasants' democracies. The argument that such a position when dealing with the Macedonians is wrong, saying it starts from an anti-Leninist theoretical basis and [that] it agrees more with the views of Rosa Luxemburg on the national question which cannot be seriously supported today, that the national independence of the Macedonians cannot occur within the framework of bourgeois regimes such as in the Norwegian example, which was discussed by such Russian Marxists as Lenin during the discussion with Rosa Luxemburg, is untenable. Such a position on the national question, despite the fact that it was condemned by the [Third] Congress, in practice is the position of the party today, as the slogans of the Emergency Congress of 1924 were not even propagandistically used after the Third Emergency Congress. (pp 118-20)

Pouliopoulos further clarified his position in 1940, when he wrote that:

Whoever rejects the existence (unresolved until today) of a *national Macedonian question* in Greek, Bulgarian and Serbian Macedonia is *without a doubt* a lapdog of the bourgeoisie. ('Communists and the Macedonian Question', p 204)

Furthermore:

Communists, faced with a beaten down or betrayed national liberation movement or with 'ethnic cleansing' and subjugating acts of their own national bourgeoisie, don't close their eyes and don't become worshippers of the 'done deed'. They will not deny the reality of the national oppression of a nation and its *desire* (existing in the heart of every Macedonian worker) to shake off the national yoke one day. Communists make these liberating desires of the Macedonian people their own, and declare loudly from now their right to self-determination, even breakaway, if they so wish. They defend daily every immediate national demand, economic, political, cultural, and thus they prepare now tomorrow's revolutionary alliance of the social revolutionary movement of the proletariat with the national revolutionary movement against the common enemy: the Balkan bourgeoisie. (pp 205-06)

Pouliopoulos had a number of pertinent things to say about the KKE. In the 'Open Letter' he writes that:

We will never build a serious Communist Party in Greece if we do not at first concentrate a certain layer of chosen proletarian and intellectual elements... Greek Communists must first of all take care to concentrate in their ranks those whose intellectual, moral and practical qualities can inspire the Greek proletariat to gather around them. (pp 110-11)

The party must educate itself: 'It is a task of all leaders to educate themselves continuously in all theoretical questions.' (p 113)
This surely applies to all members of the party. As to spheres of work:

The party is obliged above all to concentrate its attention and to use most of its forces in trade-union work, and in the proletarian centres of the country, concentrating upon workers in the unions, in their revolutionary education, and to apply revolutionary tactics not with abstract phraseology but in confronting the concrete problems of the daily struggle of the workers. (p 115)

When Stalin issued the order to embrace the 'Popular Front' tactic around 1935, Pouliopoulos condemned the move. In a pamphlet in June 1937 he pronounced that:

The policy of the Popular Front cannot give any decisive defence against fascism, as fascism has been proved to be the policy inevitably advanced by decaying capitalism in its current phase, if the proletariat doesn't overthrow it. Every other policy apart from that of the overthrow of capitalism is not only weak as regards fascism, but, on the contrary, ensures the fascist victory. (pp 157-58, translation amended)

Pouliopoulos was equally condemnatory of the 'Archaiomarxist' tendency. This began as a group within the KKE that published a journal called *Archives of Marxism* (whence its name). They were expelled in 1924 and from then on operated independently. In June 1930 the Archaio applied to join Trotsky's International Left Opposition, becoming the official section thereof until 1934, when they switched over to the 'London Bureau' ('Three and a Quarter International'). In the 'Open Letter' Pouliopoulos wrote that:

> The party must confront the Archaiomarxists as a particular Greek organisation which exploits the organisational disorder of the party and the rudimentary [the text has 'nascent'] cultural level of its members, seeking the dissolution of the party in the name of Communism, dividing in anti-Marxist fashion theory from practice, distorting the teachings of Marxism with countless slanders against the party, distorting the psychology and spirit of the workers, who, disillusioned with the party, are pushed towards the Archaiomarxists. It must educate the workers and intellectuals with care, and explain that the Archaiomarxists' corrosive propaganda is an obstacle to the creation of a strong Communist Party in Greece. (p 117)

Finally it is worth noting that Pouliopoulos refused to conceive of Marxism as a fully finished system of ideas but, on the contrary, demanded that Marxists deepen and develop it. He wrote:

> By its very nature Marxism is not a closed dogma, immovable. It presupposes the possibility and necessity of its later development. With the results of its new experience and the new advances in science, Marxism — its method itself — has demanded from the beginning not only to be checked every time so that it is proven right, but also to be enriched with new theoretical conquests. (pp 215-16)

As readers will have noticed, in my view the translation leaves something to be desired in places — although, to be fair, only in one instance is it so bad as to obscure the meaning completely. Also some occasional notes would have come in handy: not all readers will necessarily know that Ioannis Sofianopoulos/Stephanopoulos — described by Pouliopoulos as a 'common political chameleon' on page 175 — was leader of the Agrarian Party in Greece, or that Stjepan Radić was the founder and leader of the Croatian People's Peasant Party until he was shot by a Serb member of parliament in the debating chamber in 1928. Perhaps details such as these are not so important in our age of the internet. Also, Edouard Daladier is 'Daladie' on page 161, and the Catalan head of government in the Spanish Civil War, Lluis Companys, becomes Greekified as 'Cobanys' (p 173). Likewise, Jacques Doriot, a one-time French Communist who went over to fascism, appears as 'Doro' on page 167. Nonetheless, VN

Gelis is to be congratulated on bringing out this collection of a number of Pouliopoulos' writings in English and thereby helping to extend our knowledge of an important Greek Marxist who deserves to be better known.

More information about Pouliopoulos is available at http://www.marxists.org/archive/pouliop/works/index.htm. Comrade VN Gelis is publishing a series of books on Trotskyism and Greece without the support of any publishing or distribution business. We will endeavour to inform our readers of his progress. The best sources of the Pouliopoulos book are: **Kindle format:** http://www.amazon.co.uk/Pandelis-Pouliopoulos-First-Secretary-KKE-ebook/dp/B007I6ABVM; **book format:** http://www.amazon.com/Pandelis-Pouliopoulos-First-Secretary-Words/dp/1470139944.

Chris Gray

* * *

Ted Grant, *Writings: Volume One: 1938-1942: Trotskyism and the Second World War*, Well Red Books, London, 2010, pp 392, £12.99

Ted Grant, *Writings: Volume Two: 1943-1945: Trotskyism and the Second World War*, Well Red Books, London, 2010, pp 476, £14.99

The first two volumes of the writings of Ted Grant form part of an ambitious plan to publish all the articles and documents that he wrote from 1938 until his death in 2006. Some articles not written by Ted or articles that were jointly written with others have been included in these volumes, to reflect the contrasting ideas and approaches of others. Whilst it is not the 'Collected Works', it is nonetheless all the signed articles of Ted Grant that have so far been unearthed. Not all of Ted's output appears in these books because, although he probably wrote many of the editorials in *Socialist Appeal*, they were usually unsigned, and hence have not been included.

The first volume covers the period from 1938 to 1942. This was a period when the small band of Trotskyists in Britain were put to the test by the momentous events such as the outbreak of the Second World War, the Hitler–Stalin Pact and the invasion of the USSR, and the decline of the Independent Labour Party.

The only British group that came through this period strengthened was the Workers International League, whose leadership consisted of Raff (Ralph) Lee, Jock Haston and Ted Grant. The WIL oriented itself to the mass organisations; this is simply explained in 'Contribution of the WIL to the Discussions on the Tasks of the Bolshevik-Leninists'.

The first volume of 392 pages is organised chronologically into five sections, 'Prewar', 'Imperialist Slaughter', 'Proletarian Military Policy', 'The Attack on the USSR', and 'WIL Conference Documents'.

Many of the documents are taken from *Youth for Socialism*, which became

Socialist Appeal, and from *Workers International News*.

The titles of articles from *Socialist Appeal* — 'Workers Want Peace — Bosses Prepare for War', 'Down with the War'; then on the outbreak of war, 'Our War is the Class War', 'Workers Must Be Armed Against Capitalism' — all written by Ted, give a flavour of the policy that was being developed by the WIL.

The WIL was the only Trotskyist group which implemented Trotsky's Proletarian Military Policy. In the discussion within the WIL the majority led by Ted and Gerry Healy, who wrote 'Military Policy — Or Confusion', defended this policy, and Jock Haston opposed them in 'A Step Towards Capitulation'. Another document, taken from the *Internal Bulletin* of 28 February 1941, which was written by Sam Levy and Millie Kahn, criticised the article 'Arm the Workers! The Only Guarantee Against Hitler's Invasion', written by Andrew Scott, which put the majority point of view. All of these documents are in this first volume. In 'Resolution on Military Policy', Ted writes:

> Our proletarian military policy is a decisive question which separates our tendency from all other parties of the working class. It is an independent military policy designed to supplement our general political policy for the seizure of power.

The WIL connected with the workers and the workers in uniform by campaigning for the Proletarian Military Policy, which recognised that the working class didn't want to live under the Nazi jackboot, and the transitional nature of the policy explained that all workers should be armed and trained, and the control of production should rest with the workers by taking it out of the hands of the capitalists who were making super-profits.

The theme of seizure of power is taken up in 'Preparing for Power', which outlined the tasks and perspectives for the coming period. The document ends with:

> Revolutionary Audacity can achieve everything. The organisation must consciously pose itself as the decisive factor in the situation. There will be no lack of possibilities for transforming ourselves from a tiny sect into a mass organisation on the wave of revolution.

Stirring stuff and if I close my eyes I can imagine Ted delivering these lines in his South African accent with the familiar moving of his arms and fingers. What I like about this collection is the style of writing. It is simple, straightforward and easily grasped and it contains the arguments to defeat the right and left reformists in the mass organisations.

The second volume of 476 pages covers the period of 1943-45; again historic events took place which tested all parties of the working class. This volume is organised differently from the first, which is something the publishers should give more thought to when subsequent volumes are published. The first section is 'War and Revolution', which covers the end of the Third International, the fall of Mussolini, the end of the war and the events in Greece. The second section deals with issues pertaining to Britain, 'The Home Front'. The third section is a collection of letters that passed between the WIL and the Revolutionary Socialist League, Ted and Jimmy Deane and the WIL/Revolutionary Communist Party and the Fourth International. Included in this last section is the 'Criticism of the WIL *Preparing for Power*' by the RSL and the reply from the WIL written by Ted.

On the home front, Jock Haston, Roy Tearse, Heaton Lee and Ann Keen, who were all leading members of the RCP, were jailed under the Trades Dispute Act, regulation 1AA. The WIL/RCP came under attack from the Communist Party, Ernest Bevin, the miners' leaders, the *Daily Sketch* and *Daily Mail*, and the Savoy Hotel.

The volume also contains 'The Italian Revolution and the Tasks of British Workers', 'The Coming German Revolution' and 'The Changed Relationship of Forces and the Role of the Fourth International'. In the first article, published in August 1943, it is assumed that 'the coming revolution in the West would be the beginning of the end for Stalin... we are on the verge of a revolutionary wave in Europe which will last for years'. In the second article, published in October 1944:

> If the revolutionary communists of Germany together with the Fourth International everywhere, can succeed in finding a way to the masses and building strong revolutionary parties, it is they who will determine the future — that of the socialist united states of Europe.

In the third article, published in September 1945:

> But by far the greatest event of world significance is the emergence of Russia, for the first time in history, as the greatest military power in Europe and Asia... The approaching revolution in Europe can be no other than the proletarian revolution... the counter-revolution of capital in its early stages, will within a short period of time following the establishment of military government, assume a 'democratic form'.

It should be obvious to the reader that Ted was developing a different perspective from James Cannon and Pierre Frank. The RCP and Ted recognised that the USSR had emerged from the war strengthened and that what was taking place in Western Europe was a 'counter–revolution in a democratic form'.

The RSL published a 'Criticism of *Preparing for Power*' in December 1942. I read this for the first time in 1975, when *Militant* republished it together with 'Reply of WIL to the Criticism of *Preparing for Power*'. The RSL stated:

> In conclusion, we must state that the basis for all political mistakes of the WIL is to be found in the defencist position it has adopted with regard to the imperialist war since the fall of France first made the defeat of British Imperialism a real possibility.

Ted demolished the arguments of the RSL: 'The basic reason for the mistakes of the RSL lies in the fact that the leadership does not understand the revolutionary attitude towards the war.'

A likeable trait in Ted's articles is the dismissal of opponents who don't understand the ABC of Marxism. There is no doubt left in your mind about what Ted thinks. There is plenty more in this second volume, including 'Our Tasks in the Coming Revolution' published in 1944, the minutes of the fusion conference of March 1944, 'The ILP in Transition', and 'The ILP at the Crossroads'.

These two books give a view of the application of Trotskyism to the colossal events that unfolded between 1938 and 1945. If you want a cookbook of revolutionary answers, these are not the books for you. If you want to get a feel for applying the methods of Trotskyism then buy these books. They are written in a way that workers can follow, understand and learn from.

The main lessons that could be learnt from these two volumes are understanding the importance of the correct orientation towards the mass organisations, to readjust perspectives in the light of new circumstances, and not to suffers fools gladly.

Alun Morgan[52]

* * *

Selma James, *Sex, Race and Class: The Perspective of Winning: A Selection of Writings 1952-2011*, Merlin Press, London, 2012, pp 297, £14.95

Selma James has spent a lifetime involved in radical causes and working in

---

52. Alun Morgan joined the Militant in 1974, and is now a supporter of the International Marxist Tendency and the web-manager of www.revolutionaryhistory.co.uk, and has been involved with the research for both these volumes.

revolutionary movements. In the USA, she was a member of the Johnson-Forest tendency, Johnson being a pseudonym for CLR James with whom she worked closely and whom she married.

In 1952, as a 22-year-old factory worker with a small child, James wrote 'A Woman's Place', based on her experience and the experience of those around her. A Marxist, she finds confirmation of her views in Marx himself. A consideration of the position of women led her to inaugurate the national campaign called Wages For Housework. She states that only waged or paid workers are recognised as productive. Housework or caring work within the home is discounted, but this work, largely performed by women, maintains those in the home who are paid, and also produces the next generation to work in capitalist industry. For a similar purpose, children are taken by the state out of the home and sent into schools to be trained to be the next generation of workers in industry.

With regard to bourgeois feminism, James is very opposed to this, as its only regard is for women obtaining senior jobs. These women no doubt employ working-class women to take care of their home responsibilities and this does nothing to raise the level of the majority of women. The majority of women working outside the home in paid jobs find they now have two jobs, one paid and one unpaid.

James includes a chapter on breastfeeding entitled 'The Milk of Human Kindness', in which she notes that this is part of women's caring work and that babies should not be pushed onto formula. She remarks that Tony Blair invited Nestlé to advertise their formula at a Labour Party conference. She states that investment by government should be for caring not killing, and women should be paid the money set aside for the military budget.

When they do work outside the home the wages women are paid are not equal to those of men. In this respect, James is critical of the trade unions, and she considers that the fact it is much harder for women to receive equal pay to that of men is something that unions should grasp. Women's low pay undermines men's wages. She refers to women as a 'caste' and considers that waged and unwaged workers are equally important and must work together.

James organised a Prostitutes Collective, which had as its aim the defence of prostitutes against pimps and the police. To draw attention to this campaign, the group occupied The Church of the Holy Cross at Kings Cross for 12 days. The English Collective of Prostitutes was accompanied into the church by Women Against Rape and Black Women for Wages for Housework. The Payday Men's Network, who supported the wages for housework campaign, provided hot food. Similar pickets took place in Europe and the US, and collective demands were negotiated through Kate Allen, the Chair of Camden's Women's

Committee. It was agreed that the council would pay for a woman to monitor police activity in Argyle Square for one month and report on any illegal arrests that she witnessed. However, James was critical of the eventual report.

James spoke at the US Assembly of Jews in 2010 and opposed Zionism in support of Palestinian liberation. She received much support from the Assembly. James agrees that in a capitalist society men too are not free and she writes of the 200 000 men in prison in the USA at any one time. Some are put to work for companies, for which they receive no wages. This is apparently much admired by the Tory PM David Cameron who wants to introduce this system here.

James also writes about the position of women in the Third World who are unpaid carers and carry out agricultural work. In 1985, women from a number of countries attended the first conference of the UN Decade for Women in Nairobi, Kenya. An article, 'The Global Kitchen', demanded that women's unwaged work globally be counted in national statistics. James recommends Virginia Woolf's novel *The Three Guineas*, which argues that money going to support war should go to women instead. James writes that every year the Global Women's Strike has sent out a call to action on 8 March, International Women's Day. The central demand is payment for all caring work. Women in over 60 countries have taken part in this, calling for an end to poverty, investment in caring not killing, a living wage for all our work, and pay equity in the global market. In writing about the Third World, James is extremely critical of NGOs. She says their role is to assist privatisation. Almost everywhere where there has been a welfare state, the NGOs which take it over are not accountable. She is also critical of academia, which she considers has had too much power for too long. James is critical too of the various socialist and revolutionary groups and states that while we need leadership, we do not need management. The aspect of unpaid work in the home is not generally accepted by socialist organisations, and James has provided a great service in bringing it to our attention.

Sheila Lahr

* * *

Ben Lewis and **Lars T Lih** (eds), *Zinoviev and Martov: Head to Head in Halle*, November Books, London, 2011, pp 228, £14.00

> Dedicated to the United Opposition and all the victims
> of Stalinist counter-revolution.

The enormous value of this book is documentary: activists and scholars can now easily access and judge for themselves a key moment in the history of the struggle for a revolutionary party and a revolutionary International immediately after the Russian Revolution.

In the summer of 1920, the Second Congress of the Communist International got seriously to grips with the establishment of a world party of socialist revolution. This involved building an organisation out of many different and often conflicting tendencies. One thing that united them all was the huge international groundswell of support for the new Soviet state.

Delegates included revolutionary groupings of workers to one degree or another outside of political parties, such as the British shop stewards and the Spanish anarcho-syndicalists, some sectarian Marxist groups highly critical of any lapses in political theory, representatives of anti-colonial struggles, and also socialist organisations of various sizes moving away from the 'official', reformist socialist parties towards support for the Comintern or internally divided over the question.

One of the most prominent in the last category was the Independent Social-Democratic Party of Germany (USPD), which had broken from the main Social-Democratic Party of Germany (SPD) because of the latter's support for Germany's war effort in the First World War and the social truce it had made with the German ruling class for the duration.

The supporters of Rosa Luxemburg and Karl Liebknecht were avowed revolutionary Marxists who broke away from the USPD to form the Spartakus League (Spartakusbund) in January 1919, which quickly rallied to the Comintern. The main body of the USPD, on the other hand, was much more mixed.

It contained the old leader — and for years upholder of the Marxist, revolutionary tradition in the SPD — Karl Kautsky. But it also contained (from 1917 to 1919) his main 'revisionist' opponent, the man who epitomised and expressed theoretically the reformist, parliamentary and ultimately class-collaborationist outlook which came to dominate in the SPD, Eduard Bernstein.

Many of the leaders of the USPD were experienced officials of the SPD and its affiliated trade unions. The issue of the war had forced them out of the old party, but it did not alter their outlook fundamentally.

However, the military collapse of the German Reich after four years of total war and the political and social collapse it brought unleashed violent class struggles across Germany. Soldiers and sailors mutinied and joined with workers to establish proto-soviets. A socialist republic was actually established in Munich and mutated into a soviet republic as it struggled to survive armed repression.

Encouraged by 'Majority' Socialists terrified of social disintegration, reactionary paramilitary units were armed and equipped and unleashed on the revolutionaries. Early in 1919 Luxemburg and Liebknecht and Leo Jogiches were arrested and murdered. Many revolutionary workers were slaughtered.

Besides formal political organisations there were mass movements of working people, including the Revolutionary Shop Stewards, workers' own paramilitaries and groups of non-party communists and anarchists. (Quite a varied literature about these developments is starting to become available in English.)

The mass of rank-and-file members of the USPD were closer to this ferment and to what was going on further east than they were to their own leaders.

The Second Congress of the Comintern adopted a set of criteria for membership (the Twenty-One Conditions), and in the months that followed a great debate broke out in the USPD over affiliation to that organisation.

Feelings ran high on both sides, and in the upshot the USPD split, with a majority joining with Spartakus League in a United Communist Party of Germany, while most of the USPD leadership subsequently returned to their old home in the SPD.

The climax of the dispute came at the USPD's special congress in Halle in October 1920. Comintern leader Grigory Zinoviev made a speech that lasted four hours defending the Bolsheviks and inviting affiliation. Pitched against him was, among others, Julius Martov, one of the outstanding leaders of the Russian Mensheviks. These were Russian socialist opponents of the Bolsheviks, who broadly speaking supported the Russian Revolution but opposed the seizure of power by the Bolsheviks and the establishment of a state based on soviets, the councils of workers', peasants' and soldiers' representatives.

The Texts: The four documents here assembled for the first time as a whole in English are 'Twelve Days in Germany', Zinoviev's own report of the event written on his return to Russia; his address to the congress, recorded as 'World Revolution and the Third International'; 'May the USPD be Preserved', Martov's speech in reply to Zinoviev; and Zinoviev's 'Closing Words', which were not actually delivered at the congress, as his already over-taxed vocal chords had succumbed to an infection.

The undoubted leader of the right wing of the USPD and most prominent theoretician opposed to affiliation to the Comintern was Karl Kautsky. However, he was not at the congress. Many leaders were in attendance and did oppose affiliation, but until the whole proceedings of the Halle Congress can be made available in English, the selection of the two Russians, Zinoviev and Martov (neither of them members of the USPD of course) as representatives of the two opposing trends is probably the happiest.

It was indeed a confrontation of revolutionary and reformist politics.

Martov is the more intelligent and intellectually-gifted of the two speakers. He is lucid and logical and steeped in a theoretical understanding of Marxism. However, all this is mustered to serve conservative ends, to curb action, to warn against initiatives and to persuade socialists to remain in the half-way house of the USPD.

Martov has two main lines of attack. The first is to emphasise that a postwar political collapse and general crisis is a bad time to have a socialist revolution. Malignant 'elemental' forces are unleashed, he argues, which can end up who knows where. Socialists, Marxists, should oppose their mistaken fanatical zeal to remake a world that is not ready for it, but the Bolsheviks have succumbed to these forces.

Socialists should eschew this madness, remain dispassionate, knowing that the objective prerequisites for socialism must first be assembled, while workers gradually absorb enough theoretical class-consciousness to achieve and organise the new society rationally.

He views the revolutionary ferment arising from the war and its aftermath as a distemper, a dark fever which clouds minds and opens the door to every kind of breakdown.

He points out that revolutionary Russia is saddled with a peasant mass. The country is not really ripe for socialist revolution because Russian capitalism is not yet sufficiently developed. Furthermore, hopes of an international response are illusory; the country is isolated, and does not possess the resources to construct a socialist society on its own. The Bolshevik leaders are behaving irrationally and increasingly frantically. He foresees a disaster.

In his opinion, the extent and violence of revolutionary terror practised by the Soviet regime show the dangers. Martov goes into detail on this: how the Bolsheviks claim to have abolished the death penalty, only to resurrect it again in order to kill political opponents; how they take hostages in order to terrorise; how they punish people whose only 'guilt' is by association; how the leadership of the Socialist Revolutionary Party is collectively punished for the actions of a few members.

His second main argument is to show up apparent logical inconsistencies in the Bolsheviks' actions. They denounce reactionary terror against socialists, but practise terror themselves. They accuse majority socialists of allying with the bourgeoisie in the West, but happily ally themselves with murderous, genocidal Turkish nationalists such as Enver Pasha, and even establish a statelet around Vladivostok (to block Japanese incursions) with a socially very mixed regime.

In the name of the socialist revolution, they make alliances with Muslim clerics. They arouse the worst passions in the peoples of the East but have no future to offer them. Will they go on to whip up Hindus to fight the very Muslims Zinoviev is currently inciting to jihad?

In the name of 'super-Marxism', they preach the doctrine of Michael Bakunin, against which Marx fought all his life. Martov ends with a plea for a rational Western Marxist international.

Martov's speech is a diatribe against Bolshevism which obviously rests on profoundly-held beliefs. However, essentially it is sophistry. It is the deployment of logical and legalistic arguments against a living force, which is why it was applauded by the USPD leaders and simply exasperated the USPD left.

Superficially convincing, many of Martov's arguments turn out to be logic chopping. An alliance with the local élite in a colony or semi-colony in order to fight together against imperialism is not the same as joining with the imperialist Kaiser to fight the imperialist Allies. Rejecting Narodnism in the late nineteenth century is not the same as repudiating a Russian revolution in the early twentieth century with massive peasant participation as the first blow in the world revolution brought on by a general imperialist crisis. Opposing the official church in an imperialist state is not the same as defending the rights of religious groups that the same state oppresses. An alliance with one oppressed nationality or its religion does not automatically mean disrespecting another.

The rest of his arguments merely rehearse things which people knew very well. Russia was a backward country and the peasants were the biggest part of the population. The Russian Revolution could not succeed in isolation. The price of failing to overcome these two problems, many people understood, would be very high indeed.

(Incidentally, Lars T Lih asserts that: 'Martov's analysis overlaps to a considerable degree with various interpretive arguments from the Trotskyist tradition, although with the value signs changed from plus to minus.' And he goes on: 'The difference between the two interpretations mainly concern timing.' (p 165). They concern a great deal more than timing. The problems facing the Russian Revolution were fairly clear to many of the leaders at the time, and became clearer. And yet, where Martov prostrated himself before these established facts, the Bolsheviks devoted themselves to overcoming them. That is what revolutions do.)

Thought tends to strangle movement. Theoreticians continue to repeat 'truths' when reality has changed. The world during and after the First World War was profoundly altered.

This is why Zinoviev repeated (as he had at the Second Congress of the Comintern) Nietzsche's phrase about the need to 're-evaluate all values' ('*eine Umwertung aller Werte*').

Zinoviev bluntly asserts that: '… the working class is already strong enough that — if we are tightly united and openly fight for communism — we can bring the bourgeoisie to its knees… If workers are still slaves, then that is because we still have not stripped off the legacy of rotten ideology within our own ranks.'

'Who is saving the bourgeoisie?' he asks. 'The so-called social democrats.'

He is careful to deny charges that the Russian Bolsheviks dominate the Comintern and dictate to other parties, an accusation which he derides as 'the "knout" is coming from Moscow'.

He accuses the USPD right of 'fear of the revolution', for worrying about the disruption it will cause. He asserts that 'the economic preconditions' for socialism 'are present', and mocks: 'Do you first want to put capitalism back on its feet and then tear it down again?'

While socialists might have hoped there could be a smooth transition, 'the war threw a spanner in this calculation', so that the path to socialism includes famine, suffering and 'a long stage of civil war'.

Zinoviev knows that the Comintern's negative attitude towards the 'so-called Trade Union International' — 'a weapon of the international bourgeoisie' — will attract accusations of dividing workers from each other. To counter such an attack, he emphasises the revolutionary wave in the working class which animated actions such as the refusal of London dockers to load ships with arms for Poland.

He has to soothe USPD members' concerns over the Twenty-One Conditions for membership of the Comintern, especially the fact that they had been toughened up so as to exclude the right-wing USPD leaders. His core argument is that these leaders oppose Bolshevism on principle and slander the Soviet state.

He has to defend the Comintern's policy on the land and the national question against formal Marxist assertions that the working class alone is the force to achieve socialism.

Whilst Rudolf Hilferding sneers that 'the mullahs of Chiva are communists!', Zinoviev explains: '... we in the Third International are aware that we really have to speak to the workers of the whole world — and not merely from a European point of view', and: 'The Second International was restricted to people with white skin; the Third International does not classify people according to the colour of their skin.' He brushes aside the caveat that many of what he describes as 'the oppressed of all countries' are themselves 'young capitalist states'.

All these are issues which still resonate in the socialist movement.

Against the accusation that the Comintern is encouraging religious obscurantism, Zinoviev talks about what happens when women in the Orient become conscious of communism, join demonstrations and abandon their veils: 'I say to you, that is a world historical event.'

He quotes Rosa Luxemburg about breaking the resistance of the bourgeoisie 'with an iron fist', explains how in the course of the revolution the Bolsheviks in Russia and Finland were forced by bloody experience to abandon any illusions, and adds: 'It is not a matter of morality versus immorality.'

Anticipating Martov, he roars: '... you are still thinking about the revolution in a completely abstract way. You think that it will come in a hundred years. You do not want to deal with concrete circumstances as they are in Germany…'

He justifies terror against Socialist Revolutionaries, quoting an SR party resolution which called for the 'liquidation of the Bolshevik government' and offered to allow Allied troops into Russia. These people, he says, call themselves socialists but they are bourgeois agents. He rehearses the need to use terror against the bourgeoisie: 'The struggle for socialism is the most violent war known in world history, and the proletarian revolution must prepare itself with the munitions necessary in order to fight and win.'

Zinoviev defends the dictatorship of the proletariat and the Twenty-One Conditions. He accuses the USPD of confusion and vacillation: 'It stems from the fact that you are still not quite clear on these decisive questions of principle. A whole number of shades of opinion exist in your leadership and the individuals within it.'

USPD leader Crispien attacked the Comintern's policy on the land and the peasantry. (German Social Democrats had a longstanding policy of nationalisation of the land and the socialisation of agricultural production, to be run on rational, scientific lines. The Bolsheviks had nationalised the land, but left it for the time being in the hands of the peasants.) Zinoviev explains that many countries in the world only have a 'thin layer' of proletarians and that the workers are obliged to find allies among the peasants. He calls on the delegates to recognise that seizure of the land by poor and middling peasants is a revolutionary act. He accuses Crispien of wanting to 'prepare the soil from which the counter-revolution can recruit its armies'.

He explains that the Comintern was prepared to countenance situations where large agricultural units (latifundia) are taken over by peasants and broken up. ('Heckle from Crispien: "Back to the Middle Ages!"')

Zinoviev has to defend the Comintern's attitude on national questions, quoting the actual resolution that was passed on Enver Pasha at the Baku Congress, and saying that 'without this support we cannot make world revolution'.

He accepts the criticism that the system of workers' and peasants' soviets gives a voice also to backward elements, but explains that the soviets themselves 'will become very generous universities for these workers. They will soon get rid of their own prejudices.'

Describing the situation in Russia, he cannot help 'mirroring' some of the criticisms of the socialist opponents of the Bolsheviks. The situation is critical; many of the best people have sacrificed themselves in the struggle; the necessities of life are in such short supply that 'our workers from Petersburg and Moscow looked like ghosts'. 'Dodgy and shady types' have 'forced their way into the party'. But 'proletarian revolution cannot be had cheaply'.

His speech brims with confidence that the revolution can be spread 'with the bayonet and with all other possible means', that an aggressive spirit will be enough to break through to further revolutions in Western Europe, and that only the reactionary ideology of bureaucratic leaders is barring the way.

The Introductory Essays: Ben Lewis and Lars Lih have their own 'takes' on the history of Marxism which they develop explicitly elsewhere. A general discussion of their conceptions deserves serious consideration which cannot be accommodated within the scope of this review. Nevertheless the point about Zinoviev's reputation does require comment.

Years later, Zinoviev was accused of complicity in the Kirov assassination and of plotting, with Trotsky, terrorist attacks on the Soviet Union. He was — apparently despite a promise from Stalin that his life would be saved — executed in Moscow on 25 August 1936 as an enemy of the Soviet Union.

Stalin's torturers made him say:

I would like to repeat that I am fully and utterly guilty. I am guilty of having been the organiser, second only to Trotsky, of that block whose chosen task was the killing of Stalin. I was the principal organiser of Kirov's assassination. The party saw where we were going, and warned us; Stalin warned us scores of times; but we did not heed these warnings. We entered into an alliance with Trotsky.

Zinoviev was a committed Bolshevik, a close associate of Lenin and a devoted servant of the world working class and the cause of the socialist revolution. Restoring and rehabilitating his reputation in history involves reasserting that fact against the vile slanders of Stalin, Yagoda, Yezhov and their creatures.

However, his actual role in the Communist International and in the struggles in the Soviet Union has been the subject of serious criticism. He is mentioned as something of a bag-carrier for Lenin (see Pierre Broué, *Histoire de L'Internationale Communiste* (Fayard, 1997), p 21). Isaac Deutscher's character sketch of Zinoviev in *The Prophet Unarmed* (OUP, 1960), pp 77-79) sizzles off the page with a searing contrast of strengths and weaknesses:

His temper alternated between bursts of feverish energy and bouts of apathy, between flights of confidence and spells of dejection. He was usually attracted by bold ideas and policies which required the utmost courage and steadfastness to pursue. Yet his will was weak, vacillating, and even cowardly. (p 77)

Deutscher accuses Zinoviev, with Kamenev, of initiating 'the exalted glorification of Lenin which was later to become a state cult' (p 95) at the Twelfth Party Congress, and of leading the charge for the 'Bolshevisation' of the Comintern, starting at its Fifth Congress (p 146). Deutscher's account of the damage which was done to the International and Zinoviev's role within it (pp 147-48) is quite devastating.

Broué criticises Zinoviev for neglecting to prepare the Communist parties he influenced for a united fight against fascism (*Histoire de L'Internationale Communiste*, p 242) and shows him representing the 'party' or 'apparatus conservatism' which failed to recognise the need to turn to a new tactic, the 'united front' in 1921 (p 250).

Zinoviev and Kamenev allied for a period with Stalin against Trotsky. They helped to facilitate the arrival in power in the Soviet Union of a bureaucracy which had appalling consequences for the USSR and the world working class.

Deutscher's description of Zinoviev and Kamenev in the collapse of the Joint Opposition — 'whose hopes had swelled with expectations of easy success, were crestfallen... They regretted that they had ever made the attempt to rouse the cells against the Central Committee. They were anxious to beat a retreat and to placate their adversaries.' (p 291) — speaks very clearly of a political inconsistency in practice. (The volume under review is rightly 'dedicated to the United Opposition and the victims of Stalinist counter-revolution'.)

These authors are merely samples of a wider literature. No wonder Lih feels the need to redress the balance.

However, the essay in which he seeks to restore Zinoviev's reputation ('Zinoviev: Populist Leninist') does not deal with any of those matters, but 'examines his outlook as revealed in two interconnected themes: the relationship of the party to the working class as a whole, and the battle Zinoviev thought was being waged for the soul of the peasantry' (p 40).

Lih can easily show a consistency in Zinoviev's outlook on these questions on the basis of speeches and writings. However, consistency of that sort is mere words. It is no proof that Zinoviev could put up a consistent fight on the principled questions.

Hic Rhodus, hic salta! Lih's essay would be more convincing if it answered the questions set by previous scholars.

Bob Archer

* * *

John Newsinger, *Fighting Back: The American Working Class in the 1930s*, Bookmarks, London, 2012, pp 238, £12.00

This book deserves many more readers than it seems likely to get. It is to be hoped that readers of this review will play an active role in helping to invalidate that gloomy prediction. It would be especially good to find a way to facilitate broader circulation in the United States itself of this important contribution to US labour history.

John Newsinger has presented us with a taut, fact-filled, analytically incisive, extremely readable narrative of the amazing class-struggle upsurge of the US working class during the Great Depression. It covers much the same ground as the two bulky classics, Art Preis' *Labor's Giant Step* (which actually goes to 1955) and Irving Bernstein's *The Turbulent Years*, but it reflects the capable utilisation of an immense number of more recent sources and accomplishes its task in less than 240 pages. It is a remarkable achievement.

Newsinger has produced other good and valuable books, among them the informative popularisation on the history of British imperialism, *The Blood Never Dried*, the useful discussion in *Orwell's Politics*, and a splendid collection of John Reed's revolutionary journalism, *Shaking the World* (none of which is easy to secure in the United States). If someone with the skills of, say, a Professor of History at Bath Spa University were combined with the sensibilities and talents of an Orwell and a Reed at their best, we might get a volume like this — which, in fact, we do. As this suggests, the result is far from the merely 'academic'.

The story to be told involves an incredibly weak US labour movement that, thanks to a stilted prosperity of the 1920s and the extreme political myopia (not to mention bureaucratisation and outright corruption) of its own encrusted leadership, is utterly unprepared for the devastating impact of the Great Depression of the 1930s. It also involves the broader political and economic leadership of the United States which, to begin with, has been successful 'in resisting even a vestigial welfare state' into the country. When the Depression hit, this reality imposes 'immense suffering on millions of men, women and children, both middle class and working class'. But even more, the story involves the ability of the largely repressed left fringe of that movement — dedicated members of the Communist Party, the Socialist Party, the Trotskyist handful gathered in the Communist League of America, the independent American Workers Party, and others — to play a role in drawing more and more workers, and layers of the working class, into militant struggles that can win (with insurgencies of the unemployed and victorious strikes of 1934 in Toledo, Minneapolis and San Francisco).

There are some elements in the conservatised and bureaucratised American Federation of Labor (AFL) — from the registered Republican head of the mineworkers' union, John L Lewis, to the moderately socialist leaders of the garment and clothing workers' unions, David Dubinsky and Sidney Hillman —

who rebel against the AFL leadership's ban on organising new industrial unions, since that would violate the federations outmoded craft-union structures. Lewis, Dubinsky, Hillman and like-minded elements are motivated by (a) a belief that to plod along in the old ways amid the new capitalist crisis (and the employers' desperate, intensified viciousness) will result in the destruction of their own organisations, (b) a belief that the successful left-wing struggles show the way forward, and (c) the conviction that if they themselves do not seize leadership of this class-struggle upsurge, they will be outflanked and displaced by more radical elements. They break from the AFL, establishing the Congress of Industrial Organizations (CIO), and welcome the various activists of the organised left to help them to organise new, powerful industrial unions.

In a succession of amazing struggles, involving tenacious organising, mass picketing, factory occupations, pitched battles, and the immense heroism and creativity of 'ordinary' (truly extraordinary) working-class men and women, a power-shift takes place in US society. A Democratic Party President (who won the 1932 election with ringing promises of hope and change and a vague 'New Deal' for the American people) is consequently pushed much further to the left than he was inclined to go. Franklin D Roosevelt (the much-beloved FDR), denounced, or in some cases hailed, as being a traitor to his class, patiently and correctly explained that it was absolutely necessary to do what he was doing if the capitalist system was to be saved. Along with FDR, a bevy of newly-elected Democratic Party liberals pass sweeping legislation to expand the welfare state much further than had been the case even during the earlier Progressive Era, and to help enable unions to organise (tempered with the insertion of state-imposed rules and regulations, to be sure). Meaningful material gains for the working class combine with a powerful and inspiring radical spirit to make this, truly, what some have referred to, not always positively, as the Red Decade. But there would be significant limitations — some historians have seen them as inevitable and necessary, but Newsinger doesn't think so.

Of the left-wing forces in the CIO, as well as in political and cultural insurgencies of the larger society during this Red Decade, the Communist Party came to be the most influential by far. In Newsinger's view, the elemental idealism and class-struggle militancy of that organisation's membership (and of the many more who were influenced by it) were betrayed by the Stalinism to which the party leadership was committed. This does not simply involve the violations of elementary socialist democracy all too common inside the movement (and even more murderously in the Soviet Union itself) — it involves the Popular Front line developed in the Communist International and imposed on all of its affiliates. This projected the need to subordinate working-class struggles to partnerships with 'progressive' capitalists (such as FDR) who might become aligned with the Soviet Union in collective security arrangements against Hitler and other fascist elements. This resulted in US Communists — for a time powerfully influential in the CIO and other spheres — working effectively for the subordination of the labour movement to the Democratic Party. This would limit the extent of working-class victories and help pave the way for future defeats.

A number of solid qualities stand out in Newsinger's account. A devastating yet well-documented portrait emerges of FDR as an arrogant patrician reformer, who, despite his warm and generous persona, was shrewdly opportunistic to the point of cynicism. We are shown, similarly, the complex and problematic qualities of the CIO hero John L Lewis. The true heroes of this story, however, are the women and men who devoted so much of their life-energy (and in some cases the whole of their lives — there were many martyrs) to labour's cause. The concise descriptions of innumerable class battles are packed with energy, brought alive with apt touches of colour and characterisation, and are the heart and soul of this account. At the same time, there is a rich presentation of the larger context, including some fine indications of left-wing cultural developments.

Naturally, in drawing together such an immense amount of material, an author will inevitably get more than one thing wrong (to be corrected in future editions) — the one that leaped out at me (on page 203) attributes to socialist novelist Upton Sinclair authorship of Sinclair Lewis' 1935 novel *It Can't Happen Here* on the possibility of fascism in the United States. I hope many more reviewers will join me in combing through this book to find other corrections to be made. What is impressive to me, however, is how much Newsinger gets right.

As he concludes his account, Newsinger himself gives us a sense of the book's practical value:

> At a time when the US ruling class seemed to have the whip hand, bolstered both by its huge wealth and by the effects of mass unemployment, socialist and communist militants seized the initiative and forced the most powerful corporations in the world into retreat... Overwhelmingly these struggles that changed the face of America were led by young men and women fighting for the future.

Their fight is an inspiration for working people throughout the world today when we are once again confronted with an attempt to solve a grave crisis at the expense of the working class. At a time when politicians from all major parties in country after country stand revealed as wholeheartedly committed to protecting the interests of the rich and the super-rich, the experience of American workers shows the way forward and the pitfalls to avoid.

A limitation of the book — perhaps unavoidable and appropriate, given the nature of the text — is the failure to indicate important differences between the 1930s and our own realities some seven decades later. One of the most difficult for those on the left is the fact that the socialist and communist militants that Newsinger celebrates were part of a much more powerful global left-wing labour movement than exists today, with innumerable seasoned activists having considerable class-struggle experience under their belts. The organised left of our own time is in many ways much weaker, numerically and otherwise. Hopefully this fine book can be a resource in overcoming that limitation in our own reality.

Paul Le Blanc

* * *

Ngo Van, *In the Crossfire: Adventures of a Vietnamese Revolutionary*, AK Press, Edinburgh, 2010, pp 296

Ngo Van (1912-2005) was a Vietnamese revolutionary who began his political career as a Trotskyist in 1932, at the age of 19. Later, after going into exile in Paris in 1948, he became a libertarian socialist. He published several books, including *Revolutionaries They Could Not Break: The Fight for the Fourth International in Vietnam* (Index Books, London, 1995) and the monumental *Vietnam 1920-45: Révolution et Contre-révolution sous la domination coloniale* (L'Insomniaque Éditeur, Paris, 1995).

In the Crossfire, an autobiographical counterpart to *Vietnam 1920-45*, was originally published by L'Insomniaque Éditeur in 2000 as *Au pays de la cloche fêlée*, an allusion to Baudelaire's poem 'La Cloche Fêlée' ('The Cracked Bell') and to the title of a journal published in Vietnam in the mid-1920s by the Trotskyist Nguyen An Ninh (1900-1943). It is here supplemented by excerpts from Ngo Van's *Au pays d'Héloïse*, the uncompleted second part of his autobiography (about his years in France) named after Heloise, the secret lover of the medieval philosopher Abelard, who had lived near what became Ngo Van's home in Paris. It has been edited by Ken Knabb and Hélène Fleury, and was translated from the French by Hélène Fleury, Hilary Horrocks, Ken Knabb and Naomi Sager.

Trotskyism never had much impact in developed capitalist countries. Its strongest sections outside the Soviet Union have been in Sri Lanka, China and Vietnam. Ngo Van traces the origins of Vietnamese Trotskyism to Paris in 1930, where a faction formed whose returning members linked up with an Opposition that arose at around the same time in Vietnam in the Indochinese Communist Party (ICP), after the failure of an ICP-led peasant insurrection.

The Vietnamese Trotskyist movement arose not from a split in the official Communist Party, like in China, but had a largely independent origin.

In some places, the Trotskyists in Vietnam at times achieved greater influence and support than the official party, for example in working-class areas of Saigon-Cholon in 1936. They defeated the Stalinists (collaborating at the time with Vietnam's bourgeois constitutionalists) in elections to the Saigon Colonial Council in April 1939, with a slate headed by Ta Thu Thau. In later years, they led uprisings in other parts of the country. They were destroyed after the Japanese surrender in 1945 by the Stalinist-led Vietminh, which assassinated many of their leaders and suppressed their supporters.

Ngo Van starts his book by quoting Pascal's maxim that 'the only historians I trust are those who risk getting their throats cut'. Ngo Van risked this outcome more than most, as shown by his concluding list of short biographies of his comrades, most of whom were killed, or died (in or out of prison) of curable diseases. Other chapters describe, movingly and thrillingly, Ngo Van's arrest in 1936, his peasant childhood, his apprenticeship, his Trotskyist recruitment, his struggles, his imprisonment and torture alongside Stalinist prisoners by the *Sûreté*, and the revolutionary turmoil in 1945, when he and his comrades were caught in the 'crossfire' of the French colonial police and the Vietminh.

The story ends with his departure for France in 1948, to escape the French and Vietminh terrors. In exile in Paris, where he worked as an electrician in a factory, he stopped being a Trotskyist, as result of the French Trotskyists' support for Ho Chi Minh, who had massacred his comrades, and of the Hungarian rising of 1956 and his concomitant re-reading of Marx. Instead, he joined a group of libertarian socialists and anarchists around Maximilien Rubel (1905-1996), the Ukrainian-born council communist.

The book is introduced by Ken Knabb, the Situationist author, and has a brief but intimate portrait of Ngo Van by his close friend and collaborator Hélène Fleury. It is beautifully translated, copiously and expertly annotated, and illustrated with historical photographs and with paintings and drawings by Ngo Van, a well-regarded artist. A concluding editorial note explains the politics of Stalinism, from an anti-Trotskyist point of view. My only concern about the translation is the editors' use in the title they thought up for the volume of the word 'crossfire', which inappropriately implies that the Trotskyists were collateral victims of the struggle between the colonialists and the Vietminh. This view is not, in my view, supported by the author's narrative, which suggests instead that they were deliberate targets of the two rival forces.

Ngo Van's account reveals many parallels between the Trotskyist movements in China and Vietnam, coincidences (and contrasts) that merit serious comparative study beyond the scope of this brief review. The two movements had a direct tie: the Chinese Trotskyists Peng Shuzhi and Liu Jialiang fled to Saigon from China (via Hong Kong). Liu Jialiang was caught and murdered by the Vietminh, whereas Peng moved on to France.

Both movements had a strong French connection, direct in the case of the Vietnamese, many of whom became Trotskyists in France, and indirect in that of the Chinese, several of whose leaders (including Zheng Chaolin) were inducted into revolutionary politics in Paris in the early 1920s, where they spent a couple of years studying and working in industry as a prelude to study in a Comintern school in Moscow. However, Moscow played a greater role in the emergence of the Chinese Opposition, which had sources both in China and among the hundreds of Communists who fled to Moscow after Chiang Kai-shek's crackdown in 1927.

Trotskyists in both Vietnam and China enjoyed a relatively good relationship with members and even leaders of the Stalinist party until the mid to late 1930s and in some cases even after the start of Stalin's main anti-Trotskyist campaign. In Vietnam, Stalinists and Trotskyists collaborated for several years on a weekly newspaper, *La Lutte* (published in French to evade restrictions on publications in indigenous languages), to which Ngo Van also contributed. The alliance, unique in the history of world communism, ended in 1936, when the Vietnamese Stalinists started supporting the French Communist Party's (PCF's) Popular Front, which upheld French colonial rule in Indochina.

Stalin's supporters and some scholars have claimed or argued that Trotskyism outside the Soviet Union was an alien growth transplanted by foreign agents. Yet the testimony of Ngo Van — like Wang Fanxi and Zheng Chaolin's memoirs of the Chinese Trotskyist movement — suggests the opposite: anti-Trotskyism was the import, whereas the sources of Trotskyism in Vietnam and China were endogenous as well as exogenous.

In both countries, however, anti-Trotskyism eventually played a major role in the factional affairs of the official party. In China, the Moscow-educated Wang Ming tried to use anti-Trotskyism to unseat Mao Zedong as party leader, and although he failed, he did manage to plant vigorous seeds of it in Mao's party. Wang Ming fetched the ideology from Moscow, while the Vietnamese Stalinists received directives to break with the Trotskyists both from the PCF, acting on Moscow's orders, and from China, which Ho Chi Minh visited in 1938 and 1939, after spending several years in Moscow. Ho Chi Minh is said to have received the anti-Trotskyist 'line' in Yan'an (the Chinese Communist Party's (CCP's) wartime capital), where Wang Ming had unveiled it to the CCP after his return to China from Moscow in late 1937, and wrote home 'unmasking the ugly face of Trotskyism' and denouncing the Trotskyists as 'agents of fascism'. The Vietnamese Stalinists even imported some of the CCP's special usages. For example, they called the Trotskyists *Vietjian* (Vietnamese traitors), a direct echo of the Chinese *Hanjian* (Han [Chinese] traitors).

Trotskyists in both Vietnam and China also shared a sorry history of splits: each briefly united (the Chinese in 1931, the Vietnamese in 1932), but divisions soon reappeared in both. Members of both spent much of their time in prisons and penal colonies or on the run. In both countries, they were, in the end, pulverised between two millstones, the French and the Vietminh in Vietnam, and Chiang Kai-shek and the Communists in China. In both countries, they had a relatively strong base among intellectuals, and, as a result, played an important role in popularising and translating Marxist works.

In Vietnam, the Trotskyists had a greater political impact than in China, where they never achieved a mass following or political representation on elected bodies. The reasons for this difference await further study. However, it is hard to believe that the greater impact in Vietnam was a result of a more competent leadership and cadre, since the hundreds of Chinese Oppositionists in the early 1930s included scores of veteran Communists initially united under the leadership of the CCP's founder, Chen Duxiu, a towering figure in modern Chinese politics and culture.

Instead, one might look for an explanation to the nature of the state in the two countries at the time. The Chinese Trotskyists were successfully suppressed for most the 1930s by Chiang Kai-shek's newly installed Nationalist Party (the Guomindang), which used 'scientific terror' to rule the cities that the Trotskyists chose as their main battleground (unlike the CCP, which was based in the villages after 1927). The Trotskyists in Vietnam, on the other hand, confronted a colonial regime that lacked any legitimacy, especially after the Japanese surrender, and whose repressive measures were less effective. What's more, the Trotskyists in Vietnam were on a political spectrum that included a far wider range of anti-colonial parties and political and civil organisations than in China, where the Stalinists managed to dominate the political centre by skilful employment of the united-front tactic. Economic conditions in Vietnam may also have been more conducive than in China to the growth of a workers' movement. However, this was less true of South Vietnam, where the Trotskyists had their main base, than of the North, where the French encouraged plantations, extractive industries and some manufacturing and built a substantial transport infrastructure. In China, industrial development was even more uneven and the urban economy was paralysed or laid waste by a seamless succession of wars and civil wars until 1949, so the Chinese Trotskyists found it particularly difficult to build a revolutionary party among the city workers.

Another parallel is between the main protagonists and memoirists of the two movements. Knabb notes in his introduction that Ngo Van was 'the sweetest

and most gentle person', graced despite his resolute atheism 'with an almost Buddhist stoicism and equanimity'. People who met Wang Fanxi and Zheng Chaolin also noted their cultivation, compassion and complete absence of bitterness, despite their terrible suffering.
Gregor Benton

* * *

Tom O'Lincoln, *Australia's Pacific War: Challenging a National Myth*, Interventions, Melbourne, 2011, pp 194

Tom O'Lincoln here takes on not simply one but a whole number of myths. The first and most important one, and where I wholly agree with him, is that the Pacific war was no struggle against Nazism but purely an inter-imperialist bloodbath. One can have one of two views about the war against Hitler: inter-imperialist though it certainly was, it also contained elements of a Popular Front against Nazism. In contrast to the European war too, or at least that involving the Western Allies, the Pacific one was suffused with the most vicious racism, as O'Lincoln shows. There was after all a considerable debate in the United States among the different varieties of Trotskyists about the nature of the Japanese conflict.

I have minor criticisms of the book, the first being that the structure seems a bit unformed. It ends in the air without any clear conclusion. Secondly, there is the lack of an index which, as many of the people and events mentioned are unfamiliar to British readers, is a real shortcoming; in these days of word-processing and word-searching there is little excuse. An index of proper names of people and places would surely be possible and would be a considerable help. The third, perhaps a trifle unfair, is that it is addressed above all to Australian readers and some aspects, obvious to Australians, are unknown to us. Thus, on a more minor level, the cover image shows Australians in the burnt settlement of Tarakan without explaining that this was in Borneo in 1945. It is worth recalling that in this particular instance the official British naval historian, Captain Roskill, believed that the damage caused by this operation was quite counter-productive, though it is only fair to say that this was on the orders of that great fraud, General MacArthur, the hero of victory over the Bonus Marchers.

Perhaps the reason for the fact that the Pacific war played such an important and mythic role in Australian consciousness is that it was, with Gallipoli, one of the causes of the formation of that very consciousness. I can still remember the response when we told people in the Melbourne area that we were going home to Britain in 1945, the reply, 'Oh, you're going home. I've never been home.' — which was the cause for quiet amusement among the British evacuees at the time. From almost the genesis of the Commonwealth 40 years previously there had been a real fear of Japan and the 'yellow peril' in general, which was reflected in this 'colonial cringe' reply to us in 1945. Australia's own imperialism was a very minor aspect of things in 1941-45, and I think O'Lincoln rather exaggerates this. Australia clung like a child to the security given by the Royal Navy until the disasters of Singapore and Malaya, and has since clung to Uncle Sam, but as an adult. I also think that his comments on sexuality and the oppression of women and gays rather ignore the fact that this was general in all the English-speaking, indeed the 'civilised' European, world at the time. Australians were no worse and indeed in some respects, perhaps in many respects, rather better as regards their attitudes to women, since they got the vote in 1902 after all. Changes in sexual behaviour and attitudes have been gradual over at least the past 140 years. The 'past is another country and they do things differently there' and you cannot ask people to be 70 years in advance of their times however unpleasant you may regard some of their behaviour by present-day standards, unless indeed it was in direct contradiction to their stated ideals. This certainly applied to the British and Australian support for colonialism, not just their own but that of the Dutch and French, contrasted with their mouthing of calls for 'freedom' and support of the Atlantic Charter. It also applies to the racism that, on O'Lincoln's own account, sounds as if it was worse among the Americans.

One great difference between the Japanese and British imperialism lay not so much in relative humanity, though it is fair to say that the Japanese were more brutal, but in fact Japan was a young and vigorous imperialism while Britain was an old and tired one. If you compare the actions of the British in the Indian Mutiny with those of the Japanese 85 years later then the contrast is not nearly so great, if indeed there is any contrast at all. Even the treatment and death rates of prisoners in the camps by the Japanese when compared with the conditions inflicted on rank-and-file prisoners in the Great French War of 1790-1815 or the American Civil War do not seem so very different. As an example of Japanese behaviour which seems quite a lot worse than anything the British or Australians did in the Second World War, the first information on conditions in Singapore after the surrender reported not merely the tiny rations given to the PoWs together with one execution of a British Major for refusing to work for the Japanese, but in addition mass public beheadings of Chinese civilians and forcible mass prostitution of Chinese women. Though the Indians and Malays were quite well treated, they were rapidly disillusioned by these horrors inflicted on their fellow inhabitants.[53] O'Lincoln correctly points out

---

53. WO 106/2578, 'Information From Escaped Officers', a report by two Indian commissioned officers who disguised themselves as coolies and got out through Burma. They also report on the rations of the Indian PoWs. Again I have not seen this mentioned elsewhere.

the failure of Australian (and one could add American) troops to take prisoners or offer quarter, but this process started very early in the conflict among the British and not simply among the rough colonials or after savage fighting when chivalrous ideals had evaporated. I found in the National Archives a document,[54] dealing with the lessons of the Malayan campaign from a Lieutenant-Colonel HC Phillips, stating that Japanese prisoners and wounded were shot out of hand, which meant that there was no one available for interrogation. Phillips even furiously complained of the case of a British officer who had shot dead a wounded Japanese officer who was trying to surrender. I put this generalised behaviour down to unalloyed racism and not simply the stress of battle. It was all much more like matters on the Eastern Front between the Russians and Germans. Incidentally, when the British finally surrendered in February 1942 the first question that Yamashita asked Percival was how many Japanese prisoners did he have. Percival replied that he had none. In fact the British had taken a dozen prisoners, who are named in the archives but who were then sent out of Singapore three or four days before the surrender, the last reference to them being in southern Sumatra.[55] I have not seen any histories of the campaign that have picked this up, and many simply state that the British were unable to take any prisoners.

The Japanese treatment of prisoners was not invariably bad. A point O'Lincoln makes is that the Japanese too were often very short of food and the PoWs not unnaturally were the last in the queue. A further aspect not mentioned is that the Australian servicemen were accustomed to twice the meat ration of the British, who in turn had far more meat than the Indians, some of whom were vegetarians. The Australians must have suffered most. As the Japanese considered surrender as disgraceful, they must have thought that their prisoners were pretty worthless anyway, and this attitude may have been in existence for a long time. My father told me that as a small boy in Ceylon in 1905-06 he remembers seeing a shipload of Japanese ex-PoWs returning to their country from Russia after the war and was told, doubtless wrongly, that they all had to commit hara-kiri when they got back. That does suggest that even then there was a perception even amongst her allies that Japan's society and military took a harsh line against surrendering.

The Australian General Gordon Bennett, cited by O'Lincoln, who boasted of one Aussie being equal to six 'Japs', might not have been as crass as he appears

54. WO106/2579B, a very large file. Twelve prisoners were got back to Singapore, five wounded and one clearly deranged. A couple were wounded shot-down pilots. They seem all to have been shifted out of the fortress on ships in the last few days and indeed there is found in CO 980/140 a list of nine Japanese prisoners who were taken to Sumatra, two are pilots, both wounded, and thought to be officers.
55. CO 980/140.

at first sight. To be charitable, Bennett was not alone in his views and might simply have been attempting to encourage his troops. Before hostilities began there was a widespread racist view of the Japanese as barely human little yellow men unable to shoot or fly planes. Since my father's childhood hero in 1904-05 was Admiral Togo, he did not suffer from that variety of racism. After the first Japanese successes there was an equally false tendency to regard them as supermen. However, Bennett was a disgrace who deserted his soldiers when surrender loomed and was flown to Padang in a purloined Tiger Moth from whence he returned to Australia. The views of captured Australians about him, whether soldiers or officers, were unprintable and he was never employed again. Apart from Bennett, the Australian General most cited as an unpleasant reactionary by O'Lincoln is General Blamey, who is described by Max Hastings, a military historian for whom I have the greatest regard, as a 'seedy old reprobate' and whom one of his staff officers thought 'a coward and not a commander'. (When a prewar Commissioner of Police his police badge was found in a Melbourne brothel, which gave rise to some comment.) Blamey was keen on pointless Australian troop actions in New Guinea in 1943-45 against Japanese who had been cut off and who could have been left to suffer from starvation and disease. The many Australian casualties in very unpleasant conditions were just to show the Americans what valuable allies they were.

Roosevelt's Grand Strategy in the immediate pre-Pearl Harbour period by which he attempted to disarm or provoke Japan by economic sanctions is of course well known. It has certain similarities to US policy towards Iran today. As imperialist behaviour it is quite normal, but to claim that the sudden Japanese attack was 'A Day of Infamy', as is still done, is surely to ignore the fact that the US had broken the Japanese codes and was quite aware of the approximate date, even if not the hour, of the forthcoming attack, though not of its location or method. An attack, of course, that they were trying to provoke. Admiral Kimmel in Honolulu knew of the approximate date to within a day or two, and if he failed to make sufficient preparations that was his fault, not that of his government which had kept him informed. He was quite justly sacked for his pains. In the Philippines eight hours *after* the attack on Pearl Harbour, the Japanese achieved total surprise and destroyed nearly all the US planes on the ground, but MacArthur was spared Kimmel's fate, which seems odd, and I have never heard of a convincing explanation either of MacArthur's failure or the forgiveness he received. Perhaps there was still gratitude for his behaviour towards the Bonus Marchers. At almost exactly the same time as the attack on the US fleet, I can well remember the sirens going when the phone rang in our house in Singapore as I was being taken down to the air-raid shelter and my father saying to us after he had answered it: 'It's started.' So Singapore and

Malaya were not surprised, but were out-fought by the better soldiers.

War is always unpleasant, but Tom O'Lincoln has done us a service by showing how for the Australians the Pacific war was not some heroic enterprise even if many of the soldiers involved on all sides did indeed behave heroically. It is a vital source in this nasty, bloody, vilely racist, imperialist conflict in which Australia's ruling class played a subordinate but enthusiastic role.

Edward Crawford

* * *

John Riddell (ed), *Toward the United Front: Proceedings of the Fourth Congress of the Communist International, 1922*, Haymarket Books, Chicago, 2012, pp 1310, £39.99/$50.00

It is hard to review a book of the proceedings of the Fourth Congress of the Communist International, not simply because of its length — around 1200 pages — but because the documents and transcripts of the meetings are not a literary product, they simply exist as part of the historical record. A review has — at least in part — to examine the debates and decisions themselves, in the historical context of the time in which they occurred.

For one month in 1922, 350 delegates, representing around two million communists across the world, gathered in Russia to plan their work of how to take forward the struggle for working-class revolution. This fourth congress — the last which Lenin attended — is the last one considered by many to be in keeping with the revolutionary tradition of the Bolsheviks. The subsequent congress two years later saw Stalin take centre stage and the assembled delegates adopt the disastrous policy of socialism in one country.

As such a close reading of the proceedings of the Fourth Congress of the Comintern, authoritatively edited by Canadian socialist John Riddell, provides rich historical material on the debates around that most controversial of subjects — the united front. But it is not just focussed on this issue — the transcripts and verbatim reports of debates give the reader a real feeling of the Comintern at this time, of what it was like to be a delegate, the depth and range of opinions and debates. This was no monolithic rally for the troops, it was a place of meaningful discussion which would potentially decide the course of the revolutionary struggle across the world.

Riddell is right to concentrate focus on the united front. The united front is controversial because, out of all the tactics in the Communist arsenal, it is undoubtedly the most used but also the most abused, often seeing incredibly opportunist manoeuvres by revolutionaries all in the name of 'maintaining the united front'.

Like many tactics, the policy of the united front was the result of an attempt to systematise the practical work being done on the ground by revolutionary workers as they fought their bosses. The decline of the revolutionary wave across Europe had seen sizeable but minoritarian Communist parties forced into alliances with reformist workers. How to negotiate the necessary compromises that resulted from such alliances without betraying the revolutionary principles of the newly-formed Communist International was the subject of much debate at the congress. And this was not a new debate — it had begun two years previously after the publication of Lenin's pamphlet *'Left-Wing' Communism*, a direct attack on the left wing of the Communist movement who saw tactical alliances with reformists or systematic work in bourgeois institutions such as parliament as beyond the pale. The debate over interpretations of the united front are a running theme at the congress, with recognisable left and right 'deviations' on what became the generally accepted Comintern methodology expressed by delegates from the floor (for instance, Ruth Fisher's 'united front from below' approach).

An aspect of this debate centred on the question of the workers' government, and the book reveals that delegates remained in real confusion about what such a united front might look like (for example, pp 173-74). Mass struggle could pose the situation where working people formed a government, but based on what? Based on workers' councils — but then it would be an out-and-out soviet government. Or based in parliament, in which case what was its remit and how would it be different to a normal social-democratic government? Zinoviev at the congress didn't help in clarifying issues, referring to the British Labour government as a 'liberal workers' government' (pp 266-67); a coalition government, made up of social democrats, trade unionists and Communists — 'an historical possibility', he argues — and finally a workers' government that is really a workers' government — which is a synonym for the dictatorship of the proletariat (p 267). Suffice to say that it was left to the German Communist Party to seek clarity on these issues with an amendment to congress documents. Interestingly, Riddell points out that although the amendment was adopted unanimously it was left out of the Russian-language version of the documents, which are the *Ur*-text upon which many other translations, including English, were based.[56] One wonders how many other crucial amendments and resolutions have been lost down the back of the translator's desk in the history of the workers' movement.

But the congress also took an important step forwards on the 'Eastern Question', namely building revolutionary workers' organisations in the colonised and exploited Eastern countries where the working class was a clear

56. See http://johnriddell.wordpress.com/2012/01/01/a-workers-government-as-a-step-toward-socialism/.

minority of the population compared to other exploited popular groups. A continuation of debates started at the Second Congress, the session on the Eastern Question was seen in the context of the Comintern dealing with both the 'class struggle in the West and the support for the freedom struggle of the colonial and semi-colonial people in the coming years' (Overstraeten, p 650). The debate on relating to the Muslim people toiling and struggling against French imperialism is a very interesting one (funnily enough, considering the Socialist Workers Party's subsequent orientation, Ian Birchall barely mentions these important discussions in his review in *International Socialism*). The Comintern delegates regularly made appeals to the 'world proletariat and the Eastern people' (for example, p 677), arguing that British and French imperialism and colonial supremacy must be 'broken'. Ravesteyn, giving the main report on the Eastern Question, proposed a resolution which is quite clear in this viewpoint: '… in this world historic struggle for the political liberation of Islam, the revolutionary proletariat has the duty to devote its full attention and provide all possible moral support.' (p 685) The analysis of complex class forces in the semi-colonial world and the particular dynamics that open up between them in a revolutionary situation are of doubtless interest to socialists today, despite the passage of 90-odd years. The position that the Eastern national bourgeoisies are 'objectively revolutionary' when they are directing their struggle against colonialism and feudal social relations, whilst ostensibly bearing a large part of truth in terms of the bourgeois revolutionary character of such movements, eventually led to some disastrous united fronts with anti-communist forces (for instance, in Turkey) where the national bourgeois class displayed as much savage violence against the left as their cousins had been doing in Russia and Germany.

The resolutions adopted by the congress — most of which have been previously published — deal with quite specific issues and provide a wealth of interesting material. Thankfully no long-winded 'perspectives document' so beloved of Trotskyists are included, though the theses on Comintern tactics includes some brief general analysis on the direction of world politics before outlining each major tactical and strategic turn that was agreed for the organisation. The emphasis is on the United Front — the demand is that each party as part of its adherence to the Twenty-One Conditions for entry into the International (adopted in 1920) must now rigorously apply these agreed positions. The centralisation principle of the Comintern is clearly on display with quite long directives provided for the French Communist Party, which gets a whole resolution to itself, to bolster the left wing against the rest of the party.

Where the book really comes alive is in a close reading of the transcript of the debates. For instance, the opening session — ostensibly about the world situation — turns into a series of national reports from delegates, many of them from the left of the International, who were critical of the policies and direction of the previous congresses. The chair implores speakers to look at the global situation and not just their own countries — something to which many socialist activists who have been to international gatherings can relate.

The debates also reveal that many of the parties were very divided at this congress — the Hungarian, German, Polish and Czech parties all arrived at the congress with different tendencies represented. The Italian party's most vocal delegate, Bordiga, was clearly a heterodox voice at the congress, though his contributions were listened to with respect and engaged with on a non-demagogic level by the Comintern's core leadership. The congress passed a long and detailed resolution on the 'crisis' of the French party and its various factions which gave some considerable, but not uncritical, support to the left of the party in the struggle against the more reformist-inclined right wing. Interestingly, the tone of the congress is not focussed on a bureaucratic exclusion of more reformist elements, it is far more interested in the PCF staying united but 'having the arguments out'. Zinoviev's criticisms of the PCF focus on the centre and the right — he argues that only one of the three current tendencies in the PCF is truly Communist, and the PCF paper *L'Humanité* is an excellent workers' paper 'but not yet a Communist paper' (pp 103-04). The emphasis is on the PCF working through disagreements, on taking time to establish a more consistent orientation, and there is little sign of the subsequent manner of dealing with comrades who have 'deviated' from the party line.

But what hangs over all the congresses — and no less so this one — was the struggle in Germany. The German party was the biggest outside of Russia — the jewel in the crown of the Comintern — proving that Bolshevism was not just an Eastern or exclusively Russian phenomenon but was also attractive to thousands of workers in a developed 'Western' country. And the new party which was being regularly tested in the complex, unpredictable events of the continuing crisis in German politics during 1918-23 that generated outbreaks of revolutionary struggle and counter-revolutionary violence, was the axis around which most new approaches were generated and tested in practice. In a sense a lot of the purpose of the Comintern was directed at getting the orientation of the German party right — after all the Russian Communists desperately needed the revolution in Germany to succeed to get them out of their own economic (and political) impasse: as Zinoviev stated in his report to the congress 'the path of proletarian revolution leads from Russia through Germany' (p 101). This is not to undermine the importance of discussions relating to the French and Italian parties, both of which got their own resolutions adopted, but the contributions of the German delegates seem much clearer, more subtle, with the experience of the revolutionary convulsions of their own country behind them.

Connected to the issue of Germany was the first serious international discussion on the — at the time — specifically Italian phenomenon of fascism. The congress was taking place only weeks after the fascists' 'March on Rome', Benito Mussolini was at the time Prime Minister of Italy. Sadly for the delegates it does not seem clear that they were aware of the level of defeat in Italy, one of the clearest and quickest examples of a revolutionary situation (the struggles of 1918-21) becoming a counter-revolutionary nightmare on the cusp of the crushing of independent workers' organisations and democracy more generally. The Italian situation was Germany's future, but at this time that possibility seemed a million miles away from the delegates' thoughts. Certainly Bordiga's explanation of fascism is a curate's egg; despite an accurate analysis of the role of the state and the big bourgeoisie in forming fascism as a movement, he concludes that it 'added nothing to the traditional ideology and programme' of capitalism, it 'does not represent any new political doctrine' (p 413). Debatable points, considering the extent to which fascism would change the course of the twentieth century in Europe. On the other hand, Bordiga's point that fascism is a method to secure the power of the ruling classes by utilising every means available to then, including making use of the lessons of the first proletarian revolution, the Russian Revolution (p 419), demonstrates real foresight, and is something that would not be out of place in Trotsky's excellent analysis of the rise of fascism in Germany.

Speaking of Trotsky, he is noticeably absent from a lot of the discussions at the congress. Clearly already in a stage of being side-lined from the International leadership, he was only proposed as an alternate to the International Executive Committee (p 1105). He only spoke three times in plenary — once during the discussion of the five years of the Russian Revolution and then twice on France (both of which he was in commission). He did not speak once during the important discussions on the international situation, trade unions or fascism. He spoke less than Zinoviev, Radek, Sen Katayama (Japan), Béron (France) or Bordiga. Considering that within weeks of the congress finishing Trotsky would be appealing to Lenin to form a united front against Stalin, he certainly was not putting his best foot forward to make an impression at the international gathering of leaders of the Communist movement from across the world. Likewise, the congress saw several positions and orientations adopted — including the reduction in congresses from annually to every other year — which helped the consolidation of undemocratic practices at the heart of the movement, changes which at the time seemed innocuous enough, even expedient, but with the benefit of hindsight were a step on the road to the hell that would follow.

There is probably not much more to say about the book. If you believe that there is something valuable in the debates that took place at the Comintern then this book is an incredibly useful addition to your collection. Seeing the quality and depth of debate that took place at these annual meetings of revolutionary fighters in that brief but heady time after the Russian Revolution, when it seemed that capitalism was on its last legs, makes you realise that the loss of such a forum is a real loss for the movement today. Today the left is largely reduced to tiny propaganda groups — we return to an almost First International existence — but we can still struggle for a return to a situation where we — in the words of Béla Kun — are 'here not to write but to make history' (p 337).

Simon Hardy

* * *

Jean Marc Schiappa, *Buonarroti (1761-1837): L'Inoxydable*, Les Editions Libertaires, St-Georges d'Oléron, 2008, pp 274, €15

Revolutionary socialism was born amid the French Revolution, the first time that visions of the future came together with practical action in the present. Central to the process was Babeuf's organisation of 1796, in which one of his closest collaborators was Philippe Buonarroti. Jean Marc Schiappa has already written extensively on Babeuf and his followers (see my review of his *Les babouvistes* in *Revolutionary History*, Volume 8, no 4 (2004)); now he has given us a biography of Buonarroti, described as 'inoxydable' (rustproof).

Not that this is hagiography. As Schiappa notes, 'it is the nature of revolutionaries constantly to make plans, and to be constantly disrupted by events'. Schiappa shows us the interaction between an individual and the course of the Revolution which formed Buonarroti.

Born in Italy in 1761, Buonarroti was profoundly influenced by Rousseau and other eighteenth-century thinkers, but he became politically involved only after arriving in Corsica at the outbreak of the Revolution. He was probably involved in a riot shortly after his arrival, and may on this occasion have made his first contact with a young Corsican, soon to become well-known, one Napoleon Bonaparte. In April 1790 he embarked on his career as an activist when he launched his own weekly newspaper.

It was not a great success. It appears not to have reached his modest target of 400 subscribers, and was not very attractively set out. On one occasion he added a footnote so lengthy that it spread over several issues, only being completed some three months after it began. (Even our most turgid present-day papers are not quite so bad.)

In Corsica, as throughout France, there was a ferment of ideas and political clubs began to be formed. It was in this exhilarating climate that Buonarroti's ideas began to develop. He was still far from developing an opposition to private property, but he took a particular interest in questions of land ownership, and this may have started him on a path which would take him a long way from his origins.

He arrived in Paris in the spring of 1793, now a convinced Jacobin. But it was only after Thermidor, when Robespierre was overthrown, that the crucial development took place. Imprisoned in 1795, he met Babeuf; as Schiappa notes the Paris prisons at this time were 'real schools of political confrontation and education'. He soon became a close and trusted ally of Babeuf, and played a leading role in the unsuccessful 'conspiracy' of 1796. (It should be noted that 'conspiracy' was the name given to the organisation by the government which repressed it; Babeuf and Buonarroti aimed to agitate as openly as possible.) Buonarroti was never as profound or as original a thinker as Babeuf, though he was a fluent writer. But his talent was above all as an organiser, and he complemented Babeuf in the frenetic activities of the short-lived attempt to organise an insurrection against the post-Thermidor regime.

Buonarroti was arrested along with Babeuf and many others and put on trial at Vendôme — Schiappa with some justice describes this as the 'first anti-communist trial'. Babeuf was executed; Buonarroti went to prison and then spent many years in exile in Geneva and later Brussels. Babeuf's movement had been broken, and it would be three decades before a recognisably socialist movement would begin to re-emerge. But, as Schiappa's researches show, many of the individuals who had been around Babeuf continued to be active in one way or another. Buonarroti was constantly attempting to regroup such activists.

The limited forms of mass work that had been possible in 1796 were no longer appropriate, and the new organisations that Buonarroti tried to set up were of necessity much more clandestine and hierarchical. Only the inner circle was allowed to know the full communist doctrine.

Each generation of revolutionaries is different from its predecessors, yet each generation learns from the past. Here Buonarroti's role was crucial. In particular his history of Babeuf's Conspiracy, published in 1828, passed on the socialist ideas developed by Babeuf to those who would go on to make the revolutions of 1848. Without Buonarroti's tenacity that continuity might have been lost.

Buonarroti's self-sacrifice makes a striking contrast to the many who have subsequently enriched themselves off the back of the working-class movement. He survived by working as a music teacher, and his friends had to buy him a piano, and later firewood, in order that he could keep going.

Not that he was always a paragon of virtue. In his sixties he became enamoured of Sara Desbains. He then proceeded to propose to Teresa Poggi, his faithful companion who had shared jail and exile with him for over 20 years, that they should form a *ménage à trois*. Her response was predictable.

Schiappa's biography will be a valuable asset to all who want to understand the early history of our movement. The one weakness is a failure to examine more closely the relationship between Babeuf and Buonarroti. Trotskyist historians have often shied away from exploring the interesting disagreements between Lenin and Trotsky out of fear of seeming to lack solidarity with both men. Likewise Schiappa might have dealt in greater detail with the differences between Buonarroti and Babeuf.

Babeuf was a convinced atheist while Buonarroti remained a deist, believing in a supreme being. Buonarroti was an uncritical admirer of Robespierre, whereas Babeuf, though of necessity working with Robespierrists, had a much more nuanced appreciation of Robespierre's contradictions.

And Buonarroti does not seem to have shared Babeuf's passionate commitment to the equality of women. It is true that he was the author of the remarkable Draft Economic Decree, which proposed full citizenship for both sexes 150 years before it was achieved in France. But he seems to have shown little interest in the question at other times in his life.

There is, then, still more to be said about Buonarroti — and Babeuf. But Schiappa's research provides an invaluable foundation on which future study can be built.

Ian Birchall

* * *

Richard Seymour, *Unhitched: The Trial of Christopher Hitchens*, Verso, London, 2012, pp 134, £9.99

Christopher Hitchens was a most unpleasant person. Arrogant and ill-mannered, he could write quite well, but was guilty of plagiarism, repetition, evasion and downright lying. If he became a bloodthirsty, pro-imperialist jingo only after 9/11, there was much in his earlier work that prepared that move to the right.

Richard Seymour's short book offers a devastating analysis of Hitchens' work and career. It is a careful, well-documented work, based on extensive study of Hitchens' writings and discussions with those who knew him. Seymour has been accused of being tasteless in writing such a book so soon after Hitchens' death — though (at the very moment I am writing) some of his critics are dancing on the grave of Hugo Chávez.

The account is readable and presented with clear signs of polemical glee. My only slight reservation is Seymour's vocabulary. I consider myself a reasonably literate person, but every few pages Seymour seems to discover a word I don't know. Thus I discover that 'tomecide' refers not to cat-strangling, as I had supposed, but to destroying a book. This may be educational for a crossword addict like myself, but less helpful to other readers.

Seymour looks at several themes emerging from Hitchens' work — his roots in the English literary tradition from Kipling to Orwell and Larkin, his ideas on nationalism, the inadequacies of his critique of religion and his changing views on imperialism and the Middle East. But perhaps the most interesting theme developed is that of political renegacy.

Between 1967 and 1974 Hitchens was a member of the International Socialists, forerunners of today's Socialist Workers Party, in Oxford and London. Seymour examines this period of his life with interviews with and information received from Chris Harman, Alex Callinicos, Michael Rosen, Stephen Marks, John Palmer, John Rose and Martin Tomkinson.

Renegacy as spectacular as Hitchens' is relatively rare. After a meeting on left-right defectors at Marxism 2009 by Seymour and David Edgar, I remember discussing with the late Chris Harman just how many real renegades from IS/SWP we could think of. Not those who had accommodated to reformism, but those who had openly and prominently espoused the other side. We managed a grand total of five — two of them called Hitchens.

Seymour's account of Hitchens' trajectory is carefully presented; yet as one who knew the young Hitchens, I felt certain discrepancies were left unexplained. Firstly, Hitchens left little trace in the International Socialists. At the time the organisation produced a quarterly, then monthly, journal, *International Socialism*, which was well respected and had a high standard of content. Hitchens was an aspiring writer, yet he did not contribute a single article to the journal. For one year — 1972 — the journal had a *troika* of Review Editors (at all other times one person sufficed for the job), one of whom was Hitchens. He contributed just three rather anodyne book reviews.

On leaving Oxford for London, Hitchens joined the Hornsey branch of the International Socialists, of which I also was a member. I have to say that I have no memory of him making any particular impression on the branch, or of his giving a lead in any aspect of the branch's activity. I do remember that he would sweep away at the end of meetings, too important or too busy to have a drink with the rest of us hobbledehoys.

Alan Wald, in his studies of Trotskyist writers and artists like Sherry Mangan and Duncan Ferguson, has powerfully depicted the tension between creative activity and the day-to-day donkey work of a revolutionary organisation. Hitchens resolved the tension by doing as little as possible of the latter. For an ambitious young journalist, systematic trade-union work in the NUJ doubtless seemed unappealing. In his own account of his departure from the International

Socialists, Hitchens recalls his 'relief... at ceasing to hear about "rank and file"'.

Hitchens' ostensible ground for resignation was the IS position on Portugal. He disagreed with IS support for the PRP (Revolutionary Party of the Proletariat), an organisation with some Guevarist tendencies which Hitchens later damned as 'semi-Baader-Meinhof elements'. Now at the time I served on the IS International Sub-Committee; I attended many, many meetings about Portugal. Never do I recall Hitchens speaking up to put his point of view. Nor, to the best of my knowledge, did he contribute to the *Internal Bulletin*, or even write a letter to *Socialist Worker*. If he had his differences, he kept them to himself.

So in the end I can only concur with Chris Harman, who told Seymour that Hitchens 'went flat out to know the right people to make a career in journalism and began to find us a hindrance'. In an interview with Decca Aitkenhead, Hitchens implausibly claimed that he could not 'trace any connection' between his wealth and his opinions. Now there can be no doubt that Hitchens liked money and the good life. But the real key to his renegacy lies rather in a point Seymour makes in his final paragraphs, and which could have been developed further, namely what he calls 'the defeat of 1968'.

Between the French general strike and the beginning of 1974, when industrial action by miners brought down a Tory government, there was a massive upsurge of industrial struggle in Britain. There seemed a real possibility that the International Socialists could replace the Communist Party as the main militant force in the trade unions. For some on the left it seemed that their personal ambitions could be combined with adherence to the revolutionary cause. Roger Rosewell, the IS industrial organiser, doubtless dreamt of replacing Bert Ramelson. But with Labour's Social Contract the dream faded, and Rosewell and Hitchens were perceptive enough to be among the first to notice that the ship was sinking. The long haul, perhaps lasting the rest of their lives, had no charm for them.

Hitchens learnt much during his sojourn with the far left. Often he was able to use what he had learnt in a fresh political context. Thus his opposition to Clinton owed something to the traditional revolutionary critique of the Democratic Party — but it was deployed in preparing his *rapprochement* with Bush.

Hitchens is dead, but his ideas will live on. Seymour's book gives us a useful weapon to fight them.

Ian Birchall

Reiner Tosstorff, *El POUM en la revolució espanyola*, Editorial Base, Barcelona, 2009, pp 350, €20

Reiner Tosstorff's book *Die POUM in der spanischen Revolution* was published in German in 2006, on the seventieth anniversary of the Spanish Revolution. Three years later, Editorial Base published a Catalan edition, making it available for a wider readership in those regions within the Spanish state where the party of Andreu Nin and Joaquín Maurin had been strongest.

Tosstorff is one of the most prominent researchers of the history of the POUM. He obtained his PhD at the University of Johannes Gutenberg de Mainz writing a thesis on the POUM, which was published in German in 1987 by the publishing house isp-Verlag under the title *Die POUM im Spanischen Bürgerkrieg*. The thesis is still considered today to be the most ambitious work to date in the field, but its small print-run, added to the fact that it has not been translated into other languages, has restricted its availability.

The intention of the book under review is mainly informative and it contains some of the latest research published by the author. Whilst the bulk of it is focused on the history of the POUM after 19 July 1936, it also encompasses, particularly through a study of the writings of its two main leaders, the events in the run-up to the foundation of the POUM in October 1935.

Tosstorff takes the reader through the main programmatic positions of the POUM in the midst of the revolutionary process, especially in Catalonia, which was the stronghold of POUMism, not only by analysing its written positions and documents, but also by contrasting them with its political actions. Finally, he traces the history of the POUM beyond the Iberian borders, relating aspects of the party's international policies, its international relationships, and its debates with Trotskyists and other anti-Stalinist organisations. He also deals with the tragic end of the party as a result of Stalinist repression, and sets out to establish the relationship between this and the prosecution of the opposition in the USSR instigated by Stalin and carried out at the Moscow Trials, the first of which took place almost simultaneously with the start of the Spanish Revolution.

The book presents a solid analysis, based on a truly rigorous study of historical events. However, this has not prevented the narrative from adhering to the same POUMist positions in order to explain and justify the actions of the party.

The POUM: An Anti-Stalinist Marxist Unity Party: Tosstorff notes at the very beginning of the book that the POUM was an exception at a global level, since it was the result of a fusion of two groups from different currents, both opposed to Stalinism, but also undoubtedly counterposed to each other. For him, 'it was an exception and can only be understood if we take into account the huge radicalisation the country was undergoing at the time' (p 20). On the one hand, there was the Izquierda Comunista de España (ICE, Communist Left of Spain) which had been linked to Leon Trotsky, and, on the other, the Bloque Obrero y Campesino (BOC, Workers and Peasants Bloc), a party founded in 1931 as a result of a previous fusion between the Catalan Communist Party and the Catalan-Balearic Communist Federation (FCCB), which had recently been expelled from the Partido Communista di España (PCE, the 'official' Comintern section). This formation was linked to the right opposition of the international Communist movement, which had one of the pioneers of the anti-Trotskyist opposition in the USSR, Bukharin, as a reference. He himself had been expelled by Stalin as a result of his opposition to forced collectivisation and the turn to industrialisation.

Thus was constituted a party which was 'in favour of a "socialist and democratic revolution"' (p 20), a wide definition which accommodated within its ranks both Communists and anti-Stalinists. This broadness was the precise cause of one of the first divergences between Nin and Trotsky, since the latter believed that such a combination resulted in a centrist party at odds with the task of building a revolutionary party. However, this discrepancy is not pointed out by Tosstorff, who goes straight on to the differences around the Popular Front and the need or otherwise to build a new International. For the author, the formation of the POUM was the matter of an exception created by immediate political necessities, a kind of synthesis to overcome the differences amongst the anti-Stalinist forces.

But in addition to probing the immediate reasons, Tosstorff tries to track the past of both groups in search of points of contact between these clearly opposed lines. He does this by going over the biographies of the two main leaders, Nin and Maurín, and, in my opinion, overstates the common path between them, which in reality boiled down only to the fact that both had made the journey from revolutionary trade unionism, in the ranks of the CNT, to Bolshevism. At the same time, the divergent paths that both leaders took when the bureaucratisation of the USSR started to wreak havoc with the legacy of the October Revolution are played down. Furthermore, he omits any mention of some of the most bitter polemics that took place between the two organisations at the beginning of the 1930s, which centred on the character of the Spanish Revolution and the policy of the BOC, which consisted of its tailing the Catalan petty-bourgeoisie around the figure of Lluís Companys[57] in the 1934 insurrection.

57. Lluís Companys i Jover (1882-1940) was the leader of the Esquerra Republicana de Catalunya. He became President of Catalonia in September 1933, and held the post through the Civil War.

The result of the fusion was an organisation that was, as is recognised by Tosstorff himself, 'overtaken by the political importance and significance of the movement after 19 July' (p 80). Without recognising it explicitly, the author shows us a POUM which was not prepared for the revolutionary outbreak.

Although Tosstorff does not lay the blame upon the Bloc's strategies, when he deals with the party day by day during the Civil War he has to accept that it would be precisely the 'Blocist' wing, or Maurinists, who would apply the greatest pressure to adopt decisions that would militate against the consolidation of the revolution.

The most significant example, which incidentally is shown in great detail in the book, is related to the military organisation of the POUM, which was unable to apply the policy of building soldiers' committees in the POUM militias due to opposition from the former Bloc cadres to this policy. These cadres carried some weight at the front. It is rightly pointed out that, as well as the sector in Valencia where 'the Popular Army was defended unconditionally..., the leadership of the Lenin Division which was controlled by old militants of the BOC, which constituted one of the nuclei of the right wing, also opposed and complicated the application of such a policy' (p 169).

The policy of unity among all anti-Stalinist Marxists was also represented at the international level, as Tosstorff relates in a chapter devoted to this topic. It was what he calls the 'new International' of the London Bureau, of which the BOC was already part, which was opposed to Trotsky's line of founding the Fourth International. Here, gathered under one roof, were different organisations with important differences on strategies and programme that the Spanish Revolution was going to accentuate even further. This heterogeneity prevented it from acting like an International and ended up being the cause of its demise. Tosstorff explains how the right wing of the Bureau, led by the German SAP, set in motion a crisis of no return through its fervent defence of collaboration with the Popular Front and its desire to dilute the struggle against Stalinism, which was preparing to crush the Spanish revolutionary process.

For the POUM, the London Bureau 'was not an International with a uniform policy, but a place where each of the parties had to help the rest with their experiences' (p 221). But, above all, the Bureau, as well as keeping contact with other independent revolutionary groups — such as the RSAP (Netherlands) — and even with the Trotskyists, was a valuable instrument which was of great help in terms of material support and international propaganda for the POUM itself. A good illustration of this was the mobilisation of volunteers in order to fight in the POUMist ranks, which, according to Tosstorff, amounted to between 600 and 700, 10 per cent of its forces.

The POUM: A Party Overwhelmed by the Revolution: As stated above, for Tosstorff, the POUM and the rest of the workers' organisations would be overtaken by the events taking place after 19 July 1936. It is not clearly stated what that expression means, but the book gives us a clue. The POUM was founded with the aim of carrying out a 'socialist and democratic revolution'. However, when the workers' revolution erupted, its actions were at odds with those necessary to defend, strengthen and ultimately gain victory for the revolution.

By focusing on the POUM after 19 July, Tosstorff overlooks the other significant difference with Trotsky, the one which brought about the break with Nin. I am referring to the party's support for and entry into the Popular Front in the 1936 elections. For Tosstorff, it was only a matter of an argument over 'the tactic to follow in respect of the Popular Front' (p 21). In this way he reduces the differences to a mere tactical issue when in fact it was a watershed for the oppositionist movement, and, as was demonstrated by the revolution itself five months after the 1936 elections, it was going to have profound consequences in respect of the POUM's policy.

This in turn leads to Tosstorff's failure to make any connection between this 'tactical argument' and the other difference which would make the split irreversible, namely that of its entering the Generalitat. For Tosstorff again, the reason for this decision is once more related to the coerciveness of the circumstances. He tells us: 'In order not to lose contact with the anarchist workers, the POUM saw itself obliged to enter the Catalan government, expecting the new government to legalise the revolution.' (p 28) In this way, the book reproduces the arguments put forward systematically by the POUMists at the time, which were totally contrary to the most basic principal of class independence.

However, this concern of the POUM to avoid being isolated from the anarchist workers was really focused on its avoiding being isolated from the anarchist leadership. Nin himself, as the book quotes, declared in 1937: 'It is clear that there is a difference between the masses of the CNT and their leadership, but we have no choice other than to fraternise with the leadership in order to be able to exercise a certain influence on the rank and file.' (p 110) Tosstorff himself defends this, stating that 'the POUM had no other option if it did not want to see the revolution finished from the very start' (p 110), and this is the idea that pervades the book, where there is little differentiation made between the leadership and the rank and file of the anarchist movement, and where the 'anarchists' are in general considered as groups that brought together the war and the revolution. The book ignores the fact that the leadership committees of the CNT quickly became the champions of anti-fascist unity and militarisation, putting the brakes on revolutionary advances.

Tosstorff outlines the POUM's failure to make contact with left-leaning anarchist factions, such as the Friends of Durruti Group. The policy of the POUM leadership was not aimed at uniting with the most revolutionary sectors of Iberian anarchism, but rather served to please the conservative and reformist sections of the movement's leadership. Tosstorff himself recognises that the POUM's tailing of the leadership of the CNT and the FAI disqualified it from being able to capitalise on the situation and attract to its ranks, or to a revolutionary strategy, those anarchists who were starting to break from the policy of their collaborationist leadership. The book lacks a deeper analysis of the importance of these groups, in particular in Catalonia. Moreover, there is a certain undervaluing of some groups that expressed these views, as is the case with the Friends of Durruti Group. This group managed to attract between 4500 and 5000 followers in Catalonia in only two months of the group's existence, half the number of supporters the POUM managed to get in the same region.

Tosstorff recognises that the actions of the government were to undermine the gains made by the July 1936 revolution. Taking into account its organisational aspect, the committees, he explains how 'the "aim" of the new government was precisely the dissolution of the committees and not their development' (p 86). He sets out to understand the rationale for the POUM's participation in this process, arguing that its behaviour 'oscillated between an unenthusiastic acceptance and a soft critique, which meant that the POUM, deep down, did not agree with it but neither did it want to provoke a major crisis' (p 87).

However, Tosstorff does not at all hide the POUM's direct compromise in the implementation of the Generalitat's anti-revolutionary policy. In fact, he reveals an event little known or studied until now that greatly exemplifies the extent to which the POUM and Nin were prepared to compromise with the first stage of the bourgeois state's recomposition of power. We are referring to the dissolution of the Local Committee of Lerida (Comité de Lleida), under POUMist hegemony. Tosstorff tells us how 'on 30 September, a delegation composing of Nin, the Chief Minister Tarradelles (ERC), counsellors Comorera (PSUC) and Domènech (CNT), accompanied by a hundred members of the Assault Guard, forced the political institutions — and this meant, most of all, the POUM — to subordinate themselves to the new government' (p 87). A few days later, the POUM's newspaper *La Batalla* justified this excursion and Nin's participation in it, declaring that 'Andreu Nin has said that they hadn't come to stop the revolution but to shape it' (p 88); a phrase that sums up the logic reproduced by the POUM in order to justify its participation in the elaboration and application of various decrees that allowed the Generalitat to recover the normality that had reigned before 19 July 1936. Tosstorff reproduces in part this very same logic when explaining the work of the POUM in this government, presenting it as an attempt by the bourgeois government to legalise and 'shape' the revolution. He considers that the reason for the POUM's failure was the unstable relationship between forces within the POUM and the policies of the CNT.

Tosstorff applies this same logic when he reviews agrarian, military and economic policies and goes on to explain many of the revolution's weaknesses, such as the need for a sole command of the militias or the planning of the collectivised economy. These were all real problems and he points out that they were mainly rooted in the shortcomings of anarchist ideology, such as the extreme federalism that ended up building a kind of 'capitalist trade unionism' (p 133).

Nevertheless, the POUM's way of resolving these weaknesses did not diverge from that of a general policy of class collaboration with their entry into the government. It accepted the Decree of Militarisation of the Militias that would ostensibly 'resolve' the military problem, but in reality favoured the recomposition of the republican army — this is recognised by Tosstorff — and decrees such as the one on collectivisation — supported by the POUM — which included formulas for rationalisation and planning, but were in reality measures aimed at dissolving workers' control and handing authority back to the republican bourgeois state.

The form of the revolution could not be separated from its class content, as *La Batalla* stated. Whoever acted as its agent — the revolutionary committees or the republican bourgeois institutions — would determine whether it was deepened or was reversed.

The POUM, A Party Persecuted by the Forces of the Counter-Revolution: The POUM's collaboration with the Catalonian government did not spare it from the campaign of slander and persecution instigated by the Stalinists, both at a national level by the PCE and regionally by its local wing, the United Socialist Party of Catalonia (PSUC). The first measure was precisely its expulsion from the government in December 1936. Tosstorff believes that 'the balance of forces had changed very decisively in the period of common government' (p 93). The Generalitat had managed to encroach upon the conquests of July and to rebuild the state apparatus at large. The tragic fact is that up until that moment the POUM had played a part in this process, critical voices being few and far between, and there were even those who thought that they should fight to return to the government (p 93).

Looking at this new situation, Tosstorff devotes a great deal of research to studying the persecution of the POUM, from the time of the armed counter-revolutionary putsch known as the 'Barcelona May Events' — when by his account it is clear that the POUM continued to cling to the coat-tails of the

CNT leadership by calling on 7 May for the barricades to be removed (p 31) — up to the show trial of the party's leaders. He goes into great detail about the plot hatched by the diplomatic representatives of the USSR, Antonov-Ovseyenko and Orlov to set in motion a concerted slander campaign in direct collaboration with the PCE and the PSUC, the falsification of evidence for an indictment, the investigation that revealed the operation orchestrated for the disappearance and assassination of Nin, and the lesser-known process against Trotskyist militants in the SBLE (Bolshevik-Leninist Section of Spain).

Tosstorff devotes an entire chapter to this, viewing it within the framework of the propaganda campaign which had already begun in the USSR with the Moscow Trials and the international repercussions which they produced, ultimately leading to the persecution of POUM militants in the republican camp.

On this subject, Tosstorff's work represents an important contribution to the condemnation of the role of the Stalinists in the Spanish Revolution. He reports that 1000 militants of the POUM were imprisoned and 50 assassinated, then goes on to polemicise with historians, such as Bizcarrondo and Elorzo, who claim the validity of the kangaroo courts used against the POUM leadership, along with others who still endorse the slanders against the POUM in their writings.

By Way of Conclusion: Until a publisher is found who is willing to translate Tosstorff's doctoral thesis for a non-German speaking public, *El POUM en la revolució espanyola* should serve as a fine 'preview' of the author's work. It is a very good synthesis of the key standpoints and actions of the POUM and its leadership in respect of the crucial issues of the Spanish Revolution, from the decision to join the Generalitat to the positions they took — consistent with this decision — in response to the main military, economic and territorial problems. In addition, Tosstorff reveals hitherto little-known episodes which illustrate the extent of the POUM's collaboration with Companys' government in Barcelona, such as the expedition to dissolve the Lerida Committee.

The sections dealing with the Stalinists' persecution are an important contribution that shed light on the real history of the PCE and the PSUC during the Spanish Civil War, in clear alliance with the Stalinist bureaucracy of the USSR. It is a mine of empirical data that can be used against the idealised and sweetened view presented by Spanish Stalinism of its role in the Civil War, a view that it uses as its foundational myth.

Finally, on a personal note, I believe that although Tosstorff does not hide his sympathies for the POUM and shares many of the arguments used by it to justify its policies, his book does present us with the history of the POUM, a party which was overwhelmed by the revolution and ended up unintentionally working against it, and which later was crushed by a violent counter-revolution. It is the history of a project that failed because of its own internal contradictions, having been conceived without a strategy and a programme anchored in the continuity of the revolutionary Marxist tradition, which at that time was represented in the current defended by Leon Trotsky. This was a failure that can be linked to the collapse of the London Bureau, with, above all, tragic consequences for the Spanish Revolution. The strategy of unity with the right-wing anti-Stalinists, who had already shown clear signs of defending a collaborationist policy in Catalonia in 1934, far from being a 'short cut' to the building of a revolutionary party, turned out to be an insurmountable obstacle to this task.

Salvador Lou Cuartero

LETTERS

John Baird
Dear Editor
I read with interest John Plant's article about John Baird MP, which appeared in *Revolutionary History*, Volume 10, no 4. There are aspects of Baird's political career that have puzzled me for some time, and I wonder whether any of your readers could cast light on them.

The characterisation of Baird's political orientation as Trotskyist, though supported by an increasing body of evidence, runs up against what seems to me a crucial difficulty, namely that in May 1949 he voted in favour of ratification of the North Atlantic Treaty (see *Hansard*, Volume 464, column 2127, 12 May 1949). This was an issue that divided the Labour left, with a few, including Michael foot, voting for ratification. A probably larger number, including such critics of the Treaty as Ian Mikardo, Tom Driberg and William Warbey, abstained or were absent, while eight members registered formal opposition either by casting negative votes or acting as tellers for the 'No' side. This last group comprised four Labour members (Tom Braddock, Ronald Chamberlain, Emrys Hughes and Konni Zilliacus), two Communists and two CP-aligned expellees from the Labour Party. Baird thus placed himself, in this respect, on the rightward end of the Labour left spectrum — a strange position for a Trotskyist of any variety, particularly as it meant endorsement of what was generally understood to be an anti-Soviet alliance. A possible explanation, of course, is that Baird adopted Trotskyist views at a later stage of his political career. If so, when and why?

With regard to Baird's attitude to the events in Hungary, the *Daily Worker* reported on 29 October 1956 that he had delivered a speech in which he warned against 'American adventures' and added: '… if in this confused situation it later becomes apparent that the rebels are led by agent provocateurs financed by American capitalism, then the Hungarian Government would have every justification for calling in Soviet troops to defend the Socialism in Hungary.'

This was at an early stage of the Hungarian crisis, and it is not entirely clear how Baird's thinking about the matter subsequently developed. Although a Hungarian Communist organ published an article under his name taking a pro-Soviet position, the *Manchester Guardian* reported him as saying that the article mischaracterised his views. On the other hand, the late Richard Clements once told me that Baird remained deeply suspicious of the Hungarian insurrectionaries. In any event, his stance seems less clear-cut than the unequivocally pro-Soviet line adopted by the John Lawrence–Hilda Lane faction in Holborn.

Sincerely

John Chiddick
Politics Program, La Trobe University, Australia

Also available from the Merlin Press

Ian Birchall, Ed
European Revolutionaries and Algerian Independence, 1954-1962
The book considers the course of Algerian War 1954-1962, and the response of the French left and gives the fullest account in English of the role of the revolutionary left in giving political and practical solidarity to the Algerian liberation struggle. It presents substantial extracts from Sylvain Pattieu's, Les camarades des frères (Paris 2002), and will gives the fullest account of the role of Trotskyists in this period, drawing on documents and interviews with participants.
418pp, 978 0 85036 665 5 Pbk, £20.00

Bukharin & Preobrazhensky
The ABC of Communism
This book brings together the 1919 Programme of the Russian Communist Party and the Abc of Communism first published in 1920, written as an extensive popular introduction, explanation and commentary on the Programme. For ten years it was widely translated and read as the best introduction to Bolshevik theory. It is both an historical document and a comprehensive statement of communist theory. A critical afterword situates political debates and events of 1919-20.
397pp, 978 0 85036 543 6 Pbk £14.95

Chris Gray, Ed
Pierre Broué: Revolutionary Historian
This book brings together essays by Pierre Broué (1926-2005), hitherto unavailable in English, throwing light on the role of the opposition to Stalin within Russia and on the development the Fourth International up to 1945. A biographical sketch by Vincent Presumey paints a substantial, frank and illuminating portrait of an original historian and political analyst.
368pp, 978 0 85036 588 7 Pbk £14.95

Mike Jones, Ed
Rosa Luxemburg: Selected Political and Literary Writings
Rosa Luxemburg, perhaps the most remarkable and original figure among German Marxists thinkers and activists, was one of the earliest victims of fascism, murdered in Berlin, in 1919. This volume presents selected political essays, writings previously unavailable in English. Revolutionary History Series: Volume 10, Number 1.
288pp, 978 0 85036 693 8 Pbk £ 14.95

Marcel Liebman
Leninism Under Lenin
This book, a winner of the Isaac Deutscher Memorial Prize, is an antidote to the view that Stalinism is synonymous with Leninism. Liebmann highlights democratic dimensions in Lenin's thinking as it developed over 25 years. "I have not come across anything which captures so well the complexities of Lenin's positions" Ralph

Miliband. "The author of this historical study of Lenin's political activities and theories combines a sympathetic understanding of Lenin's positions with a critical approach making it one of the most informative books on Lenin that have been written." Labour Research.
477pp, 978 0 85036 261 9 Pbk £18.95

Georg Lukács
History and Class Consciousness: Studies in Marxist Dialectics
Lukács wrote the essays in the 1920's reflecting on his experiences in Hungary where he was a commissar in the short-lived Soviet Republic.
Contents: Preface (1967): What is Orthodox Marxism: The Marxism of Rosa Luxemburg: Class Consciousness, Reification and the Consciousness of the Proletariat: The Changing Function of Historical Materialism: Legality and Illegality: Critical Observations on Rosa Luxemburg's "Critique of the Russian Revolution": Towards a Methodology of the Problem of Organisation, Notes: Index.
404p, 978 0 85036 197 1 Pbk £13.95

Georg Lukács
The Ontology of Social Being: 1. Hegel
Contents: Hegel's Dialectic 'amid the manure of contradictions': Hegel's Dialectical Ontology and the Reflection Determinations: Notes.
116pp, 978 0 85036 226 8 Pbk £9.95

Georg Lukács
The Ontology of Social Being 2. Marx
Contents: Methodological Preliminaries: The Critique of Political Economy: Historicity and Theoretical Generality: Notes.
173pp, 978 0850362275 Pbk £9.95

Georg Lukács
The Ontology of Social Being: 3. Labour
139pp, 978 0 85036 255 8 Pbk £9.95

Paul Mattick
Anti-Bolshevik Communism
Contents: Introduction, Karl Kautsky: From Marx to Hitler, Luxemburg versus Lenin, The Lenin Legend, Bolshevism and Stalinism, Council Communism, Otto Rühle And The German Labour Movement, Spontaneity and Organisation, Karl Korsch: His Contribution to Marxism, Humanism and Socialism, Marxism and the New Physics, Monopoly Capital, Workers' Control.
248pp, 978 0 85036 223 7 Pbk £14.95

Leo Panitch & Colin Leys, Eds
The Communist Manifesto Now, Socialist Register 1998
Contents: Preface , Dear Dr. Marx: A Letter from a Socialist Feminist: Sheila Rowbotham; The Political Legacy of the Manifesto: Colin Leys & Leo Panitch; The

Geography of Class Power: David Harvey; Socialism with Sober Senses: Developing Worker's Capacities: Sam Gindin; Unions, Strikes and Class Consciousness Today: Sheila Cohen & Kim Moody; Passages of the Russian and Eastern Europe Left: Peter Gowan; Marx and the Permanent Revolution in France: Backgound to the Communist Manifesto: Bernard Moss; The Communist Manifesto and the Environment: John Bellamy Foster; Remember the Future? The Communist Manifesto as Historical and Cultural Form: Peter Osborne; Seeing is Believing: Marx's Manifesto, Derrida's Apparition: Paul Thomas; The Making of the Manifesto: Rob Beamish; The Communist Manifesto: Marx & Engels. 278pp, 978 0 85036 473 6 Pbk £14.95

Anton Pannekoek
Lenin as Philosopher: A Critical Examination of the Philosophical Basis of Leninism
Contents: Introduction; Marxism; Middle-Class Materialism; Dietzgen; Mach; Avenarius; Lenin; The Russian Revolution; The Proletarian Revolution. Appendix [1]: Lenin's Philosophy by Karl Korsch; Appendix [2]: Anton Pannekoek (1873-1960) by Paul Mattick.
132pp, 978 0 85036 186 5 Pbk £10.95

Cathy Porter
Alexandra Kollontai: A Biography Revised Edition
Alexandra Kollontai inspired generations of socialists in Russia with her pioneering views on sex and the family. A revolutionary activist and writer, she was the only woman in the first Bolshevik government in 1917. This second edition of Cathy Porter's biography draws on newly-published memoirs, diaries and letters to offer fresh insights into Kollontai's stormy political life. It tell of her fight for workers' democracy and women's rights, her love affairs, her disagreements with the Bolshevik party, and her last years 'in exile' as a Soviet diplomat in Norway, Mexico and Sweden.
500pp, 37 black and white photos. 978 0 85036 640 2 Pbk £20.00

Milton Keynes UK
Ingram Content Group UK Ltd.
UKHW020635060724
445093UK00007B/174